FAMILY
DAYS OUT

IN BRITAIN

Produced by the Publishing Division of the Automobile Association

Editor: Penny Hicks
Designer: Peter Gibbons
Cover design: Quadraphic Design Consultants Limited

Typeset by: Avonset, Midsomer Norton, Bath
Printed and bound in Great Britain by: Unwin Brothers Ltd, Old Woking

A CIP catalogue record for this book is available from the British Library.

Published by the Automobile Association, Fanum House, Basingstoke, Hampshire RG21 2EA.

ISBN 07495 0526 5

CONTENTS

INTRODUCTION

There is a universal cry which echoes across the land at the time of any school holiday – 'what can we do today?' This book offers hundreds of suggestions and contains places to visit of all kinds, all of which have been specially selected for their appeal to the whole family: there are theme parks for an action-packed day of exciting rides and country parks for a quiet day in the country; stately homes which offer something specially for children, such as a safari park or an adventure playground; farms to look round; steam train and canal boat rides; there are museums, such as the ever-popular Natural History and Science Museums in London and those fascinating open-air museums where history is accurately recreated and children have such a good time that they don't realise they are being educated!

The book begins with London – always a good choice for a day out – first central London and then the outer regions, which are often overlooked, but have just as much to offer. England, the Channel Islands, Isle of Man, Scotland and Wales follow, with the directory of places to visit arranged in alphabetical order of counties. Within each county towns are listed in alphabetical order.

Throughout the directory you will find the occasional full page or two-page feature on a town which has something extra to offer a family, where you could spend a good day out without every crossing the threshhold of a 'place of interest'. These include seaside resorts with piers and funfairs and other traditional attractions, and historic towns and cities, such as Bath, Oxford and York, whose streets are an attraction on their own.

Opening dates quoted in the guide are inclusive – for instance, where you see Apr-Oct, that place will be open from the beginning of April to the end of October.

Prices quoted are, as far as possible, those which are expected to be in force in 1992. However, some establishments have been unable to give us their projected prices and for those we have given 1991 prices, prefixed by an asterisk. If no price is quoted, you should check with the establishment concerned before your visit. A number of the places which do not charge admission at all may ask for a voluntary donation.

Telephone numbers always include the STD code, shown in brackets, or with a dash, before the telephone number. An exchange name is only shown if it differs from the town in the heading, but you will only need to refer to the exchange name if you are in the area and need to use the local code.

Disabled visitors should look for the wheelchair symbol which features in those entries where all or the majority of the establishment is accessible to wheelchair-bound visitors.

We strongly recommend that you telephone in advance of your visit to check the exact details, particularly regarding access to toilet and refreshment facilities.

SYMBOLS

In order to give you as much information as possible in the space available, we have used the following symbols in the guide:

☎ Telephone number
♿ Suitable for visitors in wheelchairs
✳ Indicates 1991 price
🅿 Parking at establishment

☕ Refreshments
✗ Restaurant
🐕 No dogs
🚌 No coaches

ABBREVIATIONS

In the same way, we have abbreviated certain pieces of information:

AM	Ancient Monument	Free	Admission free
AM	Ancient Monument	10p	Admission 10p
(CadW)	(Wales)	ch 20p	Children 20p
EH	English Heritage	ch 15 20p	Children under 15 20p
NT	National Trust	Pen	Senior Citizens
NTS	National Trust for Scotland	Party	Special or reduced rates for parties booked in advance
BH	Bank Holidays		
PH	Public Holidays	Party	Special or reduced rates
Etr	Easter	30 +	for parties of 30 or
ex	except		more booked in advance

LONDON

London offers the ultimate day out for any family, and the excitement of exploring this great city for the first time must be the experience of a lifetime for any child. There is a tremendous amount to see and do – pageantry, palaces, museums, galleries, parks, markets and, of course, the river. Forward planning is essential if you are to make the most of your day out and, as London is so enormous, it is a good idea to concentrate on one area at a time.

You can easily spend a day around Whitehall and St James's, taking in the Changing of the Guard ceremony at Buckingham Palace (at approximately 11.25am, daily from May to mid August, then on alternate days), the Royal Mews, Guards Museum, Westminster Abbey, the Cabinet War Rooms and the Houses of Parliament.

The Tower of London is a major attraction and it is wise to get there early. In the same area you can cross Tower Bridge by the glass-covered walkway 142 feet above the river, visit HMS Belfast, the Schooner Kathleen and May and the chilling London Dungeon.

Kensington is the place for the big museums – Natural History, Science and Geological and the Victoria and Albert – and for Kensington Palace and the fascinating Commonwealth Institute. The British Museum is in Bloomsbury and, while this could easily occupy the whole day, you might also fit in the charming Pollock's Toy Museum, the Theatre Museum or a look round Covent Garden and the London Transport Museum.

Right in the heart of London is Piccadilly and Trafalgar Square – a busy and exciting place to spend the day with attractions such as the Guinness World of Records, the National Gallery, National Portrait Gallery and the Museum of Mankind.

In addition to all that London has to offer every day, the capital also has its extra special days with annual events such as the Lord Mayor's Show on the second Saturday in November, Trooping the Colour in June, the New Year's Day Parade and the Notting Hill Carnival over August Bank Holiday weekend. The River Thames comes alive for the Head of the River Race and the Boat Race, both in March, the Doggett's Coat and Badge Race in July and Thamesday in September.

Sightseeing buses are a good introduction to London and London Transport run frequent services from Baker Street Station, Marble Arch, Piccadilly Circus and Victoria. There are also river and canal boat trips and a huge range of guided walks.

It is wise to consider very carefully the best way of getting to London and getting around once you are there – a car might seem the cheapest option for a family, but parking is expensive and difficult to find, and traffic jams can take valuable time out of your day. Travelcards can save you money and are valid on the Underground, local British Rail services, most buses and the Docklands Light Railway.

Tourist information: Victoria Station
Liverpool Street Station
Tower of London (West Gate)   Telephone: 071-730 3488

CENTRAL LONDON

WC1   British Museum

The stern façade of the British Museum belies the rich and varied treasures within which make it one of the great museums of the world, showing the works of man from many civilisations, from prehistoric to comparatively recent times. Founded in 1753, the nucleus of the museum was the collections of Sir Hans Sloane and Sir Robert Cotton. The galleries are the responsibility of the following departments: Egyptian, Greek and Roman, Western Asiatic, Japanese, Prehistoric and Romano-British, Medieval and later, Coins and Medals, Oriental Prints and Drawings and Ethnography (based at the Museum of Mankind). The museum also displays famous books and manuscripts from the British Library collections. The original building, Montagu House was demolished, and Sir Robert Smirke commissioned to build a more suitable replacement on the site, which was completed in 1852; the famous domed Reading Room was added in 1857. Among the treasures not to be missed are the Egyptian mummies, the notorious and superb Elgin marbles, two of the four existing copies of the Magna Carta, Shakespeare's signature, Nelson's plan of the Battle of Trafalgar and the Sutton Hoo treasure. There is a regular programme of gallery talks, lectures and films, and young visitors can enjoy special children's trails.

Great Russell St (Underground – Russell Sq, Tottenham Court Rd)
☎ 071-580 1788 (recorded information) & 071-323 8599

Open: all year, Mon-Sat 10-5, Sun 2.30-6. (Closed Good Fri, May Day, Xmas & 1 Jan). *Admission:* Free.
☞ ✗ licensed &. (parking by arrangement; touch tour for visually impaired) toilets for disabled shop ⚹

SW1   Cabinet War Rooms

The underground emergency accommodation provided to protect the Prime Minister, Winston Churchill, his War Cabinet and the Chiefs of Staff during the Second World War provide a fascinating insight into those tense days and nights. Among the 21 rooms are the Cabinet Room, the Map Room (where information about operations on all fronts was collected) and the Prime Minister's room, which have been carefully preserved since the end of the war. Other rooms have been restored to their original appearance.

Clive Steps, King Charles St (Underground – Westminster)
☎ 071-930 6961

Open: all year, daily 10-6. Last admission 5.15 (Closed 24-26 Dec & 1 Jan). *Admission:* £3.60 (ch £1.80, students & pen £2.70). Party 10 +.
&. toilets for disabled shop ⚹

W8   Commonwealth Institute

Discover the history, landscapes, wildlife, crafts and economies of the 50 countries of the Commonwealth on three floors of spectacular galleries, where you can visit the Caribbean, see Canada from a skidoo, climb up Mount Kenya or take a rickshaw across Bangladesh. There are also cultural events and exhibitions as well as educational programmes and special activity sheets for children, and holiday workshops. The Commonwealth Shop sells gifts and crafts from around the world. Special for 1992 is the New Worlds series of programmes in which exhibitions, visual, verbal and performing arts events, conferences etc focus on periods of history to explore the relationships between the Commonwealth and Europe.

Kensington High St (Underground – High Street Kensington)
☎ 071-603 4535

Open: all year, Mon-Sat 10-5, Sun 2-5. (Closed Good Fri, May Day, 24-26 Dec & 1 Jan). *Admission:* ✳ Free. Occasional charge for special exhibitions.
🅿 ☞ ✗ licensed &. (lift from car park) toilets for disabled shop ⚹

SW1 Green Park

The smallest of the central London parks, Green Park is aptly named, for the Tyburn stream runs just below the surface, maintaining its lush verdancy. It is situated in the triangle formed by Piccadilly, The Mall and Constitution Hill (where Charles II used to take his constitutional stroll) and was formerly meadowland. This informal character is still maintained today, for there are no flower borders here – just the springtime crocuses and daffodils which grow among the grass.

(Underground – Green Park)

W1 Guinness World of Records Exhibitions

Through the use of life sized models, videos and the latest audio-technology, thousands of world records come alive at the touch of a button. Six themed areas depict: The Human World, The Animal World, Our Planet Earth, Structures and Machines, The Sports World and The World of Entertainment.

Visitors can watch original newsreel footage whilst measuring up to the world's tallest man; select their choice of sporting records from the Sports Recall Data Bank; watch an exciting chronicle of man's exploration of space; listen to the songs that sold millions on a 50s style juke box, and much more.

The Trocadero, Coventry St, Piccadilly Circus (Underground – Piccadilly Circus)
☎ 071-439 7331

Open: all year, Mon-Sat 10am-10pm (last admission), Sun 10-9.30pm (last admission). (Closed 25 Dec).
Admission: £5 (ch 4-16 £3.20, under 3 free, pen & students £3.95). Group 10 + .
& toilets for disabled shop ✗

SE1 HMS Belfast

The largest cruiser ever built for the Royal Navy dates from 1939. She served in the Second World War, and was saved from the breaker's yard to become a floating naval museum. She is owned by the Imperial War Museum and is now permanently moored in the Pool of London, with seven decks to explore. New sound and light displays, exhibitions, art gallery and cinema bring the ship to life. Recorded audio guides available. Special events take place throughout the year. Exhibitions in 1992 include Damage Control Display opening in April and Falklands Exhibition: 10th Anniversary, opening July.

Morgans Ln, Tooley St (Underground – London Bridge)
☎ 071-407 6434

Open: all year, daily. 20 Mar-Oct 10-6, last admission 5.20; Nov-19 Mar 10-4.30, last admission 4. (Closed 24-26 Dec & 1 Jan)
Admission: ✱ £3.60 (ch, students & pen £1.80). Party.
▆ & (wheelchair lift for access on board) shop ✗

SW1 Houses of Parliament

From the time of Edward the Confessor to Henry VIII, the site of the present-day Houses of Parliament was the main residence of the monarch. Hence the often-used term the 'Palace of Westminster'. It was not until Henry VIII moved to Whitehall Palace in 1529 that the building was turned over to state institutions. A disastrous fire in 1834 destroyed most of the medieval palace and a competition was held for the design of a new Parliament building; Charles Barry was awarded the commission with his

Westminster (Underground – Westminster)
☎ 071-219 4272

To gain admission to the Strangers' Galleries join the queue at St Stephens entrance from approx. 5.30pm Mon-Thu, approx 9.30am Fri (House of Commons). From approx 2.30pm Tue, Wed & some Mons, 3pm Thu & 11am Fri (House of Lords) or by arrangement with MP (House

Gothic-style design (although Pugin was responsible for much of the creative detail). Today the building stands at 940ft long, covers eight acres and includes 1100 apartments. There are over two miles of passages. To the south stands the lofty Victorial Tower where the Union Jack flies when Parliament is in session. At the north end of the building is the clock tower which contains Big Ben, the 13¼-ton hour bell.

of Commons) or Peer (House of Lords).
Admission: Free but guides require payment if used.
&. (by arrangement) toilets for disabled shop (bookstall) ✻ ▦

W2   Hyde Park

Situated to the west of Park Lane, between Knightsbridge and Bayswater, and formerly a Royal hunting park, Hyde Park now consists of 340 acres of grass and trees, intersected by paths. The Serpentine, at its centre, provides a habitat for wild creatures which cannot find sanctuary elsewhere in the city centre. It was the venue for the Great Exhibition in 1851, but is probably best known for Speakers' Corner, near Marble Arch, where, every Sunday, anyone can stand up and say just what they please.

(Underground – Hyde Park Corner, Marble Arch)

SE1   Imperial War Museum

Founded in 1917 and established in 1920 by an Act of Parliament, this museum illustrates and records all aspects of the two World Wars and other military operations involving Britain and the Commonwealth since 1914. It has recently undergone major renovations and although the vast collections are still housed within the imposing walls of the original building in Lambeth Road, it is now a thoroughly modern museum employing all the latest technology to make its exhibitions more vital and atmospheric for the visitor. Improvements include a new, large exhibition hall, art galleries and a shop and licensed restaurant. There are always special exhibitions and the programme of events includes film shows and lectures. The Imperial War Museum has a wealth of military reference material, although some reference departments are open to the public by appointment only.

Lambeth Rd (Underground – Lambeth North)
☎ 071-416 5000
Open: all year, daily 10-6. (Closed 24-26 Dec & 1 Jan).
Admission: ✻ £3 (ch 5-16, students, UB40 & pen £1.50). Party 10+.
✗ licensed &. toilets for disabled shop ✻

W8   Kensington Gardens

This was part of Hyde Park until William III enclosed his palace gardens and today, again, the two areas are not physically divided. A change of character is apparent, though, once you cross the invisible boundary which runs from north to south across the Serpentine Bridge. Kensington Gardens are noted for their tranquility and formality and include the Round Pond, Queen Anne's Orangery, the Sunken Garden and Flower Walk.

(Underground – Queensway, Lancaster Gate)

W8   Kensington Palace State Apartments & Court Dress Collection

The birthplace of Queen Victoria and today the London residence of the Prince and Princess of Wales, Princess Margaret and Prince and Princess Michael of Kent, Kensington Palace looks out over lovely gardens and an expanse of green parkland. When the house was bought by William III in 1689, it was a more modest town house. He commissioned Sir Christopher Wren to remodel the building and it was enlarged again and decorated by William Kent for George I. It was the principal private royal residence until George II died. The State Apartments display pictures and furniture from the Royal Collection and there is a section on the Great Exhibition. The colourful Court Dress Collection exhibits some of the magnificent costumes worn at court from 1750 onwards.

Kensington Gardens (Underground – High Street Kensington)
☎ 071-937 9561

Open: all year, Mon-Sat 9-5, Sun 1-5. Last admission 4.15. (Closed Good Fri, 24-26 Dec & 1 Jan).
& toilets for disabled shop 🎴
Details not confirmed for 1992

SE1   The London Dungeon

The London Dungeon has won the British Tourist Authority's Award for Outstanding Tourist Enterprise. Its modest entrance off a street near London Bridge station will lead the visitor through to a series of slimy vaults where the seamy side of life in past centuries is convincingly re-created. Methods of torture and death, the tools of witchcraft and black magic and some of the more grisly medicinal practices are well represented. Viewing takes about an hour; this museum is not recommended for the faint-hearted.

Entry includes the 'Great Fire of London' and 'Theatre of the Guillotine' shows, both using the latest in interactive technology.

28-34 Tooley St (Underground – London Bridge)
☎ 071-403 0606

Open: all year, daily, Apr-Sep 10-5.30; Oct-Mar 10-4.30.
Admission: £5 (ch 14 & pen £3, students £4).
🍽 & toilets for disabled shop 🎴

NW1   The London Planetarium

'Solar Swoop' is the new star show at the London Planetarium, which incorporates laser effects for the first time. Two eagles come to life under the Planetarium dome and describe their adventures through the Solar System to audiences. 'Space Trail' is the new interactive 'lift-off' zone at the Planetarium, where visitors can receive up-to-date information about space through the use of touch-sensitive screens.

Marylebone Rd (Underground – Baker Street)
☎ 071-486 1121

Open: all year, daily (ex 25 Dec), star shows from 12.40, every 40 mins (earlier during wknds & holidays).
Admission: Admission fee payable.
shop 🎴

WC2   London Transport Museum

The former flower market in Covent Garden (now moved to a site in Nine Elms, SW8) has been converted to house the London Transport Museum. It is devoted to the story of London's public transport from the earliest beginnings up to the present day, and vehicles on show include steam locomotives, trams, buses, trolleybuses, railway coaches and horse buses. There are also extensive displays using

The Piazza, Covent Garden (Underground – Covent Garden, Leicester Sq)
☎ 071-379 6344

Open: all year, daily 10-6, last admission 5.15pm. (Closed 24-26 Dec).

working models and audio-visual material, and visitors can 'drive' a modern bus, a tram and a tube train. There are special events for children and families in the school holidays and a reference library is available by appointment. There are a number of exhibitions planned for 1992; telephone for details.

Admission: £3 (ch 5-16, students, UB40s & pen £1.50).
Disabled & ch under 5 free. Family ticket £7. Party 20+.
& (wheelchair available) toilets for disabled shop ✗

NW1   London Zoo

London Zoo is home to over 5000 animals, insects, reptiles and fish. Founded by Sir Stamford Raffles, the Zoo was opened to the public in 1847, and can claim the world's first aquarium, insect and reptile house. Visitors today can view rare and exotic animals, many of which are participating in captive breeding programmes. Daily events such as Animals in Action, feeding times and Animal Encounters, give visitors an insight into animal behaviour. There are reductions for groups, and free guided tours can be arranged. For youngsters there is a Children's Zoo and Discovery Centre, and a whole range of educational programmes for schools. New exhibits include the African Aviary, offering unrivalled viewing of the birds within, and the Moonlight World where day and night are reversed. Favourites at the Zoo include black rhinos Rosie and Jos, two pairs of Asiatic Lions, the first of their kind in Europe, and of course, Ming the Giant Panda.

Regents Park (Underground – Camden Town, Gt Portland St)
☎ 071-722 3333

Open: all year, daily from 10am.
Admission: ✳ £5.20 (ch £3.20, students & pen £4.30). Party.
🅿 (charged) ☕ ✗ licensed & (wheelchairs available) toilets for disabled shop ✗

NW1   Madame Tussaud's

Madame Tussaud's world-famous waxwork collection was founded in Paris in 1770. It moved to England in 1802 and found a permanent home in London's Marylebone Road in 1884. It is Britain's top visitor attraction with over two and a half million visitors a year. The wax models are extremely life-like and the collection is being changed constantly: historical figures, film stars, kings, queens, sportsmen and other popular figures are represented. There are new themed areas within the exhibition, and these include the Garden Party, 200 Years of Madame Tussauds, and Hollywood Legends. The latest figures include John Major, Nelson Mandela, Just William, Neil Kinnock, and Nick Faldo.

Marylebone Rd (Underground – Baker Street)
☎ 071-935 6861

Open: all year 10-5.30 (9.30am wknds, 9am summer). (Closed 25 Dec).
Admission: Admission fee payable.
☕ ✗ licensed & (Lift access to all exhibition areas with guide escort) toilets for disabled shop ✗

EC3   The Monument

Designed by Wren and Hooke and erected in 1671-7, the Monument commemorates the Great Fire of 1666 which is reputed to have started in nearby Pudding Lane. The fire destroyed nearly 90 churches and about 13,000 houses. This fluted Doric column stands 202ft high (Pudding Lane is exactly 202ft from its base) and visitors can climb the 311 steps to a platform at its summit. The views over the City and beyond are splendid. Because of the steps, access is almost impossible for persons with severe disabilities: there is no lift or escalator.

Monument St (Underground – Monument)
☎ 071-626 2717

Open: all year (ex 25-26 Dec, 1 Jan, Good Fri & May Day) 31 Mar-Sep, Mon-Fri 9-6, Sat & Sun 2-6; Oct-30 Mar, Mon-Sat 9-4. Last admission 20 mins before closing.
Admission: ✳ £1 (ch 16 25p).
✗

11

EC2   Museum of London

Early December 1976 saw the official opening of the Museum of London. The collections of the former London and Guildhall museums were brought together in one specially designed building, located near the Barbican development. The site adjoins a stretch of the original Roman wall which surrounded the city.

Devoted to and detailing all aspects of London life from pre-history to contemporary times, the museum offers a fascinating display presented in chronological order. The exhibits and tableaux are arranged to give the visitor a realistic view of life in the capital through the ages; archaeological levels are illustrated by a relief model of the Thames Valley which provides an apt starting point for the story. Features of special interest include the superb models of William the Conqueror's White Tower and old St Pauls; the audio-visual reconstruction of the Great Fire of London in 1666 (superbly atmospheric) and the exhibition of ceremonial London with the Lord Mayor's State Coach as its centrepiece. It is also worth looking out for the medieval hen's egg, a lift from Selfridges department store, and a 1930s Ford motor car. There is also a pro-gramme of temporary exhibitions, lunchtime lectures and evening films throughout the year.

Special events for 1992 include: 19 May-21 Jun, London Documentary Photographers; 15 Sep-Jun 1993, The Purple, White and Green (the suffragettes in London).

London Wall (Underground – St Paul's, Barbican)
☎ 071-600 3699 ext 240 or 280

Open: all year, Tue-Sat 10-6, Sun 2-6 (Closed 24-26 Dec, 1 Jan & every Mon ex BH's). Parties by arrangement.
Admission: £3 (concessions £1.50, ch under 5 free). Family ticket £7.50.
✗ licensed & (wheelchairs available, lifts & induction loops) toilets for disabled shop ⴲ

W1   Museum of Mankind

The ethnographical department of the British Museum was re-housed in 1970 at Burlington Gardens to form the Museum of Mankind. Its vast collections embrace the art and material culture of tribal, village and pre-industrial societies from most areas of the world other than Western Europe. It also houses archaeological collections from the Americas and Africa. The museum's policy is to mount a number of fascinating temporary exhibitions (usually lasting for at least a year) rather than have permanent displays on show, although there are a number of out-standing exhibits on permanent display. The reserve collection is stored in Shoreditch and can be made available for serious study. Film shows and educational services are provided.

6 Burlington Gardens (Underground – Piccadilly Circus)
☎ 071-636 1555 ext 8043

Open: all year, Mon-Sat 10-5, Sun 2.30-6. (Closed Good Fri, May Day, Xmas & 1 Jan).
Admission: Free.
🖪 & shop ⴲ

SE1   Museum of the Moving Image

A journey through cinematic history from the earliest experiments to all the technical wizardry of modern animation is what this museum offers the visitor. There are artefacts to handle, buttons to press and films to watch as well as a detailed explanation of the operations of a television studio. A fascinating insight into the world of films and television with each chapter as exciting as the last.

South Bank, Waterloo (Underground – Waterloo)
☎ 071-401 2636

Open: all year, daily 10-6. (Closed 24-26 Dec).
Admission: £5.50 (ch, UB40's, disabled & pen £4, students £4.70). Party 10+.
🖪 ✗ licensed & toilets for disabled shop ⴲ

SW3   National Army Museum

The history of the British, Indian and Colonial forces from 1485 onwards unfolds in this museum. Displayed, in chronological order, are uniforms, weapons, prints, photographs, relics and mementos together with a special display of the orders and decorations of the Duke of Windsor and those five great Field Marshals – Lord Roberts, Gough, Kitchener, Wolseley and Sir George White VC. The Picture Gallery includes portraits by Gainsborough and Reynolds as well as battle scenes and pictures of the Indian regiments. A new display looks at the British Army in the Napoleonic Wars and includes a 400-square-foot model of the Battle of Waterloo. 1992 special exhibitions will cover the Civil War, the Falklands, and the Burma Campaign.

Royal Hospital Rd, Chelsea (Underground – Sloane Square)
☎ 071-730 0717
Open: all year, daily 10-5.30. (Closed Good Fri, May Day, 24-26 Dec & 1 Jan).
Admission: Free.
🅿 ☛ ⬥ toilets for disabled shop ✻

WC2   National Gallery

In 1824 the government bought the collection of pictures accumulated by John Julius Angerstein, a London underwriter, and exhibited them at his former residence in Pall Mall. These formed the major part of the collections of the National Gallery. Further bequests and purchases were made and by 1831 space had become limited, so plans were made for a special building to house the works of art. The present neo-classical building in Trafalgar Square was opened in 1838. All the great periods of European painting are represented here although only a limited selection of British works is displayed, as most of the national collection is housed at the Tate. The gallery's particular treasures include Van Eyck's *Arnolfini Marriage*, Velazquez's *Toilet of Venus*, Leonardo da Vinci's cartoon (the Virgin and Child with Saints Anne and John the Baptist), Rembrandt's *Belshazzar's Feast* and Titian's *Bacchus and Ariadne*. The British paintings include Gainsborough's *Mr and Mrs Andrews* and Constable's *Haywain*. There are many more captivating masterpieces to be seen at the National Gallery which houses one of the finest and most extensive collections in the world. The Sainsbury Wing opened in 1991 and contains the early Renaissance works from 1260-1510. Lectures, guided tours, children's worksheets and quizzes are available. Exhibitions for 1992 include: 26 Mar-24 May, Rembrandt: The Master and his Workshop; 1 Jul-27 Sep, Manet and the Execution of Maximilian; 12 Nov-7 Feb 1993, Edvard Munch: The Frieze of Life.

Trafalgar Square (Underground – Charing Cross)
☎ 071-839 3321 & recorded information 071-839 3526
Open: all year, Mon-Sat 10-6, Sun 2-6. (Closed Good Fri, May Day, 24-26 Dec & 1 Jan).
Admission: Free. Admission charged for major exhibitions.
☛ ✗ licensed ⬥ (wheelchairs available, induction loop in theatre, lifts) toilets for disabled shop ✻

WC2   National Portrait Gallery

With the aim of illustrating British history by means of a collection of portraits of famous, and infamous, men and women, the gallery's first home was established in George Street, Westminster. After several moves the collection was finally housed in its present accommodation in 1896. Located behind the National Gallery, the building was designed in the style of an Itallian palazzo. A further wing was added in 1933. The portraits are arranged in

2 St Martin's Place (Underground – Charing Cross)
☎ 071-306 0055
Open: all year 10-5, Sat 10-6 & Sun 2-6. (Closed Good Fri, May Day, 24-26 Dec & 1 Jan).
Admission: Free (ex special exhibitions) shop ✻

chronological order from the top floor, starting with the medieval period and finishing with the present day. As well as paintings, there are sculptures, miniatures, engravings, photographs and cartoons among the displays. Special exhibitions include Michael Faraday 1791-1867 (Sep '91-19 Jan), The Portrait in British art (Nov '91-9 Feb), Eve Arnold in Britain (Nov '91-23 Feb), George Bernard Shaw (10 Apr-5 Jul), BP Portrait Award (5 Jun-6 Sep), and Allan Ramsay (16 Oct-17 Jan '92).

SW7 The Natural History Museum

The museum's collections were built up around the specimens collected by Sir Hans Sloane and which formed a part of the nucleus of the British Museum. By 1860 the continued expansion of the collections meant that a separate natural history museum was required; it was not until 1881, though, that the new museum – since 1962 officially the British Museum (Natural History) – was opened. The vast and elaborate Romanesque-style building, with its terracotta facing showing relief mouldings of animals, birds and fishes, covers an area of four acres. The exhibits cover most aspects of biology and geology. In the Whale Hall a life size model of the enormous Blue Whale can be seen, and in the Hall of Human Biology visitors can learn about the way their bodies work (including how it feels to be in the womb). Creepy Crawlies shows you how insects, spiders, crabs, and their relatives are important to humans, as both friends and foes. Ecology stresses our relationship with, and responsibility for, the natural world. The opening of a major new permanent exhibition on dinosaurs takes place in Easter. This includes new skeletons, recreated robotic models, and displays on how dinosaurs lived, why they became extinct, and how they were dug up and studied by scientists. The Earth Galleries were formerly the Geological Museum, which contains the largest exhibition on basic earth science in the world, as well as a notable collection of gemstones and a piece of the Moon. The entrance to the Earth Galleries is on Exhibition Road, separate from the Cromwell Road entrance to the main museum, but is covered by the same entrance fee. Public lectures and films are given on Tue, Thu and Sat. Leaflet available on request.

Cromwell Rd (Underground – South Kensington)
☎ 071-938 9123

Open: all year, Mon-Sat 10-6, Sun 11-6. (Closed Good Fri, May Day, 24-26 Dec & 1 Jan).
Admission: ✷ £3.50 (ch 5-18, student, UB40s & pen £1.75). Family ticket £8. Party.
☛ ⅋ toilets for disabled shop ⊁

NW1 Regent's Park

The elegant charm of this park, north of Marylebone Road, can be attributed to John Nash, who laid it out, along with the imposing surrounding terraces, as part of a plan for a new palace which was never built. It now contains London Zoo (see separate entry), a boating lake, open-air theatre, the Regent's Canal and the lovely Queen Mary's Rose Garden. There are a number of Victorian garden ornaments around the park and a group of fossil tree trunks are the only reminders that the Royal Botanic Gardens were once situated here.

(Underground – Baker Street)

W1   Rock Circus

This is the story of rock and pop music from the 1950s to the present day, told through animated wax figures and stereo sound through headsets. Rock Circus re-enacts the great performances of stars such as The Beatles, Elvis Presley, Stevie Wonder and Madonna by use of special effects, memorabilia and, often, original clothing and instruments. Waxwork figures to be unveiled during 1992 include: Bryan Ferry, James Brown, Cliff Richard.

London Pavilion, Piccadilly Circus (Underground – Piccadilly Circus)
☎ 071-734 7203

Open: all year, daily 11-9, Tue 12-9, Fri & Sat 11-10pm, holiday periods in summer 10am-10pm, Tue 12-10.
Admission: £5.95 (ch £3.95, students & pen £4.95). Family ticket £15.85.
♿ toilets for disabled shop ⌘

E1   Pirate Ships at Tobacco Dock

These two replica sailing ships, moored alongside Tobacco Dock, paint a gruesome picture of piracy on the high seas, their decks strewn with corpses as a result of a sudden and bloody raid. Below decks, 'The Three Sisters' houses an animated history of piracy, and 'The Sea Lark' vividly brings to life the story of Robert Louis Stevenson's *Treasure Island*.

The Highway (Underground – Shadwell & Wapping)
☎ 071-702 9681

Open: all year, daily 10-6.
Admission: Three Sisters £2.50 (ch £1.50). Sea Lark £1.
🅿 shop

W1   Pollock's Toy Museum

Teddy bears, board games, toy theatres, tin toys, mechanical and optical toys, folk toys and nursery furniture, are among the attractions to be seen in this appealing museum. Items from all over the world and from all periods are displayed in two small, interconnecting houses with winding staircases and charming little rooms.

1 Scala St (Underground – Goodge Street)
☎ 071-636 3452

Open: all year, Mon-Sat 10-5. (Closed Sun & Xmas).
Admission: £1.50 (ch 3-16, students & pen 50p).
♿ shop

EC2   Royal Britain

All the technical wizardry of the 20th century is employed in this unique exhibition on the history of Britain's monarchy. The visitor walks through time, beginning in the mists of prehistory and ending with a revealing look at royalty today.

Aldersgate St (Underground – Barbican, Moorgate)
☎ 071-588 0588

Open: all year, daily 9-5.30. (Closed 25 Dec).
✗ licensed ♿ toilets for disabled shop ⌘
Details not confirmed for 1992

SW1   The Royal Mews

Designed by John Nash and completed in 1825, the Royal Mews houses the State Coaches. These include the gold, fairy-tale state coach made in 1762, with panels painted by the Florentine artist Cipriani. It has been used for every coronation since that date. The collection also includes the Irish State Coach, private driving carriages and royal sleighs. The Windsor greys and Cleveland Bay carriage horses are stabled here. When the Royal Mews re-opens in April, all seven State Carriages will be displayed together for the first time.

Buckingham Palace, Buckingham Palace Rd (Underground – Victoria)
☎ 071-799 2331

Open: all year, Apr-mid Jul, Wed & Thu; mid Jul-Sep, Wed-Fri; Oct-Mar, Wed only noon-4. (Closed if carriage procession or state visit).
Admission: £2 (ch 17 £1, pen £1.50).
♿ toilets for disabled shop ⌘

15

SW1   St James's Park

Situated between Buckingham Palace and Whitehall, this is the oldest of the Royal Parks in London, drained and converted into a deer park by Henry VIII in 1532. Charles II had the park redesigned in the style of Versailles, but the park as it exists today, with its lake, plantations and walks, was created by Nash for George IV. It remains one of the most delightful and popular places to relax, both for visitors and for workers, who frequently share their sandwiches with the large variety of waterfowl on the lake. There are also band concerts and refreshment facilities.

(Underground – St James's Park)

SE1   Schooner Kathleen & May

The last British wooden, three-masted topsail schooner, is on show to the public in a berth at St Mary Overy Dock, on the South Bank of the River Thames. Exhibitions on board, and film and audio-visual displays provide added interest.

St Mary Overy Dock, Cathedral St
(Underground – London Bridge)
☎ **071-403 3965**

Open: all year, daily 10-5 (4 at wknds); Nov-Mar 11-4. (Closed Xmas, New Year & wknds Nov-Feb).
Admission: £1 (ch, students & pen 50p). Family ticket £2.50.
shop ✗

SW7   Science Museum

Of all the Exhibition Road museums, the Science Museum is the most attractive to children (and often adults too). Among the displays are many working models with knobs to press, handles to turn and buttons to push to various different effects: exhibits are set in motion, light up, rotate and make noises. The collections cover the application of science to technology and illustrate the development of engineering and industry through the ages; there are galleries dealing with printing, chemistry, nuclear physics, navigation, photography, electricity, communications and medicine. A popular feature of the museum is the 'Launch Pad', an interactive children's gallery where children of all ages can carry out their own fun experiments. 'Food for Thought' is a permanent gallery which explains the impact of science and technology on today's food. The centre-piece of the Exploration of Space exhibition is the Apollo 10 space capsule, whilst the world's oldest steam locomotive and Stephenson's *Rocket* can be seen in the huge gallery devoted to rail and road transport. The Wellcome Museum of the History of Medicine features numerous reconstructions of important events in medical history.

Exhibition Rd, South Kensington
(Underground – South Kensington)
☎ **071-938 8000**

Open: all year, Mon-Sat 10-6, Sun 11-6. (Closed 24-26 Dec & 1 Jan).
Admission: ✳ £3.50 (ch & concessions £1.75, pen £2).
🅟 ♿ toilets for disabled shop ✗

WC2   Theatre Museum

Major developments, events and personalities from the performing arts are illustrated in this appealing exhibition. Stage models, costumes, prints, drawings, posters, puppets, props and a variety of other theatre memorabilia

Russell St, Covent Garden
(Underground – Covent Garden, Leicester Sq)
☎ **071-836 7891**

are displayed. Special exhibitions include 'Slap – the Art of Stage Make-up', and 'From Page to Stage' with the *Wind in the Willows*, based on the National Theatre production. There are children's Saturday clubs, evening 'live' theatre productions, and a monthly 'Masterclass' with members of the acting profession talking about their roles in the theatre.

Open: all year, Tue-Sun 11-7.
Admission: ✳ £3 (ch under 5 free, ch, students, disabled, UB40's & pen £1.50). Party. Family ticket.
🍷 ♿ toilets for disabled shop 🍴

SE1 Tower Bridge

Nearly a century old, the fairy-tale outline of Tower Bridge remains one of the capital's most popular landmarks. Its glass-covered walkway stands 142ft above the Thames, affording a panoramic view of the river. Much of the original machinery for working the bridge is still in place and can be seen in the museum.

Walkway (Underground – Tower Hill)
☎ 071-407 0922 & 071-407 5247

Open: all year, Apr-Oct, 10-6.30; Nov-Mar 10-4.45 (last ticket sold 45 mins before closing). (Closed Good Fri, 24-26 Dec & 1 Jan).
Admission: £2.50 (ch 15 & pen £1, ch under 5 free). Party.
♿ toilets for disabled shop 🍴

EC3 Tower of London

Perhaps the most famous castle in the world, the Tower of London has played a central part in British history throughout the ages. The nucleus of the complex is the original White Tower, built by William the Conqueror as a show of strength to the population of London; it remains one of the most outstanding examples of Norman military architecture in Europe. Today it houses the Royal Armouries, the national collection of arms and armour based on the great arsenal of Henry VIII.

For a great part of its history, the Tower of London was used, among other things, as the State Prison. It was here that King Henry VIII had two of his wives executed, here that Lady Jane Grey died and here that Sir Walter Raleigh was imprisoned for 13 years. From the reign of Charles II its main use was as an arsenal, administrative centre and the headquarters of the Royal Mint (until 1812) but during both World Wars it reverted to a state prison and was used to incarcerate German spies.

The unique Yeoman Warders, or 'Beefeater' guards are not present merely as a tourist attraction: they guard the Crown Jewels which are exhibited here. Another feature of the Tower are the ravens whose continued residence is said to ensure that the Kingdom does not fail. The first new raven for 300 years was hatched in May 1989, bringing their numbers up to nine.

Tower Hill (Underground – Tower Hill)
☎ 071-709 0765

Open: all year, Mar-Oct, Mon-Sat 9.30-5.45, Sun 2-5.30 (last admission 5); Nov-Feb, Mon-Sat 9.30-4.30 (last admission 4). (Closed Good Fri, 24-26 Dec & 1 Jan. Jewel House closed 7 Jan-3 Feb).
♿ toilets for disabled shop 🍴
Details not confirmed for 1992

SW7 Victoria & Albert Museum

Covering art and design, from all countries and from all periods and styles, this museum has over seven miles of galleries. It is impossible to take it all in on one visit, and so it is advisable to buy a guide book and plan a route before

Cromwell Rd (Underground – South Kensington)
☎ 071-938 8500

setting off to see the displays. The collection was founded at Marlborough House after the Great Exhibition, and was known as the Museum of Manufactures. In 1857 it moved to its present site and was called the South Kensington Museum. Enlarged and re-designed by Sir Aston Webb at the end of the 19th century it was re-opened in 1909 by Edward VII as the Victoria and Albert Museum. There are two types of galleries: the primary ones which give a comprehensive picture of a period or civilisation; and subject galleries which contain the specialised collections. Features include a series of rooms decorated and equipped with the paintings, furniture and household accessories of particular periods in British history including the enormous 16th-century Great Bed of Ware. The Toshiba Gallery of Japanese Art and Design, the Constable Paintings, Raphael Cartoons and the costume exhibition displayed in the Octagon Court all contribute toward one of the world's outstanding collections of fine and applied arts. Exhibitions for 1992 include 'Sovereign – A celebration of 40 years of Her Majesty The Queen's accession to the throne' (Apr-Sep) and 'The Art of Death' (8 Jan-22 Mar).

Open: all year, Mon-Sat 10-5.50, Sun 2.30-5.50. (Closed Good Fri, May Day, 27 Aug, 24-26 Dec & 1 Jan).
Admission: ✱ Donations-suggested £3 (students, UB40 & pen 50p).
✗ licensed ♿ toilets for disabled shop ✖

OUTER LONDON

BAYSWATER (W2)   London Toy & Model Museum

A fine collection of commercially-made models and toys with emphasis on trains, cars and boats. To add to the interest there is an extensive garden railway.

21-23 Craven Hill (Underground – Bayswater)
☎071-262 9450 & 071-262 7905

Open: all year, Mon-Sat 10-5.30, Sun 11-5.30. (Closed 25-26 Dec & 1 Jan).
Admission: ✱ £2.70 (ch 5-15 £1.20, pen, students & UB40 £1.70). Family ticket £6. Party 15+.
☛ shop ✖

BETHNAL GREEN (E2)   Bethnal Green Museum of Childhood

This prefabricated Victorian hall houses a multitude of childhood delights. Toys, dolls and dolls' houses, model soldiers, puppets, games, model theatres and children's costume are all included in its well planned displays.

Cambridge Heath Rd (Underground – Bethnal Green)
☎ 081-980 2415 & 081-980 3204

Open: all year, Mon-Thu & Sat 10-6, Sun 2.30-6 (Closed Fri, May Day, Spring BH Mon, 24-26 Dec & 1 Jan).
Admission: Free.
🅿 ♿ toilets for disabled shop ✖

BRENTFORD   Kew Bridge Steam Museum

The Victorian pumping station has model engines, steam engines and six beam engines, of which five are working and one is the largest in the world. A forge, diesel house and old workshops can also be seen. Various events are held including a Magic of Meccano show (24/5 Apr), historic engine rally (25 May), and great model steam trials (Sep).

The Pumping Station, Green Dragon Ln (Underground – Gunnersbury)
☎ 081-568 4757

Open: all year, daily 11-5. In steam wknds & BHs. (Closed Xmas wk).
🅿 ☛ ♿ shop

CHESSINGTON   Chessington World of Adventures

Dare you ride the Vampire, the UK's only hanging roller coaster and the Dragon River Water Ride with the most exciting single drop in the UK? Plus Chessington's latest attraction, Professor Burp's Bubble Works, a unique crazy colourful musical indoor water ride for all the family. Over 100 rides and attractions including the Canyon, 5th Dimension, Smugglers' Galleon, Magic Carpet, Safari Skyway Monorail, Old Crocks Rally, the Juggler, an international circus & world famous zoo. Special Saturdays are allocated to Scouts, Cubs, Guides, Brownies and youth clubs, etc. Please telephone for details.

(on A243, M25 off junc 9)
☎ Epsom (0372) 727227

Open: – Theme Park 28 Mar-1 Nov. Zoological Gardens open all year. Last admissions 3pm.
Admission: ✲ £10.50 (£9.50). High season £10.75 (£9.75). Party 20+.
🅿 ✗ 🍷 licensed ♿ (some rides not accessible) toilets for disabled shop ⚑

CHISLEHURST   Chislehurst Caves

This labyrinth of caves has been called the enigma of Kent. Miles of mysterious caverns and passages hewn out of the chalk over some 8,000 years can be explored with experienced guides to tell the history and legends of the caves.

Old Hill (off A222)
☎ 081-467 3264

Open: all year, daily 11-4.30. (closed 25 Dec).
Admission: £2.50 (ch £1.20; longer tours: Sun & BH's only £4 (ch £2).
🅿 🍷 ♿ toilets for disabled shop

CHISWICK (W4)   Chiswick House

Considered to be one of the finest Palladian buildings in Britain, this domed mansion was built between 1725 and 1730 with magnificent interior detailing by William Kent. It has been restored to all its former glory.

Burlington Ln, Chiswick (Underground – Gunnersbury)

Open: all year, Apr-Sep daily 10-6; Oct-Mar: daily 10-4. (Closed 24 & 25 Dec).
Admission: £2 (ch £1, pen, students & UB40 £1.50).
♿ shop ⚑ (EH)

COLINDALE (NW9)   Royal Air Force Museum

Over 65 full-size original aeroplanes and other exhibits, all under cover, tell the fascinating story of flight through the ages. Extensive galleries show the political and historical impact of this means of transport and communication – including the incredible 'Battle of Britain Experience', the story of history's most famous air battle. Visitor facilities include personal stereo-audio tours; a daily free cinema programme, a Tornado flight simulator; guided tours and a regular programme of special events and exhibitions (telephone for details).

Grahame Park Way, Hendon
(Underground – Colindale)
☎ 081-205 2266

Open: daily 10-6. (Closed 24-26 Dec & 1 Jan).
Admission: ✲ £4.10 (ch & concessions £2.05). Family ticket £10. Party 10+.
🅿 ✗ licensed ♿ (wheelchair available) toilets for disabled shop ⚑

EAST HAM (E6)   East Ham Nature Reserve

This 10-acre nature reserve with grassland and woodland, has two nature trails with printed guides (braille version in preparation). One trail is suitable for all disabled visitors. There is a visitor centre with displays relating to natural history and the history of the churchyard nature reserve.

Visitor Centre, Norman Rd
☎ 081-470 4525

Open: Visitor Centre: wknds 2-5. Nature Reserve: summer, Mon-Fri 9-5, wknds 2-5; winter, Mon-Fri 9-4, wknds 2-4.
Admission: Free.
♿ (trails for wheelchairs & blind) toilets for disabled shop ⚑

GREENWICH (SE10)   Cutty Sark Clipper Ship

The fastest tea clipper to be built (in 1869) once sailed 363 miles in a single day. She has been preserved in dry dock since 1957 and her graceful lines dominate the riverside at Greenwich. Exhibitions and a video presentation on board tell the story of the ship and there is a magnificent collection of ships' figureheads. Major restoration work can be seen while the ship is open to visitors, ie shipwrights, riggers etc.

Greenwich Pier
☎ 081-858 3445 & 081-853 3589

Open: all year, daily 10-5, Sun 12-5; 6pm in summer. (Closed 24-26 Dec). Last ticket 30 mins before closing.
Admission: ✻ £3 (concessions £2). Party 15 + .
& (between deck and lower hold deck only) shop ✻

GREENWICH (SE10)   Gipsy Moth IV

Standing near the famous tea clipper is the yacht in which Sir Francis Chichester made the first single-handed sailing trip around the world, in 1966-7.

Greenwich Pier, King William Walk
☎ 081-858 3445 or 081-853 3589

Open: Apr-Oct, daily 10-6; (Sun 12.6). Last ticket 30 mins before closing.
Admission: ✻ 50p (ch 30p)
✻

GREENWICH (SE10)   Greenwich Park

On the northern perimeter of this delightful park is the largest children's playground in any Royal Park. It is famous, though, as the home of the Old Royal Observatory (see separate entry) and the Meridian which marks Nought Degree Longitude, where you can stand in the eastern and western hemispheres at the same time. Mostly laid out by Le Nôtre, whose love of symmetry is very noticeable, the park has wonderful views down over the Royal Naval College to the Thames. The Wilderness is 13 acres of woodland and wild flowers, inhabited by a herd of fallow deer.

GREENWICH (SE10)   National Maritime Museum

The National Maritime Museum tells the story of Britain and the Sea, from ancient boats and Roman trade, through centuries of boatbuilding, battles and exploration to 20th-century trade and pleasurecraft. Features include items from Henry VIII's naval fleet, skilled 17th-century Navy Board models of wooden warships, great masterpieces of battles at Trafalgar and in the Americas. See Nelson's uniform and elegant gilded Royal barges and shalltops.

Romney Rd
☎ 081-858 4422

Open: all year, Mon-Sat 10-5 (6pm in summer). (Closed Good Fri, May Day, 24-27 Dec & 1 Jan).
☛ & (wheelchair available, touch tours on request) toilets for disabled shop ✻
Details not confirmed for 1992

GREENWICH (SE10)   Old Royal Observatory

Charles II founded the Royal Observatory in 1675 'for perfecting navigation and astronomy'. It stands at zero meridian longitude and is the original home of Greenwich Mean Time. Set in the beautiful grounds of Greenwich

Greenwich Park
☎ 081-858 4422

Park, which were laid out to plans by the French gardener, Le Nôtre, who planned the grounds at Versailles, the Royal Observatory is part of the National Maritime Museum. It houses an extensive collection of historic timekeeping, astronomical and navigational instruments.

Open: all year, daily 10-5 (6pm in summer). (Closed Good Fri, May Day, 24-27 Dec & 1 Jan).
🅿 ⅓ shop ✖
Details not confirmed for 1992

HAMPTON COURT   Hampton Court Palace

The palace was started in the early 16th century by Cardinal Wolsey, Lord Chancellor to Henry VIII. When he fell out of favour he presented it to the king as a placatory gesture. Henry VIII expanded the palace by adding the hammer-beamed great hall, the immense kitchens and the Royal Tennis courts. Later monarchs (and Cromwell) left their own mark: Elizabeth I added plants from the New World to the garden, and William and Mary commissioned Wren to remodel part of the building. The result was the handsome Fountain Court, part of which was devastated by fire in recent years.

Today pictures, furniture and tapestries can be seen, and there are handsome gardens and parkland close to the River Thames. Special attractions are the kitchens, the great gatehouse, the orangery with its Mantegna paintings, the Hampton Court vine, and the maze, laid out in the time of William III.

☎ 081-977 8441

Open: all year. Palace & maze, daily 9.30-6 (4.30pm mid-Oct-mid-Mar). 5.15 (Closed 23-26 Dec & 1 Jan).
🅿 (charged) ♨ ✖ licensed & toilets for disabled shop ✖ (ex in gardens)
Details not confirmed for 1992

ISLEWORTH   Syon House

The house stands on the site of a monastery, founded by Henry V. After the Dissolution it passed into the hands of the Duke of Somerset but he was accused of treason by John Dudley. Dudley was created Earl of Northumberland and Syon House became his property. The Earldom was made a Dukedom, and in 1750 the 1st Duke of Northumberland engaged Robert Adam to renovate the mansion. Adam not only adapted the architecture but also was responsible for the furnishings and decoration – the result is spectacular, particularly in the superbly coloured ante-room and gallery library. The Tudor brick was resurfaced with Bath stone in the late 19th century; this gives the exterior a rather harsh appearance but in no way detracts from the splendours inside.

(Approach via Park Rd off Twickenham Rd)
☎ 081-560 0881/3

Open: Apr-Sep, Sun-Thu 12-5 (last ticket 4.15). Oct, Sun only.
🅿 ♨ ✖ licensed & toilets for disabled shop garden centre ✖
Details not confirmed for 1992

ISLEWORTH   Syon Park

Contained within the 55 acres that make up Syon Park is one of the inspirations for the Crystal Palace and the Great Exhibition of 1851: a vast crescent of metal and glass, the first construction of its kind in the world and known as the Great Conservatory. It was designed by Fowler in 1829. The park also boasts a six-acre rose garden which, at the right time of year, assaults the visitor's eye with its brilliant colour; a butterfly house and the largest garden centre in England. Although the horticultural reputation of Syon

(A315 off A310 to Busch Cnr, entry Park Rd)
☎ 081-560 0881/3

Open: all year, Apr-Oct, daily 10-6. Nov-Mar, 10-dusk. (Closed Xmas). Conservatory closed during winter months.
🅿 ♨ ✖ licensed & toilets for disabled shop garden centre ✖
Details not confirmed for 1992

Park goes back to the 16th century – when the use of trees purely as ornaments was looked upon as unique – its beauty today is thanks to the master of landscape design, 'Capability' Brown. It is hardly believable that the peaceful haven he has created beside the River Thames is just nine miles from the centre of London.

ISLEWORTH   Heritage Motor Museum (Syon Park)

Yet another attraction of this glorious park is an exhibition of more than 100 vehicles covering much of the story of the British motor industry. Special displays are mounted during August and September. Car club meets are held most summer weekends. The museum will be relocated to Warwickshire in October 1992.

☎ 081-560 1378

Open: all year, daily 10-5 (4pm Nov-Mar). (Closed 25-26 Dec). Closing at the end of October. Museum relocating to Gaydon, Warwickshire.
Admission: £2.50 (ch & pen £1.75). Family ticket £5.50.
P ☛ ✗ licensed ♿ (wheelchair available) toilets for disabled shop garden centre 🐕

KEW   Kew Gardens (Royal Botanic Gardens)

The world-famous gardens at Kew started as a mere nine-acre site, laid out by George III's mother, Princess Augusta in 1759 (she lived in the White House at Kew which has long since been demolished). In 1841 the gardens were given to the State and by 1904, after Queen Victoria had presented more of the surrounding land to the country, the gardens covered 300 acres – their present size. The 19th-century botanist, Sir Joseph Banks, and head gardener, William Aiton (later curator), were largely responsible for laying the foundations of the great collection of plants, shrubs and trees which exist here today; a collection which not only gives great public enjoyment but also forms part of the world's foremost botanical research centre. The west of the gardens is largely woodland and arboretum, while the formal gardens, with their lawns and neatly manicured beds are in the eastern half. The site has inspired some notable architectural features, both old and very modern. The Palm House is perhaps the most elegant: an early example of glass and wrought iron, it was completed in 1848. But the most famous landmark at Kew is the Chinese Pagoda; it stands 163ft high in ten storeys. Plants that would not otherwise be seen in Britain are grown in houses which reproduce special climatic conditions and among many other features are art galleries, one showing works for sale the other exhibiting the work of Victorian artist Marianne North. Wheelchairs are available (booking advisable) free of charge and there are purpose-built toilets for wheelchair users. Art exhibitions are changed every 6-8 weeks, and there are jazz concerts with a firework finale in the last week in July. Telephone for details.

(Underground – Kew Bridge)
☎ 081-940 1171

Open: all year. Gardens daily 9.30-between 4-6.30pm on weekdays, between 4-8pm Suns & PH, depending on the time of sunset.
Admission: Fee payable.
P ☛ ✗ licensed ♿ toilets for disabled shop 🐕

SYMBOLS

☎ Telephone number	✳ Indicates 1991 price	☛ Refreshments	🐕 No Dogs
♿ Suitable for visitors in wheelchairs	**P** Parking at Establishment	✗ Restaurant	🚌 No coaches

KEW Kew Palace

A favourite country residence during the reign of the first three Hanoverian Kings, Kew was the site of several royal houses although only three of the buildings now remain. A fairly modest red-brick building, built in the Dutch style with gables, Kew Palace was built in 1631 and used for nearly a century until 1818 when Queen Charlotte died. It was opened to the public in 1899 and remains much as it was in George III's time, reflecting the quiet country life his family enjoyed here. Family paintings and personal relics, furniture and tapestries are on display, and a charming 17th-century garden has been recreated.

Royal Botanic Gardens (Underground – Kew Bridge)
☎ 081-940 3321
Open: Apr-Sep, daily 11-5.30.
shop ✝
Details not confirmed for 1992

KEW Queen Charlotte's Cottage

The cottage is typical of the rustic-style edifices built by the gentry in the 18th century and was used by the royal family as a summer house and a place to take tea. The interior is designed to give the impression of a tent.

Royal Botanic Gardens (Underground – Kew Bridge)
☎ 081-977 9518
Open: Apr-Sep, Sat, Sun & BH 11-5.30.
shop ✝
Details not confirmed for 1992

RICHMOND Richmond Park

With its herds of deer, abundant wild life and centuries-old oaks, Richmond is a favourite haunt for visitors and naturalists. There is a formal garden at Pembroke Lodge, and the various plantations show a wealth of exotic shrubs and wild flowers. Model sail boats are allowed on Adam's Pond, where the deer drink, and the 18-acre Pen Ponds have been specially made for angling (permit required).

(Underground – Richmond)

ST JOHNS WOOD (NW8) Primrose Hill

Once part of the same hunting forest as Regent's Park, Primrose Hill retains in its name the rural character and charm that it undoubtedly had in the past. The view from the summit is panoramic and encompasses virtually the whole of central London. In 1842 its 62 acres gained gaslights, a gymnasium and respectability as a Royal Park.

TEDDINGTON Bushy Park

Situated close to Hampton Court, this is one of London's ten Royal parks, formerly hunting preserves, which were opened to the public by Charles I and Charles II. Bushy Park has a famous Chestnut Avenue which runs from Hampton Court to the Teddington Gate. This superb double row of enormous trees, laid out by Wren, is best seen in springtime.

TWICKENHAM   Rugby Football Union

A visit to the Twickenham Rugby Football ground captures the marvellous atmosphere of this popular sport on match days. Visitors are given a tour of the changing rooms, the famous double baths and the medical room, and are shown a video which lasts about 15 minutes.

There are also displays of kits and trophies presented to the RFU by other unions around the world, with a museum of the game's past history and a souvenir shop.

Rugby Rd
☎ 081-892 8161
Open: Mon-Fri, tours 10.30 & 2.15. (Closed wk before Internationals. By prior arrangement, telephone for reservations).
🅿 ✗ licensed ♿ toilets for disabled shop
Details not confirmed for 1992

WEMBLEY   Wembley Stadium

Wembley is Britain's largest and most important stadium. It was built in 1923 for the British Empire Exhibition and has a capacity of 100,000. The 1948 Olympic Games were held here, it is the home of the England football team, and it is also the venue for the annual Cup Final and other cup competitions. Other large audience events held here have included the Live Aid rock concert, and in 1977 a large conference centre attached to the stadium was opened.

The tour around the complex includes a visit to the dressing rooms. A walk up the player's tunnel, accompanied by sound effects of a roaring crowd, is one of the highlights of the visit.

Empire Way
☎ 081-902 8833
Open: all year, daily 9.45-last tour departs 4. (Closed on days of events & 25 Dec).
Admission: £3.50 (ch & pen £2.50). Party.
🅿 (charged) ♨ ♿ toilets for disabled shop ⅍

WOOLWICH (SE18)   Thames Barrier Visitors Centre

Built to prevent the possibility of disastrous flooding, the Thames Barrier spans a third of a mile and is the world's largest movable flood barrier. It is sometimes described as the eighth wonder of the world. The nearby visitors' centre and exhibition on the South Bank explains the flood threat and the construction of this £480 million project. Each month a test closure, lasting over 2 hours, is carried out and the annual full day closure of all ten gates takes place in the autumn.

Unity Way
☎ 081-854 1373
Open: all year, daily 10.30-5 (5.30 Sat & Sun). (Closed Xmas – telephone for details). Evening openings in summer and for groups – telephone for details.
Admission: ✳ £2.25 (ch & pen £1.40). Car park 50p Coach park Free. Family ticket £6.10. Party.
🅿 (charged) ♨ ✗ licensed ♿ (lift) toilets for disabled shop ⅍

SYMBOLS

☎ Telephone number	✳ Indicates 1991 price	♨ Refreshments	⅍ No Dogs
♿ Suitable for visitors in wheelchairs	🅿 Parking at Establishment	✗ Restaurant	🚌 No coaches

ABBREVIATIONS

AM	Ancient Monument	BH	Bank Holidays	ch 15 20p	Children under 15 20p
AM(CadW)	Ancient Monument (Wales)	PH	Public Holidays	Pen	Senior Citizens
		Etr	Easter	Party	Special or reduced rates for
EH	English Heritage	ex	except		parties booked in advance
NT	National Trust	Free	Admission free	Party 30+	Special or reduced rates for
NTS	National Trust for Scotland	10p	Admission 10p		parties of 30 or more booked in advance
		ch 20p	Children 20p		

ENGLAND

AVON

BATH   see page 26

BRISTOL   see page 28

PRISTON   Priston Mill

Once run by the monks of Bath Abbey, this is one of the mills that have supplied flour to the citizens for hundreds of years. Set in rolling countryside, the history and workings of the watermill are described by staff, and other attractions include a trailer ride, a nature trail, and children's play areas.

Priston Mill Farm (6m SW, off A39)
☎ **(0225) 423894**
Open: Etr-Sep, daily 2.15-5.30, Sat, Sun & BH 11-5.30.
Admission: £2.10 (ch & pen £1.40). Party. Free admission for disabled in wheelchairs.
🅿 ✗ licensed ᶜ shop ✹

WESTON-SUPER-MARE   International Helicopter Museum

A unique collection of more than 40 helicopters and autogyros is on display. This is given a further dimension by exhibits of models, photographs and components to illustrate how the aircraft work. There is a ride simulator, and the third Sun in summer months is 'Open Cockpit Day' when visitors can try out the pilots seat of a real helicopter, and enjoy a pleasure flight (weather/serviceabllity permitting). Helicopters from this museum are also featured in the Weston-Super Helidays (25/26 July), which take place on the seafront.

Weston Airport, Locking Moor Rd
☎ **(0934) 635227**
Open: all year, Mar-Oct, daily 10-6 & Nov-Feb, Thu-Sun 10.30-4.
Admission: £2.50 (ch under 5 free, 5-15 & pen £1.50). Family ticket £6.50. Party 15+.
🅿 ♥ ᶜ toilets for disabled shop

WESTON-SUPER-MARE   Woodspring Museum

This museum, housed in the workshops of the Edwardian Gaslight Company, is set around a central courtyard with displays of the Victorian seaside holiday, an old chemist's shop, a dairy, and a lion fountain with Victorian pavement mosaics. Adjoining the museum is Clara's Cottage, a Westonian home of the 1900s with period kitchen, parlour, bedroom and back yard. One of the rooms has an additional display of Peggy Nisbet dolls. Other displays in the museum include a gallery of wildlife in the district, Mendip minerals, mining and local archaeology. There are also costume rooms, an exhibition of transport, cameras, and a display on the dentist in 1900. Changing exhibitions are held in the Temporary Exhibitions Gallery.

Burlington St
☎ **(0934) 621028**
Open: all year, Mon-Sat 10-5. (Closed Xmas, New Year & Good Fri).
Admission: Free.
♥ ᶜ toilets for disabled shop ✹

In 1988 Bath was designated a World Heritage City – one of only three in the world. It has been a popular place to visit for around 2,000 years: first came the early Celtic visitors to worship Sulis, the Goddess of the Sacred Spring, then the Romans whose Baths can still be visited, later came the high society of Georgian times, whose patronage shaped the city we see today, and now today's tourists (perhaps sometimes too many of them) who come to marvel at the heritage left by their predecessors.

History is on every street and Bath's numerous museums house many exhibits of national importance, but amidst all this serious heritage there is a charming mix of the unusual and even eccentric, such as "Mr Bowler's Business" at the Bath Industrial Heritage Centre – the recreated 19th-century workshops of a local fizzy drinks maker and engineer. And who would expect this historic city to be the home of the Spitting Image Puppet Rooms with its collection of world-famous personalities in "living rubber"?

For architecture, the best bits include Royal Crescent, The Circus and Pulteney Bridge, but the city is built on hills so be prepared for some steep walking. There is always the alternative of the regular sightseeing buses, with commentary, which pick up at various points, including the magnificent Bath Abbey, or the 50-minute boat trips from the Pulteney Bridge landing stage. For picnics, or just a breather from all the buildings, Bath has lots of parks (the city has won the Britain in Bloom competition nine times); Royal Victoria Park (overlooked by the magnificent Royal Crescent), probably has the most to offer, with a lake, boating pool, superb children's play area and a seven-acre Botanical Garden.

Bath is a lively city, particularly during the arts festival in late May/early June and the carnival in early September, events which roughly mark the beginning and end of a season during which the city can suffer from a touch of tourist overload. If you can avoid the high season it is advisable to do so, particularly as few of the attractions here depend on the weather. If you plan to see a number of attractions during your visit, ask at the tourist office about combined tickets and family tickets which could save you money.

Tourist information: The Colonnades, Bath Street Telephone: (0225) 462831

☆ STAR ATTRACTIONS

American Museum

Claverton Manor is two miles east of Bath, in a beautiful setting above the River Avon. The house was built in 1829 by Sir Jeffrey Wyatville, and is now a museum of American decorative arts. A series of rooms show American life from the 17th to 19th centuries, with special sections on American Indians and the Shakers, and a distinctive collection of quilts. The gardens are also well worth seeing, and include an American arboretum. Winston Churchill made his first political speech in the grounds in 1897.

Claverton Manor (2.5m E off A36)
☎ (0225) 460503

Open: 29 Mar-3 Nov, Tue-Sun 2-5. Gardens 1-6, BH Sun & Mon 11-5.
P ☕ ♿ toilets for disabled shop
Details not confirmed for 1992

Bath Industrial Heritage Centre

The centre houses the Bowler collection, the entire stock-in-trade of a Victorian brass founder, general engineer and aerated water manufacturer, displayed so as to capture the atmosphere of the original premises. Also here is 'the Story of Bath Stone', with a replica of a mine face before mechanisation, and a Bath cabinet maker's workshop, complete with tools and original drawings. A series of temporary exhibitions will include displays from the collection of travelling exhibitions, and there will be a series of lectures throughout the year.

Camden Works, Julian Rd
☎ (0225) 318348

Open: all year, winter 10-4 (last entry 3pm), summer 10-5. (Closed 24-26 Dec).
Admission: ✻ £2.50 (ch, pen & students £1.50). Family ticket £7.
☕ shop

No 1 Royal Crescent

Bath is very much a Georgian city, but most of its houses have naturally altered over the years to suit changing tastes and lifestyles. Built in 1768 by John Wood the Elder, No 1 Royal Crescent has been restored to look as it would have done some 200 years ago. Two floors are furnished as they might have been in the 18th century, with pictures, china and furniture of the period, and there is also an interesting kitchen. Note also the first-floor windows, which are the original length: all the others in the Royal Crescent were lengthened downwards in the 19th century. The house was once the home of the Duke of York, famed for marching his 10,000 men up the hill and down again.

☎ (0225) 428126

Open: Apr-Sep, daily 11-5; Mar & Oct-13 Dec, Tue-Sun 11-4. (Closed Good Fri). Last admission 30 mins before closing.
Admission: £3 (ch, students & pen £2)
shop ✝

Roman Baths & Pump Room

The descent to the Roman baths is a step back in time. The remains give a vivid impression of life nearly 2000 years ago. The Baths, built next to Britain's only hot spring, served the sick and the pilgrims visiting the adjacent Temple of Sulis Minerva. The Spring was a sacred site lying within the courtyard of the Temple. Votive offerings and temple treasures discovered during the excavations of the Spring can be seen in the museum display.

Today, the Temple Courtyard is beneath the Pump Room. This building became a popular meeting place in the 18th century when Bath became the leading resort for fashionable society. Inside the present Pump Room there is now a restaurant where morning coffee, lunches and teas can be taken to the accompaniment of music from the Pump Room Trio. The hot spa water can also be sampled.

Abbey Church Yard
☎ (0225) 461111 ext 2785

Open: all year, Mar-Jul & Sep-Oct daily 9-6, Aug daily 9-6 & 8pm-10pm, Nov-Feb Mon-Sat 9-5, Sun 10-5. Disabled visitors free admission to ground floor areas. Last admission 30 minutes before closing.
Admission: fee payable.
✗ licensed ⴷ toilets for disabled shop ✝

Sally Lunn's Refreshment House & Museum

The history of this Tudor building can be traced to Roman times. It is the oldest home in Bath, and became a popular meeting place in the 18th century. In the cellars, a fascinating museum reveals the findings of recent excavations. Here too is the original kitchen, with its faggot oven, Georgian cooking range and a collection of baking utensils. The traditional 'Sally Lunn' is still served in the restaurant: it is a bread like the French 'brioche', made with eggs and butter, popularly believed to have been named after its first maker, who came to Bath in 1680.

4 North Pde Passage
☎ (0225) 461634

Open: all year, museum – Mon-Sat 10-5 & Sun 12-6; refreshment rooms – Mon 10-6, Tue-Sat 10am-10.30pm & Sun 12-10.30pm. (Closed 25-26 Dec & 1 Jan).
Admission: 30p (ch & pen free).
▼ ✗ licensed shop ✝▦

Bath Postal Museum

Ralph Allen, 18th-century postmaster of Bath, helped to reform England's post, and the first letters with stamps were probably posted in Bath. Together with Mr John Palmer, another Bath citizen, Mr Allen introduced the first nationwide mail coach service. The museum has displays on written communications throughout history, exhibitions and films, and of course stamps. A special exhibition will be held from April to December – Pictures in the Post.

8 Broad St
☎ (0225) 460333

Open: all year, Mon-Sat 11-5; Sun 2-5 (Apr-Oct). Parties by appointment. (Closed Good Fri, 25-26 Dec & 1 Jan).
Admission: £1.70 (ch 50p, pen, UB40 & students £1). Party 10+.
▼ ⴷ shop ✝

Bristol is one of those old seafaring towns which has rejuvenated its derelict docks into an area which attracts many visitors. Old warehouses have now been transformed to house fascinating museums telling the story of 1,000 years of Bristol's maritime and industrial history. On the water itself various watersports events are popular, but the main attraction is the SS *Great Britain*.

Those for whom Bristol is synonymous with sherry might head for Harvey's Wine Museum in Denmark Street and there are many beautiful historic houses and museums around the city. The cathedral dates from the 12th century and contains many splendid features. A short distance from the city is the famous Clifton Suspension Bridge over the Avon Gorge.

Bristol is also a cultural centre, with no less than 14 art galleries in and around the city, highly regarded concert halls and the Bristol Old Vic – one of the country's leading repertory theatres. Best shopping streets are in the Queens Road/Park Street/College Green area.

Tourist information: 14 Narrow Quay Telephone: (0272) 260767

☆ *STAR ATTRACTIONS*

Bristol Industrial Museum
The museum is housed in a converted dockside transit shed. Motor and horse-drawn vehicles from the Bristol area are shown, with locally built aircraft and aero-engines. Railway exhibits include the industrial locomotive 'Henbury', in steam about once a month. There are also machines used in local industry, and displays on the history of the port.

Prince's Wharf, Prince St
☎ (0272) 251470
Open: all year, Sat-Wed 10-1 & 2-5. Please check for BH closures.
Admission: Free.
🅿 (charged) ⅇ toilets for disabled shop ⚹

The Exploratory Hands-on-Science Centre
As its name suggests, this is a museum which invites the visitor to try things out. Bubbles and bridges, lights and lasers, mechanics and mirrors – they are all here to discover and enjoy. Come to the Exploratory and find out for yourself! There will be a special exhibition held during the summer, telephone for details.

Bristol Old Station, Temple Meads
☎ (0272) 252008
Open: all year, daily 10-5 (Closed Xmas wk).
Admission: £3.50 (ch, pen & student £2.30, ch under 5 free) Family ticket £22 (allows 10 visits/visitors, valid for 1 year). Party 10+.
🛇 ⅇ toilets for disabled shop ⚹

SS Great Britain
Designed by Isambard Kingdom Brunel, the ship was the first iron, screw-propelled ocean-going vessel, and was launched in 1843. She was restored in the dry dock where she was built, and is now the centrepiece of the revitalised Bristol docks.

Great Western Dock, Gas Ferry Rd (off Cumberland Rd)
☎ (0272) 260680
Open: all year daily 10-6, 5pm in winter. (Closed 24 & 25 Dec).
🅿 (charged) 🛇 ⅇ shop ⚹
Details not confirmed for 1992

Zoological Gardens
Set in extensive gardens, the zoo has a varied collection of mammals, birds and reptiles, and the 'World of Water'. There are outdoor activities in the school holidays, and a full programme of special events.

Clifton Down
☎ (0272) 738951
Open: all year, daily (ex 25 Dec) from 9am. Closing times vary with season.
Admission: £4.50 (ch 3-13 £2.20, pen £2.20 on Mon ex BHs).
🅿 (charged) 🛇 ✗ licensed ⅇ toilets for disabled shop ⚹

BEDFORDSHIRE

LEIGHTON BUZZARD Leighton Buzzard Railway

The original light railway was built to carry sand in 1919, and after its redundancy in 1967 the railway society took over its three and a half mile length. It is now a 2ft gauge passenger-carrying line through varied scenery with over 30 locomotives, including nine resident steam engines from West Africa, India, Spain and Britain. 1992 is the 25th anniversary of the preservation, and a major Steam Festival will be held on 2 Aug-13 Sep. Other events include a Teddy Bears' Outing (10 May), a 25th Birthday Steam Gala (21 Jun), and special Christmas trains in Dec.

Pages Park Station, Billington Rd
(.75m SE on A4146)
☎ (0525) 373888

Open: operating dates Suns, 5 Apr-4 Oct, Etr wknd & BH Mons. Also Wed & Thu 5 Aug-3 Sep. Trains run to Stonehenge Works. Return journey lasts 1hr. Trains run between 11am-3.10pm (4.30 Sun & BH Mons).
Admission: Return ticket £3.50 (ch 5-15 £1.75, pen £2.80, ch under 5 free).
🅿 ☕ ᵹ shop

OLD WARDEN The Shuttleworth Collection

Housed in seven hangars in a classic grass aerodrome, 30 working historic aeroplanes span the progress of aviation with exhibits ranging from a 1909 Bleriot to a 1941 Spitfire. A garage of roadworthy motor vehicles explores the era of the 1898 Panhard Levassor and there is a coach room of carriages from earlier years.

(2m W from rdbt on A1, Biggleswade by-pass)
☎ Northill (076727) 288

Open: all year, daily 10-4 (3pm Nov-Mar). Closed 1 wk at Xmas.
🅿 ☕ ✗ licensed ᵹ toilets for disabled shop
Details not confirmed for 1992

STAGSDEN Stagsden Bird Gardens

A breeding centre for many species of birds, including owls, cranes, pheasants, waterfowl and old breeds of poultry. There is also a fine collection of shrub roses.

(5m W of Bedford, on the A422)
☎ Oakley (02302) 2745

Open: all year, daily 11-6 or dusk. (Closed 25 Dec)
Admission: £2.50 (ch £1 & pen £2).
🅿 ᵹ shop 🐾

WHIPSNADE Whipsnade Wild Animal Park

The Park is set in 600 acres of beautiful parkland and is the home to almost 3000 animals. Wallabies, peacocks, mara and Chinese water deer roam freely among the woods, and many of the animals here are rare and endangered species in the wild. Whipsnade's conservation and breeding programmes for endangered species are known and respected worldwide. Things to see and do include Bird of Prey demonstrations, World of Sealions, Elephants at Work, Animal Encounters, Discovery Centre, Woodland Bird Walk, Wolf Wood, Chimpanzee Centre, Passage through Asia, Children's Farm, Duck Island, a steam railway and a new tiger enclosure called Tiger Falls, which allows visitors to look down into the enclosure at different points. Events at Whipsnade include an Easter Egg Hunt (17-20 May), Steam Weekend (2-4 May), Conservation Matters (25/26 July), and Bank Holiday Teddy '92 (29-31 August) – subject to change, telephone for details.

☎ (0582) 872171

Open: all year, Mon-Sat 10-6, Sun & BH 10-7 or sunset. (Closed 25 Dec). Closes earlier in winter.
Admission: ✱ £5.95 (ch under 4 free, 4-15 £3.95, pen & disabled £4.95) Cars £6.
🅿 ☕ ✗ licensed ᵹ toilets for disabled shop 🐾

WOBURN   Woburn Abbey & Deer Park

This palatial 18th-century mansion is the home of the Duke of Bedford. The house dates from 1744 but was remodelled in 1802 by Henry Holland. Originally a Cistercian abbey, the Dukes of Bedford have lived at Woburn since 1547. There is a valuable art collection in the house with paintings by Canaletto, Rembrandt, Van Dyck, Gainsborough and many others. There is also an extensive collection of 18th-century furniture, both French and English. There are 14 state apartments on view and the private apartments are shown when not in use by the family. The house stands in 3,000 acres of parkland, famous for its collection of varieties of deer. Special events are held during the year; please telephone for details.

☎ (0525) 290666

Open: Abbey Sat & Sun only Jan-28 Mar, 11-4.45; 29 Mar-1 Nov daily 11-5.45 (6.15pm Sun). Last admission 45 mins before closing time. Deer Park Sat & Sun only Jan-28 Mar, 10.30-3.45; 29 Mar-1 Nov daily 10-4.45 (5.45 Sun).
Admission: ✳ Abbey & Deer Park £5.50 (ch 7-16 £2, pen £4. Family ticket (2 adults & 2-4 ch) £12.50-£15.50. Deer Park only car & passengers £2.50. Motorcycles & passengers £1.25.
1🅿 ⬤ ✗ licensed ㋐ (wheelchairs accommodated by prior arrangement) toilets for disabled shop garden centre ⅙

WOBURN   Wild Animal Kingdom & Leisure Park

Within the 3,000 acres of parkland belonging to Woburn Abbey, is an area of over 300 acres set aside as a wild animal kingdom. A collection of many species of animal has made Woburn justifiably famous among Safari Parks. Woburn's own safari road passes through an African plains area stocked with eland, zebra, hippos and rhinos. Then through the well-keepered tiger and lion enclosures and on past bears and monkeys. The Pets Corner, Sea Lion and Parrot Shows, and Elephant Displays, are all popular attractions. The large leisure complex also offers a boating lake and adventure playground.

☎ (0525) 290407

Open: 7 Mar-1 Nov, daily 10-5.
Admission: £7 (ch & pen £4.50).
🅿 ✗ licensed ㋐ toilets for disabled shop ⅙

BERKSHIRE

BASILSDON   Beale Bird Park

Ornamental pheasants, peacocks, parrots, owls, cranes and wildfowl can be seen here in a pleasant riverside setting (a designated area of Outstanding Natural Beauty), together with Highland cattle and rare breeds of sheep, a pets corner and a tropical house. There is a craft centre, and a children's playground with paddling pools and sandpits. There is also excellent fishing in season. The park has an information/education facility, and numerous events and exhibitions are held during the year. River trips are another attraction, and a narrow gauge railway runs around the park every day. Amidst all this is the unusual focal point of the mausoleum, built by Mr Child Beale in memory of his parents, surrounded by a large and varied collection of statues, fountains and walks. Wheelchairs are available at the park and there are purpose-built toilets for wheelchair users. Events for 1992 include a craft show (14-16 Aug), Multiple Sclerosis Family Fun day (12 or 19 Jul), and various horse shows and car club days throughout the year.

Church Farm, Lower Basildon
☎ **Upper Basildon (0491) 671325 or (0734) 845172**

Open: daily, Mar-Sep 10-6. Last admission 5pm. Oct-23 Dec 10-5. Last admission 4pm.
Admission: £4 (ch under 3 free, 3-16 & disabled £2, pen £3) Party 15+.
🅿 ⬤ ㋐ toilets for disabled shop ⅙ 🖾

ELCOT   Elcot Park Resort Hotel

The hotel's 16-acre garden overlooks the Kennet valley, and has beautiful lawns and woodland. There is a magnificent display of daffodils and blossom in spring, with rhododendrons and other shrubs coming into flower a little later. It was first laid out by Sir William Paxton.

☎ **Kintbury (0488) 58100**
Open: all year, daily.
P ✗ licensed &
Details not confirmed for 1992

ETON   Dorney Court

This enchanting brick and timber house stands in a tranquil setting. It has tall Tudor chimneys and a splendid great hall and has been the home of the present family since 1510.

Dorney
☎ **Burnham (0628) 604638**
Open: Etr wknd, then Sun & BH Mon in May; Jun-Sep, Sun-Tue 2-5.30 (last admission 5pm).
Admission: £3 (ch 9 £1.50).
P ☞ shop ✗

MAIDENHEAD   Courage Shire Horse Centre

Visitors are free to wander around and meet the horses, or take a free tour with an experienced guide who will introduce you to the horses and explain the care and history of the 'gentle giants' of the equestrian world. See the harness maker at work, and certain days will find the farrier or cooper in attendance. Dray rides are also available. Events include Vintage Day (17 May), Rural Craft Fayre (6/7 Jun), Exemption Dog Show (19 Jul), Owl Hawk and Falconry Day (13 Sep), and Heavy Horse Show (17/18 Oct).

Cherry Garden Ln, Maidenhead Thicket (off A4, .5m W of A4/A423/A423M Jct)
☎ **Littlewick Green (062882) 4848**
Open: Mar-Oct, daily 10.30-5.
Admission: £2.80 (ch & pen £2).
P ☞ & toilets for disabled shop

RISELEY   Wellington Country Park & National Dairy Museum

The park consists of 600 acres of woodland and meadows, set around a lake in the countryside between Reading and Basingstoke. The National Dairy Museum in the grounds outlines the history of the dairy industry in Britain. There is also a Thames Valley Time Trail, which traces the development of earth and mineral resources in the area. Other attractions are the collections of small domestic animals, a deer park and a miniature steam railway. Five nature trails are marked out, in addition to a fitness course and adventure playground. It is also possible to do some fishing, sailing, windsurfing or rowing. Events for 1992 include Easter fun and crafts (19/20 Apr), a horticultural show (2 Aug), and a Shetland Pony show (5 Sep).

(off B3349)
☎ **Reading (0734) 326444**
Open: all year, Mar-Oct, daily 10-5.30 & winter wknds 10-dusk.
Admission: £2.70 (ch 5-15 £1.20). Party 20+.
P ☞ & (fishing platform for disabled) toilets for disabled shop

WINDSOR   see page 32

SYMBOLS			
☎ Telephone number	* Indicates 1991 price	☞ Refreshments	✗ No Dogs
& Suitable for visitors in wheelchairs	P Parking at Establishment	✗ Restaurant	🚍 No coaches

Outside London, Windsor offers one of the most popular days out in Britain and, as the official residence of the Queen, is the only other place which can offer a similar degree of Royal pageantry, with a Changing of the Guard ceremony at 11am daily from May to early August and on alternate days for the rest of the year. The annual Garter Ceremony at St George's Chapel is a spectacular procession followed by a service to commemorate the founding of the Most Noble Order of the Garter. In addition, visiting Heads of State are sometimes entertained at the Castle and are usually received in the town and driven through the streets in horse-drawn carriages, amid much pomp and pageantry. Windsor has a long Royal history. The Saxons had a Royal Manor here and the present castle was begun by William the Conqueror in about 1070. Most successive monarchs added to the castle and now, covering some 13 acres, it is the largest inhabited castle in the world.

There is more to see in the town than anyone could manage in a single day's visit, and concentrating on the main attractions is, of course, a priority. But try to return and take in the Curfew Tower with its splendid medieval vaulted dungeons and secret passages, the Albert Memorial Chapel, converted by Queen Victoria as a memorial to her late husband, the impressive Guildhall and the Old Town, with its network of cobbled streets and many historic associations, or the famous Eton College, just across the river.

An excellent introduction to the town would be to take one of the guided walking tours which leave the Tourist Information Centre at regular intervals and take in the most interesting parts. Or take the Round Windsor Sightseeing Tour on an open-topped bus, departing from the High Street and Central Station every 15 minutes every day. Tickets are purchased on the bus or in advance from the "Guide Friday" office at the station. To really see the town in style, horse-drawn carriages are available for hire outside the station. There are also regular boat trips on the Thames of varying distances lasting from 35 minutes to 3½ hours.

If you have the time, or need an active break from all the sightseeing, there are lovely riverside walks, or venture into Windsor Great Park, 4,000 acres of woodland, farms and open fields, much of which is open to the public, notably the lovely Savill Garden and Valley Garden and Virginia Water.

Tourist information: Windor and Eton Central Station Telephone: (0735) 852010.

☆ *STAR ATTRACTIONS*

Windor Castle

☎ (0753) 831118

The castle, which covers 13 acres is the official residence of H.M. The Queen and the largest inhabited castle in the world. It was begun as a wooden fort by William the Conqueror, but has been added to by almost every other monarch. Henry II erected the first stone building, including the famous Round Tower. Among the many alterations since then were those made in the 14th century by Edward III; the 17th century when the Castle began to be altered from a fortress to a palace; and the 19th century when Edward III enlarged the royal apartments and also founded the Order of Knights of the Garter, based at Windsor. Substantial rebuilding was done during the reign of Charles II and Sir Jeffrey Wyattville (1766-1840) was the architect for alterations made by George IV. The castle is in three parts – the Upper Ward which includes the State Apartments, the Middle Ward, with its Round Tower, and the Lower Ward where St George's Chapel is situated. From the Round Tower there are views of 12 counties.

Open: all year - Castle precincts, but subject to closure at short notice.
Admission: Precincts - free.
♿ toilets for disabled shop ✗

State Apartments

There are 16 State Rooms in the Castle, each one not only historically interesting in itself but also a treasure house of superb furniture, porcelain, armour and, especially, paintings. The rooms are decorated with carvings by Grinling Gibbons and ceilings by Verrio. On the walls is a selection from The Queen's unique collection of pictures by painters such as Van Dyck and Rembrandt. These apartments are generally open to the public but may have to be closed at short notice for some Royal functions.

Windsor Castle
☎ (0753) 831118

Open: all year, except when Her Majesty The Queen is in official residence. Telephone (0753) 831118 for information. *Admission:* £4 (ch £1.50, pen £2.50) & toilets for disabled shop ✻

St George's Chapel

The chapel is an impressive feature of Windsor Castle. Begun in 1475 by Edward IV, and completed in the reign of Henry VIII, it is a fine example of Perpendicular architecture which, with its large windows, gives a light and spacious effect. The magnificent fan vaulting on the ceiling, the chantries, the ironwork and intricate carving on the choir stalls, all add to this superb building. The choir stalls are dedicated to the Order of Knights of the Garter founded by Edward III. Each stall displays the arms of every knight who has sat there and above it are the banner and crested helm of the present holder. To celebrate the Queen's 40th accession to the throne, a Flower and Music Festival will be held on 6-11 May (to be confirmed).

Windsor Castle
☎ (0753) 865538

Open: weekdays 10-4, Sun 2-4. (Closed 6 Jan-3 Feb, 26 Apr, 12-16 Jun, 24-25 Dec & occasionally at short notice). *Admission:* ✻ £2.50 (ch & pen £1.50) Family ticket £6. & shop ✻

Queen Mary's Dolls' House

The exquisite dolls' house, designed for Queen Mary in the 1920s by Lutyens, is displayed at Windsor Castle. Every piece of furniture, decoration, tableware and equipment in the miniature house has been carried out in perfect detail on a scale of 1:12.

Windsor Castle
☎ (0753) 831118

Open: all year, times vary with season. *Admission:* £1.50 (ch 70p, pen £1.30). shop ✻

Royalty & Empire Exhibition

Situated opposite Windsor Castle, Royalty and Empire recreates the events which celebrated Queen Victoria's Diamond Jubilee in 1897, using full-size wax figures created by the famous Tussaud's waxworks and displayed in the original surroundings of the historical events to evoke the atmosphere of the times.

One particularly outstanding feature of the exhibition is a theatre show, unique in Europe, which has moving and speaking life-size models of famous Victorians.

Windsor & Eton Central Station, Thames St
☎ (0753) 857837

Open; all year, daily 9.30-5.30 (4.30 in winter). (Closed 25 Dec & part Jan). ▆ & toilets for disabled shop ✻ Details not confirmed for 1992

Windsor Safari Park

Windsor Safari Park offers visitors an 'African Adventure' in the heart of Berkshire! Explore the new Egyptian Entrance and Moroccan Village. Catch one of the new Safari Roadtrains to come close to some of nature's most spectacular and dangerous animals, and don't miss the new Funicular Railway which passes the Elephant Gardens. See the many exciting shows including the Birds of Prey display and the famous Seaworld Show. Enjoy the Port Livingstone area which contains a host of exciting attractions including Limpopo Crocodiles, Swamp Devils and African Queen Riverboat Ride. The entrance price includes admission to all the shows and attractions.

Winkfield Rd (SW of town on B3022)
☎ (0753) 830886

Open: all year, daily from 10am. (Closed 25 Dec). *Admission:* ✻ Telephone for admission prices. 🅿 ▆ ✗ licensed & toilets for disabled shop ✻

BUCKINGHAMSHIRE

BEACONSFIELD   Bekonscot Model Village

Bekonscot is the oldest model village in the world, first opened in 1929. The layout of little cottages, farms and countryside (including a gauge 'one' railway) is based on a scale of 1 inch to 1 foot. There is a purpose-built toilet for wheelchair users and four narrow-gauge wheelchairs are available on loan.

Warwick Rd, New Town (2m junc 2 M40, 4m junc 16 M25)
☎ (0494) 672919
Open: 29 Feb-1 Nov daily 10-5.
Admission: £2.50 (ch £1.25, pen & students £2). Party 13+.
🅿 ☕ ♿ toilets for disabled shop ✗

CHALFONT ST GILES   Chiltern Open Air Museum

The museum aims to preserve traditional Chilterns buildings by rebuilding them here. Among the buildings dismantled and brought to the site are a toll house, cart sheds, stables, granaries, a forge, barns and an Iron Age house. There is a nature trail through the 45 acres of parkland and there is also an adventure playground. Numerous events are held throughout the year including Children's Day (4 May), a Transport Festival (16-17 May), a Harvest Celebration (10-11 October), and a Victorian Christmas Weekend (5-6 Dec).

Newland Pk, Gorelands Ln (off B4442)
☎ (02407) 71117
Open: Apr-1 Nov, Wed-Sun & BH 2-6.
Admission: £2.50 (ch 16 & over 60's £2, ch under 5 free). Family ticket £8.
🅿 ☕ ♿ toilets for disabled shop

QUAINTON   Buckinghamshire Railway Centre

This is one of the largest collections pertaining to industrial and main-line standard-gauge railways, with many items from the last century. Visitors can take a ride in a vintage steam train and see a display of locomotives and rolling stock. A small museum houses other memorabilia. Fans of Thomas the Tank Engine will enjoy the chance to meet the Fat Controller and his friendly engines, and will even be able to climb aboard the coaches and take a ride – May 3 & 4, September 26 & 28; toddlers 18 months-5 years – £3, everyone over 5 – £5.

Quainton Rd Station (off A41)
☎ (029675) 720 & 450 (info)
Open: Apr-Oct, Sun & BH Mon; Jun-Aug, Wed; 5-20 Dec, Sat & Sun.
Admission: £3.50 (ch & pen £2). Family ticket £9.50.
🅿 ☕ ♿ toilets for disabled shop

WADDESDON   Waddesdon Manor

In 1874 Baron Ferdinand de Rothschild acquired this Buckinghamshire hilltop which became the site for the Destailleur designed château, around which is set one of the finest late Victorian formal gardens and parks designed by Laine. Restoration plans for the gardens include shrubberies and additional bedding to the fountain terrace. The elegant cast iron rococo-style aviary, built in 1889, contains mainly softbill birds and some parrots.

(gates off A41)
☎ Aylesbury (0296) 651211
Open: Grounds & Aviary only 18 Mar-23 Dec, Wed-Fri 12-5, Sat, Sun, Good Fri & BH Mon 12-6.
Admission: Grounds & Aviary £3 (ch under 5 free, ch 5-17 £1.50).
🅿 ☕ ♿ toilets for disabled shop ✗ (NT)

WEST WYCOMBE   West Wycombe Caves

The entrance to West Wycombe caves is halfway up the hill that dominates the village. On the summit stands the parish church and the mausoleum of the Dashwood family. The caves are not natural but were dug on the orders of Sir Francis Dashwood between 1748 and 1752. Sir Francis, the Chancellor of the Exchequer, was also the founder of the Hell Fire Club, whose members were reputed to have practised black magic. The caves, which extend to approximately one-third of a mile underground, are supposed to have been one of their venues. The entrance consists of a large forecourt with flint walls, from which a brick tunnel leads into the caves, where tableaux and curiosities are exhibited in various chambers, including the Great Hall of Statues.

(on A40)
☎ **High Wycombe (0494) 524411**

Open: all year, Mar-Oct, daily 11-6; Nov-Feb, Sat & Sun 1-5.
Admission: £2.50 (ch & pen £1.25). Party 20 + .
🅿 ☕ & shop garden centre 🐾

CAMBRIDGESHIRE

CAMBRIDGE   see page 36

DUXFORD   Duxford Airfield

This former Battle of Britain fighter station has hangars dating from the First World War. It is now home to most of the Imperial War Museum's collection of military aircraft, armoured fighting vehicles, midget submarines and other large exhibits. There are over 120 historic aircraft on the airfield, and also on display is the Duxford Aviation Society's collection of civil aircraft, including the prototype Concorde 01. Special themed exhibits include a US 8th Air Force Exhibition. Major flying displays are held in summer, and pleasure flights can be taken during summer weekends. Those with aircraft may apply to land them at the airfield; those without can try the popular flight simulator. Cinema shows are held on summer Sundays, and there is an adventure playground. 1992 events include Classic Fighter Display (4/5 July), and Duxford '92 (13 Sep).

(off junc 10 of M11 on A505)
☎ **Cambridge (0223) 835000**

Open: all year, mid Mar-Oct daily 10-6; Nov-mid Mar daily 10-4. (Closed 24-26 Dec & 1 Jan)
Admission: ✻ Telephone for admission prices.
🅿 ☕ & (wheelchair available) toilets for disabled shop 🐾

HAMERTON   Hamerton Wildlife Centre

A wildlife breeding centre, dedicated to the practical conservation of endangered species including otters, gibbons, monkeys, marmosets, lemurs, wildcats, meerkats and many more. There is also a large and varied bird collection, with several species unique to Hamerton. Over 120 species in all, many new for 1992. Other attractions include a children's play area, and undercover viewing of many mammals. Special events for 1992 include falconry demonstrations, teddy bear's picnic and an annual birthday party.

☎ **(08323) 362**

Open: Summer daily 10.30-6; winter daily 10.30-4. (Closed Xmas)
Admission: £3 (pen £2.50 & ch 5-14 £1.50). Party 15 +
🅿 ☕ ✗ & shop 🐾

Cambridge is one of the loveliest cities in Britain, a university city since medieval times, with a maze of ancient college courtyards and gardens to explore. Behind the colleges runs the River Cam, with lawns fringed by tall trees – an area known as The Backs. You can walk here, see the river by punt – there are chauffered punts for those who have not mastered this difficult art – or take a two-hour river sightseeing tour. Guided walking tours of the city are also arranged by the Tourist Information Office.

The oldest college is Peterhouse, founded by the Bishop of Ely in 1280, the newest is Robinson, built at the end of the 1970s. In the intervening years, the other colleges were founded by various wealthy patrons including monarchs such as Henry VI, Henry VII and Henry VIII who were jointly responsible for Cambridge's greatest glory – Kings College Chapel.

Cambridge today is a lively place with entertainment all year and a number of annual events such as the arts festival in July, the famous Cambridge Folk Festival, the Midsummer Fair and the funfair and fireworks display on 5th November. Avoid the period from May to mid-June when exams are in progress and colleges will be closed.

Tourist information: Wheeler Street Telephone: (0223) 322640

☆ STAR ATTRACTIONS

Cambridge & County Folk Museum
The timber-framed White Horse Inn is an appealing setting for the folk museum. It houses items covering the everyday life of the people of Cambridgeshire from 1650 to the present day. There are also temporary exhibitions. Special exhibitions and craft days take place throughout the year, including 'To Market, To Market' – an exhibition on shops and shopping through the ages (Mar-May); Roman and Victorian Cambridge (Jun-Oct); and a Christmas exhibition in Dec.

2/3 Castle Street
☎ (0223) 355159

Open: all year, Mar-Sep, Mon-Sat 10.30-5, Sun 2-5. Oct-Feb, Tue-Sat 10.30-5, Sun 2-5. (Closed Mon ex school hols & pre-booked school parties). Last admissions 30 mins before closing.
Admission: £1 (ch 5-16, students, UB40s & pen 50p)
&. (braille & tape guides) shop 🍴

Fitzwilliam Museum
The Fitzwilliam is one of the oldest museums in Britain, and is housed in an imposing building designed for the purpose in 1834. The museum has particularly good English and Continental ceramics and English glass, with some outstanding Oriental work, and paintings by Titian, Veronese, Canaletto and many other famous names. There are Egyptian, Greek and Roman antiquities, medieval illuminated manuscripts, ivories, miniatures, carvings and armour.

Trumpington St
☎ (0223) 332900

Open: all year Tue-Sat 10-5, Sun 2.15-5 plus Etr Mon, Spring & Summer BH. (Closed Good Fri, May Day & 24 Dec-1 Jan).
Admission: Free.
🍽 &. (preferably pre-arranged) toilets for disabled shop 🍴

Scott Polar Research Institute
The institute is an international centre for polar studies, and has a museum with displays of Arctic and Antarctic expeditions, with special emphasis on those of Captain Scott. Other exhibits include Eskimo work and other arts of the polar regions. Also shown are displays on current scientific exploration. A special exhibition is shown every summer.

Lensfield Rd
☎ (0223) 336540

Open: all year, Mon-Sat 2.30-4. (Closed some public & university hols).
Admission: Free.
shop 🍴

University Botanic Garden
The garden was founded in 1762, mainly for the study of medicinal plants. It now covers a 40-acre site and has interesting collections of plants in botanical groups, a chronological bed (with plants in order of introduction), a scented garden, and a conservation garden containing rare species.

Cory Lodge, Bateman St
☎ (0223) 336265

Open: all year Mon-Sat 8-6, Sun 10-6 (dusk in winter).(Glasshouse 11-12.30 & 2-4.
Admission: ✱ Sun only £1 (ch 3-17 50p). Free for ticket holders-particulars from Director
&. toilets for disabled 🍴

LINTON   Linton Zoological Gardens

Conservation and education are the main concerns of this zoo which was established in 1972. The many species of animals and birds are housed in landscaped enclosures as like their natural habitats as possible. Especially interesting are the Sumatran tigers, giant Aloabra tortoises – the largest herd outside the tropics, a fine collection of owls, binturongs and the famous Toco toucans – the only young to be bred in Britain were born here. All around the enclosures are fine shrubberies and exotic trees. Special events are planned and details can be obtained from the zoo.

Hadstock Rd
☎ **Cambridge (0223) 891308**
Open: daily 10-6 or dusk (ex 25 Dec). Last admission 45 minutes before closing time.
🅿 ☛ ㅎ toilets for disabled shop 🐩
Details not confirmed for 1992

PEAKIRK   Wildfowl & Wetlands Trust

Over 600 ducks, geese and swans represent more than 100 different species in an attractive water garden. There is a magnificent flock of Chilean flamingoes and trumpeter, black necked and coscoroba swans. Andean geese and many other rare and unusual waterfowl can be seen. A visitor centre provides information on the birds and the Trust.

☎ **Peterborough (0733) 252271**
Open; all year, daily. Summer 9.30-6.30 (Last admission 5.30). Winter 9.30-dusk. (Closed 24-25 Dec).
🅿 ☛ ㅎ toilets for disabled shop 🐩
Details not confirmed for 1992

WANSFORD   Nene Valley Railway

This standard-gauge steam railway runs between Peterborough and Wansford and onto Yarwell Junction. It is based at Wansford Station, which also has an international collection of steam locomotives and rolling stock. There is a small museum of railway memorabilia from the days of steam. Special events are arranged throughout the year for steam enthusiasts and their families.

Wansford Station (A1 west of Peterborough)
☎ **Stamford (0780) 782854**
Open: mid Jul-Aug, Tue-Fri; Mar-Dec, Sun; Apr-Oct & Dec, Sat & BH Mon. Also other selected dates – telephone for details.
🅿 ☛ ㅎ (disabled access to trains) toilets for disabled shop
Details not confirmed for 1992

WIMPOLE   Wimpole Hall

Although Wimpole Hall is one of the grandest mansions in East Anglia, it is perhaps the 360 acres of parkland that make it unusual. The parkland was devised and planted by no less than four of the country's celebrated landscape designers, Charles Bridgeman, 'Capability' Brown, Sanderson Miller and Humphrey Repton. Under the pasture lie the remains of a medieval village with evidence of tracks and ridge-and-furrow farming. The house, which was given to the National Trust in 1976, dates back to 1640, but was altered into a large 18th-century mansion with a Georgian façade. The inside is the work of a number of important architects. Lord Harley's library and the gallery are the work of James Gibbs, and the Yellow Drawing Room was designed by Sir John Soane in about 1793. The chapel has a wonderful painted *trompe l'oeil* ceiling by Sir James Thornhill.

(junc of A14 & A603)
☎ **Cambridge (0223) 207257**
Open: 28 Mar-1 Nov, Tue-Thu, Sat, Sun 1-5, BH Sun & Mon 11-5. (Closed Good Fri).
Admissions: £4.40 (ch £2). Party 15+.
🅿 ✗ licensed ㅎ (braille guide) toilets for disabled shop 🐩 (ex park only)
(NT)

WIMPOLE Wimpole Home Farm

When built in 1794, the Home Farm was one of the most advanced agricultural enterprises in the country. The group of thatched and timbered buildings was designed by Sir John Soane for the 3rd Earl of Hardwicke. The Great Barn, now restored, holds a display of farm machinery and implements of the kind used at Wimpole over the past two centuries. On the farm there is a wide selection of rare breeds of domestic animals, including the black- and-white Bagot goat which was rescued from extinction. In the stables, there are once more the rare breed of Suffolk Punch horses. A special children's corner and a woodland play area are additional attractions.

☎ Cambridge (0223) 207257

Open: 28 Mar-1 Nov, daily (ex Mon & Fri) 10.30-5. Open BH Mons. (Closed Good Fri).
Admission: ❄ £3.40 (ch £1.50). Party 15+.
P ☕ ♿ (braille guide) toilets for disabled shop 🐕
(NT)

CHESHIRE

CAPESTHORNE Capesthorne Hall

Home of the Bromley-Davenport family, the house was built in 1722 and contains interesting furniture, pictures, silver and Americana. There is a Georgian chapel, and a family theatre. The grounds include a children's play area, and angling is available in season. There are gardens, lakes, a nature trail and woodland walks, and numerous events are held throughout the year, including craft fairs in costume (11/12 Apr and 26/27 Sep), kit car show (17 May), firework and laser concert (13 Jun) and horse trials (19 Aug).

(On A34 between Congleton and Wimslow)
☎ Chelford (0625) 861221 & 861779

Open: Apr Suns; May & Aug-Sep Wed & Sun; Jun-Jul Tue-Thu & Sun. Park & Garden 12-6, Hall 2-4.
Admission: Park, Garden & Chapel £1.75 (ch 50p). Park, Gardens, Chapel & Hall £3.50 (ch £1 & pen £3). Family ticket £7.50. Party 20+
P ☕ ✕ licensed ♿ toilets for disabled shop

CHESTER see page 39

CHOLMONDELEY Cholmondeley Castle Gardens

Ornamental gardens, with an ancient private chapel, a lakeside picnic area, and some rare breeds of farm animals. There are lovely lakeside and woodland walks. Special events are held throughout the year, please telephone for details.

(off A49/A41)
☎ (0829) 720383

Open: Etr-Sep, Sun & BH 12-5.30.
Admission: £2.50 (ch 75p, pen £1.50). Party.
P ☕ ♿ toilets for disabled shop garden centre

ABBREVIATIONS

AM	Ancient Monument	BH	Bank Holidays	ch 15 20p	Children under 15 20p
AM(CadW)	Ancient Monument (Wales)	PH	Public Holidays	Pen	Senior Citizens
		Etr	Easter	Party	Special or reduced rates for parties booked in advance
EH	English Heritage	ex	except		
NT	National Trust	Free	Admission free	Party 30+	Special or reduced rates for parties of 30 or more booked in advance
NTS	National Trust for Scotland	10p	Admission 10p		
		ch 20p	Children 20p		

In 1779 Boswell, the biographer of Dr Johnson, declared that 'Chester pleases my fancy more than any town I ever saw . . .' and today its countless visitors would certainly agree with the sentiment. The history of the city is splendidly preserved in the remains of the largest Roman amphitheatre ever uncovered in Britain, the Roman City Walls, the magnificent cathedral, 900 years old in 1992, and perhaps the most famous feature of all – the Rows. These two-tiered galleries of shops date from the Middle Ages and still preserve their picturesque black and white frontages even though they now lead into the best in modern high street shopping.

The best introduction to the city must be a walk around the top of the ancient walls – a circuit of two miles which takes in all the sights, including the famous Eastgate Clock which dates from 1897. You may like to join a 'route march' from the Tourist Information Centre, led by Chester's sole surviving Roman Legionary in full battle gear.

Amidst the bustle of the city, Grosvenor Park provides a haven of peace and relaxation, with an Edwardian bandstand overlooking the River Dee and boat trips available.

Tourist information: Town Hall Telephone: (0244) 313126

☆ *STAR ATTRACTIONS*

The Cheshire Military Museum _____
Exhibits from the history of the Cheshire Regiment, Cheshire Yeomanry, 5th Royal Inniskillin Dragoon Guards, and 3rd Carabiniers.

The Castle
☎ (0244) 347203 & 327617

Open: all year, daily 9-5. (Closed 30 mins lunchtime & 1-2 Jan, Good Fri & 19-31 Dec).
Admission: 50p (ch 20p).
shop

Chester Visitor Centre _____
Over 2000 years of Chester's history are illustrated by a video and a life-size reconstruction of a scene in the Chester Rows during Victorian times. There is a tourist information desk and guided tours depart regularly from the Centre. Craft fairs take place on Bank Holiday weekends.

Vicars Ln (opp Roman Amphitheatre)
☎ (0244) 318916 & 351609

Open: all year daily, Apr-Oct 9am-9pm, Nov-Mar 9am-7pm.
♥ & shop
Details not confirmed for 1992

Chester Zoo _____
This is one of Europe's finest zoological gardens, with 5500 animals in 110 acres of enclosures and landscaped gardens. There is a tropical house and an aquarium, and waterbus rides can be taken. A new mono-rail system is the latest attraction.

Upton-By-Chester (2m N of city centre off A41)
☎ (0244) 380280

Open: all year, daily 10-dusk. Last admission 3.30 Winter, 5.30 Summer. (Closed 25 Dec).
Admission: ✳ £5 (ch 3-15 & pen £2.50).
P ♥ ✗ licensed & (wheelchairs for hire) toilets for disabled shop ✹

DISLEY Lyme Park

Surrounded by wild moorland, Lyme Park is an Elizabethan house at the core, but it was transformed in the 17th and 18th centuries. Notable features include the handsome Palladian front and courtyard, the elaborate Baroque ceiling of the grand staircase, and the intricate woodcarvings in the saloon, probably by Grinling Gibbons. Earlier Elizabethan decorative carving can be seen in the drawing room and the Long Gallery. The house's fine pictures and furnishings include Mortlake tapestries. The Hall is interpreted in 1910 with guides in costume of the Edwardian servants of Lord Newton. The house is set amidst 15 acres of formal and informal Victorian gardens, and is surrounded by a 1377 acre country park. Other attractions include a Visitors' Centre, 1910 Tearooms, an Adventure Playground, Orienteering, a Countryside Centre, Pitch and Putt, and Fishing. Details of events are available on request.

☎ (0663) 762023

Open: – Hall, Good Fri-4 Oct, 2-5. (Closed Mon & Fri ex BH's). Freeflow – 23 May-13 Jun & 18 Jul-3 Sep, & all Sun, otherwise Guided Tours. Telephone for Xmas opening times. Park all year, Gardens all year (ex 25 & 26 Dec).
Admission: ❊ for Car & Occupants (Park & Garden incl) £3. Hall £1.95 (ch & pen £1, under 5 free). NT members free. Party ticket (5 persons) £4.95.
P ☕ ♿ (by arrangement) toilets for disabled shop
(NT)

ELLESMERE PORT Boat Museum

The museum occupies a historic dock complex at the junction of the Shropshire Union and Manchester Ship Canals. These docks were one of the most important points for transferring goods between sea-going vessels and the smaller craft of the inland waterways. There are over 60 craft to see, ranging from a small weedcutter to a 300-ton coaster. Visitors may go aboard some of them, and there is a boat trip. Other attractions include restored warehouses, workshops, blacksmith's forge and dock workers' cottages. Four of the original steam engines which once drove the hydraulic power system survive, and two are in steam on the first Sunday of each month and Bank Holidays. Craft fairs and other special events take place throughout the year, including Easter craft fair and boaters gathering (Good Friday – Easter Monday), International dance festival (May Bank Holiday), model boats convention (August Bank Holiday), and Christmas Craft Fair with Santa (Nov 28/29). The museum also has displays on canals, canal horses and the town.

Dockyard Rd
☎ 051-355 5017

Open: Summer daily 10-5. Winter daily (ex Fri) 11-4. (Closed 25 & 26 Dec).
Admission: ❊ £4 (ch £2.70, pen & students £3). Family ticket £12.50.
P ☕ ♿ (resources pack for blind & deaf) toilets for disabled shop

JODRELL BANK SCIENCE CENTRE & ARBORETUM Jodrell Bank Science Centre & Arboretum

The Science Centre stands at the feet of one of the largest, fully steerable radio telescopes in the world, the Lovell telescope, a landmark both in Cheshire and in the world of astronomy. Interactive exhibits enable visitors to 'get to grips' with science. There are shows every half-hour in the Planetarium and outside, visitors may walk through 35 acres of tree-lined walkways in the Arboretum, beautiful in every season, and visit the Environmental Discovery Centre. 1992 is International Space Year, so there will be a number of events held in connection with BISY'92 – British Industry In Space Year. These include the official opening of the Environmental Discovery Centre and the new exhibition 'The Tree Planet'.

☎ Lower Withington (0477) 71339

Open: Sat before Etr-Oct, daily 10.30-5.30; Nov-Sat before Etr, wknds only 12-5 (daily Xmas hols). (Closed 25, 26 Dec & 1 Jan).
Admission: £3.20 (ch 5-16 £1.80, pen £2.40) includes Exhibition, Planetarium, Arboretum & Environmental Discovery Centre. Family ticket £10. Infants not admitted to the Planetarium.
P ☕ ♿ toilets for disabled shop 🐕

KNUTSFORD Tatton Park

Tatton Park is one of the great playgrounds of the north-west, with gardens and a 1000-acre country park offering fishing, swimming, sailing and walking, as well as various events throughout the year. The centrepiece is the great Georgian mansion, whose gardens were first laid out by Humphry Repton, followed in the 19th century by Sir Joseph Paxton, who designed the Italian-style terraces in front of the house. Later, in the 20th century, Japanese gardeners created a Japanese garden with a Shinto temple beside one of the lakes, and also to be seen are an orangery and a fern house, as well as colourful expanses of flowers.

The park is big enough to absorb its visitors and still provide room for wildlife, and the mere is especially interesting for its wildfowl in winter. A variety of signposted walks includes an historic landscape trail.

The house itself has sumptuous furnishings and pictures including two Canalettos. Also of interest are the kitchens and cellars. The Home Farm is stocked with animals and working as it was fifty years ago. Old Hall is the original medieval manor house and a guided tour transports you through five hundred years of Tatton history. An adventure playground is the newest feature. There is a regular programme of special events.

(3.5m from M6, junc 15, or M56, junc 7)
☎ (0565) 654822
Open: Good Fri or Apr-Sep, Park 11-7, Mansion, Gardens, Old Hall & Farm 12-5. (Closed Mon ex BH Mon); Oct-Good Fri or Mar, Park 11-5, Gardens 12-4. (Closed Mon & 24-25 Dec), Farm Sun only 12-4, Shop 11.30-4.30. (Last admissions 1hr before closure).
🅿 (charged) ☛ ✗ licensed ♿ (Old Hall & Farm not accessible) toilets for disabled shop garden centre ฅ (ex in Park & Gardens) (NT)
Details not confirmed for 1992

NANTWICH Stapeley Water Gardens

Claiming to be the World's largest water garden centre, Stapeley Water Gardens has 50 acres of display lakes, gardens, pools and fountains plus 'The Palms' with sharks, piranhas, koi carp, giant Amazon water lilies and exotic blooming plants. The Stapeley Yesteryear Collection displays fully restored military, vintage cars, and a Churchill tank. Special event for 1992: 14 Jun- 19 Jul, The Wildlife Photographer of the Year.

London Rd, Stapeley (off junc 16 M6, 1m S of Nantwich on A51)
☎ (0270) 623868 & 628628
Open: daily 9-6, wknds & BHs 10-7. (Winter 9-5, wknds & BHs 10-6). The Palms Tropical Oasis open from 10am, closing times as Garden Centre.
Admission: The Palms Tropical Oasis £2.50 (ch £1.25, pen £1.85). The Yesteryear collection £2.50 (ch £1.25, pen £1.85). Joint ticket £4.50 (ch £2.20, pen £3.30).
🅿 ☛ ✗ licensed ♿ (wheelchair loan service) toilets for disabled shop garden centre ฅ

NESTON Liverpool University Botanic Gardens (Ness Gardens)

A place of learning and also a place of beauty containing fine trees and shrubs, rock terraces, water gardens, herbaceous borders and rose collections. The visitor centre has a slide show and exhibitions. Plants may be purchased in the gift shop. For children there is an exciting adventure playground. There is also a regular programme of lectures, courses and special events throughout the year for which tickets must be obtained in advance.

Ness Gardens (off A540 near Ness-on-Wirral
☎ 051-336 2135 & 051-336 7769
Open: all year, Nov-Feb, daily 9.30-4; Mar-Sep, daily 9.30-dusk.
Admission: ❋ £2.80 (ch 10-18 & pen £1.80). Family ticket £7.
🅿 ☛ ✗ licensed ♿ toilets for disabled shop garden centre ฅ

STYAL   Quarry Bank Mill & Styal Country Park

This 18th-century cotton mill and the village built by the owners for the millworkers form one of the most fascinating Industrial Revolution sites in Britain. The mill is set in a lovely valley and there are pleasant walks through woodland or by the deep ravine of the River Bollin. It has been restored to working order and the great iron waterwheel is turning once again to help produce cloth (on sale). There are three floors of textile machinery and also demonstrations of hand-spinning and weaving, with galleries illustrating the millworker's world, textile-finishing processes and the founders (the Greggs) as pioneers of the factory system. In the village are well-preserved mill-hands cottages, chapels and shops, plus the house where the young pauper apprentices lived.

Quarry Bank Mill
☎ Wilmslow (0625) 527468
Open: Mill all year, Apr & May, Tue-Sun & BH Mon 11-5; Jun-Sep, daily 11-5; Oct-Mar, Tue-Sun 11-4. Apprentice House & Gardens, Tue-Fri, as Mill opening times during School Hols, Wed-Fri 2pm-Mill closing time during school term. Sat & Sun as for Mill. (Closed Mon all year ex BH Mon).
🅿 (charged) ● ✕ licensed ♿ toilets for disabled shop ⚲ (ex in Park)
(NT)
Details not confirmed for 1992

WIDNES   Catalyst – The Museum of the Chemical Industry

A unique new museum exploring the chemical industry and its impact on our lives, past and present, with working exhibits, computer games and films. A rooftop observation gallery offers superb views, and the adjacent Spike Island Waterside Park offers walks by the River Mersey, St Helens Canal and an industrial archaeology trail.

Mersey Rd
☎ 051-420 1121
Open: all year, Tue-Sun daily 10-5. (Closed Mon ex BH's, Good Fri, 24-26 Dec & 1 Jan).
♿ toilets for disabled shop ⚲
Details not confirmed for 1992

CLEVELAND

MIDDLESBROUGH   Captain Cook Birthplace Museum

Opened to mark the 250th anniversary of the birth of the voyager in 1728, this museum illustrates the early life of James Cook and his discoveries with temporary exhibitions. Located in spacious and rolling parkland, the site also offers outside attractions for the visitor, including a conservatory of tropical plants, and assorted animals and fowl housed in small and accessible paddocks. There are Captain Cook Birthday Celebrations on 25th October.

Stewart Park, Marton (3m S on A172 at Stewart Park, Marton)
☎ (0642) 311211
Open: all year, summer Tue-Sun 10-6, winter 9-4. Last ticket 30 mins before closing. (Closed 25-26 Dec & 1 Jan).
Admission: ✳ 85p (ch & pen 40p). Family ticket £1.80.
🅿 ● ♿ (lift to all floors) toilets for disabled shop ⚲

SKINNINGROVE   Tom Leonard Mining Museum

The museum offers visitors an exciting and authentic underground experience on the site of the old Loftus mine, and a chance to see how the stone was drilled, charged with explosives and fired. Exhibits include a collection of original tools, lamps, safety equipment, old photographs and domestic objects, providing a glimpse of mining life both above and below ground.

Deepdale
☎ (0287) 642877
Open: Etr-Oct, daily 1-5 (last admission 4pm). Parties by arrangement.
Admission: £1 (ch 50p)
🅿 ♿ shop ⚲

CORNWALL

BODMIN   Pencarrow

This Georgian house is still a family home, and has a superb collection of pictures, furniture and china. The 50 acres of formal and woodland gardens include a Victorian rockery, Italian and American gardens, a lake, an ice house and an ancient British encampment. There are over 600 different rhododendrons and an internationally acclaimed conifer collection. There are also a craft centre and a children's play area.

Washaway (4m N on unclass road off A389)
☎ St Mabyn (020884) 369

Open: Etr-15 Oct, Mon-Thu & Sun, 1.30-5; BH Mon & Jun-10 Sep 11-5. (Last tour of the House 5pm).
Admission: ✳ House & Garden £3 (ch £1.20). Gardens only £1 (ch 50p). Party.
🅿 ☕ ♿ toilets for disabled shop & plant shop 🐕 (ex gardens)

CALSTOCK   Cotehele

The granite house dates from 1485 and was built for the Edgcumbe family. They moved south to Mount Edgcumbe in the 16th century, and have left Cotehele virtually untouched, apart from some building work in 1627. Inside there are tapestries, embroideries, furniture and armour; and outside there is a beautiful garden on different levels. It has a medieval dovecote. There is a restored manorial water mill in the valley below, and an outstation of the National Maritime Museum. The restored sailing barge 'Shamrock' can be seen from the quay.

St Dominick (2m E of St Dominick)
☎ Liskeard (0579) 50434 & 51222

Open Apr-Oct, daily 11-5.30; (11-5 in Oct). Last admission 30 mins before closing. House only closed Fri. Nov-Mar garden only open daylight hours.
Admission: House, Garden & Mill £4.80. Garden, Grounds & Mill £2.40. Party.
🅿 ✕ licensed ♿ (Braille guide) toilets for disabled shop 🐕 (NT)

DOBWALLS   Dobwalls Family Adventure Park

Dobwalls invites visitors to ride on its two-mile stretch of miniature American railroads. There are steam and diesel locos, and visitors can take the Rio Grande ride through the forests or the Union Pacific route over the prairies. Ten scaled-down locomotives include the Union Pacific Big Boy, and there are tunnels, embankments, lakes and canyons. Also at Dobwalls is Adventureland – eight action-packed areas filled with adventure play equipment including aerial cableways and three totally enclosed slides. There are also remote-controlled model boats and American-style trucks and trailers, a shooting gallery, Aquablasters and an Edwardian 'penny' amusement arcade.

(0.5m N of A38)
☎ Liskeard (0579) 20325 & 21129

Open: Etr-Oct, daily 10-6 (last admission 4.30pm). Nov-Etr telephone for details.
Admission: Fee payable.
🅿 ☕ ♿ (motorised & manual wheelchairs available) toilets for disabled shop

GOONHAVERN   World in Miniature

There are four major attractions for the price of one at this enchanting theme park. Visitors can stroll amongst the world's most famous landmarks such as the Taj Mahal and the Statue of Liberty, all in miniature scale, set in spectacular gardens. Then there is Tombstone, a wild-west town

Bodmin Rd
☎ Truro (0872) 572828

Open: Apr-Jun & Sep-Oct, daily 10-4 (5pm Jul-Aug).

complete with saloon, bank, shops, livery stable and jail. The Adventure Dome is the original super cinema 180 direct from the USA where you experience the thrills and spills of two great films without leaving your seat. Finally, there are the Gardens, twelve acres of beautifully landscaped garden with over 70,000 plants and shrubs.

Admission: ❄ £3.95 (ch 4-14 £2.75, pen £3.50).
P ☕ ♿ toilets for disabled shop garden centre

GWEEK Seal Sanctuary & Marine Animal Rescue Centre

A hospital and 10 pools are provided here for sick and injured seals washed in on Cornwall's beaches. There is an exhibition centre with audio-visual displays on seals and their relations. Other attractions include a nature trail and an aquarium. Visitors will also find indentification of the Helford River Wildlife and bird species by means of viewing and interpretation areas. Conservation is a very important aspect of the work here, reflected in the imaginative pollution exhibition on display.

☎ Mawgan (032622) 361

Open: all year, daily 9.30-6. (4pm in winter).
Admission: ❄ £3.80 (ch £1.85)
P ☕ ♿ (wheelchairs available) toilets for disabled shop

HELSTON Flambards Village Theme Park

Three award-winning, all-weather attractions can be visited on one site here. Flambards Victorian Village is an evocative recreation of streets, shops and house interiors from the turn of the century, including a 'time capsule' chemist's shop. Britain in the Blitz is a lifesize wartime street featuring shops, a pub and a living room with Morrison shelter; and Cornwall Aero Park covers the history of aviation from 'those magnificent men in their flying machines' to Concorde. Cornwall's Exploratorium, is a 'hands on' science playground for the whole family. There is an adventure playground and many rides from the gentle to the daring, including Flambards Family Log Flume, The fabulous Cyclopter Monorail, Balloon Race, Space Mission, Superbob and Dragon Coaster. There will be new rides for 1992, plus The Amazing Flambards Maze, Hall of Miscellany, exciting games of skill, and a huge children's playground and picnic area. Facilities for the disabled include purpose-built toilets for wheelchair users, free loan of wheelchairs and a free map guide. On Easter Monday 1992 the annual Easter Bonnet Parade and competition takes place. 1992 will also see the introduction of 'Images of the Blitz', an exhibition of some of the most remarkable photographs of our time by some of the world's best photographers. A telethon charity fund raising event will take place on 4th May.

Culdrose Manor (.5m S on A3083)
☎ (0326) 573404 & 574549

Open: 15 Apr-1 Nov, daily 10-last admission 4pm. Extended opening 27 Jul-3 Sep, last admission 5.30pm. Park closes 8pm.
Admission: £7.50 (ch 4-13 £6.50, pen £3.95).
P ☕ ♿ (wheelchairs available) toilets for disabled shop garden centre 🐕̸

LAND'S END Land's End

The most westerly point of mainland England draws countless visitors to its dramatic cliff scenery. On a clear day the Isles of Scilly, 28 miles away, can be seen together with the Wolf Rock Lighthouse and the Seven Stones Reef, where the Torrey Canyon met its end in 1967. The 200-acre site is the setting for wild coastal walks and amazing natural rock formations; and innovative

☎ Penzance (0736) 871501

Open: all year, site & exhibitions 10-dusk. Times adjustable during winter.
Admission: £4.95 (ch £2.50 & pen £4.50). Disabled visitors free.
P (charged) ☕ ✕ licensed ♿ toilets for disabled shop 🐕̸ (ex grounds)

exhibitions have been set up to trace the geology, wildlife and maritime history of the area. On the southernmost tip of the peninsula are two small smugglers' coves linked by a tunnel which local miners carved through the headland. On view are the last labyrinth, an audio-visual show and the art gallery.

LAUNCESTON Launceston Steam Railway

A four-mile round trip behind a century-old steam locomotive is an appealing prospect; there are also displays of stationary steam engines and a model railway. A motor and motorcycle museum and a specialist bookshop on transport are other features of a visit here.

Newport
☎ (0566) 775665

Open: Good Fri-21 Apr & Oct, Tue & Sun, then Jun-Sep, daily 10.30-4.30. (Closed Sat). Also Santa Specials Dec, Sat & Sun 1-4, also 24 & 26 Dec.
Admission: ✻ £3.30 (ch £2.20, pen £2.80). Family ticket £10.50. Dogs 50p.
P ☕ ♿ shop

LOOE Monkey Sanctuary

A protected breeding colony of rare Amazon woolly monkeys enjoys life here in the wooded grounds of Murrayton monkey sanctuary. Visitors can get close to the monkeys but are advised to bring children under four on dry days only. Talks are given morning and afternoon.

St Martins (4m E off B3253)
☎ (05036) 2532

Open: 2 wks Etr then May-Sep, Sun-Thu 10.30-5.
Admission: ✻ £3.50 (ch £1.70 & pen £2.50).
P ☕ ♿ toilets for disabled shop 🐕̸

MAWNAN SMITH Glendurgan

This delightful garden, set in a valley above the River Helford, was started by Alfred Fox in 1820. The informal landscape contains beautiful trees and shrubs from all over the world, including the Japanese loquat, Mexican cypress and tree ferns from New Zealand. There is also a walled garden, a maze and a Giant's Stride which are popular with children. House not open.

☎ Bodmin (0208) 74281

Open: Mar-Oct, Tue-Sat & BH Mon 10.30-5.30 (last admission 4.30). (Closed Good Fri).
Admission: £2.50.
P ♿ (Braille guide) toilets for disabled 🐕̸ (NT)

MEVAGISSEY World of Model Railways

Over 2000 British, Continental and American models are on display in this museum, which also features an impressively realistic layout for the models to run through, with urban and rural areas, a 'working' fairground, an Alpine ski resort with cable cars, and a Cornish china clay pit, all reproduced in miniature.

Meadow St
☎ (0726) 842457

Open: 2 wks Etr, then Spring BH-Oct 11-5. (Closed half term in Oct).
Admission: £1.95 (ch & pen £1.45)
♿ shop

NEWQUAY Dairy Land

Dairy Land was the first farm diversification of its kind in the UK. Here, visitors can watch while the cows are milked to music on a spectacular merry-go-round milking machine. The life of a Victorian farmer and his neighbours

Tresillian Barton , Summercourt (on A3058)
☎ Mitchell (0872) 510246

is explored in the Countrylife Museum, and a Farm Nature Trail demonstrates farming and nature in harmony with informative displays along pleasant peaceful walks. Children will have fun getting to know the farm animals in the safety of the Farm Park and Playground.

Open: Etr & May-Sep, daily 10.30-5.30; Apr & Oct, daily 12-5.
Admission: ✳ £3.95 (ch 3-15 £2.80, pen & disabled £3.65). Party.
🅿 ☞ ✗ licensed ය (wheelchairs for loan; disabled viewing gallery – milking) toilets for disabled shop 🏂

NEWQUAY   Newquay Zoo

Education and conservation are the key issues at this exciting Zoological Theme Park. Apart from the usual attractions such as the Monkey enclosures, penguin pool, tropical house and lion house all of which have been designed for maximum 'creature comfort' the park also boasts a Maze, an Oriental Garden, an activity Play Park and a Tarzan Trail Assault Course. The latest attraction is a Tortoise enclosure to house the tortoises that the Zoo is given each year.

Trenance Park
☎ (0637) 873342
Open: Apr-Nov, daily 10-5.
Admission: ✳ £3.60 (ch £2.20).
🅿 (charged) ☞ ය shop 🏂

PADSTOW   Padstow Tropical Bird Gardens

These well established gardens continue to breed many birds from all corners of the world. Many of the sub-tropical plants growing here are labelled – a thoughtful gesture to gardeners – and a heated walk-in tropical house enables visitors to see free-flying exotic birds at close quarters in a near-natural habitat. Similarly, the planted butterfly house gives the opportunity to view all stages in the life-cycle of butterflies. 'Butterfly World' is a comprehensive exhibition of the world's butterflies, many displayed in their natural habitat.

Fentonluna Ln
☎ (0841) 532262
Open: all year 10.30-7 (4pm in winter) last admission 1hr before closing. (Closed 25 Dec.)
☞ ය shop
Details not confirmed for 1992.

PENDEEN   Geevor Tin Mines

A working tin mine and museum provide an insight into the methods and equipment used in the mining of tin. Guided tours enable visitors to see the tin treatment plant and a video film illustrates the techniques employed. An underground tour in what is probably Europe's deepest visitor mine completes an enjoyable day out.

☎ Penzance (0736) 788662
Open: Etr-Oct 10-5.30. Last surface tour 4pm. Last admission 5pm. Other times by appointment.
🅿 ☞ ය toilets for disabled shop
Details not confirmed for 1992

POLPERRO   Land of Legend & Model Village

A glimpse of old Cornwall may be caught here through animated models in a replica of old Polperro, set amid a garden of exotic plants. There are commentary listening posts to guide visitors around and a photographic exhibition of Polperro's history.

The Old Forge
☎ (0503) 72378
Open Etr-Oct, Sun-Fri 10-9.
☞ shop
Details not confirmed for 1992

ST AGNES   St Agnes Leisure Park

The leisure park is set in several acres of mature land-scaped gardens. Attractions include Cornwall in miniature, the Lost World of the Dinosaurs, a Super X Simulator, an animated circus, the haunted house and fairyland. The park is illuminated after dark.

(S on B3277)
☎ (087255) 2793

Open: 29 Mar-5 Jul & 11 Sep-1 Nov, daily 10-6; 6 Jul-10 Sep, daily 10am-10pm.
Admission: Fee payable.
🅿 🍴 ♿ shop

ST AUSTELL   Wheal Martyn Museum

The Wheal Martyn Museum tells the story of Cornwall's most important present-day industry: china clay production. The open-air site includes a complete 19th-century clayworks, restored for this purpose. There are huge granite-walled settling tanks, working water-wheels and a wooden slurry pump. Other exhibits include a 220ft pan kiln, horse-drawn wagons and two steam locomotives used in the industry, and a restored 1914 Peerless lorry.

The story of china clay in Cornwall over two centuries is shown using indoor displays. There is also a short slide and sound programme, and a working pottery. Outside again there are nature trails, a children's adventure trail and the spectacular viewing area of a modern china-clay pit.

(2m N on A391)
☎ (0726) 850362

Open: Apr-Oct, 10-6 (last admission 5pm).
🅿 🍴 ♿ toilets for disabled shop
Details not confirmed for 1992

TREDINNICK   Cornish Shire Horse Centre

This 120-acre farm specialises in Shire Horses, and visitors can see mares with foals. There are two horse shows a day which take place under cover and are fully seated, and cart rides are also available. The work of the blacksmith is also on display and there is a museum of carriages, a video room and the largest display of show harnesses in the country.

Trelow Farm (off A39)
☎ Rumford (0841) 540276

Open: Good Fri-Oct daily 10-5.
Admission: £3.95 (ch £2.50 & pen £3.50)
🅿 🍴 ✗ licensed ♿ shop

TRELISSICK GARDEN   Trelissick Garden

A beautiful woodland park of some 370 acres overlooking the Falmouth estuary. The park was mainly laid out between 1844 and 1913 but the gardens were designed later, between 1937 and 1955. The grounds have been immaculately kept and offer spectacular views from walks through beech trees and oaks.

The location of the garden, near the sea and sheltered by woodland, has allowed many unusual and exotic plants to be grown. There are sub-tropical plants and some from such distant places as Chile and Tasmania. The gardens are particularly noted for their camellias, magnolias and hydrangeas, of which there are over 100 kinds. There is also a large walled garden with fig trees and climbers, and a shrub garden. Plants are available in the garden shop. There is also an Art and Craft Gallery by the House Farm Courtyard.

☎ Truro (0872) 862090 & 865808

Open: Mar-Oct, Mon-Sat 10.30-5.30, Sun 1-5.30 (closes at 5 in Mar & Oct). Woodland walks open Nov-Feb. Last admission 30 mins before closing.
Admission: £2.80.
🅿 (charged) ✗ licensed ♿ (Braille guide) toilets for disabled shop 🐾 (ex in woodland walk & park)
(NT)

WENDRON   Poldark Mine and Heritage Complex

This Cornish tin mine has three levels open to the public; an 18th-century village, museums and a cinema showing a film on the history of Cornish mining. On the surface there are restaurants, shops, gardens and children's amusements. The area around the mine has been laid to lawn and shows the West Country's largest collection of working antiquities, including a 40ft beam engine.

(on B3297)
☎ Helston (0326) 573173
Open: Etr-Jun & Sep-Oct, daily 10.30-5.30 (last admission 4); Jul-Aug daily 10-6. (last admission 4.30).
Admission: Fee payable.
🅿 ☕ ✕ licensed ⅙ shop garden centre 🐾 (ex grounds)

CUMBRIA

ALSTON   South Tynedale Railway

Running along the beautiful South Tyne valley, this narrow-gauge railway follows the route of the former Alston to Haltwhistle branch. At present the line runs between Alston and Gilderdale. Special events for 1992 include: 27 May, Children's Day; 25-26 Jul, Steam Enthusiasts' Weekend; 11 Oct, Open Day.

The Railway Station, Hexham Rd
☎ (0434) 381696
Open: 17-26 Apr daily; May, wknds, BHs & daily 23-31; Jun-Sep, Tue-Thu & wknds (daily Jul-Aug & 1-6 Sep); Oct Sun only. Trains leave at 11.15, 12, 2, 3 & 4pm. Santa specials in Dec.
Admission: £1.60 (ch 80p) return fare. Party 10+.
🅿 ☕ ⅙ toilets for disabled shop

APPLEBY-IN-WESTMORLAND   Appleby Castle Conservation Centre

The grounds of this beautifully preserved Castle provide a natural setting for a Rare Breeds Survival Trust Approved Centre, featuring rare breeds of British Farm animals and also a large collection of waterfowl and unusual birds. The fine Norman Keep and Great Hall of the house are open to the public. Clifford family paintings and some items of the Nanking cargo are on display in the Hall. The information centre has an exhibition of watercolours by local artists, open daily.

☎ (07683) 51402
Open: 16 Apr-Sep, daily 10-5.
Admission: ✳ prices not confirmed.
🅿 ☕ ⅙ toilets for disabled shop

CONISTON   Steam Yacht Gondola

Launched in 1859, the graceful 'Gondola' worked on Coniston Water until 1937, and came back into service in 1980. Now visitors can once again enjoy her silent progress and old-fashioned comfort.

Pier Cottage
☎ (05394) 41288
Open: Apr-1 Nov to scheduled daily timetable. Trips commence 11 at Coniston; on Sat 12.05. Piers at Coniston, Park-a-Moor at SE end of lake & Brantwood. Ticket prices on application & published locally.
🅿 🐾
(NT)

DACRE   Dalemain

The stately home of Dalemain was originally a medieval pele tower, which was added to in Tudor times and later, with the imposing Georgian façade completed in 1745. It has splendid oak panelling, Chinese wallpaper, Tudor plasterwork and fine Queen Anne and Georgian furniture. The rooms include a Victorian nursery and a housekeeper's room. The tower contains the Westmorland and Cumberland Yeomanry Museum, and there is a countryside museum in the 16th-century cobbled courtyard. The grounds include a deerpark and gardens, and there is an adventure playground. The 7th annual Rainbow Craft Fair will be held on 25-26 July.

☎ **Pooley Bridge (07684) 86450**

Open: 19 Apr-4 Oct, Sun-Thu 11.15-5. Last entry 5pm.
Admission: £3.50 (ch under 5 free, ch 16 £2.50). Family Ticket £9. 50. Gardens only £2.50 (ch free). Wheelchair users free.
🅿 ☕ ✗ licensed ♿ toilets for disabled shop garden centre 🐕

GRIZEDALE   Visitor Centre

Grizedale Forest was the first Forestry Commission estate where special efforts were made to provide information and other facilities for visitors. The centre illustrates the story of Grizedale from wildwood to its present role as an area managed for timber, wildlife and recreation. There is a conservation tree nursery, and a number of waymarked walks can be followed, ranging from the one-mile Millwood Habitat Trail to the nine-mile Silurian Way. Routes for cyclists are also provided, and there are woodland sculptures, observation hides, orienteering, children's play area and many picnic sites. The area gives wonderful views, with the possibility of seeing some of the woodland red and roe deer.

Forestry Commission
☎ **Satterthwaite (0229) 860373**

Open: 29 Mar-4 Nov, daily 10-5.
Craft/Sculpture Gallery 50p
🅿 (charged) ♿ (woodland trails suitable for wheelchairs) toilets for disabled shop

HOLKER   Holker Hall & Gardens

The hall dates from the 16th century, although it was rebuilt in grand Victorian style after a fire, and has been owned by the Cavendish family for over 200 years. It has notable woodcarving and stonework, and fine paintings and furniture. The 25 acres of formal and woodland gardens include water features such as the limestone cascade. Given world-class status for the last two years by the Good Gardens Guide, they are a source of beauty and tranquillity. Other attractions include patchwork and printing displays, a Victorian/Edwardian kitchens exhibition, a craft and countryside exhibition, an adventure playground, a toddlers area, and the magnificent Lakeland motor museum. Holker is also home to the Great Garden and Countryside Festival in June each year. There are also horse trials in July, and a hot air balloon rally in September.

Grange-over-Sands
☎ **Flookburgh (05395) 58328**

Open: Apr-Oct, Sun-Fri 10.30-6. Last admission 4.30 (Motor Museum 5pm).
Admission: charge made.
🅿 ☕ ♿ toilets for disabled shop

KESWICK   Cars of the Stars Motor Museum

This unusual museum features celebrity TV and film vehicles, displayed in authentic 'sets'. Some notable exhibits to look out for are *Chitty Chitty Bang Bang*, James Bond's Lotus cars, Laurel and Hardy's Model T, the *MASH* Jeep and Noddy's car. 1992 will see the introduction to the collection of the original Batmobile. A Road Safety Week will be held in June and in August there will be a James Bond Weekend – details on application.

Standish St
☎ **(07687) 73757**

Open: 2 Mar-2 Jan, daily 10-5.
Admission: £1.80 (ch & pen £1.20). Family ticket £5.
🅿 ☕ ♿ toilets for disabled shop

KESWICK Mirehouse

Undoubtedly a great place for children – there are four adventure playgrounds – but Mirehouse has its fair share of cultural interest, and a walk along the beautiful lake shore will take you past the place where Tennyson wrote much of 'Morte d'Arthur'. Inside the 17th-century house there is much original furniture adorning the graceful rooms. Portraits and manuscripts of Francis Bacon, Carlyle and, of course, Tennyson are on display. Outside, the flowers in the walled garden attract the bees and butterflies, and make this sheltered spot perfect for picnics.

(3m N on A591)
☎ (07687) 72287

Open: Apr-Oct. House: Wed, Sun & BH Mon 2-5. Grounds: daily 10.30-5.30. Parties by arrangement.
Admission: ❄ House & grounds £2.20 (ch £1.10). Grounds only 70p (ch 50p)
P ☕ ♿ 🐕 (ex in grounds on lead)

MARYPORT Flying Buzzard & VIC 96

Full guided tours of the Flying Buzzard, a 1951 Clyde tug, bringing to life the story of the ship and her crew. Also explore the VIC 96, and visit the hold – a new hands on display for all the family. A chance to try your hand at tying knots, raising and lowering sails and climbing into a hammock. Special events for 1992 include Steam Weekends.

Elizabeth Dock, South Quay, Maryport Harbour
☎ (0900) 815954

Open: all year – Etr-Oct daily 10.30-4.30; Nov-Etr, telephone to confirm details.
Admission: £1.50 (ch £1). Family ticket £4.25
shop

MUNCASTER Muncaster Castle & Owl Centre

Diverse attractions are offered at this castle, the seat of the Pennington family since the 13th century. Inside is a fine collection of 16th- and 17th- century furnishings, embroideries and portraits, whilst the grounds have a nature trail, a commando course and a profusion of rhododendrons, camellias, magnolias and azaleas. There is also an extensive exhibition of owls, as this is the headquarters of the British Owl Breeding and Release Scheme. Closed circuit television on some nests allows a closer look , and there are continuous owl videos throughout the day in the Old Dairy Theatre. Flying displays take place daily at 2.30pm, weather permitting.

☎ Ravenglass (0229) 717203 & 717393 (owl centre)

Open Apr-Nov, Castle Tue-Sun & BH 1.30-4.30; Garden & Owl Centre, all year, daily 12-5. Parties by arrangement in the morning.
Admission: Castle & Gardens £4.50 (ch 14 £2.50). Gardens & Owl Centre only £2.80 (ch 14 £1.50). Family ticket available. Party.
P ☕ ✕ ♿ toilets for disabled shop garden centre

RAVENGLASS Ravenglass & Eskdale Railway

This narrow gauge (15inch) miniature steam railway was laid in the 19th century to carry iron ore from the mines at Boot. It began to carry passengers and then other freight, including quarried stone, once the mines were closed. The railway was given the nickname 'Owd Ratty' after its contractor, a man called Ratcliffe. It is now a passenger line, where both steam and diesel locomotives are used during the summer months to pull the open and saloon coaches. The railway runs through beautiful countryside for the seven mile journey from Ravenglass, on the coast, up to the terminus at Dalegarth. Purpose-built toilets for wheelchair users at Ravenglass and Eskdale; special coaches on trains for wheelchair passengers (prior notice advisable).

(close to the A595)
☎ (0229) 717171

Open: trains operate daily 4 Apr-1 Nov & 26 Dec-1 Jan; wknds only 15 Feb-29 Mar & 7-15 Nov.
Admission: Return fare £5.20 (ch 5-15 £2.60). Family ticket £13.
P (charged) ☕ ✕ licensed ♿ (special coach) toilets for disabled shop

SKELTON Hutton-in-the-Forest

One of the major stately homes in the Lake District, the house has been occupied by the Vane family since the 17th century. The original 14th-century pele tower was added to mainly in the 17th and 19th centuries. The house contains pictures, tapestries and furniture of many periods. The gardens, park and woodland include a walled garden, topiary, fine specimen trees, a lake and a nature trail. 'Meet the Gardener' afternoons can be arranged.

☎ (08534) 449

Open: 28 May-27 Sep, Thu, Fri & Sun; BH Sun & Mon (fr Etr) 1-4. Grounds daily (ex Sat) 11-5. Groups any day booked in advance from 1 Apr.
Admission: £2.80 (accompanied ch under 7 free, ch £1). Grounds £1 (ch 50p).
P ☕

WINDERMERE Lake District National Park Visitor Centre

Brockhole, built in 1899 for a wealthy businessman, is a large house, set in 32 acres of landscaped gardens, standing on the eastern shore of Lake Windermere. It became England's first National Park Visitor Centre in 1969. It offers a 'Living Lakeland' exhibition on the evolution and development of the National Park, audio-visual displays and films on the Lake District. In the grounds there is a Nature Trail, a children's Squirrel Nutkin Trail and the Beatrix Potter Grotto. Special events during the school holidays are a big attraction. There are also a Compass Course and daily boat trips on the lake.

Brockhole (on A591)
☎ (05394) 46601

Open: 12 Apr-1 Nov, daily from 10am. (Closing time varies with season).
Admission: ✻ £2 (ch 5-16 £1). Party 15+.
P ☕ ✕ licensed ♿ (scented garden) toilets for disabled shop 🐕 (ex in grounds)

WINDERMERE Windermere Steamboat Museum

A unique display of Victorian and Edwardian steamboats which reflects the enormous part boating has played over many years in the history of Lake Windermere – a popular lake for both motorboat and sailboat enthusiasts. Many of the exhibits in this extensive collection are still afloat and in working order. The museum also contains various displays concerning life on and around the lake. A Model Boat Regatta is held on 16/17th May and other special events and exhibitions are added attractions during the summer, including in 1992 a Classic Motor Boat Rally on 1st and 2nd August.

Rayrigg Rd (.25m N Bowness Bay)
☎ (05394) 45565

Open Etr-Oct daily, 10-5. Steamboat trips subject to availability & weather.
Admission: ✻ £2.20 (ch £1.40). Family ticket £5.80. Party 12+
P ☕ ♿ toilets for disabled shop

DERBYSHIRE

BUXTON Buxton Micrarium

The Micrarium is a fascinating museum, and the first of its kind. Visitors view the displays through push-button, remote-controlled microscopes, seeing the wonders of nature magnified.

The Crescent
☎ (0298) 78662

Open: 4 Apr-Sep, daily 10-5 (Feb-Mar wknds only).
Admission: £2.25 (ch £1.25 & pen £1.75)
♿ shop 🐕

BUXTON   Poole's Cavern (Buxton Country Park)

The natural limestone cavern lies in 100 acres of woodland. There is a visitor centre with a video show and Roman exhibition. Also on show is an exhibition on the cave and woodland, including archaeological finds from a cave dig.

Green Ln
☎ (0298) 26978
Open: Good Fri-end Oct, daily 10-5. (Closed Wed in Apr, May & Oct).
🅿 ᜕ (wheelchairs available) toilets for disabled shop 🐾 (ex in park)
Details not confirmed for 1992

CASTLETON   Blue-John Cavern & Mine

The cavern is a remarkable example of a water-worn cave, and measures over a third of a mile long, with chambers 200ft high. It contains 8 of the 14 veins of Blue John stone, and has been the major source of this unique form of fluorspar for nearly 300 years.

Buxton Rd
☎ Hope Valley (0433) 620638 & 620642
Open: all year daily 9.30-6 (or dusk) (telephone for winter opening times); (Closed 25-26 Dec & 1 Jan).
Admission: ✳ £3.50 (ch £1.50, pen £2.50).
Party. shop

CASTLETON   Peak Cavern

This is one of the most spectacular natural limestone caves in the Peak District, and has an electrically lit underground walk of about half a mile. Ropes have been made for over 500 years in the 'Grand Entrance Hall', and traces of a row of cottages can be seen.

(on A625)
☎ Hope Valley (0433) 620285
Open: Etr-end Oct, daily 10-5.
Admission: £2.40 (ch £1.20)
🅿 shop

CASTLETON   Speedwell Cavern

Visitors descend 105 steps to a boat which takes them on a one-mile underground exploration of the floodlit cavern with its 'bottomless pit'.

Winnats Pass (off A625, 5m W of Castleton Village)
☎ Hope Valley (0433) 620512
Open: all year, daily 9.30-5.30. (Closed 25-26 Dec & 1 Jan).
Admission: ✳ £4 (ch 14 £2.50). Party.
🅿 shop

CHATSWORTH

Chatsworth is the palatial home of the Duke and Duchess of Devonshire, and has one of the richest collections of fine and decorative arts in private hands. Inside there is a splendid painted hall, and a great staircase leads to the even finer chapel, which is decorated with marble, paintings, statues and paintings on walls and ceiling. There are magnificent pictures, furniture and porcelain, and a memorable *trompe l'oeil* painting of a violin on the music room door. The park is one of the finest in Britain. It was laid out by 'Capability' Brown, but is most famous as the work of Joseph Paxton (later Sir Joseph), who became head gardener in the 19th century. Notable features include the Cascade and the Emperor Fountain, which sends up a jet of

☎ Baslow (0246) 582204
Open: House & Garden open 29 Mar-Nov, daily 11-4.30. Farmyard & Adventure Playground, 29 Mar-Sep 10.30-4.30.
Admission: House & Garden £4.75 (ch £2.20 & pen £3.75). Family ticket £11. Garden only £2.25 (ch £1.10). Farmyard & Adventure Playground prices under review.
🅿 (charged) ♥ ✗ licensed ᜕ toilets for disabled shop garden centre 🐾 (ex gardens)

water to 290ft. Other attractions are the farming and forestry exhibition and the adventure playground. Guided tours are available at extra cost. Numerous events are held throughout the year, including an Angling Fair on 9th and 10th May and a Country Fair on 5th and 6th September.

CRESWELL   Creswell Crags Visitor Centre

The deep narrow gorge of Creswell Crags is pitted with 24 caves and rock shelters which were used for seasonal camps by Stone Age hunter-gatherers. Unusual finds from within the caves include pieces of decorated animal bone and the remains of animals which have long since become extinct, such as the woolly mammoth. A visitor centre at one end of the gorge explains the importance of the site, with an exhibition and an audio-visual showing what life was like in prehistoric times. From there, a trail leads through the gorge, where visitors can look into the caves through grills, although the caves cannot be entered. There is a picnic site at the centre, and various events are held. There are purpose-built toilets for wheelchair users, and wheelchairs are available on loan.

off Crags Rd (1m E off B6042)
☎ Worksop (0909) 720378

Open: all year, Feb-Oct, daily, 10.30-4.30; Nov-Jan, Sun only 10.30-4.30.
Admission: Free.
🅿 ♿ toilets for disabled shop

CRICH   National Tramway Museum

Vintage electric, horse-drawn and steam tramcars from Britain and other parts of the world can be seen at this unique museum. Many of the trams are in working order, and visitors can take unlimited rides on the trams which may once have clanged through the streets of Oporto, Prague or Paisley, but now run along a one-mile tramway with wonderful views over the Derwent Valley. The tramway period street includes the reconstructed façade of the Georgian assembly rooms from Derby. There are also depots, a video theatre, and numerous exhibitions and displays throughout the year, including an Electric Trams Easter Parade (19 & 20 April), Father's Day Special – dad's chance to drive a train (21 June), and a Teddy Bear's Outing (12 & 13 September).

Matlock Rd (off B5035)
☎ Ambergate (0773) 852565

Open: 4 Apr-1 Nov Sat, Sun & BH's. 13 Apr-24 Sep, Mon-Thu. Also Fri 17 & 24 Apr, 29 May, 4 Jul-28 Aug. Additional opening during 19-30 Oct 10-5.30 (6.30 Sat, Sun & BH).
Admission: £3.70 (ch £2.10 & pen £3.10). Family £10.50. Party 10 + .
🅿 ♥ ♿ (ex trams) toilets for disabled shop

ELVASTON   Elvaston Castle Country Park

The 200-acre park was landscaped in the early 19th century, and became one of Britain's first country parks in 1968. Restored after 30 years of neglect, it includes elaborate topiary gardens from the 19th-century scheme, and a walled kitchen garden now planted out as an Old English Garden with herbaceous borders, roses and scented herbs. The old estate workshops have been restored as an Estate Museum, with exhibitions of black-smithing, saddlery and other traditional crafts associated with country houses at the turn of the century. There are also nature trails and numerous walks, exhibitions and displays, and a caravan and campsite.

Borrowash Rd
☎ Derby (0332) 571342

Open: all year, daily 9-dusk. Museum Etr-Oct, Wed-Sat 1-5, Sun & BH's 10-6.
🅿 (charged) ♥ ♿ toilets for disabled shop
Details not confirmed for 1992

ILKESTON   The American Adventure Theme Park

This is one of Britain's few fully themed parks, based on the legend of a whole continent. The experiences of a day out here are widely varied, from the heartpounding action of the Missile Rollercoaster in Spaceport USA, the wet and wild excitement of the Great Niagara Rapids ride or the Cherokee Falls log flume to the gentle excursion across Lake Reflection aboard a Mississippi paddle steamer, watching a shoot-out in Silver City, seeing the glamour of Lazy Lil's Saloon Show or experiencing the carnival atmosphere of Mexicoland.

Pit Ln
☎ **Langley Mill (0773) 769931 & 531521**

Open: fr Etr. Telephone for details.
Admission: ✽ £8.70 (ch £7.70, pen & disabled £4.10).
🅿 🍴 ✗ licensed ♿ (free wheelchair hire) toilets for disabled shop 🐕

MATLOCK   Riber Castle Wildlife Park

Dominated by the ruins of the fairy-tale fortress built by the larger-than-life figure of John Smedley, who made Matlock a fashionable Victorian health resort, the Riber Castle Wildlife Park covers 25 acres of land at the top of the 853ft high Riber Hill. Specialising in rare breeds and endangered species of birds and animals, the park is home to lynx, otters, reindeer, Arctic foxes, and owls, many on breeding and release programmes; there is also a children's playground. The house is now a roofless shell but still looks imposing and is a good vantage point from which to view the local gorge. The 'Riber Round Up' MG rally is held in September.

(off A615)
☎ **(0629) 582073**

Open: all year, daily from 10am. (Summer last admission 5pm, winter 3-4.30pm).
Admission: ✽ £3.50 (ch 5-15 £2, pen £3).
🅿 🍴 ♿ toilets for disabled shop 🐕 (in animal section)

MATLOCK BATH   The Heights of Abraham

High on a hill above the village of Matlock Bath are the Grounds of the Heights of Abraham. Until recently the climb to the summit was only for the very energetic, but now alpine-style cable cars provide a leisurely and spectacular way of reaching the top from their starting point near Matlock Bath Railway Station. Once inside the Grounds there is plenty to do for the whole family. Two famous show caverns provide fascinating tours, one is introduced by a multivision programme and the other tells the story of a 17th-century lead miner. A coffee shop, licensed restaurant and picnic sites take advantage of the superb views. There is also a nature trail, the Victorian Prospect Tower and play area. In a sparkling waterscaped setting is the High Falls Gallery and a gift shop.

(on A6)
☎ **Matlock (0629) 582365**

Open: daily Etr-Oct 10-5 (later in high season) for Autumn & Winter opening telephone for details.
Admission: ✽ £4.50 (ch £2.50, pen £3.75). Party 20 + .
🍴 ✗ licensed ♿ toilets for disabled shop

MATLOCK BATH   Peak District Mining Museum

This rewarding display, ideal for families, explains the history of Derbyshire lead industry from Roman times to the present day. The geology of the area, mining and smelting processes, the quarrying and the people who worked in the industry, are all illustrated by a series of static and moving exhibits and an audio-visual display. The museum also features an early 19th-century water pressure pumping engine – the only one of its kind in Britain.

The Pavilion (off A6)
☎ **Matlock (0629) 583834**

Open: all year, daily 11-4 (later in summer season). (Closed 25 Dec).
Admission: £1 (ch, students, disabled & pen 50p). Family £2.50. Party.
🅿 (charged) ♿ shop 🐕

MATLOCK BATH   Temple Mine

In the process of being restored to how it was in the 1920s and 1930s, this old lead and fluorspar workings makes interesting viewing. A self-guided tour illustrates the geology, mineralisation and mining techniques.

Temple Rd (off A6)
☎ **Matlock (0629) 583834**

Open: Etr-Oct, daily 11-4, (longer hours in summer); Oct-Nov & Jan-Etr, wknds only 1-4.
Admission: 80p (ch, students, disabled & pen 40p) shop ⍦

RIPLEY   Midland Railway Centre

This centre not only operates a regular steam-train passenger service, but also provides the focal point for a fascinating industrial museum project. Its aim is to depict every aspect of the golden days of the Midland Railway, and its successors. The working section of the railway line extends for some three and a half miles between Butterley Station and Riddings. Exhibits range from the steam locomotives of 1866 to the diesels of 1967. There is also a large section of rolling stock spanning the last 100 years. 'Specials' run from the centre include Wine and Dine trains and Santa Specials. Also of interest is the narrow-gauge railway and an award-winning country park. There are purpose-built toilets for wheelchair users at Butterley Station and special accommodation is available on the trains. Every Sunday from 29th March to 27th September will be a Gala Day.

Butterley Station (1m N on B6179)
☎ **(0773) 747674 & 749788**

Open: trains operate all year Sun; Apr-Oct & Dec Sat; 17-26 Apr, 23-31 May, Aug-6 Sep & 26-31 Oct daily; 30 Jun-16 Jul Tue-Thu & Sat-Sun; 21-31 Jul Tue-Sun. Train times 1130-1615.
Admission: ✽ £3.95 (ch £2 & pen £3.50). Family ticket £9.90. Party 15+. Sun & BH Mon (Apr-Oct) £4.50 (ch £2.25 & pen £4). Family ticket £11.25.
🅿 (charged) ⍦ ✗ licensed ♿ toilets for disabled shop

DEVON

ARLINGTON   Arlington Court

Built in 1822, Arlington Court is filled with a fascinating collection of *objets d'art:* pewter, shells and model ships as well as furniture and costumes from the 19th century. The biggest attraction, however, is the collection of carriages and horsedrawn vehicles, and rides are available. Around the house is a landscaped park grazed by Shetland ponies and sheep. There is a Victorian garden and a conservatory, and nature trails may be followed through the woods and by the lake.

☎ **Shirwell (0271) 850296**

Open: Apr-1 Nov, Sun-Fri 11-5.30; also Sat of BH wknds. Footpaths through Park open all year during daylight hours.
Admission: House & grounds £4.40. Grounds only £2.20.
🅿 ✗ licensed ♿ (wheelchairs available) toilets for disabled shop ⍦ (ex in park) (NT)

BEER   Pecorama Pleasure Gardens

The gardens are high on a hillside, overlooking the delightful fishing village of Beer. A miniature steam and diesel passenger line offers visitors a stunning view of Lyme Bay as it runs through the Pleasure Gardens. These feature 'Melody Close' and the 'Top Spot' where entertainment is staged during high season. Other attractions include an aviary, putting green, crazy golf and children's activity area. The main building houses an exhibition of railway modelling in various small gauges, displayed in settings around the house and gardens. There are souvenir and railway model shops, plus full catering facilities.

Underleys
☎ **Seaton (0297) 21542**

Open: Times & days vary according to season.
Admission: Fee payable.
🅿 ⍦ ♿ toilets for disabled shop ⍦ (ex in certain areas)

BICKINGTON   Gorse Blossom Miniature Railway and Woodland Park

Unlimited rides are allowed on the three-quarter mile, seven and a quarter inch gauge steam railway line, set amid 35 acres of woodland, about half of which is open to the public. Other attractions include woodland walks, a nature trail, woodland assault course, toytown village and children's play area.

☎ (0626) 821361
Open: 28 Mar-6 Oct, daily 10-last admission 4.30.
🅿 ✿ ♿ toilets for disabled shop ✗
Details not confirmed for 1992

BICKLEIGH   Bickleigh Castle

The 'castle' is really a moated and fortified manor house, and was formerly the romantic home of the heirs of the Earls of Devon and later of the Carew family. The small detached thatched chapel is said to be the oldest complete building in Devon. It dates from the Norman period and, like the medieval Gatehouse, survived the destruction which followed the Civil War. The Carew family acquired the house in the 16th century, and it was Admiral Sir George Carew who commanded the 'Mary Rose' on her first and last voyage. He drowned with his men when the ship capsized and sank. There is an exhibition on the ship and on Tudor maritime history, with a feature on peacetime maritime disasters, mainly that of the 'Titanic'. Also in the house is a museum of domestic objects and toys from the 18th century onwards, and a display of gadgets used by World War II spies and POWs – the most complete collection known. More traditional features of interest include the Great Hall, armoury (including fine Civil War armour), guardroom, Elizabethan bedroom and the 17th-century farmhouse. The garden is moated and the tower can be climbed for views of the Exe Valley and of the castle complex.

(off A396 take A3072 from Bickleigh Bridge)
☎ (0884) 855363
Open: Etr wk (Good Fri-Fri), then Wed, Sun & BH to late May BH, then daily (ex Sat) to early Oct.
Admission: £2.80 (ch 5-15 £1.40). Family ticket £7.50. Party 20+
🅿 ✿ ♿ shop ✗

BICKLEIGH   Bickleigh Mill – Devonshire's Centre

The picturesque old working watermill on the River Exe has been converted into a most comprehensive Craft, Gift and Garment Centre with attractive restaurant. Cows and goats are milked by hand at the adjacent Heritage Farm. The land is worked by shire horses who support the many rare breeds of animals and poultry. The Agricultural Museum and popular Motor Centre are situated alongside.

Additionally the complex has its own fishing, bird and otter centres with riverside picnic and children's areas serviced by its own shop. A British Tourist Authority award winner.

☎ (08845) 419
Open: all year, Jan-Mar Sat & Sun only 10-5, Apr-Dec, daily 10-6 (5pm Nov & Dec)
🅿 ✿ ✗ licensed ♿ toilets for disabled shop
Details not confirmed for 1992

BICTON   Bicton Park Gardens

Bicton Park offers many attractions, but the central one is over 50 acres of colourful gardens, shrubs, woodlands, lakes, ponds and fountains, with an Italian garden and a wonderful restored palm house. This has tropical and sub-tropical areas, where bananas and other exotica flourish. There are also fuchsia, geranium and orchid houses.

East Budleigh (2m N of Budleigh Salterton on A376)
☎ Colaton Raleigh (0395) 68465
Open: Apr-Sep daily, 10-6; Mar & Oct, daily 10-4.

A modern building houses the James Countryside Museum, which has farm tools, wagons and a cider press among its fascinating displays. Not to be forgotten either are the fun world and adventure playground, Bicton Woodland Railway, crazy golf, bird garden and tropical house. There is also an open-air arena for equestrian and other events. 9 August 1992 is Clowns International Charity Day and around 70 clowns from around the world will gather at Bicton to entertain the visitors and help raise money for local children's charities.

Admission: £4.70 (ch 3-15 £3.70, pen £3.95). Return ticket £1.50 (ch £1). Party 20+.
🅿 ✗ licensed & (adapted carriage on woodland railway) toilets for disabled shop garden centre

BLACKMOOR GATE   Exmoor Bird Gardens

These landscaped gardens have a waterfall,streams and a lake with penguins, swans and other water birds. There are aviaries with tropical and other birds, and some animals can also be seen, such as wallabies, guanaco, pigs, coati, chipmunks, ponies, monkeys and goats. There is a 'Tarzanland' for children.

South Stowford (off B3226)
☎ **Parracombe (05983) 352**

Open: daily, Apr-Oct 10-6; Nov-Mar 10-4.
Admission: £3.50 (ch 3-16 £2.25, under 3 free).
🅿 ☕ ✗ licensed & toilets for disabled shop
🐾

BOVEY TRACEY   Parke Rare Breeds Farm

Over 200 acres of parkland in the wooded valley of the River Bovey make a beautiful setting for the farm, which was established to preserve pure old breeds of domestic animal. Some of the breeds at Parke were common in the Middle Ages, and can be traced back to prehistoric times. They may not be very commercial, but they are an essential reservoir of genes which have been lost in the development of modern farm breeds. In the walled garden there is a fascinating collection of poultry, peafowl, ducks and geese, while in the fields there are pigs, goats, sheep and cattle, including the rare Belted Welsh Black cattle. There is also a pets corner and a play area. Another great attraction of Parke is the walks which can be taken through woodland beside the river and along the route of the old railway track. The headquarters of the Dartmoor National Park is also here, and has an information centre.

Parke Estate
☎ **(0626) 833909**

Open: Good Fri-Oct, daily 10-6 (last admission 5pm).
🅿 ☕ & toilets for disabled shop (NT)
Details not confirmed for 1992

BUCKFASTLEIGH   Buckfast Abbey

The story of Buckfast Abbey is a remarkable one. The monastery was originally founded in 1018, but the monks left during the Dissolution in the 16th century. Monks returned to the site in 1882 and considered restoring it; in 1907 four (mostly inexperienced) monks began rebuilding the church; and now Buckfast Abbey is once again a religious community. The church was built on the old foundations, using local blue limestone and Ham Hill stone. One of the most beautiful features is the great modern east window, which was the work of Father Charles, a craftsman in stained glass. Other monks have other skills: in beekeeping, farming, and the making of Buckfast tonic wine. Monthly concerts are held at the abbey, and there is a flower festival in July (20- 25), and there are children's activity days on Wednesdays throughout August.

☎ **(0364) 42519**
Open: all year daily 5.30am-9.30pm. (Shops, tea room 9-5.30). Etr-Oct (exhibition) 10.30-4.30.
Admission: Free. (Exhibition 60p, ch 30p).
🅿 (charged) ☕ ✗ licensed & (braille plan, wheelchair available) toilets for disabled shop
🐾

BUCKFASTLEIGH   Buckfast Butterfly Farm & Dartmoor Otter Sanctuary

Visitors can wander around a specially designed, under-cover tropical garden, where free-flying butterflies and moths from many parts of the world can be seen. The otter sanctuary has four large enclosures with underwater viewing and there are special observation holts.

(off A38)
☎ (0364) 42916

Open: Good Fri-Oct, daily 10-5.30 or dusk (whichever is earlier).
Admission: ✳ £3.25 (ch £2 & pen £2.75)
🅿 ☕ Ꭽ shop ✗

BUCKFASTLEIGH   South Devon Railway

The Buckfastleigh & Totnes line was a rural branch which served the middle of the Dart Valley for 98 years before it was closed by British Rail. It is run now as an educational charity, and makes an interesting way to see the Dart Valley and learn about its past. The store of Great Western rolling stock includes a number of locomotives, and there are extensive grounds at Buckfastleigh. The steam-hauled trains run from Buckfastleigh on a one-hour round trip. Special events include: Vintage Car Gathering, Thomas the Tank Engine Day, Autumn Transport Gathering and Santa Trains.

Buckfastleigh Station
☎ (0364) 42338

Open: daily Etr-Sep, 10-5.30. Also selected days early & late season. Santa trains in Dec.
Admission: £5 (ch £3.60, pen £4.50) includes train fare, station & grounds. Party.
🅿 ☕ Ꭽ toilets for disabled shop

CHITTLEHAMPTON   Cobbaton Combat Collection

Second World War British and Canadian military vehicles, war documents and military equipment can be seen in this private collection. There are over fifty vehicles including tanks and a recent Warsaw pact section. There is also a section on 'Mum's War' and the home front. The children's play area includes a Sherman tank.

Cobbaton
☎ Chittlehamholt (0769) 540740

Open: Apr-Oct, daily 10-6. Winter Mon-Fri 10-4.
Admission: £2.75 (ch £1.50, pen £2.25)
🅿 Ꭽ shop

CHUDLEIGH   see **Lower Ashton**

CLOVELLY   The Milky Way

This award-winning attraction gives visitors the oppor-tunity to try hand milking one of their 160 dairy cows or help with the feeding of baby animals (12.30-4pm). The high-tech milking parlour is also on show and there is an adventure playground and a Countryside Collection of machinery, implements and farmhouse scenes of yester-year. There is also a working pottery on site, and, new for 1992, the North Devon Bird of Prey Centre, with twice daily falconry displays.

(on the main A39, 2m from Clovelly)
☎ Bideford (0237) 431255

Open: Apr-Oct, daily 10.30-6.
Admission: £3.50 (ch £2, under 3 free, pen £3).
🅿 ☕ Ꭽ toilets for disabled shop

COMBE MARTIN   Bodstone Barton Farmworld

Set in an area of outstanding natural beauty, Bodstone Barton is a 17th- century farm covering 160 acres. The farm is run by both traditional and modern methods, and visitors can see goats and cows being milked by hand or machine. Attractions include an adventure playground, and

Berrydown (2m S, off A3123)
☎ (0271) 883654

Open: all year, daily May-Sep 10-6, Oct-Apr 12-5.

rides by tractor, trailer and horse-drawn cart. There is a nature trail to follow, with an abundance of wildlife to be seen. A large collection of agricultural and domestic items are on show, with 20,000 square feet under cover. Many crafts are demonstrated here, including spinning, spar-making and pottery; there is a blacksmith and visitors can watch heavy horses being groomed, harnessed and worked. There are lots of rides and regular live entertainment, including a weekly barn dance and barbeque in the season. Please phone for details.

Admission: £3.75 (ch £2.50, disabled £1.50 & pen £3).
P ☕ ✗ licensed & toilets for disabled shop ⅍

COMBE MARTIN   Combe Martin Wildlife Park

Twenty acres of woodland complete with streams, cascading waterfalls, ornamental gardens, tropical plants and rare trees make this the most natural wildlife park in Britain. Otters living in the streams have produced 29 young in the last five years and for something completely different, visitors can see Meerkats 'on guard', living in the largest enclosure in the world – a man- made desert. There is also a large selection of primates, mammals and birds. Special events for 1992 include 'Prehistoric World'.

(off A399)
☎ (0271) 882486

Open: Mar-Nov, daily 10-4.30.
Admission: £4 (ch & pen £3). Party 10 + .
P ☕ ✗ licensed & (car service) shop ⅍

DARTMOUTH   Woodland Leisure Park

A beautiful 60-acre park with ten play zones featuring Tarzan swings, death slides, mega assault course, tube slide, a three-stage free-fall slide and a special toddlers' play village. There is an international bird and fish collection, an undercover bee observatory, and a new 15-acre animal farm complex with hundreds of animals under cover. Beautiful Sika deer, tiny Russian hamsters, and many more friendly pets to meet and feed. There are also 30 acres of woodland with super nature walks and ornamental ponds. Live entertainers appear daily during school holidays, and special events during the summer season include a teddy bears' picnic, an army display team, and a country fun day.

Blackawton (W, off B3207)
☎ Blackawton (080421) 598

Open: all year, 31 Mar-Oct, daily 9.30-6.30; Nov-30 Mar, daily 10-dusk.
Admission: £3.50 (ch £2.50 & pen £2)
P ☕ & toilets for disabled shop

EXETER   Underground Passages

A unique medieval water system with an introductory exhibition. Not recommended unless fit and healthy – definitely not suitable for those inclined to claustrophobia. Flat shoes are essential. All tours are guided, and there is an introductory 10-minute videoplus exhibition.

Boots Arcade, High St
☎ (0392) 265858 & 265887

Open: Etr-Oct, daily, tours variable. Nov-Etr afternoons only.
Admission: ✱ £1.25 (ch, students & pen 75p).
shop ⅍

FARWAY   Farway Countryside Park

A collection of traditional and modern breeds of farm animals can be seen in the park, which covers 108 acres of beautiful countryside with magnificent views over the Coly Valley. Attractions include pony and donkey cart rides and trekking, nature trails and a grass ski slope.

(1.5m S on unclass rd A4 signed on B3174)
☎ (040487) 224 & 367

Open: Good Fri-Oct, daily 10-6 (last admission 5pm).
Admission: ✱ £2 (ch £1, pen £1.50).
P (charged) ☕ & toilets for disabled shop

ILFRACOMBE   Watermouth Castle

Overlooking a beautiful bay, this 19th-century castle is one of North Devon's finest. It caters enthusiastically for the public, offering such unique experiences as a mechanical musical demonstration and the Watermouth Waltzing Waters. Other attractions include a tube slide, carousel and Gnomeland.

(3m NE off A399)
☎ **(0271) 863879**

Open: Good Fri & 31 Mar-4 Apr, Sun-Thu 11-4; 7 Apr-16 May & 23 Sep-24 Oct, Sun-Thu 2-4; 19 May-28 Jun & 2-22 Sep, Mon-Fri 11-4, Sun 1-4; 30 Jun-1 Sep Sun-Fri 10-4; 27 Oct-3 Nov Sun-Thu 1-4.
Admission: ✻ £4.50 (ch £3.50 & pen £4)
🅿 ☛ ♿ (special wheelchair route) toilets for disabled shop ✖

LOWER ASHTON   Canonteign Falls & Country Park

Lakes, wildfowl, a children's play area and miniature horses can be found in this beautiful country park. Covering 80 acres of ancient woodland, this unspoilt valley is also the setting of the highest waterfall in England.

☎ **Christow (0647) 52666**

Open: all year, Apr-Oct, daily 10-6; Nov-Mar Sun only 10-5.
🅿 ☛ ✗ licensed shop
Details not confirmed for 1992

LYDFORD   Lydford Gorge

The spectacular gorge has been formed by the River Lyd, which has cut into the rock and caused swirling boulders to scoop out potholes in the stream bed. This has created some dramatic features, notably the Devil's Cauldron close to Lydford Bridge. At the end of the gorge is the 90ft-high White Lady Waterfall.

(off A386)
☎ **(082282) 441 & 320**

Open: Apr-1 Nov, daily 10-5.30. (Nov-Mar, waterfall entrance only, daily 10.30-3).
Admission: £2.60
🅿 ☛ shop (NT)

MORWELLHAM   Morwellham Quay

When copper was discovered in the hills near Tavistock the town reached new heights of prosperity. Morwellham was the nearest point to which sea-going ships could navigate and became the greatest copper port in Queen Victoria's Empire. Once the mines were exhausted the port area disintegrated into unsightly wasteland, until 1970 when a charitable trust was set up for its restoration. It is now a thriving and delightful open-air museum. Cottages have been faithfully renovated, complete with pig in the back yard, and visitors can meet a blacksmith, cooper, assayer, quay workers and coachmen, all dressed in period costume to help recreate history in this picturesque old port. There are also underground rides into a copper mine, heavy horse-drawn wagons, slide shows and other displays. Unspoilt countryside, riverside and woodland trails surround the museum.

☎ **Tavistock (0822) 832766 & 833808**

Open: all year (ex Xmas wk) 10-5.30 (4.30 in winter). Last admission 3.30 (2.30 in winter).
Admission: ✻ £5.60 (ch £3.95, pen & students £4.95). Party.
🅿 ☛ ✗ licensed shop

PAIGNTON   Paignton & Dartmouth Steam Railway

Steam trains run for seven miles from Paignton to Kingswear on the former Great Western line, stopping at Goodrington Sands, a popular beach, and at Churston, connecting with the ferry crossing to Dartmouth. The line runs Santa Specials during December, and dining specials are also available.

Queens Park Station, Torbay Rd
☎ **(0803) 555872**

Open: Jun-Sep daily 9-5.30 & selected days Oct-Nov & Mar-May.
Admission: ✻ Dartmouth return £5.50 (ch £3.80). Family ticket £17. Party 20 +
☛ ♿ shop (at Paignton & Kingswear)

PAIGNTON   Paignton Zoo

This is one of England's largest zoos set in 75 acres of botanical gardens. Animals in the collection, which first opened nearly 70 years ago, include lions, tigers, elephants, giraffe, rhinoceros, zebra, flamingos, crocodiles and ostrich. The Zoo is very committed to conservation and participates in captive breeding programmes for endangered species. A special feature is the lake with Gibbon islands where five Gibbon families roam freely. Children are well catered for with an adventure playground, 'meet the animals' area and the Ark family activity centre – an indoor area with lots to do and learn about wildlife on our planet. Other features include a nature trail which follows a route past disused lime kilns, and a jungle express miniature railway and keeper talks during the summer.

Totnes Rd (1m, on A385)
☎ (0803) 527936
Open: all year, daily 10-6.30 (5pm in winter). Last admission 5pm (4pm in winter). (Closed 25 Dec).
Admission: ✲ £4.90 (ch 3-14 £3, pen £4.20). Party 15 + . Reduction for disabled. P ☜ ✗ licensed ৬ (free wheelchair loan-booking advisable) toilets for disabled shop garden centre ⋊ (kennels available)

PLYMOUTH   Plymouth Dome

This high-tech visitor centre takes you on a journey through time, exploring the sounds and smells of an Elizabethan street, walking the gun-deck of a galleon, sailing with the epic voyages from Plymouth Sound, dodging the press gang, strolling with film stars on an ocean liner and witnessing the devastation of the blitz. Use high-resolution cameras to zoom in on ships and shoreline, or access computers to identify naval vessels. Examine satellite weather pictures as they arrive from space, keep up to date with shipping movements and monitor the busy harbour on radar. An excellent introduction to Plymouth and a colourful interpretation of the past.

The Hoe
☎ (0752) 603300 & 600608 (recorded message)
Open: all year, daily, Etr-May 9-6; Jun-15 Sep 9-7.30pm; 15 Sep-Nov 9-6; Dec-Mar 9-5.30. (Closed 25 Dec).
Admission: ✲ Jul-Sep £2.50 (ch £1.65 & pen £2); rest of year £2.10 (ch £1.45 & pen £1.85). Family ticket £7.10. Party.
☜ ৬ (induction loop for hard of hearing, wheelchairs available) toilets for disabled shop ⋊

PLYMPTON   Dartmoor Wildlife Park & Westcountry Falconry Centre

The collection of over 100 species of animals and birds is set in 30 acres of Devonshire countryside. Special attractions include a large group of big cats, bears, wolves, seals, deer, waterfowl and reptiles. You may touch, talk to and learn about living animals in 'Close Encounters of the Animal Kind' – an indoor attraction giving first hand experience of wild creatures. Falconry displays are given (weather permitting) and there are pony rides at weekends and bank holidays.

(3m NE at Sparkwell, N of A38)
☎ Cornwood (075537) 209 & 343
Open: daily, 10-dusk.
P ☜ licensed ৬ toilets for disabled shop
Details not confirmed for 1992

SIDMOUTH   Vintage Toy & Train Museum

A splendid display of toys, games and children's books, covering the 50 years from 1925 to 1975. The exhibits include the first and last Dinky Toy, Hornby '0' gauge trains and Minic clockwork vehicles, together with a selection of Britain's military and farm figures and Cadbury's free gift with cocoa – Cococubs. 1992 will see a special display of French Hornby Gauge '0' trains made in the Paris Meccano factory during the 1930s.

1st Floor, Fields Department Store, Market Place
☎ (0395) 515124 ext 34
Open: 14 Apr-Oct, Mon-Sat 10-5. (Closed BH).
Admission: £1 (ch 3-14 & pen 50p).
P ☜ shop ⊞

TIVERTON Tiverton Castle

Dating from 1106, the castle dominates the River Exe. It
was originally moated on three sides with the Exe as the
fourth defence. One remaining circular Norman tower
remains from the original four, and there is also a medieval
gatehouse with walls 5ft thick. The castle was a Royalist
stronghold during the Civil War but was taken by the
Roundheads in 1645. It houses a fascinating clock collection
in the tower, and one of the finest collections of Civil War
armour and arms in the country. Visitors are encouraged to
add their stitches in history to the New World tapestry.
The 350th anniversary of the start of the English Civil War
will be commemorated at the Castle this year.

☎ (0884) 253200 & 071-727 4854

Open: 17 Apr-Sep, Sun-Thu 2.30-5.30.
Admission: £2.50 (ch 7-16 £1.50, disabled
half price).
🅿 ☕ ♿ shop

TORQUAY Babbacombe Model Village

Set in four acres of beautifully maintained, miniature
landscaped garden, the village contains over 400 models
and 1200ft of model railway. Authentic sound effects have
been added, to create a whole new dimension. In summer,
when the village is open until late, it is illuminated. Special
'Close Encounters' can be seen early and late season,
featuring UFOs and a laser show.

Hampton Av, Babbacombe
☎ (0803) 328669

Open: all year, Etr-Sep, daily 9am-10pm;
Oct 9-9pm; Nov-Etr 9am-dusk. (Closed 25
Dec).
Admission: £3.20 (ch £2)
🅿 (charged) ♿ ('touch & see' board for
blind) toilets for disabled shop garden centre

TORQUAY Kents Cavern Showcaves

Recognised as one of the most important archaeological
sites in Britain, these showcaves provide a set of unique
experiences. This is not only a world of spectacular natural
beauty, but also a priceless record of past times, where a
multitude of secrets of mankind, animals and nature have
become trapped and preserved over the last 500,000
years. One hundred and seventy years after the first
excavations and with over 70,000 remains already
unearthed, modern research is still discovering new clues
to our past.

The showcaves are visited along well-lit paths and tours
are accompanied by 'storytellers' who bring to life past
scenes using props and the natural setting of the caves.

The Caves, Wellswood (1.25m NE off
B3199)
☎ (0803) 294059 & 215136

Open: daily (ex 25 Dec). Apr-Jun & Sep-Oct
10-6; Jul & Aug 10-9 (6pm Sat); Nov-Mar
10-5. Last tour 45mins before closing time.
Admission: £2.90 (ch 5-15 £1.90 ch under 5
free). Party 20+.
🅿 ☕ ♿ shop ✗

YEALMPTON The National Shire Horse Centre

Some fine old farm buildings are at the hub of this 60-acre
farm with over 40 Shire horses. With the revival of interest
in the gentle giants, the farm has become the National
Shire Horse Centre. Visitors are able to see not only the
heavy horses and their foals, but a variety of other
creatures as well. A butterfly house permits a range of
exotic butterflies to be seen in their real habitat. A craft
centre, showing the skills of the saddler and the falconer,
among others, is in the barns. Daily displays of falconry (at
1pm and 3.30pm) and parades of the Shire horses (at
11.30, 2.30 and 4.15) are given throughout the year.
Children are well catered for with a pets area, cart rides

(On A379, Plymouth to Kingsbridge)
☎ Plymouth (0752) 880268 & 880806
(recorded info)

Open: all year, daily 10-5. (Closed 24-26
Dec).
Admission: ✴ £4.40 (ch £2.99, pen £3.95)
🅿 ☕ ✗ licensed ♿ toilets for disabled shop
garden centre

and an adventure playground with free-fall slide. Special events include Bank Holiday Specials, a Western Weekend (3rd wknd Jul), a Steam and Vintage Rally (2nd wknd Aug), and a Classic Car Show (1st Sunday in Sep).

DORSET

ABBOTSBURY   Abbotsbury Sub Tropical Gardens

Sheltered by a curtain of trees, the twenty acre Sub Tropical Gardens have a Mediterranean-type climate that allows rare and tender plants to flourish. The gardens were started in 1760, and have a walled garden in the centre which is a mass of azaleas, camellias and rhododendrons.

Beach Rd (on B3157)
☎ **(0305) 871387**
Open: mid Mar-mid Oct, daily 10-6. Open in winter months at reduced rate.
🅿 ☛ &. (wheelchair for hire) toilets for disabled shop garden centre
Details not confirmed for 1992

ABBOTSBUY   Abbotsbury Swannery

Monks founded the swannery in the 14th century, and it is still a breeding ground for the only managed colonial herd of mute swans. The swans can be seen safely at close quarters, and the site is also home or stopping point for many wild birds. Reeds are harvested for thatching, and there is a 17th-century duck decoy. Mid-July this year sees the biennial swan round-up. A spectacular event where around eight hundred swans are herded toward the head of Fleet Lagoon. This enables staff to give each bird a general health check and repair or renew any damaged rings.

New Barn Rd
☎ **Weymouth (0305) 871242 & 871684**
Open: Apr-Oct, daily 9.30-4.30. Winter visiting for waterfowl is available, phone for details.
🅿 &. (wheelchair loan, herb garden for blind) toilets for disabled 🐕
Details not confirmed for 1992

BOURNEMOUTH   Terracotta Warriors

The Terracotta Warriors experience transports you back to the third century BC to see the First Emperor, Quin Shi Huang in life and death. Descend to a dramatic life-size reconstruction of part of the Terracotta Army excavation, and finally see the especially-recreated Terracotta Warriors displayed in all their glory.

Old Christchurch Ln
☎ **(0202) 293544**
Open: all year, daily 9.30-5.30 (9pm Jul-Aug). (Closed 24-26 Dec).
Admission: ✳ £2.85 (ch £1.70 & pen £2.35).
shop 🐕

SYMBOLS

☎ Telephone number	✳ Indicates 1991 price	☛ Refreshments	🐕 No Dogs
&. Suitable for visitors in wheelchairs	🅿 Parking at Establishment	✗ Restaurant	🚫 No coaches

ABBREVIATIONS

AM	Ancient Monument	BH	Bank Holidays	ch 15 20p	Children under 15 20p
AM(CadW)	Ancient Monument (Wales)	PH	Public Holidays	Pen	Senior Citizens
EH	English Heritage	Etr	Easter	Party	Special or reduced rates for
NT	National Trust	ex	except		parties booked in advance
NTS	National Trust for Scotland	Free	Admission free	Party 30+	Special or reduced rates for
		10p	Admission 10p		parties of 30 or more booked
		ch 20p	Children 20p		in advance

BOVINGTON CAMP
The Tank Museum (Royal Armoured Corps & Royal Tank Regiment)

You can climb inside some of the exhibits at Bovington Camp as well as look at them. There are over 250 examples of wheeled and tracked armoured fighting vehicles from 17 different countries, dating from 1915 onwards and including a cut-away Centurion tank. There are also separate displays of armaments, uniforms, medals, guns and other equipment. Videos and working models can be seen, and four new exhibition halls cover the development of the tank. Special events include: Military Model and Wargamers Fair (23-25 May), Tank Militaria and Auto Jumble (13 & 14 Jun), and Military Day/Battle Day (26 July).

(off A352)
☎ Bindon Abbey (0929) 403463 & 403329

Open: all year, daily 10-5. Last admission 4.30. (Closed 10 days over Xmas).
Admission: ✽ £4 (ch & pen £2). Family ticket £8. Party 10+. Servicemen free.
🅿 ✗ licensed ♿ (wheelchair available) toilets for disabled shop ⚑

BROWNSEA ISLAND

Although it is popular and easy to reach from Poole, Brownsea still offers peace, seclusion and a sense of timelessness. Visitors can wander along woodland paths, lounge on beautiful beaches, admire the fine views of Corfe Castle and the Dorset coast, or join a guided tour of the 250-acre nature reserve managed by the Dorset Naturalists' Trust. The island is perhaps most famous, however, as the site of the first scout camp, held by Lord Baden-Powell in 1907. Scouts and Guides are still the only people allowed to stay here overnight.

The lack of development on the island is due to its last private owner, Mrs Bonham Christie. She kept it as a kind of huge garden for animals, birds and flowers, and let peacocks roam free. Their descendants still thrive here, as do native red squirrels, and sika deer, introduced in 1896. A less welcome newcomer is the destructive mink. The island is also famous for its dragonflies, moths and butterflies, but most of all for its birds. The brackish lagoon supports a colony of Sandwich and common terns, with numerous waders in autumn and spring, and ducks in winter. There is also a heronry, one of Britain's largest.

(located in Poole Harbour)
☎ Canford Cliffs (0202) 707744

Open: Apr-11 Oct, daily 10-8 or dusk if earlier; check for time of last boat.
Admission: £1.90 (ch £1). Family ticket £5. (Apr, May, Jun & Sep). Party 15+.
🍴 ♿ toilets for disabled shop ⚑
(NT)

CANFORD CLIFFS   Compton Acres Gardens

The nine and a half acres of Compton Acres incorporate Japanese, Roman and Italian gardens, rock and water gardens, and heather gardens. There are fine views over Poole Harbour and the Purbeck Hills.

Canford Cliffs Rd (on B3065)
☎ (0202) 700778

Open: Mar-Oct, daily 10.30-6.30.
Admission: £3.30 (ch £1, student & pen £2.40). Party.
🅿 🍴 ♿ toilets for disabled shop garden centre ⚑

SYMBOLS

☎ Telephone number	✽ Indicates 1991 price	🍴 Refreshments	⚑ No Dogs
♿ Suitable for visitors in wheelchairs	🅿 Parking at Establishment	✗ Restaurant	🚌 No coaches

DORCHESTER   Dinosaur Museum

Britain's only museum devoted to dinosaurs has an appealing mixture of fossils, skeletons, life-size reconstructions and interactive displays such as the 'feelies'. There are audio-visual presentations, and the idea is to provide an all-round family attraction with new displays each year.

Icen Way
☎ (0305) 269880
Open: all year, daily 9.30-5.30. (Closed 24-26 Dec).
Admission: ✻ £2.35 (ch £1.70, pen £2.05).
& shop

POOLE   Great Poole Model Railway

A '00' gauge scenic layout covers more than 1000 sq ft of this model museum. 'Life in Space' and 'Smugglers and Pirates' are two of the displays on show.

Henning's Wharf, The Quay
☎ (0202) 687240
Open: all year daily Apr-May 9.30-5.30, Jun-Sep from 9.30, Oct-Nov 10-5, Dec-Mar 10.30-5, later at wknd. (Closed 25 Dec).
Admission: £2.25 (ch £1.25, pen £1.95). Family ticket £6.
♥ & shop

SHERBORNE   Sherborne Museum

On show in this museum is a model of Sherborne's original Norman castle, as well as a fine Victorian doll's house and other domestic and agricultural bygones. There are also items of local geological, natural history and archeological interest, including Roman material. Photographs of the Sherborne Missal of 1400 are on display. The latest addition is a 15th-century wall painting originally from a house near the museum. 1992 will see a temporary exhibition in the spring celebrating the 40th anniversary of the accession of Queen Elizabeth II, and an exhibition in the summer entitled 'It's a small world'.

Abbey Gate House, Church Ln
☎ (0935) 812252
Open: Apr-Oct, Tue-Sat 10.30-12.30 & 2.30-4.30, Sun 2.30-4.30; Nov-Dec, Thu & Sat 10.30-12.30 & 2.30-4.30. (Closed end Dec-Mar).
Admission: 50p (ch 15p).
& shop ⋈

SHERBORNE   Sherborne Old Castle

The castle was built between 1107 and 1135 by Roger, Bishop of Salisbury but was captured and destroyed by Cromwell's forces in the Civil War. The ruins of the main buildings, the curtain wall and the towers and gates date from Norman times. The castle came into Sir Walter Raleigh's possession in 1592.

☎ (0935) 812730
Open: all year, Apr-Sep, daily 10-6; Oct-Mar, Tue-Sun 10-4. (Closed 24-26 Dec & 1 Jan).
Admission: £1.10 (ch 55p, students, pen & UB40 85p).
🅿 & ⋈
(EH)

ABBREVIATIONS					
AM	Ancient Monument	BH	Bank Holidays	ch 15 20p	Children under 15 20p
AM(CadW)	Ancient Monument	PH	Public Holidays	Pen	Senior Citizens
	(Wales)	Etr	Easter	Party	Special or reduced rates for
EH	English Heritage	ex	except		parties booked in advance
NT	National Trust	Free	Admission free	Party 30+	Special or reduced rates for
NTS	National Trust for	10p	Admission 10p		parties of 30 or more booked
	Scotland	ch 20p	Children 20p		in advance

SHERBORNE   Worldwide Butterflies & Lullingstone Silk Farm

Set in the grounds of lovely Compton House is the superb collection of butterflies from all over the world, flying free in reconstructions of their natural habitats, including natural jungle and a tropical palmhouse. The collection has been built up over 30 years and there are active breeding and hatching areas on view as well as an extensive specialist library for research. Compton is also the home of the Lullingstone Silk Farm which produced unique English-reared silk for the last two coronations and the Queen's and the Princess of Wales's wedding dresses. At the farm the complete process of silk production is shown by exhibits and film.

Compton House, Over Compton (entrance on A30, 2.5m W)
☎ Yeovil (0935) 74608
Open: Apr-Oct, daily 10-5.
Admission: Fee payable.
🅿 ☕ ﹠ shop ✻

SWANAGE   Swanage Railway

When the branch railway line from Wareham was closed in 1972, Swanage railway station was fortunately saved from destruction, and a band of enthusiasts started work on rebuilding the line. As part of the reconstruction of the railway serving the Isle of Purbeck, steam train rides of about six miles are available. There is an exhibition with a model railway in a museum coach at the station, and special events are held throughout the year for the railway enthusiast. 1992 special events include a Victorian weekend on 20-21 June.

Station House
☎ (0929) 425800 & 424276 (timetable)
Open: all year, wknds & BH; Jun-Sep, daily 10.30-5.30; Santa Specials every wknd in Dec.
Admission: £3.90 (ch 5-15 £1.95, under 4 free) return. Family ticket £9.
🅿 (charged) (wine & dine specials on Sat eves) ﹠ (special disabled persons coach) toilets for disabled shop

VERWOOD   Dorset Heavy Horse Centre

The Horse Centre has become home to some of the finest champion heavy horses in the country. Breeds kept here include the Shire, Percheron, Ardennes, Clydesdale, Canadian-Belgian and Suffolk Punch. There are commentaries at 11.30, 2.30 and 4.15. There are also Shetland ponies, and a display of harness farm wagons and farm implements.

Edmondsham Rd (1.25m NW, signposted from Verwood)
☎ (0202) 824040
Open: Good Fri-Oct, daily 10-5.30. Commentaries at 11.30, 2.30 & 4.15.
Admission: £2.95 (ch £1.95, pen £2.50). Party 12 + .
🅿 ☕ ﹠ toilets for disabled shop

WEYMOUTH   The Deep Sea Adventure & Titanic Story

This exciting exhibition is an adventure story detailing the struggle to recover wealth from the sea. The exhibition brings the subject to life by the use of animation, lighting and sound effects. The latest addition to the exhibition is 'The Titanic Story: Signals of Disaster', a major collection of actual Titanic signals. Events for 1992 include: Titanic Week (12-18 Apr), Oyster Festival (23/24 May), Trawler Race (25 May), and the National Historic Diving Rally (6 Sep). There are also diving displays, given at set times mainly, during July and August.

9 Custom House Quay, Old Harbour
☎ (0305) 760690
Open: all year, daily 10-5.30; winter 10-4.30. Jul & Aug also open 10am-10pm. (Closed 24-26 Dec).
Admission: £2.95 (ch 14 £1.95, ch 15-16 , pen & students £2.50). Party 10 + .
﹠ (lift) toilets for disabled shop ✻

WEYMOUTH   Sea Life Park

The Sea Life Park is part of the beautiful Lodmoor Country Park. Here you can marvel at the mysteries of the deep and discover exotic tropical creatures through the spectacular marine life displays, the ocean film theatre, the shark observatory, tropical jungle and blue whale splash pool. There is also Captain Kidd's Adventureland and a lakeside picnic area. Special events throughout the year; please telephone for details.

Lodmoor Country Park
☎ (0305) 788255
Open: all year, daily from 10am. (Closed 25 Dec).
Admission: ✳ fee payable.
🅿 (charged) ☕ ♿ toilets for disabled shop ✶

CO DURHAM

BEAMISH   The North of England Open Air Museum

This open air museum, set in 200 acres of beautiful Co. Durham countryside, vividly recreates life in the North of England around the turn of the century. Visitors are able to take a tram ride into the living past and stroll down the cobbled street of The Town to see the fully stocked Co-operative shops, the Dentist's home and surgery, the Solicitor's office, the Music Teacher's home and then quench their thirst in the Sun Inn. Nearby is the Railway Station, with signal box, goods yard and weighbridge house, where locomotives are often in steam. Just a tram ride away at the Colliery Village, guided tours are given underground at a real drift mine, a steam winding engine demonstrates how coal was drawn to the surface and visitors can see the cosy pit cottages, where home-made bread is often baked in a coal-fired oven. The farmyard at Home Farm is a lively place, with lots of ducks, geese and hens, and the farmer's wife can be seen going about her daily chores in the farmhouse kitchen. In the dairy the delicious Beamish cheese is made. Events for 1992 include the Northern Vintage Transport Association Display (23-25 May), an MG car club meet (25 July), and a Prize Leek Show (19/20 Sep).

(off A693 & A6076)
☎ Stanley (0207) 231811
Open: all year, Apr-Oct daily 10-6; Nov-Mar daily (ex Mon) 10-5. Last admission 4pm. Phone for details of Xmas opening.
Admission: ✳ Summer:£5-£6 (ch & pen £4). Winter £3 (ch & pen £2.50). Party.
🅿 ☕ ♿ toilets for disabled shop ✶ (ex in grounds)

DARLINGTON   Darlington Railway Centre & Museum

The museum is housed in North Road Station, built 17 years after the world's first passenger train ran along the Stockton and Darlington line. The building has been carefully restored and part is still in use for train services. The prize exhibit is 'Locomotion', which pulled the first passenger train and was built by Robert Stephenson & Co in 1825. Several other steam locomotives are also shown, together with an early railway coach of about 1845 and a chaldron (coal) wagon. There are also models and other exhibits relating to the Stockton and Darlington and the North Eastern Railway companies. Locomotive restoration work takes place in the former goods shed nearby. There is a Railway Carnival in September (tel for details).

North Rd Station (0.75m N off A167)
☎ (0325) 460532
Open: daily 9.30-5 (Closed Xmas & New Year); Last admission 4.30pm.
Admission: ✳ £1.40 (ch 5-15 70p & pen £1). Party.
🅿 ♿ toilets for disabled shop ✶

DURHAM Durham Castle

This Norman castle, built to protect the cathedral and home of the Prince Bishops, contains the original crypt chapel, the 13th-century Great Hall and 15th-century kitchens. Since 1832 it has been the University College, the first college of Durham University.

☎ 091-374 3800

Open: Guided tours Mon, Wed & Sat afternoons during termtime, daily during vacations.

DURHAM Durham Heritage Centre

The Heritage Centre provides a fascinating look at the city through entertaining exhibitions, reproduction 18th-century costumes and an audio-visual history. Brass rubbing facilities are available.

Open: June-Sep 2-4.30 daily (ex Fri).

DURHAM Botanic Gardens & Visitor Centre

This 18-acre botanic garden is the newest in England with a large collection of North American trees, a series of small gardens and woodland walks. Two greenhouses house the cacti and succulents and a tropical 'jungle'.

☎ 091-374 2671

Open: daily 10-4.

STAINDROP Raby Castle

The stronghold of the powerful Nevill family until 1569, and the home of the Vane family since 1626. The fortress is built around a courtyard and surrounded by a moat (now dry). The castle was erected during Saxon times but is substantially 14th century, with parts added in nearly every century. It has an impressive gateway; and nine towers of which the tallest is 80ft; a vast medieval hall; and a Victorian octagonal drawing-room. The 14th-century kitchen, with its collection of Victorian copper cooking utensils, was in use daily until 1954. The castle contains fine pictures from English, Dutch and Italian schools, interesting furniture and ceramics, and a good carriage collection. There are about five acres of gardens and an additional 200-acre park with both red and fallow deer. Home Farm Open Days are on 3/4 June, 10-4pm.

(1m N, off A688)
☎ (0833) 60202

Open: 18 Mar-22 Apr; May-Jun, Wed & Sun; Jul-Sep, Sun-Fri; BHs May, Spring & Aug, Sat-Wed 1-5. Park & gardens 11-5.30, (last admission 4.30).
Admission: Castle, Gardens & Carriage Collection £2.75 (ch £1.30, pen £2.25). Park, Gardens & Carriage Collection £1 (ch & pen 75p). Party.
P ☕ ♿ toilets for disabled shop 🐕 (ex in Park)

TANFIELD Tanfield Railway

The Causey Arch, the first large railway bridge and the largest single span arch in Britain of its era, is the centrepiece of a woodland full of picturesque walks around a deep valley. The story of the early railway and collieries is told on a series of display boards, giving an interesting break in a return journey from Tanfield. You can ride in carriages that first saw use in Victorian times, and visit Marley Hill shed, built in 1854, inside which you can see the stationary steam engine at work driving some of the vintage machine tools. The blacksmith is also often at work forging new parts for the restoration work.

(on A6076)
☎ 091-274 2002

Open: all year, summer daily 10-5; winter daily 10-4. Trains – Etr-Sep, Sun & BH Mon (also Thu & Sat Jun-Aug); Oct-Nov & Jan-Etr, Sun pm service; Dec, North Pole Express. Telephone for details.
Admission: charge made.

EAST SUSSEX

ALFRISTON   Drusillas Park

This famous small zoo features many special areas including 'Out of Africa' with its meerkat mound, otter valley, world of owls, flamingo lagoon and beaver country. There are also beautiful gardens, an adventure playground, a railway, and a farm area introduced in 1991. Special events for 1992 include many charity days, half-term activities, and a Rose and Gardeners Day (Jul).

☎ **Eastbourne (0323) 870234**

Open: all year, daily 10-5 or dusk if earlier, (ex Xmas).
Admission: £4.50 (ch 3-12 £3.95, concessions £2.95). Incl zoo & railway ride & children 3-12 playland. Grounds free.
🅿 ☕ ✗ licensed ♿ toilets for disabled shop garden centre 🐾

BRIGHTON   see page 70

EASTBOURNE   Coastal Defence Museum

The museum is housed in one of the Martello towers built in the 1800s to fend off invasion by Napoleon. After the Napoleonic Wars they were used by a predecessor of the coastguard service. This one now has displays on defence methods and equipment of the Napoleonic period to the Second World War and an exhibition of over 1,000 model soldiers provided by the British Model Soldier Society.

King Edward's Pde
☎ **(0323) 410440**

Open: Etr-Oct, daily 9.30-5.30.
Admission: 60p (ch & pen 30p). Party 10 + .
shop 🐾

EASTBOURNE   'How We Lived Then' Museum of Shops & Social History

Over the last 30 years, Jan and Graham Upton have collected over 50,000 items which are now displayed on three floors of authentic old shop settings, transporting visitors back to the age of their grandparents. Grocers, chemists, iron-mongers, tailors, cobblers, photographers, jewellers, music and toy shops are all represented in fascinating detail, as well as a Post Office, complete with dour post mistress. Other displays, such as seaside souvenirs, wartime rationing and Royal mementoes, help to capture 100 years of social history. The gift shop includes old fashioned sweets, reproduction tins, advertisements and tin-plate and Victorian-style greetings cards.

20 Cornfield Ter
☎ **(0323) 37143**

Open: daily Feb-Dec, 10-5.30 (last entry 5pm).
Admission: £1.50 (ch 5-15 85p, pen £1.25). Party
♿ shop

EXCEAT   The Living World

This is a living exhibition of small creatures: butterflies, bees, spiders, snails, moths, scorpions, marine life and others, in settings that are as near to nature as possible. The displays of this unique mini zoo are based in two old Sussex barns, situated in a 700-acre Country Park within the Heritage Coastline.

Seven Sisters Country Park
☎ **Alfriston (0323) 870100**

Open: all year, mid Mar-1 Nov, daily; Nov-mid Mar, wknds & school holidays 10-5.
Admission: ✲ £2 (ch & pen £1.20, ch under 5 free). Family ticket £5.70. Wheelchair users free.
🅿 ☕ ✗ ♿ toilets for disabled shop

Brighton has been a favourite resort for over 200 years, its early popularity due largely to the patronage of the Prince Regent, later George IV. He built the exotic Royal Pavilion as his holiday home and splendid Regency terraces soon sprang up to accommodate his entourage. These elegant squares and crescents retain their original charm and distinguish this sophisticated resort today.

Brighton can truly be said to have something for everyone. Its five-mile seafront may have a pebble beach and be prone to sea breezes off the Channel, but it is fun – definitely the place to sample traditional seaside amusements, including a Victorian pier with shell-fish stalls and sticks of Brighton rock. More modern is the Marina Village, with shops, pubs and restaurants overlooking the vast moorings surrounded by breakwaters.

The Lanes are a warren of narrow, car-free streets where the old fishing village once stood, now a mass of antique shops and little restaurants.

Brighton is at its most lively during the International Festival in May, but all year round you will find top class entertainments and events. The Beach Deck west of Palace Pier has free shows during the summer, including children's events.

Tourist information: Marlborough House, 54 Old Steine Telephone: (0273) 23755

☆ STAR ATTRACTIONS

Royal Pavilion

The pavilion was the marine palace of the Prince Regent (George IV). It began as a farmhouse which the prince rented after his secret marriage to Mrs Fitzherbert. The farmhouse was transformed into a neo-classical villa by Henry Holland, and the villa was in turn transformed by John Nash into the present building. The prince was interested in Indian exteriors and in the fantastic Chinoiserie decorations inside. Today the furniture includes pieces lent by HM the Queen. Queen Victoria's Apartments and the extensive structural restoration of the pavilion are now complete.

Old Steine
☎ (0273) 603005

Open: all year, Jun-Sep, daily 10-6; Oct-May, daily 10-5. (Closed 25-26 Dec). *Admission:* ✳ £3.10 (ch £1.60, pen, students & UB40's £2.30). Party 20+. ☞ ♿ (facilities for the blind by arrangement) toilets for disabled shop ✗

Sea Life Centre

This is one of eight sea life centres in Britain specialising in British marine creatures from all around the coast of Britain. On show is everything from worms to octopus, from sharks to stingrays as well as special pools where you can actually touch the sea creatures.

Marine Pde
☎ (0273) 604233 & 604234

Open: all year, daily (ex Xmas day), from 10am. Last admission 5.15 (4.15 in winter). *Admission:* ✳ £3.75 (ch 14 £2.75, pen £3, under 3 free). Family ticket £11. Party 10+. ☞ ♿ toilets for disabled shop ✗

A special section of the Sea Life Centre is devoted to the recreation of the Victorian aquarium as it was 130 years ago. This includes many weird and wonderful fish – look out for George, the Centre's 3ft grouper!

HALLAND   Bentley Wildfowl & Motor Museum

Hundreds of swans, geese and ducks from all over the world can be seen on lakes and ponds and also flamingoes, cranes and peacocks. There is a fine array of veteran, Edwardian and vintage vehicles, and the house has splendid antiques and wildfowl paintings. On 3-4 May there will be a Craft Fair here.

☎ (0825) 840573
Open: 21 Mar-Oct, daily 10.30-4.30 (5pm Jul & Aug). Nov-Feb & part of Mar, wknds (Closed Jan).
Admission: £3.10 (ch 4-15 £1.50, pen £2.40). Family ticket £8.
🅿 ☕ ♿ (wheelchairs available) toilets for disabled shop ✗

HASTINGS   Hastings Castle & 1066 Story

The ruins of the Norman castle stand on the cliffs, close to the site of William the Conqueror's first motte-and-bailey castle in England. It was excavated in 1825 and 1968, and old dungeons were discovered in 1894. 'The Story of 1066', which opened recently in the Castle grounds, is an exciting audio-visual experience about the Castle and that famous battle.

Castle Hill
☎ (0424) 718888
Open: 11 Apr-27 Sep, daily 10 (last admission 5.30);28 Sep-1 Nov, daily 11 (last admission 4).
Admission: ✻ £2 (ch £1.50, pen £1.75). shop ✗

HASTINGS   Smugglers Adventure

A Smuggler's Adventure is a themed experience housed in a labyrinth of caverns and passages deep below the West Hill. Visitors first tour a comprehensive exhibition and museum, followed by a video theatre, before embarking on the Adventure Walk – a trip through several acres of caves with life-size tableaux, push-button automated models and dramatic scenic effects depicting life in the days of 18th-century smuggling.

St Clements Cave, West Hill
☎ (0424) 422964
Open: all year daily, Etr-Sep 10-5.30; Oct-Etr 11-4.30. (Closed 25 Dec).
Admission: £3 (ch £2, pen & students £2.50). Family ticket £9.35.
shop ✗

SHEFFIELD PARK   Sheffield Park Garden

Originally landscaped by Capability Brown, in about 1775, to create a beautiful park with five lakes and a cascade, further extensive planting was done at the beginning of the 20th century. This has given Sheffield Park a superb collection of trees, with particular emphasis on trees that give good autumn colour. In May and June masses of azaleas and rhododendrons give colour and later there are magnificent waterlilies on the lakes. The gardens and woodland cover nearly 200 acres.

(5m E of Haywards Heath off A275)
☎ Danehill (0825) 790655
Open: Apr-8 Nov, Tue-Sat 11-6 or sunset if earlier, Sun & BH Mon 2-6 or sunset; Sun in Oct, 1pm-sunset. Last admission 1hr before closing. (Closed Good Fri & Tue following BH Mon).
Admission: £3.20 (ch £1.60) Apr & Jun-Sep; £3.70 (ch £1.90) May, Oct & Nov.
🅿 ☕ ♿ toilets for disabled shop ✗ (NT)

SHEFFIELD PARK STATION
Sheffield Park Station, Bluebell Railway & Museum

As its name suggests this five-mile long, revived steam-railway line runs through woodland that is a mass of bluebells in the springtime. There is a regular service throughout the year and on certain Saturdays between April and October there are Evening Pullman Dinner

(4.5m E of Haywards Heath, off A275)
☎ Newick (082572) 3777 & 2370 (Train Information)
Open: all year, trains run Jan & Feb Sun; Mar, Apr & Nov wknds; May Wed, Sat &

trains. It is also possible to charter trains with catering for private functions. Part of the station is a museum and there is the largest collection of locomotives and carriages in the region. There are many special events organised for 1992, among them the English Food and Wine Fair on 20-21 Jun, and the Autumn Steam Gala on 12-13 Sep.

Sun; Jun-Sep daily; Oct wknds & Half Term week; Dec Santa Specials. For timetable and information regarding trains contact above. *Admission:* ✳ 3rd class return fare £4.50 (ch 3-13 £2.25). Family ticket £11. Museum & locomotive sheds only, £1 (ch 50p). Supplementary available for 1st class travel & new extension section.
🅿 ☕ ✗ licensed ♿ toilets for disabled shop

ESSEX

CASTLE HEDINGHAM   Colne Valley Railway & Museum

The old Colne Valley and Halstead railway buildings have been rebuilt here. Stock includes seven steam locomotives plus forty other engines, carriages and wagons, in steam from Easter to December. There is also a five-acre riverside nature and picnic area. Visitors may also dine in style in restored Pullman carriages while travelling along the line. There are several 'Specials' running during 1992.

Castle Hedingham Station (4m NW of Halstead on A604)
☎ Hedingham (0787) 61174

Open: all year, daily 10-dusk. Steam days, rides from 12-4.30. (Closed 23 Dec-1 Feb). *Admission:* Steam days £3 (ch £1.50, pen £2); Family ticket £9. Non-steam days (to view static exhibits only) £1.50 (ch 75p, £1); Family ticket £4.50.
🅿 ☕ ✗ licensed ♿ shop 🐾

COLCHESTER   Colchester Zoo

The zoo has one hundred and fifty types of animals, the most exciting collection in East Anglia. Visitors can meet the elephants, handle a snake, and see parrots, seals, penguins and birds of prey all appearing in fun, informative daily displays. There is also a lakeside miniature railway, amusement complex, several eating places and gift shops, all set in forty acres of beautiful gardens. Special events include a Teddy Bears' Picnic, special days for Brownies, Scouts and Mother and Toddler groups; please phone for details.

Stanway Hall, Maldon Rd (3m W of town B1022)
☎ (0839) 222000

Open: all year, daily from 9.30. Last admission 5.30pm (1hr before dusk out of season). (Closed 25 Dec). *Admission:* ✳ £4.50 (ch 3-13 £2.50, pen £4, disabled £1.90).
🅿 ✗ licensed ♿ toilets for disabled shop 🐾

NEWPORT   Mole Hall Wildlife Park

Set within the grounds of a part-Elizabethan hall, which is not open to the public, this wildlife park has a large collection of birds and animals in pools and enclosures. It offers a rare opportunity to see otters feeding and at play, and other creatures are housed in attractive pens within a garden setting where many waterfowl roam free. A signposted walk takes visitors through a deer paddock. The butterfly house and insect pavillion allow visitors to wander through a tropical environment with exotic plants and beautiful free-flying butterflies. A small tea shop provides a welcome break, and a gift shop sells interesting items pertaining to natural history, displays of butterflies and mementoes. From March 1992 onwards there will be a large pool for Koi and other fish (open to adults only).

Widdington
☎ Saffron Walden (0799) 40400

Open: all year, daily 10.30-6 (or dusk). (Closed 25 Dec). Butterfly House open mid Mar-mid Nov. *Admission:* £3.50 (ch £2.25, pen £3). Party.
🅿 ☕ shop 🐾

WALTHAM ABBEY   Hayes Hill Farm

A traditional-style farmyard which has been opened to the public. Visitors can see a range of farm animals, kept in the traditional way, plus tools and machinery from earlier times. The centrepiece of the farm is a restored 16th-century barn. On Sundays and Bank Holidays there are demonstrations of traditional crafts. Your visit also includes a look around Holyfield Hall Farm, a working commercial dairy and arable farm of some 435 acres. There are 150 Fresian cows, and milking takes place at 2.45pm every day. Booked guided tours are available.

Stubbings Hall Ln, Crooked Mile
☎ **Nazeing (099289) 2291**
Open: all year, Mon-Fri 10-4.30, wknds & BH 10-6.
Admission: ✳ £1.60 (ch & pen £1). Party.
🅿 ⅋ toilets for disabled shop

GLOUCESTERSHIRE

BERKELEY   Berkeley Castle

Home of the Berkeleys for over 800 years, the castle is all one might expect – a great rambling place surrounded by 14ft thick walls, with a Norman keep, a great hall, medieval kitchens and some splendid apartments. It is most famous for the dungeon where Edward II was gruesomely murdered in 1327, at the instigation of his wife and the Earl of Mortimer. Outside there are Elizabethan terraced gardens and an extensive park. There is also a particularly good butterfly farm, with hundreds of exotic butterflies in free flight.

(on B4509 1.5m W of A38)
☎ **Dursley (0453) 810332**
Open: Apr, daily 2-5; May-Sep weekdays 11-5, Sun 2-5. Oct Sun only 2-4.30; BH Mon 11-5. (Closed Mon ex BH).
Admission: £3.40 (ch £1.60, pen £2.80).
🅿 ⅋ shop ✗

BOURTON-ON-THE-WATER   Birdland

The eight-acre garden of birds was created by Len Hill, nicknamed the 'Penguin Millionaire' because of his conservation interests. It contains a fine collection of penguins, new aviaries, a tropical house and birds at liberty, including macaws, parrots, cockatoos and lorikeets.

(on A429)
☎ **Cotswold (0451) 20689 & 20480**
Open: all year, Apr-Oct, daily 10-6; Nov-Mar, daily 10-4. (Closed 25 Dec).
Admission: ✳ £3.50 (ch £2.80 & pen £3). Party 10+.
⅋ shop

BOURTON-ON-THE-WATER   Cotswolds Motor Museum

Housed in a water mill on the River Windrush, the museum has cars and motorcycles from the vintage years up to the 1950s, with a collection of 800 advertising signs and some 8000 pieces of automobilia. Also here is the Childhood Toy Collection and Father Christmas Workshop.

☎ **Cotswold (0451) 21255**
Open: Feb-Nov, daily 10-6.
⅋ shop
Details not confirmed for 1992

SYMBOLS

☎ Telephone number	✳ Indicates 1991 price	⬛ Refreshments	✗ No Dogs
⅋ Suitable for visitors in wheelchairs	🅿 Parking at Establishment	✗ Restaurant	⛟ No coaches

BOURTON-ON-THE-WATER   Folly Farm Waterfowl

Two miles from Bourton, this conservation centre in the Cotswolds has a series of pools and lakes with over 160 types of waterfowl, ducks, geese and poultry, including many rare and endangered species.

(2.5m W on A436)
☎ **(0451) 20285**

Open: all year, Apr-Sep daily 10-6; Oct-Mar 10-4.
Admission: £2.70 (ch £1.60, pen £2).
P ☛ ㋡ toilets for disabled shop garden centre

BOURTON-ON-THE-WATER   Model Village

The model is built of Cotswold stone to a scale of one-ninth, and is a perfect replica of the village. It includes a miniature River Windrush, a working model waterwheel, churches and shops, with tiny trees, shrubs and alpine plants.

Old New Inn
☎ **Cotswold (0451) 20467**

Open: all year 9-6.30 (summer), 10-dusk (winter). (Closed 25 Dec).
Admission: £1.20 (ch 90p, pen £1). Party 20+.
P ☛ ✗ licensed shop

CLEARWELL   Clearwell Caves Ancient Iron Mines

The mines were worked in Iron Age times, and the industry grew under the Romans. Over half a million tons of ore were extracted in the 19th century, and the last commercial mining was in 1945. Today nine large caverns can be seen, with deeper trips for the more adventurous. There are engine rooms and exhibits of local mining and geology from the Forest of Dean, including several vintage stationary engines. Educational visits are a speciality. Special events for 1992 include: 20 Jun, Midsummer Party (100ft underground); 31 Oct, Halloween Party; 1-24 Dec, A Christmas Fantasy.

☎ **Dean (0594) 32535**

Open: Mar-Oct daily 10-5. Other times by arrangement. Santa's secret workshop 1-24 Dec – Mon-Fri 2-6, Sat-Sun 10-5.
Admission: £2.50 (ch £1.50, pen £2)
P ☛ ✗ ㋡ shop ⚥

CRANHAM   Prinknash Bird Park

Nine acres of parkland and lakes make a beautiful home for black swans, geese and other water birds. There are also exotic birds such as white and Indian blue peacocks and crown cranes, and the park supports fallow deer and pygmy goats. The Golden Wood is stocked with ornamental pheasants, and leads to the restored (and reputedly haunted) monks' fishpond, which contains trout. There is a very different kind of Pets Corner, with the emphasis on beauty.

Prinknash Abbey
☎ **Gloucester (0452) 812727**

Open: all year, daily 10-5 (4 in winter). Park closes at 6pm (5 in winter).
Admission: ✳ £2.20 (ch & pen £1.10). Party.
P ☛ shop ⚥

GLOUCESTER   National Waterways Museum

In October 1990, this museum was judged to be one of the top seven museums in Europe in the European Museum of the Year Awards. The judge's report said 'It has used a strong poetic sense to unlock the images always latent in technology, and has revealed canal and river travel not only as a means of transport, but as a way of life with a character of its own'.

Llanthony Warehouse, The Docks
☎ **(0452) 307009**

Open: all year, daily 10-6; (winter 10-5). (Closed 25 Dec).
Admission: ✳ fee payable.
P (charged) ☛ ㋡ toilets for disabled shop ⚥

For centuries goods were transferred at Gloucester Docks between inland craft bound for Wales and the Midlands, and larger vessels which could negotiate the Severn Estuary. The heyday of the docks came after the opening of the Gloucester and Berkeley Canal in 1827, and many of the warehouses built in the 19th century still stand. The museum is housed in the Llanthony warehouse, a seven-storey brick building with cast-iron columns, which now shows the role of inland waterways in Britain's fortunes. A traditional canal maintenance yard has been re-created alongside, there are boats to visit, and demonstrations are given of the crafts and skills needed to run the canals. Special events for 1992 include a Crafts Weekend on 3-4 May and a Tugs Weekend on 20-21 June.

GUITING POWER Cotswold Farm Park

Cotswold sheep, Old Gloucester cows and many other rare breeds of farm animals can be seen here in a typical Cotswold farm setting. The aim is to ensure the survival of the old breeds, and education is an important part of the farm's work. There are seasonal events such as lambing in April, shearing in June (list of events available on application), and local crafts are on sale.

Bemborough (3.5m NE on unclass road)
☎ Cotswold (0451) 850307
Open: Apr-Sep, daily 10.30-6.
Admission: £2.50 (ch £1.25, pen £1.75)
🅿 ☛ ᕱ toilets for disabled shop ✗

LITTLEDEAN Littledean Hall

The largest known Roman temple in rural Britain was unearthed here in 1984 and the manor itself was built in Norman times; its north front is on the site of a Saxon hall of the 11th century. The house has always been lived in, and remains relatively untouched since the 19th century. Inside there are interpretive displays and a reconstruction of a Saxon lord's hall. The grounds offer beautiful walks, some of the oldest trees in Dean, fish pools in the walled garden and, of course, the Roman excavations. A new museum is currently under development.

☎ Dean (0594) 824213
Open: Apr-Oct, daily 2-5.30. (Closed Sat).
Admission: ✳ £2.50 (ch £2, pen £2.25).
🅿 ᕱ ✗ (ex in grounds)

LYDNEY Dean Forest Railway

Just north of Lydney lies the headquarters of the Dean Forest Railway where a number of locomotives, coaches, wagons and railway equipment are on show and guided tours are available by arrangement. There is also a gift shop, museum, riverside walk and forest trail. Events for 1992 will include a Vintage Rally (18 Oct), Thomas the Tank Engine (20/21 Jun and 19/20 Sep), and 'Santa Specials' in Nov and Dec.

Norchard Steam Centre, New Mills (1m N at New Mills on B4234)
☎ Dean (0594) 843423
Open: all year, daily for static displays. Steam days: Sun, Apr-Sep; Wed in Jun & Jul; Tue-Thu Aug & all BH's (ex Xmas & New Year).
Admission: ✳ £2.50 (ch £1.50 & pen £2). Party 20 + . Prices include train ride (steam days only).
🅿 ☛ ᕱ toilets for disabled shop

SYMBOLS			
☎ Telephone number	✳ Indicates 1991 price	☛ Refreshments	✗ No Dogs
ᕱ Suitable for visitors in wheelchairs	🅿 Parking at Establishment	✗ Restaurant	🚌 No coaches

MORETON-IN-MARSH   Cotswold Falconry Centre

Conveniently located by the Batsford Park Arboretum, the Cotswold Falconry gives daily demonstrations in the art of falconry. The emphasis here is on breeding and conservation, and eagles, hawks, owls and falcons may be seen flying.

Batsford Park (1m E on A44)
☎ **Blockley (0386) 701043**
Open: Mar-Nov, 10.30-5.30. (Last admission 5pm).
🅿 ⅃ shop garden centre 🐾
Details not confirmed for 1992

NEWENT   The National Birds of Prey Centre

Jemima Parry-Jones is becoming increasingly famous for her displays of falconry at shows and fairs all over the country. This is the 'home-base' for her exceptional collection of birds of prey. Trained birds can be seen at close quarters in the 'Hawk Walk' and there are also breeding aviaries, a gift shop, bookshop, coffee shop and children's play area. Weather permitting, birds are flown four times daily, giving an exciting and educational display.

(1m SW on unclass Clifford's Mesne Road)
☎ **(0531) 820286**
Open: Feb-Nov, daily 10.30-5.30.
Admission: ✳ £3.75 (ch £1.95).
🅿 ⬤ ⅃ toilets for disabled shop 🐾

NEWENT   Newent Butterfly & Natural World Centre

In a beautiful setting with magnificent views, The Butterfly Centre has a collection of tropical butterflies flying free in an exotic environment. There is also a live insect gallery, a reptile area and a children's zoo. Aviaries of birds include fancy fowl, waterfowl, peacocks, and many others.

Springbank, Birches Ln
☎ **(0531) 821800**
Open: Etr-Oct, daily 10-5.
Admission: ✳ £2.95 (ch £1.95, ch under 4 free, pen £2.75).
🅿 ⅃ shop 🐾

SLIMBRIDGE   Wildfowl & Wetlands Trust

Slimbridge was started as a wildfowl reserve in 1946 by Sir Peter Scott. Since then it has become one of the most famous in the world, having the largest and most varied collection of swans, geese and ducks to be seen. Slimbridge has six flocks of flamingos, which is the largest gathering of these birds in any country. There are both captive and wild birds and a substantial number of rare and endangered birds at Slimbridge. In a severe winter, up to 8000 birds may fly into the refuge, which now covers some 800 acres of flat fields, marsh and mudflats on the River Severn. First-class viewing facilities are available and, in winter, towers and hides provide remarkable views of the migrating birds. There is a permanent educational exhibition and also a Tropical House. Facilities for the disabled include purpose-built toilets for wheelchair users, and a braille trail with taped commentaries.

(off A38 & M5 junc 13 or 14)
☎ **Cambridge (Glos) (0453) 890333**
Open: all year, daily from 9.30 (Closed 24-25 Dec)
🅿 ⬤ ✗ licensed ⅃ toilets for disabled shop 🐾
Details not confirmed for 1992

SOUDLEY   Dean Heritage Centre

Set around an old watermill and its tranquil mill pond in a beautiful wooded valley, the unique heritage of the Forest of Dean is portrayed through museum displays entitled 'Dean – the Story of a Forest', with a reconstructed cottage, coal mine, 12ft overshot waterwheel, beam engine and audio-

Camp Mill (on B4227)
☎ **Dean (0594) 822170**
Open: all year, daily, Apr-Oct 10-6, Nov-Mar 10-5. (Closed 25-26 Dec).

visual sequences. There are also nature trails, including one suitable for wheelchairs, picnic areas and barbecue hearths as well as a smallholding. Added attractions are an adventure playground, craft shop and craft workshops. Many special events take place throughout the year.

Admission: ✷ £2.30 (ch £1.25, students, pen & UB40 £1.75). Party 20 + . Season tickets available.
P ☛ ⅊ toilets for disabled shop ✗ (ex in grounds)

WINCHCOMBE   Sudeley Castle & Gardens

Little remains of the original medieval castle, once the home of Catherine Parr, the last wife of Henry VIII. There was considerable destruction during the Civil War, including Catherine Parr's tomb, and the castle was reconstructed in 1858 by Sir Gilbert Scott who incorporated the 15th-century remains into his design. Good furniture, porcelain and tapestries can be seen, and the art collection includes notable paintings by Turner, Rubens and Van Dyck. The award-winning gardens have been extended recently; centrepiece is the Queen's Garden, a traditional Tudor rose garden. The eight-acre garden is complemented by Sudeley Castle Roses, a specialist plant centre. A special events programme runs throughout the year including jousting, craft fairs and concerts. There is also a waterfowl collection and a children's log fortress.

☎ (0242) 602308

Open: Apr-Oct daily; grounds 11-5.30, castle apartments noon-5.
Admission: £4.75 (ch £2.50). Grounds only £3.10 (ch £1.40). Family ticket £12. Season ticket £17.25 (ch £8.50). Family ticket £34.50. Ground season ticket £11. Party 20 + .
P ✗ licensed ⅊ shop garden centre ✗

GREATER MANCHESTER

BURY   East Lancashire Railway & The Bury Transport Museum

Opened in 1987, the track is 8.5 miles long, stretching along the scenic Irwell Valley and reviving memories of the golden age of steam. The journey includes two tunnels, viaducts and views of the West Pennine Moors between Bury, Ramsbottom and Rawtenstall. Special events for 1992 include: Big Engine weekends on 27 January and 22nd February; a Mother's Day special on 29 March and Diesel weekends in June and October.

Bolton St Station
☎ 061-764 7790 (wknds) & 061-705 5111 (day)

Open: Weekend service & BHs, Santa specials Dec; (Closed Xmas & New Year).
Admission: Bury-Rawtenstall £5 (ch £2.50). Bury-Ramsbottom £3 (ch £1.50).
P ☛ ⅊ (station area only suitable) toilets for disabled shop

MANCHESTER   Granada Studios Tour

Enter the world of television at Granada Studios Tour in the heart of the City Centre. Only here can you walk down Coronation Street, Downing Street and Baker Street in just one day. Visit the Giant Room, from the popular children's programme Return of the Antelope, where chairs loom overhead. See the spectacular Magic Show, then take part in a comedy debate in the House of Commons. Explore the history of cinema at Projections, experience Motion Master where the seats move with the action, and see a spectacular 3-D and laser show, the latest addition to this award-winning tour. You should allow a possible five hours for your visit.

Special events for 1992 include: 16 Apr, Charlie Chaplin's birthday promotion; 4 Jul, American Independence Day.

Water St
☎ 061-832 9090 & 061-833 0880

Open: all year, 26 Mar-29 Sep, Tue, Thu-Sun & BH Mon 9.45-7pm, Wed 9.45-11.30pm. (Closed Mon); 2 Oct-12 Apr, Wed-Fri 9.45-5.30, Sat, Sun & BH Mon 9.45-6.30. (Closed Mon & Tue). Telephone for details during school half term. (Closed 24 & 25 Dec.)
Admission: ✷ £8.75 (ch 12 £5.95). Family ticket £26.50. Party.
P (charged) ☛ ✗ licensed ⅊ (ex Theatre) toilets for disabled shop ✗

MANCHESTER Manchester United Museum & Tour Centre

This Museum was opened in 1986 and is the first purpose-built British football museum. It covers the history of Manchester United in word, pictures, sound and vision, from its inception in 1878 to the present day. A new Trophy Room was added in September 1991. More than 400 exhibits are regularly on display.

Subject to availability, a tour includes a visit to the Museum, then into the stadium, players' lounge, dressing rooms and down the players' tunnel to view the pitch and stadium.

Old Trafford (2m from city centre, off A56)
☎ 061-877 4002

Open: all year Tue-Sun & most BH Mons 9.30-4. (Closed 25 Dec).
Admission: Ground Tour, Museum & Trophy Room £4.95 (ch & pen £2.95). Museum & Trophy Room only £2.95 (ch & pen £1.95).
P ☕ ♿ toilets for disabled shop 🐕̸

MANCHESTER Museum of Science & Industry

National Heritage Museum of the Year in 1990, the Museum of Science and Industry offers endless fascination for adults and children. Located on the site of the oldest passenger railway in the world, its permanent exhibitions include the Power Hall, the Air and Space Gallery, the 'Making of Manchester' and 'Underground Manchester' – an exhibition of water sanitation and sewerage. Other exhibitions include the Electricity Gallery, the 'Out of This World' Space Gallery, cameras and microscopes, the printing and textile galleries, Machine Tools Gallery and 'Xperiment' – the interactive science centre. Recent additions include 'Energy for the Future' and the new Gas Gallery, telling the story of 200 years of Britain's gas history in a lively and entertaining way.

Liverpool Rd, Castlefield
☎ 061-832 2244

Open: all year, daily 10-5. Last admission 4.30. (Closed 23-25 Dec).
Admission: £3.50 (ch, students, pen, UB40 & disabled £1.50 ch under 5 free). Party 10+.
P (charged) ☕ ✕ licensed ♿ toilets for disabled shop 🐕̸

WIGAN Wigan Pier

Wigan Pier was once a music hall joke but today the pier, and its warehouses have been converted into a lively museum. The 'pier' was a wharf for loading coal on the Leeds-Liverpool Canal, and the theme of the museum is life as it was in the town at the turn of the century. There is a mock-up of a coal mine, and an escalator for sorting coal, as well as the interior of a pub, a miner's house and a school. Actors bring these to life by involving visitors as guests to the house or pupils in the school. There is also an exhibition called The Way We Were. Across the canal is a textile mill with the world's largest working mill engine and other textile, colliery and rope-making machines. The two parts are connected by a waterbus or by bridges and a canal walk. Since 1984 several festivals have been held at Wigan Pier each year: a Jazz Festival in July, an Arts Festival in September and another in December.

Wallgate
☎ (0942) 323666

Open: all year, daily 10-5. (Closed 25-26 Dec).
P ☕ ♿ (ex for steam engine) toilets for disabled shop 🐕̸
Details not confirmed for 1992

SYMBOLS

☎ Telephone number	✻ Indicates 1991 price	☕ Refreshments	🐕̸ No Dogs
♿ Suitable for visitors in wheelchairs	P Parking at Establishment	✕ Restaurant	No coaches

HAMPSHIRE

ALRESFORD   Mid Hants Railway

Best known as the Watercress Line, this steam railway runs along ten miles of the old Winchester to Alton line, between Alresford and Alton. The train travels through beautiful Hampshire countryside with views of hills and watercress beds. At Ropley several steam locomotives are being restored. There are special activities throughout the year; telephone for details.

Watercress Line
☎ (0962) 733810 & 734200
Open: main operating periods: Sun, Jan-Mar. wknds & BH's end Mar-Oct. Mid wk running begins Jun-mid Jul. Daily mid Jul-1st wk Sep (check timetable). "Santa Special" wknds Dec, booking essential.
🅿 ☕ ✗ licensed ♿ (ramps for trains) toilets for disabled shop
Details not confirmed for 1992

ANDOVER   Finkley Down Farm Park

A wide range of farm animals and poultry can be seen here, including some rare breeds. The pets corner has tame, hand-reared baby animals that can be stroked and petted. There is also a Countryside Museum, housed in a barn, Romany caravans and rural bygones to see, an adventure playground and a large picnic area.

(signposted from A303 & A343)
☎ (0264) 352195
Open: Apr-1 Oct, daily 10.30-6. Last admission 5pm.
Admission: Charge made.
🅿 ☕ ♿ toilets for disabled shop

ASHURST   New Forest Butterfly Farm

The butterfly reserve is set in a glasshouse planted as a tropical garden, with lemon and banana trees, passion flowers and a mass of other plants and shrubs needed by the different types of butterfly. The species come from all over the world, with a separate area devoted to butterflies of Britain. There are also dragonfly ponds, and other creatures to be seen include tarantulas, scorpions, praying mantises, ants and locusts.

Longdown (off A35)
☎ Southampton (0703) 292166
Open: 11 Apr-1 Nov, daily 10-5.
Admission: £3.30 (ch 3-14 £2.30 & pen £3). Party 15+.
🅿 ☕ ♿ (ex woodland walk) toilets for disabled shop garden centre 🐾

BEAULIEU   Beaulieu: National Motor Museum

The venerable 16th-century house of Beaulieu is worth seeing just for its lovely setting by the Beaulieu River, but it has become most famous as the home of the National Motor Museum. This is one of the world's largest collections of vehicles and motoring memorabilia, with the extra attraction of 'Wheels', a feature which takes visitors on an automated trip through a spectacular display of 100 years of motoring. Other attractions are a high-level monorail through the grounds, veteran bus rides and a model railway. Special events are held throughout the year, including, in 1992, Boat Jumble on 12 Apr; Day for the Disabled 6 Jun; Countryside Show 28 Jun; Autojumble & Automart 12-13 Sep, and a Fireworks Fair on 31 Oct.

(on B3054)
☎ (0590) 612345
Open: all year – Palace House & Gardens, National Motor Museum, Beaulieu Abbey & Exhibition of Monastic Life, Etr-Sep 10-6; Oct-Etr 10-5. (Closed 25 Dec).
Admission: ✳ £6.50 (ch £4.50, pen & students £5). Party 15+.
🅿 ☕ ♿ toilets for disabled shop

The main house itself has a collection of fine paintings and furnishings, with costumed figures showing generations of the Montagu family, which has lived here since 1538. The house is only the gatehouse of the great abbey which once stood here, and ruins of other monastic buildings can be seen in the grounds. There is also an exhibition of monastic life.

BREAMORE   Breamore House, Countryside & Carriage Museums

The handsome manor house was built in around 1583 and has a fine collection of paintings, china and tapestries. The museum has good examples of coaches and steam engines, and uses reconstructed workshops and other displays to show how people lived, worked and travelled a century or so ago. On the weekend of 9th and 10th May the Breamore Museum Special (11am – 6pm) is a mini rally almost all under cover; on Sunday 14th June the Breamore Horse Show is in aid of the Wessex Medical School Trust. Other special events include: 23-25 May, Breamore Craft Show, open 10.30am; 19-20 Sep, Craft Show, open 10.30am.

(on A338)
☎ Downton (0725) 22468

Open: Apr Tue, Wed & Sun & Etr, May-Jul & Sep, Tue-Thu & Sat, Sun & all BH, Aug, daily 2-5.30.
Admission: Combined tickets £3.50 (ch £2); Party & pen rate available.
🅿 ☕ ♿ toilets for disabled shop 🐾

BUCKLER'S HARD   Bucklers Hard Village & Maritime Museum

This is a historic shipbuilding village, where wooden warships, including some of Nelson's fleet, were built from New Forest oak. In its busy days the wide main street would have been used for rolling great logs to the 'hard' where the ships were built, and the village would have been stacked high with timber. The 18th-century homes of a shipwright and labourer, and a master shipbuilder's office can be seen. A typical inn scene has been reconstructed, complete with costumed figures, smells and conversation. The Maritime Museum tells the story of the local shipbuilding industry, and also has items from the voyages of Sir Francis Chichester, who moored his boats here. On the last Sunday in July 1992 The Bucklers Hard Village Festival recaptures all the atmosphere of the village fete.

(off B3054)
☎ Bucklers Hard (0590) 616203

Open: all year, Etr-Spring BH 10-6; Spring BH-Sep 10-9; Oct-Etr 10-4.30. (Closed 25 Dec).
Admission: £2.30 (ch £1.50, pen & student £1.85). Party 15+
🅿 ☕ ✕ licensed ♿ shop

GOSPORT   Royal Navy Submarine Museum & HMS Alliance

The great attraction of this museum is the chance to see inside a submarine. There are guided tours of *HMS Alliance*, a World War II vessel. *Holland I*, which was the Royal Navy's first submarine and dates from 1901. It was salvaged in December 1982 after 69 years under the sea. The more conventional part of the museum covers the development of submarines from their earliest days. There is an emphasis on British boats, but an international view is also given, and there are models of practically every kind. Outside, the dominant presence of the modern Royal Navy gives an exciting, topical flavour to a visit.

Haslar Jetty Rd
☎ Portsmouth (0705) 529217

Open: all year, Apr-Oct 10-4.30, Nov-Mar 10-3.30. (Closed 24-25 Dec & 1 Jan).
Admission: £3 (ch & pen £2). Party 12+
Joint tickets available for HMS Warrior or Royal Marines Museum.
🅿 ☕ ♿ shop 🐾

HIGHCLERE Highclere Castle

This splendid early Victorian mansion stands in beautiful parkland. It has sumptuous interiors and numerous Old Master pictures. Also shown are early finds by the 5th Earl of Carnarvon, one of the discoverers of Tutankhamun's tomb. Special events for 1992 include: 23-25 May, Craft Fair; 27 Jun, Classical Concert with Fireworks; 3-5 Jul, Flower Festival.

☎ (0635) 253210

Open: Jul-Sep, Wed-Sun 2-6; Aug BH Mon 11-6. Last admission to Castle 5pm.
Admission: £3.90 (ch £2.50, pen £3.40)
P ☕ ♿ (wheelchair available) toilets for disabled shop garden centre 🐕

LIPHOOK Hollycombe Steam Collection

This all-encompassing collection of steam-driven equipment includes a Bioscope show, a fairground organ, a steam roundabout, a big wheel, a steam farm, an engine room of a paddle steamer, demonstrations of threshing and steam rolling, traction engine rides and a steam locomotive which runs through a woodland setting up to spectacular views of the South Downs. As if all this wasn't enough there are also woodland gardens for walks and a miniature railway. Special events take place on 23-25 May, a Festival of Steam; 6-7 Jun; 29-31 Aug and 19-20 Sep.

(1.5m SE on unclass rd)
☎ (0428) 724900

Open: 18 Apr-11 Oct, BH & Sun, also 17-31 Aug, rides 2-6.
Admission: £4 (ch £3 & pen £3.50). Party 15+
P ☕ ♿ shop 🐕

MARWELL Marwell Zoological Park

Devoted to the conservation and breeding of rare wild animals, Marwell has a worldwide reputation. The animals are housed in spacious enclosures or can be seen grazing in paddocks, and there is an enclosure where animals can be approached and stroked by children. Covering 100 acres of parkland, the collection includes over 1000 animals, and some of the species here no longer exist in the wild. New animals are being added constantly. There is also a gift shop and many attractions for younger children, including a children's farmyard, Wallaby Wood and road trains. Numerous events are held throughout the year, including a Christmas 'Winter Wonderland'.

Colden Common
☎ Owslebury (0962) 777406 & 777407

Open: all year, daily (ex 25 Dec), 10-6 (or dusk). Last admission 4.30pm or 1 hour before dusk (whichever is earliest).
Admission: £5.20 (ch 3-14 £4) Party 20+. Free to orange badge holders.
P ☕ ✕ licensed ♿ toilets for disabled shop 🐕

MIDDLE WALLOP Museum of Army Flying

This award-winning museum tells the story of army flying from the 19th- century to the present day. Exhibits include kites, balloons, photographs, dioramas, vintage aircraft and 'hands on' exhibits. Pilot training flights can be seen during the week and museum aircraft often fly at weekends (weather permitting). There is a restaurant with panoramic views over the airfield. Special events for 1992 include, amongst others: 9-10 May, Middle Wallop International Air Show; 21 Jun, Tiger Moth Rally; 1 Aug, Kite Flying Championships; 8 Aug, Model Aircraft International Rally.

(on A343)
☎ Andover (0264) 384421

Open: all year, daily 10-4.30. (Closed Xmas-New Year). Evening visits by special arrangement.
Admission: ✻ £3 (ch, pen £2). Family ticket £8. Party.
P ✕ licensed ♿ (lifts to upper levels) toilets for disabled shop 🐕 (ex in grounds)

OWER   Paultons Park

Paultons Park has 140 acres of beautiful parkland, extensive gardens and stands on the edge of the New Forest. Around 1000 exotic species of animals, birds and wildfowl have their home here. There are hours of pleasure for children in Kids Kingdom, the Magic Forest, Pet's Corner and Land of the Dinosaurs. There is a 10-acre lake with a working waterwheel and a miniature Rio Grande Railway. Other attractions include the Bumper Boats, Go-Karts and a six-lane Astroglide. Visitors can also enjoy a glimpse of the past in the Romany and Village Life Museums, and during the summer holidays there is live entertainment.

(exit junc 2 M27, signed off A36)
☎ **Southampton (0703) 814455**

Open: 14 Mar-1 Nov, daily 10-6.30. Last admission 4.30pm. Rides close 5.30pm. Earlier closing spring & autumn.
Admission: fee payable.
🅿 ☛ ✗ ᕋ (free wheelchair available) toilets for disabled shop ✗

PETERSFIELD   The Bear Museum

Teddy Bears are the theme of this museum, which children will love because they are allowed to cuddle and play with the exhibits. A variety of dolls and bears are displayed in the Victorian-style nursery while downstairs is the 'Teddy Bear's Picnic' where children are encouraged to sing along to the famous song and join in the fun of the large picnic scene. Dolls and bears can be brought here for repair and there is also a shop.

38 Dragon St
☎ **(0730) 65108**

Open: Mon-Sat 10-5 & Sun 11-5. (Closed 2 weeks in summer, phone for details).
Admission: Free.
🅿 ᕋ shop ✗

PORTSMOUTH & SOUTHSEA   see page 84

ROMSEY   Broadlands

Famous as the venue chosen by the Prince and Princess of Wales for their honeymoon, Broadlands was the home of the late Lord Mountbatten and is now lived in by his grandson, Lord Romsey. An elegant Palladian mansion in a beautiful landscaped setting on the banks of the River Test, Broadlands was also the country residence of Lord Palmerston, the great Victorian prime minister. Visitors may view the House with its fine furniture and pictures and mementoes of the famous, enjoy the superb views from the Riverside Lawns or relive Lord Mountbatten's life and times in the Mountbatten Exhibition and spectacular new Mountbatten A-V Presentation. Special events for 1992 include: 13-14 Jun, Broadlands Country Fair; 7-9 Aug, Hampshire Craft Show; 12 Sep, Romsey Show.

(main entrance on A31 Romsey by-pass)
☎ **(0794) 516878**

Open: 16 Apr-27 Sep, 10-4. (Closed Fri ex Good Fri & Aug).
Admission: £4.75 (ch 12-16 £3.15, (ch under 12 free), pen, students & disabled £3.80).
Party 15+
🅿 ✗ ᕋ toilets for disabled shop ✗

ABBREVIATIONS						
AM	Ancient Monument	BH	Bank Holidays	ch 15 20p	Children under 15 20p
AM(CadW)	Ancient Monument	PH	Public Holidays	Pen	Senior Citizens
	(Wales)	Etr	Easter	Party	Special or reduced rates for
EH	English Heritage	ex	except		parties booked in advance
NT	National Trust	Free	Admission free	Party 30+	Special or reduced rates for
NTS	National Trust for	10p	Admission 10p		parties of 30 or more booked
	Scotland	ch 20p	Children 20p		in advance

SOUTHAMPTON   Southampton Hall of Aviation

The Hall of Aviation was inspired by the development of the famous Spitfire aeroplane at the nearby Supermarine Aviation Works at Woolston. The Spitfire evolved from aircraft built for the Schneider Trophy air races, which the company won in 1931 with the Supermarine 6B. There is a Supermarine S6A on display as well as one of the last Spitfires produced, the Mark 24, and other aircraft of local interest.

The museum is built around a huge Sandringham flying-boat which visitors can board. It was operated out of Southampton Airport by Imperial Airways (BOAC) to all parts of the British Empire. There are also exhibits on aviation production and engineering in the south of England.

Albert Rd South
☎ (0705) 635830

Open: all year, Tue-Sat 10-5, Sun 12-5. Also BH Mon & School Holidays. (Closed Xmas). *Admission:* £2.50 (ch £1.50, pen & students £2). Family ticket available. Party.
& (lift to all levels) toilets for disabled shop ⚑

STRATFIELD SAYE   Stratfield Saye House

The house was built in 1630 and given by the nation to the first Duke of Wellington in 1817, after his victory over Napoleon at the Battle of Waterloo. Stratfield Saye has remained the home of the Dukes of Wellington and contains a unique collection of paintings, prints, and furniture as well as many momentoes of the lst Duke, including his magnificent funeral carriage. It weighs 18 tons and is 17ft high. The Wellington Exhibition shows the life and times of the great statesman soldier, and in the grounds is the grave of Copenhagen, his mighty horse.

(off A33)
☎ Basingstoke (0256) 882882

Open: May-last Sun in Sep, daily ex Fri.
🅿 ✗ licensed & toilets for disabled shop ⚑ (ex in grounds)
Details not confirmed for 1992

STRATFIELD SAYE   Wellington Country Park & National Dairy Museum

(For full entry, see Riseley, Berkshire)

☎ Reading (0734) 326444

WEYHILL   The Hawk Conservancy

In the heart of attractive Hampshire countryside, this conservancy has a specialist collection of birds of prey from all over the world. The enclosures in which the birds are kept are very simple and the range of hawks, falcons, eagles, owls, vultures and kites are easily seen. There are impressive demonstrations of falconry every day (at noon, 2pm, 3pm and 4pm), weather permitting, and also the exciting opportunity for visitors to hold or fly some of the birds themselves.

(off A303)
☎ Andover (0264) 772252

Open: Mar-last Sun in Oct, daily from 10.30 (last admission spring & winter 4pm, summer 5pm).
🅿 ✗ & toilets for disabled shop ⚑
Details not confirmed for 1992

WINCHESTER   see page 86

SYMBOLS			
☎ Telephone number	✳ Indicates 1991 price	▼ Refreshments	⚑ No Dogs
& Suitable for visitors in wheelchairs	🅿 Parking at Establishment	✗ Restaurant	▦ No coaches

The main attraction at Portsmouth is undoubtedly its maritime history and the collection of historic ships – the *Victory, Mary Rose* and *Warrior* in the Royal Navy's Dockyard; the submarines *Alliance* and *Holland I* at Gosport. You can also get a good view of the warships and merchant ships of today by taking a boat trip around the harbour from The Hard, just outside the dockyard gates. A board tells you what ships are in port as well as the times of trips. Trips are also available from the beach landing stage beside Clarence Esplanade, Southsea.

Portsmouth is not the prettiest of cities, but the Old Town with narrow winding streets and views of the harbour inlet known as The Camber, is worth a visit. The Cathedral is in High Street, as is the Golden Barque, which sailors touch for luck. Port Solent is a recent marina development for the leisure sailor with shops and restaurants overlooking the moorings.

Southsea is the resort area of these twin towns, where you will find all the traditional fun of the seaside, including piers and a funfair. If the sea is too cold for a dip, there is a Pyramids Leisure Centre with wave pool, water chutes and poolside bars, all in an 84°F controlled temperature.

Tourist information: The Hard Telephone: (0705) 826722
102 Commercial Road Telephone: (0705) 838382

☆ *STAR ATTRACTIONS*

The Mary Rose Ship Hall & Exhibition

The spectacular raising of the Mary Rose in 1982 is remembered by millions. Remarkably preserved in the Solent silts for 437 years, Henry VIII's warship was a Tudor time capsule, complete with everyday possessions, clothing, food, tools and weapons of her 700 men. Now the Mary Rose is one of Britain's major tourist attractions, offering a fascinating family day out. In her special dry dock workshop in Portsmouth's historic dockyard, the great oak hull is constantly sprayed with chilled water to conserve her timbers. Visitors can witness the reinstatement of much of the decking removed before the recovery, and will also enjoy special hi-tech 'Acoustiguide' radio commentary which is provided. In the Mary Rose Exhibition a twelve minute audio-visual presentation on the discovery, raising and conservation of the ship highlights the enormous endeavour which has gone into the world's most ambitious underwater archaeological project. The visitor will then enjoy all the more the fascinating exhibition of the Mary Rose's treasures: a themed display of many of the 20,000 artefacts recovered, including longbows, cannon, gaming boards, clothing, combs, pewterware, lanterns, a shaving bowl – even the contents of the barber surgeon's chest, with syringes and jars of ointment! Special events for 1992 include: 10-11 Oct, a weekend of celebrations – the 10th Anniversary of the Raising. On 4-5 Jul there will be a summer celebration of the same.

HM Naval Base
☎ (0705) 839766 & 750521

Open: all year, daily, Mar-Oct 10-5.30 (last visitors 4.30pm), Jul & Aug 10-6.45 (last visitor 5.45); Nov-Feb, daily 10.30-5 (last visitors 4pm). (Closed 25 Dec).
Admission: £3.90 (ch & students £2.50, pen £3). Family ticket £10.50-£13.
& (to all but one gallery of Ship Hall) toilets for disabled shop ✗

Spitbank Fort

This massive granite and iron fortress was built in the 1860s as part of the coastal defences against Napoleon. The interior is a maze of passages connecting over 50 rooms on two levels. A Victorian cooking range is still in working order, as are the forge and 402ft well from which fresh water is obtained. Because of its location one mile out to sea, it provides a panoramic viewpoint of the Solent.

☎ Fareham (0329) 664286 & (0831) 608383

Open: Etr-Oct. (Weather permitting).
Admission: ✳ £4 (ch £2.50) includes ferry charge. Boat ride takes approx 20 mins, visitors should allow 2hr to view. Ferries depart Gosport & Clarence Pier.
▼

HMS Victory

Still in commission and manned by regular serving officers and men, Lord Nelson's famous flagship at the Battle of Trafalgar is, because of her age and historic significance, the world's most outstanding example of maritime restoration. A tour around her decks gives some idea of the sailors' way of life in Nelson's day, and visitors can see the spot where the Admiral received his fatal wound, and the surgery below decks where he eventually died.

HM Naval Base
☎ (0705) 839766

Open: Mar-Oct, daily 10-4.50; Nov-Feb, daily 10.30-4.30. (Closed 25 Dec).
Admission: £3.90 (ch £ 2.50, pen £3). Family £10.50. Prices include Royal Naval Museum.
🅿 (charged) ⅃ (lower gun deck) toilets for disabled shop ✗

HMS Warrior 1860

Originally launched in 1860, HMS Warrior was the world's first iron-hulled armoured warship. Restored, with painstaking accuracy over a period of eight years in Hartlepool, she is now a permanent feature beside The Hard in Portsmouth. She gives an insight into life aboard a 19th-century warship, enhanced by the staff on board dressed in the correct uniform of the period. Special events are planned in August for 'Victorian Navy Days'.

Victory Gate, HM Naval Base
☎ (0705) 291379

Open: all year, Mar-Jun & Sep-Oct 10-5.30; Jul-Aug 10-7; Nov-Feb 10.30-5. (Last admission 1 hr before closing).
Admission: £3.70 (ch & student £2.20, pen £3). Family ticket £10-£13. Party.
🍴 ✗ ⅃ (upper deck only) toilets for disabled shop ✗

Royal Naval Museum

This is the only museum exclusively devoted to the overall history of the Navy. A panorama of Trafalgar, with sound-effects, is complemented by relics of Lord Nelson, his officers and men. Uniforms, medals, figureheads and model ships are on show, and there are displays on such subjects as 'The Rise of the Royal Navy', 'Sailing Navy', 'The Victorian Navy', 'The Navy in the 20th Century', and to bring the picture right up to date, 'The Modern Navy'.

HM Naval Base
☎ (0705) 733060

Open: all year, daily 10.30-5. (Closed 25 Dec).
Admission: £1.80 (ch & pen £1.30). Family ticket £4.90.
🍴 ⅃ (exhibit for sight impaired groups by prior arrangement) toilets for disabled shop ✗

The Royal Marines Museum

The Royal Marines Museum offers a series of exhibitions depicting the history of the corps through the ages. An audio-visual show demonstrates the Marine involvement in the Falklands War, there's a chance to walk through a chilled display of conditions in the far north, and a 16th-century gallery showing life at sea, with graphic descriptions of punishments and food. Outside there is a junior commando assault course, and the chance to climb aboard a Falklands landing craft.

☎ (0705) 819385

Open: all year, Etr-Aug daily 10-5.30; Sep-Etr daily 10-4.30. (Closed 3 days Xmas)
Admission: £2.50 (ch & students £1.25, pen £1.50) Family ticket £6
🅿 shop ✗

D-Day Museum & Overlord Embroidery

The story of D-Day is told from the viewpoint of those involved in both sides of history's biggest seaborne invasion, through audio-visual shows, displays, military vehicles and the 272ft long Overlord Embroidery.

Clarence Esplanade (adjacent to Southsea Castle)
☎(0705) 827261

Open: all year, daily 10-5.30. Last admission 4.30. (Closed 24-26 Dec).
Admission: £3 (ch £1.80, pen £2.25). Family ticket £7.80. Oct-Mar: £2.25 (ch £1.35, pen £1.70). Family ticket £5.85.
⅃ (Induction loops available for the hard of hearing). toilets for disabled shop ✗

Cumberland House Natural Science Museum & Butterfly House

The geology and natural history of the area are explained, with a full-size reconstruction of a dinosaur, and aquarium and free-flying butterflies. There are seasonal displays of woodland, downland and marshland ecology.

Eastern Pde
☎ (0705) 827261

Open: all year, daily 10.30-5.30. Last admission 5pm. (Closed 24-26 Dec).
Admission: ✳ £1 (ch 60p, pen 75p). Family ticket £2.60. Oct-Mar: 75p (ch 45p, pen 55p). Family ticket £1.95.
🅿 shop ✗

Winchester is full of history, which goes back to the founding of the Roman city of Venta Belgarum – their main street followed the same line as the one you will see today and their rebuilt walls can still be seen by the Weirs. Later, it was the capital of Alfred the Great, King of Wessex, whose statue dominates the Broadway, the place where William the Conqueror claimed the throne of England, and the place where the Domesday Book was written. Mary Tudor married King Philip of Spain here and William Rufus and the Anglo-Saxon kings are buried in the cathedral. This magnificent building, 556 ft from east to west, is the longest medieval cathedral in Europe and one of the most beautiful. The Cathedral Close is one of the most attractive parts of the city – try to visit the 13th-century Pilgrim's Hall which is open when not in use by the cathedral choir school.

Among Winchester's other historic buildings is the Hospital of St Cross, Britain's oldest charitable institution, founded in 1136, Wolvesey Old Bishop's Palace and Winchester City Mill, built over the river in 1744. The city also has an interesting Heritage Centre and a number of museums and art galleries. The army are represented here too and at the historic Peninsula Barracks you can visit the Royal Green Jackets Museum, The Royal Hussars Museum, the Light Infantry Museum and the Ghurka Museum; the Royal Hampshire Regiment Museum is in Southgate Street.

Winchester has an excellent shopping centre and a lively programme of events throughout the year including concerts at the cathedral, a folk festival in May, carnival in June and Winchester Hat Fair in July with two days of lively street entertainment. Summer guided walks are available from the tourist information centre, including a popular drama tour.

Tourist information: The Guildhall, Broadway Telephone: (0962) 840500

☆ STAR ATTRACTIONS

The Great Hall of Winchester Castle _____
The only remaining portion of William the Conqueror's first castle, it was completed in 1235 and is a fine example of 13th-century architecture. Purbeck marble columns support the roof and on the west wall hangs the Round Table purported to belong to King Arthur. A small medieval garden known as Queen Eleanor's Garden, leads off the Hall.

The Castle
☎ (0962) 846476

Open: all year, Mar-Oct daily 10-5; Nov-Feb, daily 10-4. (Closed Good Fri & 25-26 Dec).
Admission: Donations.
ᒼ shop ⅄

Winchester College _____
Founded and built by Bishop William of Wykeham in 1382, Winchester College is one of the oldest public schools in England. The college has greatly expanded over the years but the original buildings remain intact. The chapel, and during school term, the cloisters and Fromond's Chantry are open to the public. Also open is the War Cloister, which is reached by Commoners' Gate. Dedicated in 1924, it contains memorials to Wykhamists who died in World War I and all battles since then.

College St
☎ (0962) 868778

Open: Guided tours Apr-Sep daily (ex Sun am) 11, 1 & 3.15.
Admission: ✳ £2 (ch £1.50).
ᒼ toilets for disabled shop ⅄

HEREFORD & WORCESTER

BEWDLEY   Bewdley Museum

The Shambles is an 18th-century row of butcher's shops, and makes an interesting setting for the attractive museum devoted to the crafts and industries of the Bewdley area, with displays of charcoal burning, basket making and coopering. There are also craft workshops within the museum, where demonstrations are often held. For those interested in the industrial side, there is a restored brass foundry and the sawyard area gives occasional demonstrations of a 19th-century horizontal reciprocal saw. A working water wheel and hydraulic ram pump can also be seen and there are daily demonstrations of rope-making and clay-pipe making. A range of events, demonstrations and exhibitions take place throughout the year. These will include workshops on coracle making, stickdressing, working in willow, and skepmaking.

The Shambles, Load St
☎ (0299) 403573
Open: Mar-Nov, Mon-Sat 10-5.30 (inc BH), Sun 11-5.30.
Admission: ✳ 55p (ch & pen 20p, accom ch free). School party Free.
& shop

BEWDLEY   Severn Valley Railway

(For full entry see Bridgnorth, Shropshire)

☎ (0299) 403816 & (0746) 764361

BEWDLEY   West Midland Safari & Leisure Park

A wildlife park with over 40 species of wild and exotic animals. Ride tickets can also be bought for the variety of rides in the leisure area. Attractions include a pets corner, a sealion show, a reptile house, a parrot show, and a deer park.

Spring Grove (on A456)
☎ (0299) 402114
Open: Apr-Oct, daily 10-5.
Admission: ✳ £3.50 (ch 4 free). Book of ride tickets 5-£1.50, 10-£3 or 20-£5. Unlimited ride wristband £3.50.
🅿 ☕ & toilets for disabled shop garden centre

BROADWAY   Broadway Tower Country Park

This 65ft tower was designed by James Wyatt for the 6th Earl of Coventry, and was built in 1799. There are exhibitions on three floors, and an observation room with telescope, giving wonderful views over 12 counties. Around the tower is a country park with farm animals, an adventure playground, nature walks, a barbeque, ball game areas and giant chess and draughts boards.

☎ (0386) 852390
Open: Apr-Oct, daily 10-6.
Admission: £2.25 (ch & pen £1.50). Family ticket £7. Party.
🅿 ☕ ✗ licensed & toilets for disabled shop

BROMSGROVE   Avoncroft Museum of Buildings

The aim of the museum is to save interesting buildings by re-erecting and restoring them here. A working post mill and a blacksmith's shop, a cockpit and a merchant's house are neighbours on the 15-acre site with an 18th-century

Redditch Road, Stoke Heath (2m S, off A38)
☎ (0527) 31886

dovecote, an earth closet and a 1946 prefab. One of the more unusual exhibits is a Georgian icehouse from Tong Castle in Shropshire. It consists of a deep, brick-built pit, where ice could be stored in winter for use in summer. The latest acquistion is the great 14th-century roof from the Gueston Hall, once a monastic establishment adjoining Worcester Cathedral. An interesting feature of the museum is that the people who work on the buildings have had to relearn traditional skills such as building in wattle and daub. Visitors can sometimes see the skills being used as buildings are added to the museum. There are wheelchair ramps to the shop and tearoom, and a wheelchair is available on loan.

Open: Jun-Aug daily 11-5.30; Apr, May, Sep & Oct 11-5.30 (Closed Mon). Mar & Nov 11-4.30 (Closed Mon & Fri). Open BHs. *Admission:* £2.80 (ch £1.40, pen £1.95). Family ticket £7.40.
🅿 ☂ ᕫ toilets for disabled shop

GOODRICH   Goodrich Castle

The castle stands above the River Wye, and gives wonderful views in all directions. It was built in around 1150 and then expanded in the 13th and 14th century, using the red sandstone rock on which it stands, so that rock and castle seem to merge together. The castle was not severely tested until the Civil War, when it was held by Royalists and was battered by 'Roaring Meg' – a cannon said to have fired 200-pound balls. The siege ended after four and a half months, by which time the castle had lost its water supply. Parliament ordered the slighting of the castle, but the remains are still extensive and impressive.

☎ Symonds Yat (0606) 890538
Open: all year, Apr-Sep, daily 10-6; Oct-Mar, Tue-Sun 10-4. (Closed 24-26 Dec & 1 Jan).
Admission: £1.50 (ch 75p, pen, students & UB40 £1.10)
🅿
(EH)

KIDDERMINSTER   Severn Valley Railway

(For full entry see Bridgnorth, Shropshire)

☎ Bewdley (0299) 403816 & (0746) 764361

ROSS-ON-WYE   The Lost Street Museum

Discover this unique Edwardian Street, lost in time, with its fully stocked, life-size shops. This is probably the largest privately-owned collection of music boxes, toys, dolls, wireless, gramaphones, motor cycles, costumes and advertising in the country. There are demonstrations of musical boxes and automata, quizes with cash prizes and the pub boasts a fine collection of old amusement machines.

Palma Court, 27 Brookend St
☎ (0989) 62752
Open: Feb-Nov, Mon-Sat 10-5; Sun 11-5. Dec-Jan, telephone for opening times.
☂ ᕫ
Details not confirmed for 1992

SYMONDS YAT (WEST)   The Jubilee Park

The world-famous Jubilee Maze, built to celebrate the Queen's Jubilee in 1977, and the Museum of Mazes showing paths of mazes and labyrinths through the ages. Also The World of Butterflies, where hundreds of colourful butterflies from all over the world fly free in their large tropical indoor garden. Special events for 1992 include: Spring Festival and Easter Maze Festival; Sep-Oct, Autumn Crafts Exhibition; Nov 1-Christmas, Winter Wonderland.

☎ (0600) 890360
Open: Feb-24 Dec, attractions – daily 11-5.30, restaurant and information – daily 10.30-5.30. Open evenings Aug until 10pm, Nov-Dec Thu-Sat until 8pm.
Admission: ✳ £2.50 (ch £1.50 & pen £2). Prices include admission to Jubilee Maze, Museum of Mazes and Amazing Puzzle Shop.
🅿 ☂ ✕ ᕫ toilets for disabled shop garden centre ⚑ (ex in grounds)

HERTFORDSHIRE

HATFIELD   Hatfield House

Robert Cecil built the great Jacobean mansion in 1607-11. It replaced an older palace where Elizabeth I had spent much of her childhood, and is full of Elizabethan associations, important portraits of the queen, and historic possessions such as her silk stockings, perhaps the first pair worn in England. There are also other celebrated pictures, tapestries and armour, including some from the Spanish Armada. Newer attractions include a William IV kitchen (1833) and the National Collection of Model Soldiers.

Around the house are the great park and gardens, including a parterre planted with yews and roses, a scented garden and knot garden with typical plants of the 15th to 17th centuries. Hatfield is still the home of the Cecils, who at one point had a private waiting room at the nearby railway station.

Special events for 1992 are: Living crafts: 7-10 May; National Patchwork Championships 4-7 Jun; Festival of Gardening 20-21 Jun; Bentley Drivers Club Concours 27 Jun.

(2m from junc 4 A1(M) on A1000)
☎ (0707) 262823
Open: 25 Mar-11 Oct. House: weekdays 12-4.15, Sun 1.30-5. (Closed Mon ex BH 11-5 & Good Fri). Gardens: daily 11-6.
Admission: House Park & Gardens £4.30 (ch £2.90, pen £3.50). Park, Gardens & Exhibitions £2.40 (ch £1.80, pen £2.20). Party 20 + .
🅿 ☕ ✗ licensed ♿ toilets for disabled shop garden centre ✗ (ex in park)

KNEBWORTH   Knebworth House, Gardens & Country Park

Home of the Lytton family since 1490, the original Tudor manor was transformed in 1843 by the spectacular high Gothic decoration of Victorian novelist Sir Edward Bulwer Lytton. The interior includes a superb Jacobean Great Hall with a splendid plaster ceiling and magnificent panelling (the reredos, which stretches across the width of the room, is 17th century). He was a well known statesman and author and counted among his friends many famous people, including Dickens and Disraeli, who were all guests at Knebworth. There is a fascinating exhibition on the British Raj and some fine furniture and portraits. Outside, the formal-style gardens were simplified by Lutyens (who built several buildings in the town) and the 250-acre park now includes many attractions for visitors. There is a miniature railway, an extensive adventure playground, and a deer park. Knebworth is a popular venue for special events and activities, including in 1992 jousting tournaments (3/4 May), car rallies, and a fireworks and laser symphony concert (5 Jul). Telephone for details.

(direct access from junc 7 A1(M) at Stevenage)
☎ Stevenage (0438) 812661
Open: 4 Apr-17 May, Sat, Sun, BH & school holidays; 23 May-6 Sep, daily (ex Mon). Also wknds 12 Sep-4 Oct. House & Garden 12-5; Park 11-5.30. (Closed Mon ex BHs, 27 Jun & 31 Jul-3 Aug).
Admission: £4 (ch & pen £3.50); Park & Playground only: £2.50. Party.
🅿 ☕ ✗ licensed ♿ shop ✗ (ex in park)

ST ALBANS   Verulamium Museum

Verulamium was one of the largest and most important Roman towns in Britain. By the 1st century it was declared a 'municipium', which gave its inhabitants the rights of Roman citizenship. No other British city was granted this honour. The town was attacked by Boadicea in AD61, but rebuilt after her defeat.

St Michaels
☎ (0727) 819339
Open: Apr-Oct, weekdays 10-5.30, Sun 2-5.30; Nov-Feb, weekdays 10-4, Sun 2-4.

89

The site is set within a 100-acre park. A mosaic and under floor heating system can be seen in situ, and the museum shows finds, including mosaics, wall paintings, jewellery, pottery and other domestic items.

Following refurbishment in 1991, the museum has new displays including recreated Roman rooms, excavation videos, hands-on discovery areas and computer data bases accessible to visitors. Regular talks and demonstrations at weekends.

Admission:£1.80 (ch, pen & students 90p). Family ticket £3.95.
🅿 (charged) ᕕ shop ⚔

TRING   Zoological Museum

This most unusual museum was founded in the 1890s by Lionel Walter, 2nd Baron Rothschild, scientist, eccentric and natural history enthusiast. It is famous for its magnificent collection of thousands of mammals and birds, and there are also displays of reptiles, fishes, insects and domestic dogs. There is even a well known exhibition of dressed fleas. Extinct, rare, exotic and bizarre specimens in a unique Victorian setting. Exhibitions are organised throughout the year (details on request).

Akeman St
☎ (044282) 4181

Open: all year, Mon-Sat 10-5, Sun 2-5. (Closed Good Fri, 24-26 Dec & 1 Jan).
Admission: ✳ £1 (ch 15, UB40 & pen 50p).
🅿 ᕕ toilets for disabled shop ⚔

WARE   Scott's Grotto

Scott's Grotto, built in the 1760s by the Quaker poet John Scott, has been described by English Heritage as "one of the finest in England". Recently restored by the Ware Society, it consists of underground passages and chambers decorated with flints, shells, minerals and stones, and extends 67ft into the side of the hill. Please wear flat shoes and bring a torch.

Scott's Rd (off A119)
☎ (0920) 464131

Open: Apr-Sep, Sat & BH's 2-4.30. Other times by appointment only.
Admission: Donations

HUMBERSIDE

BEVERLEY   Museum of Army Transport

The museum tells the story of army transport from horse drawn waggons to the recent Gulf conflict: everything from prototype vehicles to Montgomery's Rolls Royce and the last Blackburn Beverley aircraft. There are also other exhibits to be explored including 'Women at the wheel' (their role in the war) and an area for children. Special events in 1992 include a Toy and Train Fair on 1 Mar and 10 May, and the 'El Alamein' exhibition on 23 Oct.

Flemingate
☎ Hull (0482) 860445

Open: all year, daily 10-5. (Closed 24-26 Dec).
Admission: ✳ £2.50 (ch 5-16 & pen £1.50). Children under 16 must be accompanied. Party 10+.
🅿 ☕ ᕕ toilets for disabled shop ⚔

SYMBOLS			
☎ Telephone number	✳ Indicates 1991 price	☕ Refreshments	⚔ No Dogs
ᕕ Suitable for visitors in wheelchairs	🅿 Parking at Establishment	✗ Restaurant	🚫 No coaches

BRIDLINGTON   Sewerby Hall

The house was built around 1714-20, and is now an art gallery and museum of history and archaeology. It contains the Amy Johnson Trophy Room, and the gardens are full of interest, especially the walled gardens. There is also a miniature zoo and aviary.

☎ (0262) 673769 (Park) & 677874 (Hall)

Open: all year, Park & grounds 9-dusk. From Spring BH-mid Sep game facilities are available to public. Art gallery & museum, Good Fri-last Sun in Sep.
🅿 (charged) ♥ ♿ (garden for the blind) toilets for disabled shop
Details not confirmed for 1992

ELSHAM   Elsham Hall Country Park

Attractions include an animal farmyard, clocktower shop and art gallery, carp-feeding jetty, an arboretum and an adventure playground. There are nature trails and quizzes, a Craft Centre with working craftsfolk, a tea room and an award-winning restaurant. The latest addition is a Falconry Centre with an excellent selection of birds of prey. There are special events planned throughout the year, especially during the school holidays.

(on M180/A15 Humber Bridge junc)
☎ Barnetby (0652) 688698

Open: all year, mid Sep-Maundy Thu, Sun & BH 11-4; Etr Sat-mid Sep, daily 11-5. (Closed Good Fri & 25-26 Dec).
Admission: ✳ £3 (ch & pen £2, ch under 3 free). Party 20+.
🅿 ♥ ✗ licensed ♿ (fishing facilities for disabled) toilets for disabled shop garden centre 🐾

HORNSEA   Hornsea Pottery Leisure Park

This retail and leisure park on Yorkshire's east coast combines bargain factory shopping – everything from clothes, toys, shoes, pottery, furniture, and bedding plus designer clothes shops. Family leisure attractions include Butterfly World, Birds of Prey Conservation Centre, Yorkshire Car Collection, Minidale Farmyard and Model Village plus adventure playground. Special events for 1992 include unusual car rallies and a Santa's party and Children in Need 'aerobathon' in November.

Rolston Rd
☎ (0964) 534211

Open: all year, daily from 10-5 (Closing at 6pm school summer holidays, 4pm Nov-Feb). Xmas week phone for details. Amenities charged individually.
🅿 ♥ ✗ licensed ♿ toilets for disabled shop 🐾 (ex in park)

POCKLINGTON   Penny Arcadia

This museum houses the world's most comprehensive collection of antique and veteran coin-operated amusement machines. An audio-visual screen show, stage presentation, guided tours and demonstrations introduce you to the world of the slot-machine.

Ritz Cinema, Market Place
☎ (0759) 303420

Open: May-Sep, daily 10-5 (Jun-Aug), 12.30-5 (May & Sep). Other times by arrangement.
Admission: £3 (ch 15 & pen £2). Party.
🅿 ♿

SANDTOFT   Sandtoft Transport Centre

Set up primarily for the preservation and operation of trolley buses this developing museum now boasts over 60 vehicles from many parts of Britain and the Continent. There are some working models among the exhibits which include motorbuses and other transport memorabilia. (Leave M180 at junction 2, S of motorway on A161 for about quarter of a mile, then take unclassed road.)

Belton Rd
☎ Weybridge (0932) 851650

Open: Etr-Sep, Sun & BH's 12-6.
🅿 ♥ ♿ shop
Details not confirmed for 1992

SCUNTHORPE   Normanby Hall Country Park

A whole host of activities and attractions are offered in the 350 acres of grounds that surround Normanby Hall including golf, riding, nature trails, gift shop and a farming museum. Deer herds can be spotted grazing in the parkland and many species of wildfowl have their home here. Inside the Regency mansion there are fine rooms decorated and furnished in period style. Special events include car rallies, craft fairs, demonstrations and guided walks

Normanby (5m N on B1430)
☎ (0724) 720588
Open: Park all year, daily. Hall: Etr-Oct, Mon-Fri 11-5, Sat & Sun 1-5; Nov-Etr by appointment only. Farming Museum: Etr-Oct, daily 1-5; Nov-Etr by appointment only. *Admission:* Free.
🅿 (charged) ☙ ✗ licensed ⅁ toilets for disabled shop

KENT

BEKESBOURNE   Howletts Park Zoo

Howletts is one of John Aspinall's animal collections in Kent. It has the world's largest breeding gorilla colony, and also to be seen are tigers, small cats, free running deer and antelope, snow leopards, bison, ratel and the UK's only herd of breeding elephants.

(off A257)
☎ Canterbury (0227) 721286
Open: all year, daily 10-5 or dusk. (Closed 25 Dec).
🅿 ☙ ⅁ toilets for disabled shop ⅄
Details not confirmed for 1992

BELTRING   Whitbread Hop Farm

Set amidst picturesque countryside and hop gardens, this is the largest group of Victorian oast houses and galleried barns in the world. They house two award-winning museums, one on rural crafts, the other devoted to hop farming through the ages. There are also displays of farming machinery, carts and other bygones, but perhaps the greatest attractions are the Whitbread Shire Horses. The many facilites include a gift shop and restaurant, coarse fishing, a craft centre and a play area for children, and there are nature trails to follow. Numerous events are held throughout the year, including jazz festivals, country fairs, motor shows, flower and garden shows, a hot air balloon show, and even Highland games.

☎ Maidstone (0622) 872068
Open: 4 Mar-23 Dec, daily 10-6. (Last admission 5pm).
Admission: £4.25 (ch, pen & disabled £3). Extra charges on special event days.
🅿 ☙ ✗ licensed ⅁ (audio tours for partially sighted) toilets for disabled shop

CANTERBURY   see page 94

CHATHAM   Historic Dockyard

A Royal dockyard until 1984, now an 80-acre working museum with 47 Scheduled Ancient Monuments which form the most complete Georgian/early Victorian dockyard in the world. Eight museum galleries cover 400 years of shipbuilding history, and include the award-winning 'Wooden Walls' which shows through sights, sounds and smells, how 18th-century warships such as HMS Victory were built here. Visitors can see a working ropery, sail and flag-making, crafts workshops in action, and witness the

☎ Medway (0634) 812551
Open: all year, Apr-Oct, Wed-Sun 10-6 (last admission 5pm); Nov-Mar, Wed, Sat & Sun 10-4.30 (last admission 3.30pm).
Admission: £5.20 (ch 5-16 £2.60, student & pen £4.50). Party.
🅿 ✗ licensed ⅁ (wheelchair available) toilets for disabled shop

restoration of the Victorian sloop, Gannet, in dry dock. Impressive buildings include huge covered slips, a Georgian Officers' Terrace, and the Commissioner's House (1703), Britain's oldest intact naval building whose pleasant garden is open to visitors. Guided tours and horse-drawn wagon rides are available. Special events for 1992 include a Mad Hatter's Tea Party (20 Apr), a model railway exhibition (13-14 Jun), and a heavy horse day (26 Jul).

CHILHAM   Chilham Castle Gardens

The 'castle' is an imposing hexagonal Jacobean house with an older keep, overlooking the the River Stour. It is not open, but the spacious gardens can be visited. Immediately below the house are terraces planted with roses and wisteria, then come trees and yew hedges, a rose garden, a vegetable garden and a herb garden. There is some handsome topiary, and there are wide lawns adorned with stone urns. Woodland and lakeside walks can be taken, and various events are held in the grounds during the year. Also there is the Raptor Centre, where birds of prey can be seen. Events for 1992 include horse trials (16/17 May), a festival of transport (24/25 May), a country fair (1/2 August), Midsummer Mania (23/24 Aug), and a Firework Fantasia (1 Nov).

☎ Canterbury (0227) 730319

Open: Garden only 12 Apr-18 Oct, daily 11-6. (Last admission 5pm).
Admission: Garden: Tue-Thu, Sat & Sun £3 (ch £1.50); Mon & Fri £2.50 (ch £1.25). Parties 20 + .
🅿 ☛ ⅋ shop

DOVER   Dover Castle and Hellfire Corner

The Norman castle has a massive keep built by Henry II in the 1180s, with chapels, a 242ft-deep well, and massive walls and towers. The castle was strengthened and adapted in later centuries. It stands on cliffs which have been fortified since Iron Age times, but the oldest building there now is the Roman lighthouse, the Pharos. The Saxon church of St Mary de Castros is also near the castle. It has been restored but still shows Saxon and Normanwork. Secret tunnels underneath the castle were built in Napoleonic times and were more recently used during the Second World War to plan the evacuation of Dunkirk. A new exhibition is based here called Hellfire Corner.

☎ (0304) 201628

Open: all year, Apr-Sep, daily 10-6; Oct-Mar, daily 10-4. (Closed 24-26 Dec & 1 Jan).
Admission: £4.50 (ch £2.30, students, pen & UB40 £3.40).
🅿 ☛ ⅋ shop ⚲
(EH)

DOVER   Old Town Gaol

High-tech animation, audio-visual techniques and 'talking heads' take visitors back to Victorian England to experience the horrors of life behind bars, listening, as they walk through the reconstructed courtroom, exercise yard, washroom and cells, to the stories of the felons and their jailers. You can even, if you so wish, try the prisoners' beds or find out what it is like to be locked in a 6ft x 4ft cell!

Dover Town Hall, Biggin St
☎ (0304) 201066

Open: May-Oct, Mon-Sat 10-5. (Closed Mon & Tue in winter ex Public Hols). Telephone (0304) 242766 for recorded information.
Admission: ❋ £2.50 (ch & pen £1.25).
🅿 (charged) ⅋ shop ⚲
Entries for Dover contd on p.95

Most of the interesting parts of Canterbury are in the old city, still partly enclosed by its medieval walls, built on Roman foundations. As in the days of Chaucer's pilgrims, most visitors make straight for the magnificent cathedral which stands in peaceful precincts at the heart of the city. The tombs of Henry IV and his queen, Joan of Navarre, and that of Edward, the Black Prince, are among the many important monuments, but the cathedral is most famous as the site of the martyrdom in 1170 of St Thomas Becket.

Canterbury has countless old buildings including Eastbridge Hospital, where medieval travellers stayed, St Dunstan's Church, which houses the head of Sir Thomas More, brought here after being cut off by Henry VIII, St Augustine's Abbey and the picturesque Weavers' Cottages. There are open-topped bus sightseeing tours, which start at Canterbury East railway station, and guided walks from the tourist information centre. River tours and horse-drawn carriage tours are also available. Canterbury is busy with visitors throughout the summer, but is at its most lively during the Arts Festival in October and Cricket Week in August.

Tourist information: 34 St Margaret's Street Telephone: (0227) 766567

☆ *STAR ATTRACTIONS*

Blean Bird Park
Exotic tropical birds can be seen flying in a natural setting among the trees. The garden has the largest breeding collection of macaws, cockatoos and parakeets in England. There are also owls, peacocks, pheasants and other birds, with a pets' corner, a small collection of mammals, and a woodland walk.

Honey Hill, Blean (3m NW on A290)
☎ (0227) 471666

Open: Mar-Nov 10-6.
Admission: ✳ £2.50 (ch £1.50, pen £2).
🅿 ☞ ⟁ toilets for disabled shop ⴵ

Canterbury Heritage
An award-winning new museum in a breath-taking medieval building on the riverbank close to the Cathedral, shops and other attractions. The tour starts in Roman times and continues up to the present day. Some of the most exciting of the city's treasures are shown: Roman cavalry swords and a silver spoon hoard, Anglo-Saxon gold, and Viking finds. The displays include (among many others) a reconstruction of Becket's tomb; a medieval street with a pilgrim badge shop; Christopher Marlowe (he was born in Canterbury); the city in the Civil War; and Stephenson's locomotive 'Invicta'. The latest feature to be added is the Rupert Bear Collection.

Poor Priests' Hospital, Stour Street
☎(0227) 452747

Open: all year, Mon-Sat 10.30-5 & Sun (Jun-Oct) 1.30-5 (last admission 4pm). (Closed Good Fri & Xmas).
⟁ shop ⴵ
Details not confirmed for 1992

The Canterbury Tales
At Canterbury Tales you can step back in time to the 17th-century and experience the sights, sounds and even the smells of the period. Meet the people, see their animals and visit their homes, inns and workshops and become one of Chaucer's happy band of pilgrims walking from Southwark to Canterbury and the miracle-working tomb of St Thomas Becket. The whole thing is brought vividly to life using the latest electronic presentation techniques. Commentary is available in English, French, Dutch, German, Italian and Spanish. A special children's tape is available, with 24 hours' notice. Events for 1992 include a medieval street theatre.

Saint Margaret's St
☎ (0227) 454888

Open: all year, Apr-Sep daily 9.30-5.30; Jan-Mar & Oct-Dec, Mon-Fri 10-4.30 & Sat-Sun 9.30-5.30.
Admission: ✳ £3.75 (ch 6-16 £2.50, under 6 free, students & pen £3). Family ticket £11.
☞ ⟁ toilets for disabled shop ⴵ

DOVER   The White Cliffs Experience

The White Cliffs Experience tells the story of Britains's frontline town from the Roman Invasion to the Second World War. Comprising a Historium, Museum and Archaeological Gardens, and using the latest technology, history is brought to life in an informative way. Visitors can witness the Roman Invasion, talk to the Romans and even take a turn rowing in a Roman Galley. Time and Tide is a living cartoon where Corporal Crabbe and Her Cliffness tell the story of Dover from Norman to Victorian Times. Finally, it's Dover 1944 and visitors can experience the blitzed streets complete with air-raid warning sirens.

Market Sq
☎ Deal (0304) 214566
Open: all year, 24 Feb-1 Nov, daily 10-7; 4 Nov-23 Feb, Wed-Sun 10-5. Please telephone to confirm opening times.
Admission: £4 (ch £2.50, under 5 free, pen £3.50).
♥ ﺙ (Lifts, parking arranged) toilets for disabled shop 🐾

HAWKINGE   Kent Battle of Britain Museum

Once a Battle of Britain Station, today it houses the largest collection of authentic relics and related memorabilia of British and German aircraft involved in the fighting. Also shown are British and German uniforms and equipment, and full-size replicas of the Hurricane, Spitfire and Me 109 used in Battle of Britain films.

Aerodrome Rd (on A260)
☎ (030389) 3140
Open: Etr-Sep, daily 11-5; Oct, daily 11-4.
🅿 ﺙ shop 🐾
Details not confirmed for 1992

HERNE COMMON   'Brambles' Wildlife Park

The 20-acre park has a nature trail leading through woodland where fallow and sika deer, mara, guanaco, wallaby, owls, Scottish wildcats and red foxes may be seen. Small rare breed farm animals, ponies and a miniature donkey may be fed with the food sold at the gate. There is also a walk-in rabbit enclosure and an indoor garden, an adventure playground and under-fives' playground.

Wealdon Forest Pk
☎ Canterbury (0227) 712379
Open: Etr-Oct, daily 10-5.
Admission:£2 (ch £1.20, pen £1.50).
🅿 ♥ ﺙ shop 🐾

HEVER   Hever Castle & Gardens

This enchanting, double-moated, 13th-century castle was the childhood home of Anne Boleyn. In 1903 it was bought and restored by the American millionaire William Waldorf Astor, and now shows superb Edwardian craftsmanship and an exhibition on scenes from the life and times of Anne Boleyn. Astor also transformed the grounds, creating a Tudor village (available for conferences and corporate hospitality), a lake, a spectacular Italian garden filled with antique sculptures; maze and a fine topiary. Special events planned for 1992 include jousting tournaments throughout the summer and a traditional day of dance on 6th June. There are ramps in the gardens and purpose-built toilets for wheelchair users; some wheelchairs are available on request.

☎ Edenbridge (0732) 865224
Open: 17 Mar-8 Nov, daily. Castle 12-6, Gardens 11-6. Last admission 5pm. Private guided tours for pre-booked groups available all year.
Admission: Castle & Gardens £4.80 (ch 5-16 £2.40, pen £4.30). Family ticket £12. Gardens only £3.40 (ch 5-16 £2, pen £2.90). Family ticket £8.80. Party 15+.
🅿 ✕ licensed ﺙ (Wheelchairs available) toilets for disabled shop garden centre

---

SYMBOLS

☎ Telephone number	✳ Indicates 1991 price	♥ Refreshments	🐾 No Dogs
ﺙ Suitable for visitors in wheelchairs	🅿 Parking at Establishment	✕ Restaurant	🚫 No coaches

LYMPNE   Port Lympne Zoo Park, Mansion & Gardens

The only pair of Sumatran rhinos in the western world have their home in John Aspinall's 300-acre zoo park along with hundreds of other rare animals: Indian elephants, wolves, bison, black and snow leopards, Siberian and Indian tigers, monkeys and chimpanzees. The newly opened gorilla pavilion is now the home to Djoum and his family from Howletts. The mansion designed by Sir Herbert Baker is surrounded by 15-acres of spectacular gardens. Inside, the most notable features include the recently restored Rex Whistler Tent Room, Moroccan Patio and hexagonal library where the Treaty of Paris was signed after the First World War. The recently completed Spencer Roberts mural room has illustrations of over 300 animals and birds from South East Asia adorning its walls. Safari trailers journey through some of the animal paddocks during peak times; please telephone to check availability.

☎ Hythe (0303) 264646

Open: all year, daily 10-5, 4pm in winter (Closed 25 Dec).
Admission: ✻ £6 (ch 4-14 & pen £4)
🅿 ✗ licensed ৬ toilets for disabled shop ⌁

MAIDSTONE   Leeds Castle

Named after Led, Chief Minister of Ethelbert IV, King of Kent in AD 857, this castle was described by Lord Conway as 'the loveliest castle in the world'. Visitors may well agree with the sentiment. Built on two islands in the middle of a lake and set in 500 acres of landscaped parkland, it was converted into a royal palace by Henry VIII, and remained a royal residence for over three centuries. Today it has been beautifully restored and furnished; it has some beautiful pictures and other treasures, and, more unusual, a museum of medieval dog collars. Outside there are the Culpeper Flower Garden, the greenhouses, aviaries and vineyard, the 14th-century barbican and mill, the maze and grotto, and water and woodland gardens. The Fairfax Hall, a 17th-century tithe barn, is the venue for 'Kentish Evenings' each Saturday night (except during Aug) and is a fully licenced self-service restaurant during normal opening hours. There are also many special events run throughout the year, including an Open Air Classical Concert, an International Balloon Fiesta, and a Festival of English Wines.

(4m E on B2163, off M20/A20)
☎ (0622) 765400

Open: 16 Mar-Oct daily 11-5; Nov-Mar Sat & Sun 11-4. (Closed 27 Jun, 4 Jul & 7 Nov prior to special events). Open by special appointment at other times. Also daily in Xmas wk (26 Dec-1 Jan).
Admission: Castle & park £6.20 (ch £4.20, students & pen £5.20); Park & gardens £4.70 (ch £2.70, students & pen £3.70). Family ticket £17, Park & gardens only £12.50. Party 20 + .
🅿 ✗ licensed ৬ (Braille information, induction loops & wheelchair lift) toilets for disabled shop garden centre ⌁

MATFIELD   Badsell Park Farm

A pleasant day in the country for all the family is offered at this attractive 180-acre fruit and arable farm. Children are able to handle young farm animals and pets in the Animal Park and Pet Area. There are nature trails to follow in beautiful countryside, a butterfly house with live tropical species, and picnic facilities. An Information Room gives details of farming and wildlife, including live insect displays. Strawberries, apples and other fruit and vegetables can be picked in season. Children's birthday parties are a speciality and pony and tractor rides are available by arrangement.

Crittenden Rd
☎ Paddock Wood (0892) 832549 & 833436

Open: 25 Mar-15 Nov daily 10-5.30.
Admission:£2.50 (ch & pen £2)
🅿 ☕ ৬ shop ⌁ (ex on nature trail)

NEW ROMNEY   Romney Hythe & Dymchurch Railway

The world's smallest public railway has its headquarters here. The concept of two enthusiasts coincided with Southern Railway's plans for expansion, and so the thirteen-and-a-half mile stretch of 15in gauge railway came into being, running from Hythe through New Romney and Dymchurch to Dungeness Lighthouse.

☎ (0679) 62353 & 63256

Open: daily Etr-Sep, also wknds in Mar & Oct. For times apply to: The Manager, RH & DR., New Romney, Kent.
Admission: Charged according to journey.
🅿 (charged) ☕ ዼ shop

PENSHURST   Penshurst Place

The original manor house was built by Sir John de Pulteney between 1340 and 1345 and is perfectly preserved. Successive owners enlarged it during the 15th, 16th and 17th centuries, and the great variety of architectural styles creates an elaborate and dramatic backdrop for the extensive collections of English, French and Italian furniture, tapestries and paintings. The world-famous, chestnut-beamed great hall is the oldest and finest in the country, and the collection in the Toy Museum is much loved by children. The house is surrounded by magnificent formal gardens laid out in authentic Tudor style. The leisure area includes an adventure playground, a country-side exhibition and nature trail. The Kent Craft and Hobby fair is held here on May 2-4 and September 18-20. There are also special activities and events on all Bank Holidays; telephone for details.

(on B2176)
☎ (0892) 870307

Open: House & gardens Apr-4 Oct, daily 12.30-5.30;Grounds & venture playground only open weekends from 7 Mar, 12.30-5, then until 1 Nov.
Admission: House & Grounds £4 (ch £2.25, pen & students £3.50). Grounds, Toy Museum & Venture playground £3 (ch £2, pen £2.50). Party 20+.
🅿 ☕ ✗ licensed ዼ shop ⍢

SWINGFIELD MINNIS   The Butterfly Centre

A tropical greenhouse garden with scores of colourful free-flying butterflies from all over the world among exotic plants such as bougainvillea, oleander and banana. The temperate section houses British butterflies, with many favourite species and some rarer varieties.

McFarlanes Garden Centre
☎ (0303) 83244

Open: 28 Mar-11 Oct, daily 10-5.
Admission: £1.95 (ch £1.20 & pen £1.30). Family ticket £5.35-£5.85
🅿 ☕ ዼ shop garden centre ⍢

LANCASHIRE

BLACKPOOL   see page 98

CHARNOCK RICHARD   Camelot Adventure Theme Park

This 130-acre theme park brings the legend and pageantry of the medieval world of Camelot to life every day with jousting tournaments, falcony displays, Merlin's Magic Show and Puppet Show. There are over 100 rides and attractions here, including The Tower of Terror and The Beast. There is also a three-star hotel and conference centre in the grounds with 147 rooms in total, where family weekends and parties are a speciality.

☎ Eccleston (0257) 453044

Open: Apr-Oct. Telephone for further details.
Admission: ✲ £7.45 (ch under 4 free).
🅿 ☕ ✗ ዼ toilets for disabled shop ⍢

There is no other resort like Blackpool, which attracts more visitors (16.8 million a year) than the whole of Greece and its islands and has more holiday beds (120,000) than the whole of Portugal. It may not be the most sophisticated of towns, but it is enormous fun, with its famous tower, amusement arcades, fortune tellers, variety shows and fun fair rides, and it is at its best when it is busy.

Its seven miles of sandy beach has a promenade, donkey rides and three piers, each with amusements and shows. The Sandcastle is a large under-cover leisure pool with waves, water chutes and the like, while the Lido caters for more serious swimming. As far as the sea is concerned, look out for boards giving details of cleanliness tests.

One of the more simple pleasures of Blackpool is to take a ride along the Prom in a tram – Blackpool was the first town to use electric trams (in 1885) and now has the only surviving public tram service. During the annual autumn illuminations some of the trams are specially decorated to become part of this fantastic light show.

Tourist information: 1 Clifton Street Telephone: (0253) 21623/25212;
87A Coronation Street Telephone: (0253) 21891

☆ *STAR ATTRACTIONS*

Pleasure Beach
This 40-acre amusement park is crammed full of traditional fairground rides and the terrifying up-to-the-minute rollercoasters you would expect to find at any top theme park. Beaver Creek is for children up to about 10 years; its attractions include a log flume and the Beaver Club which organises a variety of activities.

Promenade
☎ (0253) 41033

Open: from 7 Mar to 11 Apr weekends only 1-6pm, then daily from 11am. Summer closing time depends on season, but is usually around 10.30-11pm.
Admission: charges for individual rides.

Blackpool Tower
Don't miss the lift ride to the top of the 518ft tower for far-reaching views on clear days. The entertainment complex at the foot of the tower includes the Tower Ballroom, with its famous Wurlitzer organ, the aquarium, adventure playground and Tiny Tots Soft Play Area.

Promenade
☎ (0253) 22242

Open: from 15 May daily 10am-11pm
Admission: fee payable

Zoological Gardens
There are over four hundred large and small animals kept in the 32 acres of landscaped gardens. There is a miniature railway and a children's play area, and also a mother and baby room..

East Park Dr
☎ (0253) 65027

Open: all year daily, summer 10-6; winter 10-5 or dusk. (Closed 25 Dec).
Admission: ✽ £2.95 (ch & pen £1.50).
🅿 ☕ ✗ licensed ♿ toilets for disabled shop
🐾

LEIGHTON HALL

Early Gillow furniture is displayed among other treasures in the fine interior of this neo-Gothic mansion, which has a gallery with resident artist. Outside a large collection of birds of prey can be seen, and flying displays are given at 3.30pm each afternoon (weather permitting). Special events for 1992: 12-13 Sep, Rainbow Craft Fair; 18 Oct, Doll Fair.

☎ **Carnforth (0524) 734474**

*Open:*May-Sep, Sun, Tue-Fri & BH Mon from 2pm. (Last admission 4.30). School parties pre-booked from 10am. Other times by arrangement.
Admission: £2.80 (ch £1.80, pen £2.30). Party 25+.
🅿 ☕ ♿ toilets for disabled shop ⅓ (ex in park)

MARTIN MERE   Wildfowl & Wetlands Trust

The Wildfowl Trust acquired 360 acres of the most primitive part of this old marsh and have re-created some of the open water habitats, many of which were lost when the land was drained for agriculture in the 17th century. The vast lake and variety of small ponds are now visited by thousands of wild geese, swans, ducks and waders; there are also three flocks of flamingoes among a permanent collection of birds numbering around 1600. In winter the refuge attracts Whooper swans from Iceland and more exciting still, Bewick's swans which have travelled well over 2000 miles from Siberia. The lake is overlooked by comfortable hides and the attractive visitor centre (built from Norwegian logs) contains an exhibition gallery, educational centre and a welcome coffee shop. Facilities for the disabled include wheelchair loan, purpose-built toilets for wheelchair users, braille notices around the grounds and tarmac paths. The Trust is signposted from the A565 at Mere Brow.

☎ **Burscough (0704) 895181**

Open: all year, daily 9.30-5.30 earlier in winter (ex 24-25 Dec).
🅿 ☕ ♿ toilets for disabled shop ⅓
Details not confirmed for 1992

MORECAMBE   Frontierland – Western Theme Park

Themed on the American Wild West, there are over 30 rides and attractions for all the family with wood and steel roller coasters, dark rides, American carousel, and an all-weather fun house with live country and western and magic shows in the main season. The Sky Ride offers great views across Morecambe Bay. Special events for 1992 include: 15-17 May, Country and Western Festival; 9 May and 12 Sept, Cub and Brownie Days; 4 Jul, Independence Day.

The Promenade
☎ **(0524) 410024**

Open: 12-26 Apr & 24 May-27 Sep, daily; 21 Mar-11 Apr & May Day-23 May, wknds only; Also school hol wk in Oct.
Admission: fee payable.
🅿 (charged) ☕ ♿ toilets for disabled shop

RIBCHESTER   Museum of Childhood

Twice winners of the Best of England's North-West Tourist Attractions Award, this nostalgic collection of toys, games, models, dolls, dolls' houses, miniatures and curios is housed in an atmospheric museum. There are over 250,000 objects on display and over fifty dolls houses. There is a working model fairground and special exhibitions including the Warneken Collection of embroidered dolls, the General Tom Thumb cabinet, the Titanic Bear and the famous Professor Tomlin's Flea Circus. There are normally at least four special events planned each year – details on application. From April there will be a special exhibition to commemorate the 80th anniversary of the liner Titanic.

Church St
☎ **(0254) 878520**

Open: all year, Tue-Sun, also BH Mon, 10.30-5. Last admission 4.30pm.
Admission: ❋ £1.95 (ch £1.25, pen £1.75). Family ticket £6.40.
🅿 shop

LEICESTERSHIRE

COTTESMORE   Rutland Railway Museum

The museum has an extensive collection of industrial locomotives and rolling stock, many of which were used in local ironstone quarries. A number are demonstrated in use over three quarters of a mile of the mineral branch built for the quarries. This line is also used to give passenger rides.

Cottesmore Iron Ore Mines, Sidings, Ashwell Rd (off B668)
☎ Stamford (0780) 62384 & 63092

Open: wknds for viewing, with free diesel-hauled rides on request, site conditions permitting. Steam operating days: 30 Mar-1 Apr, 5, 6 & 25-27 May, 7 Jul, 4 & 24-26 Aug & 29 Sep, 11-5.
🅿 ☕ ♿ shop
Details not confirmed for 1992

LOUGHBOROUGH   Great Central Railway

This private steam railway runs over seven miles from Loughborough Central to Leicester, with all trains calling at Quorn and Woodhouse. The locomotive depot is at Loughborough Central, together with a museum. A buffet car is run on most trains. Special events for 1992 include three steam galas, two Thomas Tank Engine weekends, bonfire night fireworks display and Santa specials in December.

Great Central Rd
☎ (0509) 230726

Open: Sat, Sun & BH Mon & midweek May-Sep.
Admission: £5 (ch & pen £2.50). Family ticket £12.50.
🅿 ☕ ✕ licensed ♿ (Disabled coach added to train by prior request) shop

MARKET BOSWORTH   The Battlefield Steam Railway Line

Together with a regular railway service (mainly steam) from Shackerstone to Shenton, there is an extensive railway museum featuring a collection of rolling stock and a multitude of other relics from the age of steam rail travel. With the opening of the extension in April 1992 of the line to Shenton (site of the Battle of Bosworth Field), the return passenger trip is 9 miles. Special events throughout the year include Friends of Thomas the Tank Engine days, a Teddy Bears' Picnic, Halloween Special, Bonfire Special and Santa Specials on December weekends.

(5m NW on unclass rd at Shackerstone station
☎ Tamworth (0827) 880754 & (0827) 715790 (wknd)

Open: all year, Station & Museum, Sat & Sun, 11.30-5.30. Passenger steam train service operates Apr-Oct, Sun & BH Mon only.
Admission: Shackerstone station: 50p (ch 5-15 free). Return train fare £4 (ch £2). Family ticket £11.
🅿 ☕ ♿ shop

MARKET BOSWORTH   Bosworth Battlefield Visitor Centre & Country Park

The Battle of Bosworth Field was fought in 1485 between the armies of Richard III and the future Henry VII. The visitor centre gives the viewer a comprehensive inter-pretation of the battle by means of exhibitions, models and a film theatre. There are also illustrated trails around the battlefield, and special medieval attractions are held in the summer months. Full details of admission fees for special events and free leaflets are available on application.

Sutton Cheney (2.5m S)
☎ (0455) 290429

Open: all year – Country Park & Battle trails all year during daylight hours. Visitor Centre Apr-Oct, Mon-Sat 1-5.30, Sun & BH Mon 1-6. Parties all year by arrangement.
Admission: ✳ Visitor Centre £1.50 (ch & pen £1). Party 20 + . Special charges apply on event days.
🅿 (charged) ☕ ♿ (parts of footpath network not suitable) toilets for disabled shop 🐶 (ex country park)

OADBY   Farmworld

Winner of the 1989 Best of Tourism Award for The Shires of Middle England, Farmworld is a working farm that offers a feast of fun and surprises for all the family. Children will enjoy the Children's Farmyard and the playground, while their parents might appreciate the Edwardian Ale-house and the craft workshops and demonstrations. There are also Shire horses and cart rides, lakeside and woodland walks, nature trails and ancient and modern machinery displays.

Stoughton Farm Park, Gartree Rd (off A6 & A47)
☎ **Leicester (0533) 710355**
Open: all year, daily 10-5.30 (5 in winter). (Closed 25-26 Dec & 1 Jan).
Admission: £3.50 (ch 2-4 £1.25, ch 5-16 £1.75, pen £2.50). Party.
🅿 ☕ ৬ (specifically designed viewing gallery) toilets for disabled shop ⛄

SWINFORD   Stanford Hall

This William and Mary house on the River Avon, was built in the 1690s by Sir Roger Cave. The Ballroom is notable for its decoration and the chimney-piece and the house contains antique furniture, paintings and family costumes. There is a replica of Percy Pilcher's flying machine of 1898. In the grounds are a walled rose garden, an old forge, and a motor cycle museum. A craft centre based in the old stables can be seen on most Sundays. Outdoor pursuits include fishing and a nature trail and the large number of events arranged for 1992 include car and motorcycle owners club rallies, National Hovercraft Racing Championships on 23-25 May and 29-31 Aug, The 10th Rugby Raft Races on 28 Jun and a craft fair on 3-4 Oct.

(1m E)
☎ **Rugby (0788) 860250**
Open: Etr-Sep, Sat, Sun, BH Mon & Tue following 2.30-6; noon on BH & Event Days (House 2.30).
Admission: House & Grounds £2.80 (ch £1.30); Grounds only £1.50 (ch 70p); Motorcycle Museum 90p (ch 20p). Party 20+.
🅿 ☕ ৬ (museum also accessible) toilets for disabled shop ⛄ (ex park)

TWYCROSS   Twycross Zoo

Set up during the 1960s, Twycross Zoo Park specialises in primates, and also includes gibbons, gorillas, orang-utangs and chimpanzees. There is a huge range of monkeys from the tiny tamarins and spider monkeys to the large howler monkeys.

There are also various other animals such as lions, tigers, elephants and giraffes, and a pet's corner for younger children. Other attractions include a Sealion Pool with spectacular waterfall, Penguin Pool with underwater viewing and a Children's Adventure Playground.

(1.5m NW off A444)
☎ **Tamworth (0827) 880250**
Open: all year, daily 10-6 (4 in winter). (Closed 25 Dec).
Admission: £3.80 (ch £2, pen £2.60). Party.
🅿 ☕ ৬ toilets for disabled shop ⛄

LINCOLNSHIRE

BELTON   Belton House Park & Gardens

For many people Belton is the perfect country house, a handsome but not overwhelming grand mansion. It was the home of the Brownlow family for nearly three centuries before being given to the National Trust, and the family still has a flat in the house. The ground floor has a succession of state rooms, with the Marble Hall as its centrepiece. The name comes from the black and white marble floor, which is original. The walls are decorated with intricate wood

(3m NE Grantham on A607)
☎ **Grantham (0476) 66116**
Open: Apr-Oct, Wed-Sun & BH Mon (Closed Good Fri). House open 1-5.30 (last admission 5pm). Grounds open 11-5.30.

carvings of birds, fruit, flowers and foliage, which have been attributed to Grinling Gibbons but are probably by Edmund Carpenter. There are more remarkable carvings in the formal saloon, which also has ornate plasterwork on the ceiling. Splendid furnishings and decorations throughout the house include tapestries and hangings, both old and modern, lovely garden scenes by Melchior d'Hondecoeter, family portraits, porcelain and fine furniture. Not to be forgotten are the rolling grounds and gardens, including an orangery and formal Italian garden, laid out in the 19th century. There are some attractive sculptures, and an adventure playground for children. An open-air concert is planned for 27 June.

Admission: £3.80 (ch £1.90).
P ✕ licensed ♿ toilets for disabled shop 🐕̸ (ex in grounds)
(NT)

BELVOIR Belvoir Castle

Although Belvoir Castle has been the home of the Dukes of Rutland for many centuries, the turrets, battlements, towers and pinnacles of the house are a 19th-century fantasy. Amongst the many treasures to be seen inside are paintings by Van Dyck, Murillo, Holbein and other famous artists. Also here is the museum of the 17th/21st Lancers, the 'death or glory boys'. The castle's lovely terraced gardens are adorned with sculptures. Jousting tournaments will be held on 24-25 May, 28 Jun, 26 Jul, 30-31 Aug, 13 Sep.

(between A52 & A607)
☎ Grantham (0476) 870262

Open: Apr-Sep, Tue-Thu, Sat-Sun & BH Mon 11-5. Also Oct. Sun only.
Admission: £3.20 (ch & pen £2.20). Party 20+.
Jousting days 50p extra per person.
P ☕ ✕ licensed ♿ toilets for disabled shop garden centre 🐕̸

LINCOLN Lincoln Castle

Situated in the centre of Lincoln, the Castle, built in 1068 by William the Conqueror, dominates the Bailgate area alongside the great Cathedral. In addition to its many medieval features, Lincoln Castle has strong 19th-century connections and the unique Victorian prison chapel is perhaps the most awe-inspiring. The beautiful surroundings are ideal for historical adventures, picnics and special events which take place throughout the year. Among these is a Folk Festival in May and a Vintage Vehicle Rally in September.

Castle Hill
☎ (0522) 511068

Open: all year, British Summer Time Mon-Sat 9.30-5.30, Sun 11-5.30. Winter time Mon-Sat 9.30- 4, Sun 11-4. Last admission 30 mins before closing. (Closed 25-26 Dec & 1 Jan).
Admission: ✻ 80p (ch, pen & students 50p). Party 20+.
♿ (video theatre also accessible) shop 🐕̸

SKEGNESS Skegness Natureland Marine Zoo & Seal Sanctuary

The Zoo houses a specialised collection of animals including seals, penguins, tropical birds, aquarium, reptiles, Pets' Corner etc. Also free-flight tropical butterflies (May-Oct). Natureland is well known for its rescue of abandoned seal pups, and has successfully reared and returned to the wild a large number of these beautiful creatures. The new Seal Hospital Unit incorporates a public viewing area. Additional attractions include the Seal Life exhibition, floral displays and an Animal Brass Rubbing House.

North Pde
☎ (0754) 764345

Open: all year, Apr-Jun & Sep 10-5; Jul & Aug 10-6.30; Oct-Mar 10-4.30. (Closed 25-26 Dec & 1 Jan).
Admission: £2.50 (ch £1.50, pen £2). Party.
☕ ♿ shop

SPALDING   Butterfly & Falconry Park

The Park contains one of Britain's largest walk-through tropical houses, in which hundreds of butterflies from all over the world fly freely. Outside are 15 acres of butterfly and bee gardens, wildflower meadows, wildfowl and conservation ponds, nature trail, farm animals and a pets corner. At the new Falconry Centre, falcons, hawks and owls can be seen, the falcons give two displays every day.

Long Sutton
☎ **Holbeach (0406) 363833**

Open: 28 Mar-Sep, daily 10-6, Oct 10-5.
Admission: £2.80 (ch £1.80, pen £2.50).
Party.
🅿 ▮ ₺ (wheelchairs available) toilets for disabled shop garden centre ❌

SPALDING   Springfields Gardens

The 25-acre gardens provide an amazing spectacle in the spring when more than a million bulbs are blooming among the lawns and lakes. There are also glasshouses and a magnificent bedding display with over 200,000 plants during the summer season. Flower parade early May; other events throughout the year will be held in the new Exhibition Centre which opens in April.

Camelgate (on A151, signposted)
☎ **(0775) 724843**

Open: 27 Mar-4 Oct, daily 10-6.
Admission: £2.50 (accompanied ch free, pen £2.30). Special Events £3.
🅿 ▮ ✗ licensed ₺ (Free wheelchair hire) toilets for disabled shop garden centre ❌

MERSEYSIDE

LIVERPOOL   Animation World

A permanent exhibition of cartoon and animation, including hands-on displays, workshops and model studios and fantasy sets. Also original sets, models and drawings from children's favourite TV characters such as Count Duckula, Danger Mouse and Wind in the Willows.

Britannia Pavilion, Albert Dock
☎ **051-707 1828**

Open: all year, daily 10-6.
Admission: ✳ £3 (ch £2.50, pen & UB40 £2.70)
🅿 ₺ toilets for disabled shop ❌

LIVERPOOL   The Beatles Story

Winner of the English Tourist Board's 'Come to Britain' award 1991, the sights and sounds of the sixties can be relived at The Beatles Story. You can take a trip to Hamburg, 'feel' the cavern beat, 'tune in' to flower power, board the yellow submarine and battle with a Beatle brain computer.

Britannia Pavilion, Albert Dock
☎ **051-709 1963**

Open: all year, daily 10-6 (last admission 1 hr before closing). (Closed 25 & 26 Dec).
Admission: ✳ £3 (ch, pen & students £2, ch under 5 free). Family ticket £7.50
🅿 ₺ toilets for disabled shop ❌

LIVERPOOL   Croxteth Hall & Country Park

Visitors can step back in time and join an Edwardian house party when they visit the displays in Croxteth Hall: the Edwardian rooms are furnished with period pieces and character figures. The grounds of this former home of the Earls of Sefton contain a Victorian walled garden, a unique collection of rare breed animals, a miniature railway and an adventure playground. Croxteth Hall is a popular venue for special events; it also boasts an award-winning educational service.

(5m NE of city centre)
☎ **051-228 5311**

Open: all facilities daily 10.30-5 in season (phone for details); Some facilities remain open through winter, hours on request.
Admission: ✳ Hall 90p; Farm 90p; Walled Garden 50p. Inclusive ticket £2 (ch & pen £1).
🅿 ▮ ₺ toilets for disabled shop ❌ (ex in park & grounds)

LIVERPOOL   Liverpool Football Club Visitors Centre Museum

Come to Anfield and enjoy the magnificent display of trophies and mememtos representing the achievement of one of soccers most successful clubs. Experience and share some of the great moments in the club's history, captured on video.

Anfield Rd
☎ 051-263 2361
Open: all year, Mon-Fri. Tours starting at 2 & 3pm. (Closed Xmas wk).
Admission: ✳ £1.50 (ch & pen £1). Party 20+.
🅿 ⅃ shop ⑂

LIVERPOOL   Merseyside Maritime Museum

A large award-winning museum in restored 19th-century docklands, which includes a Boat Hall, Cooperage, and the Albert Dock Warehouse, containing varied displays about the Port of Liverpool. There are floating craft, outdoor exhibits of maritime crafts and demonstrations. Permanent displays include Emigrants to a New World, Art and the Sea and World of Models Galleries. From 12 May-25 October the Tall Ships exhibition will be open – a major photographic display of the work of David E Smith showing ships and crew at work.

Albert Dock
☎ 051-207 0001
Open: all year, daily 10.30-5.30 (last admission 4.30pm). (Closed Good Fri, 24-26 Dec & 1 Jan).
Admission: £1.50 (ch, pen, students & UB40's 75p). Family ticket £4.
🅿 (charged) ⬤ ✗ licensed ⅃ (Lifts & free wheelchair) toilets for disabled shop ⑂

PRESCOT   Knowsley Safari Park

A five-mile drive through the reserves enables visitors to see lions, tigers, elephants, rhinos, monkeys and many other animals. Extra attractions include a children's amusement park and pets' corner plus sealion shows and a miniature railway.

☎ 051-430 9009
Open: Game reserves Mar-Oct. Other attractions Etr-Sep. Daily 10-4.
Admission: £8 per car (incl all occupants). No soft-topped cars (safari bus available). Coach passengers £2.30 (ch 2-15 & pen £1.30).
🅿 ⬤ ⅃ toilets for disabled shop ⑂ (kennels provided)

SOUTHPORT   Southport Railway Centre

A thousand feet of standard gauge rail connects the museum to the British Rail system. Within the museum, are ex-British Rail locomotives as well as several industrial locomotives, and also on display are local buses, tramcars, traction engines and a variety of other vehicles, making up what is possibly the largest preservation centre of its type in north-west England. Special events are held from February to December (Santa Specials).

Derby Rd
☎ (0704) 530693
Open: all year, Oct-May, Sat & Sun 1-5; Jun-Sep, Sat & Sun 11-5; Jun & first wk Sep wkdays 1-4.30; Jul & Aug wkdays 10.30-4.30. Also BH periods 11-5.
Admission: Non Steam Days £1.50 (ch 80p, pen £1.20). Steam Days £1.80 (ch £1, pen £1.40).
🅿 ⬤ ⅃ toilets for disabled shop

SOUTHPORT   Southport Zoo

Within its five acres, the zoo has large and small mammals, duck and flamingo pools, and an assortment of aviaries. An aquarium and a reptile house with an alligator beach are unusual attractions. There is also a mandrill house, a Pets' Corner, Penguin Pool and a variety of monkeys. The new extension to the Zoo includes a giant tortoise house and enclosure, baby chimp house, and children's play area.

Princes Park
☎ (0704) 538102
Open: all year (ex 25 Dec) 10-6 in summer, 10-4 in winter,
Admission: ✳ £2.20 (ch £1.30, pen £1.70). Party 25+
⬤ ⅃ toilets for disabled shop

NORFOLK

BANHAM Banham Zoo & Appleyard Craft Court

Situated in over 20 acres of parkland and garden, this zoo specialises in rare and endangered species of animals and birds. Especially featured is the collection of monkeys and apes. There are also snow leopards, zebras, otters, seals, maned wolves, camels, macaws and flamingoes. Other facilities include an ice cream parlour, an indoor activity centre featuring a themed story room and new children's outdoor play area, plus a putting green and appleyard craft courtyard, adjoining the zoo complex. Special events are planned throughout the year including an Owl Week in February and a Conservation Week in October.

The Grove (on B1113)
☎ Quidenham (095387) 771

Open: all year, daily 10-6.30 (or dusk if earlier). (Closed 25-26 Dec).
Admission: ✻ £5 (ch 5-15 & pen £3). Disabled & party rates available.
P ☕ ♿ (wheelchair available) toilets for disabled shop 🐕

BRESSINGHAM Bressingham Steam Museum & Gardens

Alan Bloom is an internationally recognised nurseryman and also a steam enthusiast, and has combined his interests to great effect at Bressingham. There are four steam-hauled trains: a 9.5in gauge, a 15in gauge running through five miles of the wooded Waveney Valley, a 2ft gauge running through two miles of Europe's largest hardy plant nursery and a standard gauge engine giving footplate rides alongside the driver. There are six acres of informal gardens, with 5000 species of perennials and alpines, grouped in island beds; and there is a collection of 50 road and rail engines, mostly restored to working order. A steam roundabout is another attraction, and Norfolk fire museum is housed here. Various events are held here during the year including the 6th Annual Fire Rally on 2-6 August.

(on A1066)
☎ (037988) 386 & 382

Open: Apr-Oct, daily, 10-5.30. Also 29 Nov-20 Dec. Steam Days on Sun, Thu, BHs & Wed (Jul & Aug).
Admission: ✻ £3.50 (ch £2.50) Party 20+
P ☕ ✕ licensed ♿ toilets for disabled shop garden centre 🐕

CAISTER-ON-SEA Caister Castle, Motor Museum, Tower & Grounds

The collection consists of vehicles from 1893 to the present day. In the same grounds is the moated castle built by Sir John Falstaff (the original of Shakespeare's Falstaff) when he returned from Agincourt. The walls surround a 98ft tower, and also here is the 1951 Festival of Britain Tree Walk, removed from Battersea Park.

Caister Castle
☎ Wymondham (057284) 251

Open: Grounds mid May-Sep daily ex Sat 10.30-5.
P ☕ ♿ toilets for disabled shop

COCKLEY CLEY Iceni Village & Museums

A village of the Iceni tribe has been reconstructed here, as it was 2,000 years ago, on the site where it was believed there was an Iceni encampment. There is also a museum, in a 15th-century cottage forge, with models and exhibits of local life from prehistoric times to the present day; and there is a museum of agricultural equipment, vintage engines and carriages. The nearby flint church dates back to around 630. There is also a nature trail and picnic area.

(off A1065)
☎ Swaffham (0760) 721339 & 24588

Open: Apr-Oct, daily 12-5.30 (Jul-Sep 11-5.30).
Admission: £2.50 (ch 5-16 £1, pen & students £1.50). Party 10+.
P ♿ toilets for disabled shop

FILBY   Thrigby Hall Wildlife Gardens

The 250-year-old park of Thrigby Hall is now the home of animals and birds from Asia, and the lake has ornamental wildfowl. There are tropical and bird houses, a unique blue willow pattern garden and tree walk and a summer house as old as the park. An enormous jungled swamp hall is now open, with special features such as underwater viewing of large crocodiles.

(on unclass rd off A1064)
☎ **Great Yarmouth (0493) 369477**
Open: all year, daily 10-5.
Admission: £3.30 (ch £2, pen £2.80).
🅿 ☞ & (wheelchairs available) toilets for disabled shop 🖘

GRESSENHALL   Gressenhall Norfolk Rural Life Museum & Union Farm

This museum portrays the history of Norfolk over the past 200 years. Housed in what used to be a workhouse, it has displays on all aspects of rural life, with special emphasis on agriculture, rural crafts and village life, with working reconstructions. Union Farm is a typical small mixed farm of the 1920s with heavy horses and rare breeds of sheep, cattle, pigs and poultry. There is a nature trail around the farm.

Beech House (2.5m NW on unclass rd at Gressenhall)
☎**Dereham (0362) 860563**
Open: 12 Apr-1 Nov, Tue-Sat 10-5, Sun 2-5.30. Also BH Mons 10-5.
Admission: ✶ £2 (ch 60p, concessions £1).
🅿 ☞ & toilets for disabled shop 🖘

HORSHAM ST FAITH   City of Norwich Aviation Museum

Run entirely by enthusiastic volunteers, this museum offers displays relating to the aeronautical history of the local area, supported by a fine collection of aircraft, engines and equipment featuring the Vulcan bomber. Some of the aircraft cockpits are open to visitors. The location of the museum also offers a good vantage point for viewing aircraft using the airport.

Old Norwich Rd
☎ **Norwich (0603) 625309**
Open: all year, Apr-Oct Sun 10-5 (also Tue & Thu eves 7.30pm-dusk May, Jun, Jul & Aug only); Nov-Mar Sun 10-3.30
Admission: 75p (ch 25p & pen 50p)
🅿 & shop 🖘

HOUGHTON   Houghton Hall

This splendid Palladian house in beautiful parkland was built for Sir Robert Walpole. The staterooms have decorations and furniture by William Kent, and the harness room, coach house and stables may be seen (complete with heavy horses and Shetland ponies). There is a model soldier collection.

(1.25m off A148)
☎ **East Rudham (048522) 569**
Open: Etr Sun-last Sun Sep, Thu, Sun & BH's 12.30-5.30.
🅿 ☞ & toilets for disabled shop
Details not confirmed for 1992

REEDHAM   Pettitts Feathercraft & Animal Adventure Park

Pettitts have aviaries where peacocks, ornamental pheasants, birds of prey and parrots are displayed. There are also waterfowl on show in their gardens, which are surrounded by a picnic area. The arts of feather craft and dip-and-carve American-style candles are demonstrated, and the products are on sale. Other attractions include a miniature horse stud, deer petting park, crazy golf, a large adventure playground with amusement rides, live entertainment and children's shows; and a half mile miniature railway. A gnome village and an American-style locomotive ride around the grounds are newly opened for 1992, also a

(on B1140)
☎ **Great Yarmouth (0493) 700094**
Open: Etr Sun-Oct, daily 10-5.30. (Closed Sat).
Admission: £3.50 (ch & pen £2.50). Disabled & helpers £2.50. Party.
🅿 ☞ ✕ & toilets for disabled shop

6-acre car park. Easy access makes Pettitts suitable for the elderly and disabled, there are purpose-built toilets for wheelchair-users and wheelchairs can be taken on a specially adapted truck on the train. Special events are planned throughout the season.

SAXTHORPE   Mannington Gardens & Countryside

The moated manor house, built in 1460 and still a family home forms a centre- piece for the pretty gardens which surround it. Visitors can enjoy the roses – the chief feature of the gardens – and also lovely countryside walks. Special events take place throughout the season, including Nature Discovery Days for children. Special events for 1992 include: 24 May, Countryside Activities Day; 27-28 Jun, Rose Festival; 6 Sep, Charities Fair.

(2.25m NE)
☎ **(026387) 4175**

Open: Gardens May-Aug, Wed-Fri 11-5; also Sun noon-5 Etr-Oct. Walks open every day from 9am. Hall open by prior appointment only.
Admission: Garden £2 (accompanied ch 16 free, students & pen £1.50). Walks free (car park for walkers 50p).
🅿 (charged) ☛ ዿ toilets for disabled shop garden centre ✗

SHERINGHAM   North Norfolk Railway

A steam railway with trains operating on certain days from Easter to October, with extra days as the season progresses and a daily service in August. On Sundays, lunch is served on the train. At the station is a collection of steam locomotives and rolling stock, some of which are undergoing or awaiting restoration. These include several industrial tank engines and ex-Great Eastern mainline engines. The rolling stock includes suburban coaches, the Brighton Belle, Pullmans and directors' private saloons and a vintage buffet saloon. There is also a museum of railway memorabilia and a souvenir and book shop.

Sheringham Station
☎ **(0263) 822045**

Open: Etr-Oct; Aug (daily); Dec (Santa special). Telephone (0263) 825449 for timetable.
✷ Return £4.50 (ch £2.30, pen £3.60). Family ticket £12.50. Party 20+.
☛ ዿ shop

SNETTISHAM   Park Farm

You can see farming in action here with lambing in the spring, sheep shearing in May and deer calving in June and July. Sheep, goats, lambs, rabbits, turkeys, ducks, chickens, ponies, piglets etc can be seen in the paddocks, there is a Sheep Centre and you can take a safari ride around the estate to see the magnificent herd of red deer. There is a large adventure playground, an indoor adventure area, mini golf and pedal buggies for the children and an indoor picnic area. Special events for 1992 include: 16-17 May, Craft Fayre; 23-25 May, Sheep Shearing with world champion shearer.

☎ **Dersingham (0485) 542425**
Open: 29 Mar-1 Nov, daily 10.30-5.
Admission: ✷ £3 (ch £2, pen £2.50). Party 10+.
🅿 ☛ ዿ toilets for disabled shop ✗ (ex on farm trails)

THURSFORD GREEN   Thursford Collection

This exciting collection specialises in organs, with a Wurlitzer cinema organ, fairground organs, barrel organs and street organs among its treasures. There are live musical shows every day; featuring all the material organs

(1m off A148)
☎ **Fakenham (0328) 878477**
Open: Apr-Oct, daily 1-5. (Jun-Aug 11-5).

and the Wurtlizter show, extra Wurlitzer concerts are given by the leading organists on Tuesdays at 8pm throughout the summer. The collection also includes showmen's engines, ploughing engines and a 2ft gauge steam railway, as well as farm machinery. There is a children's play area and a breathtaking 'Venetian gondola' switchback ride.

Admission: ✻ £4 (ch 4-14 £1.80, pen £3.60, ch under 4 free). Party 15+.
P ☕ ♿ toilets for disabled shop 🐕

WELLS-NEXT-THE-SEA Wells & Walsingham Light Railway

The railway covers the four miles between Wells and Walsingham. It is unusual in that it uses ten and a quarter inch gauge track and is the longest track of this width in Britain. The line passes through some very attractive countryside, particularly noted for its wild flowers and butterflies. This is the home of the unique Garratt Steam Locomotive specially built for this line.

(A149 Cromer Rd)
(Wells Station Sheringham Rd (A149); Walsingham Station Egmere Rd)

Open: Good Fri-Sep, daily.
£3.50 (ch £2.20). Return.
P ☕ ♿ shop

WELNEY Wildfowl & Wetlands Trust

Probably the best time to visit this refuge on the Ouse Washes is during the winter, when the 920-acre site is home to some 5000 migratory swans and vast numbers of wild ducks and geese. Bewick and whooper swans as well as wigeon and pintail ducks can be seen.

In the spring, the whole refuge is alive with nesting birds including redshank, snipe, ruff and blacktailed godwit, and in the summer there is a trail to view the resident wildfowl. There are numerous hides and also a spacious observatory. On winter evenings the lagoon is floodlit to show hundreds of wild Bewick's swans.

Pintail House, Hundred Foot Bank (off A1101, N of Ely)
☎ Ely (0353) 860711

Open: all year, daily 10-5. (Closed 24-25 Dec).
P ☕ ♿ toilets for disabled shop 🐕
Details not confirmed for 1992

WEST RUNTON Norfolk Shire Horse Centre

The Shire Horse Centre has a collection of draught horses and nine breeds of mountain and moorland ponies. There are also exhibits of horse-drawn machinery, waggons and carts, and harnessing and working demonstrations are given twice every day. Other attractions include a photographic display of draught horses past and present, talks and a video show. There is a riding school on the premises as well. There are many events planned for 1992 from a programme of working demonstrations, mornings and afternoons, to day events such as sheep dog days or timberloding days.

West Runton Stables (on A149)
☎ (026375) 339

Open: Good Fri-Oct, Sun-Fri, 10-5. Shire Horse demonstrations 11.15 & 3. School parties by appointment.
Admission: ✻ £3 (ch £1.50, pen £2). Party 10+.
P ☕ ✕ ♿ toilets for disabled shop

WITCHINGHAM, GREAT Norfolk Wildlife Park

This wildlife park offers a large collection of British and European wildlife. The animals can be viewed in semi-natural surroundings set in 40 acres of beautiful parkland. Britain's only team of trained reindeer pull their wheeled sledge round the park, and there are tame animals to fascinate both young and old. There are also exciting Commando play areas, an electonic Theme Hall, a narrow gauge Steam Railway and a trout pool.

(on A1067)
☎ Norwich (0603) 872274

Open: all year, daily 10.30-6 or dusk.
P ☕ ♿ shop 🐕
Details not confirmed for 1992

YARMOUTH, GREAT Merivale Model Village

Set in attractive landscaped gardens, this comprehensive miniature village is built on a scale of 1:12. The layout includes a two and a half inch gauge model railway, radio-controlled boats, and over 200 models set in an acre of landscaped gardens. There are additional amusements, children's rides and remote-controlled cars. During the summer, from June to October, the gardens are illuminated after dusk.

Wellington Pier Gardens, Marine Pde
☎ Great Yarmouth (0493) 842097

Open: Etr 9.30-6, Jun-Sep 9.30-10
Admission: ✻ £2 (ch 3-14 £1)
☕ ♿ shop

NORTH YORKSHIRE

BENINGBROUGH Beningbrough Hall

Beningbrough was built around 1716, and its structure has hardly been altered since then. It houses 100 pictures from the National Portrait Gallery in London. Perhaps the finest feature of the house is the Great Staircase, built of oak with wide parquetried treads and delicate balusters carved to imitate wrought iron. Ornately carved wood panelling is a feature of several of the rooms, notably the drawing room. The other side of country house life can be seen in the restored Victorian laundry, which has its original stoves, drying racks and other equipment. The gardens include formal areas, a conservatory and a wilderness play area. Events for 1992 include: 4 Apr-4 May, exhibition of etchings by Janet Evans; 28 Jun, Edwardian picnic with music – in costume – 1-5pm; 16 Aug, Family fun day – 1pm.

(off A19. Entrance at Newton Lodge)
☎ (0904) 470666

Open: 4 Apr-Jun & Sep-Oct, Tue-Thu, wknds, Good Fri & BH Mon; Jul-Aug, daily (ex Mon) 11-5. Last admission 4.30pm. Grounds, shop & restaurant 11-5.30.
Admission: House, garden & exhibition: £4 (ch £2) Family ticket £10. Garden & exhibitions: £2.50 (ch £1.20) Family £6.20. Party.
P ✕ licensed ♿ toilets for disabled shop 🐕 (NT)

CARLTON Carlton Towers

The Yorkshire home of the Dukes of Norfolk, Carlton Towers was first built in 1614, on land owned by the family since the Norman Conquest. It was altered in the 18th and 19th centuries, and its present appearance is a product of the 1870s, when it was remodelled in an ornate, High Victorian manner. The elaborate state rooms with their sumptuous decorations were designed by John Francis Bentley, the architect of Westminster Cathedral. A priest's hiding place can be seen, and there are collections of interesting paintings, furniture, silver and heraldry. Various events are held including: 23-26 May, a Spring Bank Holiday flower festival; 26 Jul, Annual Vintage Car Rally; 29-31 Aug, Festival of Fashion and Craft.

☎ Goole (0405) 861662

Open: May-Sep, Sun & BHs. Parties any day by arrangement, plus Thu evening when a guided tour will be given, approx one and a half hours.
Admission: £2.50 (ch £1.50, under 5 free, pen £2). Guided tours 20+.
P ☕ ♿ toilets for disabled shop 🐕

DANBY The Moors Centre

The former shooting lodge provides information on the North York Moors National Park, with an exhibition, video and bookshop information desk. There are riverside and woodland grounds, with terraced gardens, a children's play area and a brass-rubbing centre. Special events are held in summer.

Lodge Ln
☎ Guisborough (0287) 660654

Open: all year, Apr-Oct, daily 10-5; Nov-Mar, Sun 11-4; (Guided walks Jul-Aug, Sun only).
Admission: Free.
P ☕ ♿ (woodland & garden trails) toilets for disabled shop 🐕

ELVINGTON   Yorkshire Air Museum & Allied Air Forces Memorial

The aim of this museum is to preserve part of a typical wartime airfield as a memorial to the allied air and ground crews who served in World War II – in particular, the many thousands who served in the Yorkshire and Humberside area. Visitors can see many of the fine aircraft including the last Lightning, and enter the original Flying Control Tower. Displays include engines, models and photographs and there is even a friendly NAAFI offering modern home cooking. The whole museum recreates the sights, sounds (and even the smells!) of an authentic wartime base.

☎ (090485) 595

Open: 29 Mar-10 Nov, Tue-Thu 11-4, Sat & Sun noon-5, BH's 11-5.
🄿 ⯑ ✗ licensed ♿ shop
Details not confirmed for 1992

KIRBY MISPERTON   Flamingo Land Zoo & Family Funpark

With an 18th-century house as a backdrop, this vast 'adventure playground' has appeal for all the family. Funfair rides, exhibitions, a large lake and over 1,000 animals are just some of the many attractions.

The Rectory (off the A169)
☎ (065386) 287

Open: Apr-Sep, daily 10-5 or 6 according to season. Also school hol & wknds in Oct 10-5.
Admission: ✴ £6 (ch under 4 free). Party 20+.
🄿 ⯑ ♿ (parking) toilets for disabled shop

MALTON   Castle Howard

In its dramatic setting of lakes, fountains and extensive gardens, this 18th- century palace was designed by Sir John Vanbrugh. Principal location for the TV series 'Brideshead Revisited', this was the first major achievement of the architect who later created the lavish Blenheim Palace near Oxford. Castle Howard was begun in 1699 for the 3rd Earl of Carlisle, Charles Howard, whose descendants still call the place 'home'. The striking façade is topped by an 80ft painted and gilded dome. The interior has a 192ft Long Gallery, as well as a Chapel with magnificent stained glass windows by the 19th-century artist, Edward Burne-Jones. Besides the collections of antique furniture, porcelain and sculpture, the Castle contains a number of important paintings, including a portrait of Henry VIII by Holbein and works by Rubens, Reynolds and Gainsborough. The grounds include the domed Temple of the Four Winds by Vanbrugh, and the richly designed family Mausoleum by Hawksmoor. The Rose Garden contains both old-fashioned and modern varieties of roses.

Ray Wood is a 30-acre area with unique collections of rare trees, shrubs, rhododendrons and azaleas, while Stable Court houses the internationally famous Costume Galleries which contain the largest private collection of period costume in Britain. Displays are changed annually and include a replica collection of Crown Jewels.

☎ Coneysthorpe (065384) 333

Open: 1-24 Mar Grounds only. 25 Mar-1 Nov, Grounds & Plant Centre 10, House & Costume Galleries 11. Last admissions 4.30pm.
Admission: £5.50 (ch £2.50, pen £4.50). Party 12+.
🄿 ⯑ ✗ licensed ♿ (chairlift, free adapted transport to house) toilets for disabled shop garden centre ⯑

SYMBOLS			
☎ Telephone number	✴ Indicates 1991 price	⯑ Refreshments	⯑ No Dogs
♿ Suitable for visitors in wheelchairs	🄿 Parking at Establishment	✗ Restaurant	⯑ No coaches

MALTON   Eden Camp Modern History Theme Museum

The story of the peoples' war – the drama, the hardships, the humour – unfolds in this museum devoted to civilian life in World War II. The displays, covering the blackout, rationing, the Blitz, the Homeguard and others, are housed in a former prisoner-of-war camp built in 1942 for German and Italian soldiers. Large toilet cubicles with handles for wheelchair visitors; tapes and braille cards for the blind. On 30-31 May, a 50th anniversary display will include 50 years as a POW camp and 5 years as a museum.

(junc of A64 & A169)
☎ (0653) 697777
Open: 14 Feb-23 Dec, daily 10-5. Last admission 4pm.
Admission: £3 (ch & pen £2). Party 10+.
🅿 ♨ ♿ (taped tours, Braille guides) toilets for disabled shop

MIDDLEHAM   Middleham Castle

The town of Middleham (much of which is a conservation area) is dominated by the 12th-century keep which saw its great days during the Wars of the Roses. The seat of the Neville family, the Earls of Warwick, it was the home for a time of the young King Richard III, then Duke of Gloucester, who married the Earl's daughter Anne Neville.

☎ Wensleydale (0969) 23899
Open: all year, Apr-Sep, daily 10-6; Oct-Mar, Tue-Sun 10-4. (Closed 24-26 Dec & 1 Jan).
Admission: £1.10 (ch 55p, pen, students & UB40 85p).
shop (EH)

NEWBY HALL & GARDENS

This late 17th-century house had its interior and additions designed by Robert Adam, and contains an important collection of classical sculpture and Gobelin tapestries. In addition to the formal Gardens' 25 acres are a miniature railway, an adventure garden for children, and a woodland discovery walk. Special events take place throughout the year, including on 16-17 May, Carriage Driving; 14 June, Country Fair; 20-21 June and 19-20 Sep, Craft Fairs; 19 Jul, Historic Vehicle Rally.

(4m SE off B6265)
☎ Boroughbridge (0423) 322583
Open: 28 Mar-29 Sep, Tue-Sun & BH's; Gardens 11-5.30; House 12-5. Last admission 5pm.
Admission: House & Garden £4.80, (ch & disabled £2.70, pen £3.80). Gardens only £2.70 (ch & disabled £2, pen £2.30). Party.
🅿 ♨ ✗ licensed ♿ (wheelchairs available, maps of wheelchair routes) toilets for disabled shop garden centre ♥

NORTH STAINLEY   Lightwater Valley Theme Park

Set in 125-acres of country park and lakeland, Lightwater Valley offers a selection of rides and attractions suitable for all the family. Enjoy the white-knuckle thrills of the world's biggest roller coaster, Soopa Loopa, the Rat and the Wave or, for the less adventurous, there is the steam train, boating lake or country sports. There is also live family entertainment and shopping malls.

(on the A6108)
☎ Ripon (0765) 635368 & 635321
Open: 11-26 Apr; 2-4, 9-10, 16-17 & 23-31 May; Jun Wed-Sun; Jul-Aug daily; 1-6 Sep & wknds; Oct Sun only.
✳ Telephone for details.
🅿 ♨ ✗ licensed ♿ toilets for disabled shop ♥

PICKERING   North Yorkshire Moors Railway

Operating through the heart of the North York Moors National Park between Pickering and Grosmont, steam trains cover a distance of 18 miles. Beautiful Newtondale Halt gives walkers easy access to forest and moorland. The locomotive sheds at Pickering are open to the public. 1992 marks the Railway's 25th anniversary.

Pickering Station
☎ (0751) 73535
Open: Etr-Oct, daily. Dec, Santa Specials.
Admission: ✳ Return fr £4.80. Special rates for pen (ex Jun-Aug). Family ticket.
🅿 (charged) ♨ ✗ licensed ♿ (ramp for trains) toilets for disabled shop
For **Ripon** and **Sutton-on-the-Forest** see page 114

With its medieval streets and city walls, its splendid Minster and its Viking heritage, York has plenty to occupy more than just a single day out. Although it has a sizeable city, its main attractions are fairly concentrated within the old walls and a good introduction would be to walk around the top of those sections which still stand. From here you will get some of the best views of the Minster, the largest Gothic cathedral in northern Europe where you can see remnants of Roman, Anglo-Saxon and Norman work alongside the mightly 20th-century underpinning. There is some remarkable stained glass and a wonderful view from the tower. The World of the Minster, housed in the 15th-century timber-framed St William's College, offers an insight into the life and times of Minster people over 800 years.

Don't miss a stroll down The Shambles, where the buildings haven't changed much since the Middle Ages. Other places to see include the 14th-century Merchant Adventurer's Hall, Fairfax House, a Georgian mansion, Treasurer's House and Clifford's Tower, all that is left of York Castle. The ruins of St Mary's Abbey are a backdrop to the medieval miracle plays which are performed in the botanical garden each summer, and the interesting Yorkshire Museum is nearby. Free guided walks leave the Tourist Information Office twice daily and sometimes in the evening too; there are also boat trips on the River Ouse.

Tourist information: De Grey Rooms, Exhibition Square Telephone: (0904) 6212756

☆ *STAR ATTRACTIONS*

Jorvik Viking Centre

Jorvik was the Viking name for York. Between 1976 and 1981 archaeologists made some remarkable discoveries about Jorvik, during a dig in an area known as Coppergate. In 1984 the Viking Centre was opened over the site of the original excavations. The dig shed a totally new light on the Viking way of life and has revealed many details of tools, clothing, crafts and trade. The Centre displays the archaeological remains – leather, textiles, metal objects and even timber buildings – in a detailed and vivid reconstruction. First there is an audio-visual display to explain exactly who the Vikings were. Then, 'time-cars' carry visitors through a 'time tunnel' from World War II back to Norman times and then to a full-scale recon-struction of 10th-century Coppergate. The busy street scene includes a crowded market, a river wharf with a fully-rigged sailing ship and a family at home. This is all made more authentic by voices speaking in Old Norse and even smells such as cooking, fish, pigsties and rubbish! Finally the tour passes through a reconstruction of Coppergate during the dig of the 1970s. The visit ends in the Skipper Gallery which has a display of some of the 15,000 small objects found during the dig.

Coppergate
☎ (0904) 643211

Open: all year, Apr-Oct daily 9-7; Nov-Mar daily 9-5.30. (Closed 25 Dec).
Admission: ✳ £3.50 (ch £1.75). (pen £2.60 Nov-Mar only).
⅊ (time car designed to take a wheelchair) toilets for disabled shop ⍾

The York Dungeon

The blood and thunder of Britain's past comes to life in the York Dungeon, where life-size tableaux depict super-stition, pain, torture and death in spine-chilling detail. From the moment you enter, eerie sound effects and dramatic lighting create a fascinating atmosphere. The cold chill of horror is based on the realities of our ancestors' lives, through carefully researched historical facts.

12 Clifford St
☎ (0904) 632599

Open: all year, daily from 10am
Admission: ✳ £2.75 (ch & pen £1.75, under 5's free)
⅊ shop

Museum of Automata

The Museum of Automata appeals to adults and children alike, with a unique collection of ingenious machines spanning 2000 years from simple articulated figurines from ancient civilisations to modern day robots. The French Gallery contains a throng of musicians, clowns, artists and eccentrics from Parisian cafe society, brought to life by video, sound and lighting. Visitors can crank exhibits into action in the Contemporary Gallery, and there's a reconstruction of a saucy 1950s seaside pier.

Tower St
☎ **(0904) 655550**

Open: all year, daily 9.30-5.30. (Closed 25 Dec)
Admission: ❊ £2.85 (ch £1.50, pen & students £2.20)
♿ toilets for disabled shop 🐕

National Railway Museum

Wednesday 15 April 1992 will be the first time visitors will see the greatly expanded National Railway Museum with its new displays and exhibitions telling the story of British railways up to the present day. The opening of the Great Hall will enable the Museum to double its display space and focus on the technical aspects of railway development. Visitors will see famous locomotives explaining the evolution of motive power with displays highlighting design and safety on railways as well as the Channel Tunnel. The exhibition 'The Great Railway Show' will continue to highlight the social history connected with travelling by train, including the story of Royal travel.

Leeman Rd
☎ **(0904) 621261**

Open: all year, Mon-Sat 10-6, Sun 11-6. (Closed 24-26 Dec & 1 Jan).
Admission: ❊ £3 (ch £1.50 under 5 free, pen £2). Party 15+.
P (charged) ✕ licensed ♿ ("Please Touch" evenings) toilets for disabled shop 🐕

Rail Riders World

One of the biggest and best model railway museums in Britain, Rail Riders World has two very intricate railway layouts. The larger one is set in town and country landscapes. It comprises hundreds of buildings, about 5,500 tiny trees, over 2,000 lights and around 2,500 people and animals. As many as 20 trains can run in this model at the same time, including the Royal Train, the Orient Express, Inter City 125 and the latest freight and passenger trains.

The second model is a much smaller layout and shows a typical German town at night, brightly lit by numerous tiny lights. There are push buttons for children, amid these detailed and accurate scale models.

York BR Station, Tearoom Square
☎ **(0904) 630169**

Open: daily 10-6 (Last admission 5.30pm). (Closed 24-26 Dec, 15 Jan-9 Feb & 19 Feb-1 Mar).
♿ shop 🐕
Details not confirmed for 1992

York Castle Museum

Four centuries of everyday life are exhibited in the Castle Museum, imaginatively displayed through reconstructions of period rooms and two indoor streets, complete with cobbles, a Hansom cab and a park. The museum is housed in the city's prison and is based on an extensive collection of 'bygones' acquired at the beginning of the century. It was one of the first folk museums to display a huge range of everyday objects in an authentic scene. The Victorian street includes a pawnbroker, a tallow candle factory and a haberdasher's. There is even a reconstruction of the original sweet shop of the York chocolate manufacturer, Joseph Terry. An extensive collection of many other items from musical instruments to costumes, and a gallery of domestic gadgets from Victorian times to the 1960s entitled 'Every home should have one' are further attractions to this remarkable museum. The museum also has one of Britain's finest collections of Militaria; this includes a superb example of an Anglo-Saxon helmet – one of only three known.

The Eye of York
☎ **(0904) 653611**

Open: all year, Apr-Oct Mon-Sat 9.30-5.30, Sun 10-5.30; Nov-Mar, Mon-Sat 9.30-4, Sun 10-4. (Closed 25-26 Dec & 1 Jan).
Admission: £3.35 (ch, pen, students & UB40 £2.35). Family ticket £9.40. Party 20+.
☕ ♿ toilets for disabled shop 🐕

RIPON   Fountains Abbey & Studley Royal

Founded by Cistercian monks in 1132, Fountains Abbey is the largest monastic ruin in Britain. It was acquired by William Aislabie in 1768, and became the focal point of his landscaped gardens at Studley. These include formal water gardens, ornamental temples, follies and magnificent views. They are bordered by a lake and 400 acres of deer park. Other interesting features include Fountains Hall, built between 1598 and 1611 using the stone from the abbey ruins. Special events for 1992 include: 20 Jun, Music in the Water Garden – City of London Sinfonia plus fireworks, 8pm; 26 Dec, Boxing Day Pilgrimage – Walk from Ripon Cathedral to Fountains Abbey (4 miles) and return.

(2m SW off B6265)
☎ Sawley (0765) 620333

Open: all year. Abbey & garden: Jan-Mar, Nov & Dec, daily (ex 24 & 25 Dec, & Fri Nov-Jan), 10-5 or dusk if earlier; Apr-Jun & Sep 10-7; Jul & Aug 10-8; Oct 10-6 or dusk if earlier. Fountains Hall: Apr-Oct 11-6; Nov-Mar 11-4. St Mary's Church: 29 Mar-Sep, 1-5.
Admission: Jan-Mar: £2.70 (ch £1.30). Family ticket £6.70. Apr-Oct: £3.50 (ch £1.60). Family ticket £8.60. Nov-Mar 1993: £3 (ch £1.50). Family ticket £7.50. Party 15+.
🅿 ▣ ৬ toilets for disabled shop (NT)

SUTTON-ON-THE-FOREST   Sutton Park

An early Georgian house (built in 1730). Sutton Park contains some fine antique furniture by Chippendale and Sheraton, paintings and a good collection of porcelain. The grounds have superb terraced gardens, a lily pond and a Georgian ice house. There are also delightful woodland walks and a nature trail as well as spaces for caravans.

(on B1363)
☎ Easingwold (0347) 810249

Open: Gardens Etr-Oct, daily from 11am. House Etr wknd then May-Sep, Wed & BH Sun & Mon from 1.30. Private parties by arrangement daily ex Sat.
Admission: £3 (ch £1.50, pen £2.50). Gardens only £1 (ch 50p). Party.
🅿 ▣ ৬ shop ✷ (ex gardens)

YORK   see page 112

NORTHAMPTONSHIRE

HOLDENBY   Holdenby House Gardens

The gardens have been restored in the style of Elizabethan times (when this was the largest house in England), and have fragrant and silver borders. Also here are a museum, rare breeds of farm animals and a falconry centre. There is a children's farm and craft shop. Special events are planned for May; on Easter Sunday and Monday there will be an Easter Egg Hunt, and in September a Falconry Fair will be held.

(off A50 or A428)
☎ Northampton (0604) 770074

Open: Etr-Sep, BH & Sun 2-6; Jul & Aug, Thu 2-6. Parties 20+ by appointment Mon-Fri. Falconry Centre open Mon-Sat noon-5.
Admission: Gardens £2.50 (ch £1.20, pen £1.70). House & Gardens £3.50 (ch £1.20).
🅿 ▣ ৬ (gravel paths) toilets for disabled shop garden centre ✷

ABBREVIATIONS					
AM	Ancient Monument	BH	Bank Holidays	ch 15 20p	Children under 15 20p
AM(CadW)	Ancient Monument	PH	Public Holidays	Pen	Senior Citizens
	(Wales)	Etr	Easter	Party	Special or reduced rates for
EH	English Heritage	ex	except		parties booked in advance
NT	National Trust	Free	Admission free	Party 30+	Special or reduced rates for
NTS	National Trust for	10p	Admission 10p		parties of 30 or more booked
	Scotland	ch 20p	Children 20p		in advance

STOKE BRUERNE   Canal Museum

The three storeys of a former corn mill have been converted to hold a marvellous collection of bygones from over two centuries of the canals. The museum is near a flight of locks on the Grand Union Canal. Among the hundreds of exhibits is the reconstructed interior of a traditional narrow boat, complete with furniture, crockery, brassware and traditional art. There are genuine working narrowboats on show and the opportunity for a boat trip through the mile-long Blisworth Tunnel nearby. On 27-28 June there will be a national exhibition by waterways artists in a marquee by the canal, 11am-9pm, admission free.

(4m S junc 15 M1)
☎ Northampton (0604) 862229
Open: Nov-Etr, Tue-Sun 10-4; Etr-Oct daily 10-6. (Closed Xmas).
Admission: £1.90 (ch & pen £1.20). Family ticket £5.
🅿 & toilets for disabled shop 🎪

WEEDON BEC   Old Dairy Farm Craft Centre

There are sheep, pigs, peacocks, ducks and donkeys. Features include a British wool collection, live sheep exhibits, craft workshop, gifts, Liberty materials, antiques and farm shop. The Barn Restaurant serves homemade food.

Upper Stowe (2m S of Weedon off A5)
☎ Weedon (0327) 40525
Open: all year, daily 10-5.30. (Closed 25 & 26 Dec).
🅿 ☕ ✗ & toilets for disabled shop 🎪
Details not confirmed for 1992

NORTHUMBERLAND

BAMBURGH   Bamburgh Castle

Rising up dramatically on a rocky outcrop, Bamburgh Castle is a huge, square Norman castle. It was restored in the 19th century by Lord Armstrong, and has an impressive hall, an armoury with a large collection of armour from HM Tower of London. Guide services are available.

☎ (06684) 208 & 515
Open: daily, Apr-last Sun Oct; Jul & Aug from noon; Apr-Jun & Sep-Oct from 1pm.
Admission: ✳ £2.20 (ch £1, pen £1.80). Party.
🅿 (charged) ☕ & shop 🎪

BARDON MILL   Vindolanda (Chesterholm)

Vindolanda was a Roman fort and frontier town, with remains dating back to the 3rd and 4th centuries. It was started well before Hadrian's Wall, and became a base for 500 soldiers. The headquarters building is well preserved, and a special feature is a full-scale reconstruction of Hadrian's turf and stone wall, complete with turret and gate tower. The civilian settlement lay just west of the fort, and has been excavated. A vivid idea of life for both civilians and soldiers can be gained at the excellent museum in the country house of Chesterholm nearby. It has displays and reconstructions, and its exhibits include homely finds such as sandals, shoes and a soldier's sewing kit. There are also formal gardens. Excavation will be in progress during the summer months.

Vindolanda Trust
☎ (0434) 344277
Open: daily from 10 am. (Closed Jan & Dec).
Admission: £2 (ch £1, student & pen £1.50).
🅿 ☕ & toilets for disabled shop 🎪

CARRAWBROUGH   Roman Wall (Mithraic Temple)

A farmer found the Mithraic Temple in 1949. It was
excavated to reveal three altars to Mithras which date from
the third century AD. They are now in the Museum of
Antiquities in Newcastle, but there are copies on the site.
The temple is on the line of the Roman wall near the fort of
Brocolitia.

(on B6318)
Open: any reasonable time.
Admission: Free.
🅿
(EH)

CHILLINGHAM   Chillingham Castle

After a period of neglect, the castle has been brought back
to life by a new owner. It dates back to the 12th century,
and has a great hall and state rooms where antique
furniture, tapestries, arms and armour are displayed.
There are formal gardens, woodland walks and a lake. A
BASC country fair will take place on 10 May.

☎ Chatton (06685) 359 & 390
Open: Etr wknd & May-Sep, daily (ex Tue)
1.30-5. (Last admission 4.30pm).
Admission: £2.50 (ch £1.80, ch under 5
Free, pen £2). Party 20+.
🅿 ☕ shop ⛶

CHILLINGHAM   Chillingham Wild Cattle Park

The park at Chillingham boasts an extraordinary survival: a
herd of wild white cattle descended from animals trapped in
the park when the wall was built in the 13th century; they
are the sole surviving pure-bred examples of their breed in
the world. Binoculars are recommended for a close view.
As the cattle are aggressive and should not be approached,
visits are made with a warden.

(Off B6348)
☎ Chatton (06685) 250
Open: Apr-Oct, daily 10-12 & 2-5, Sun 2-5.
Closed Tue.
🅿 ⛶
Details not confirmed for 1992

CORBRIDGE   Corbridge Roman Site

The remains of a Roman 'Corstopitum', built around
AD210, include granaries, portico columns and the prob-
able site of legionary headquarters. Finds from excavations
of the site are displayed in a museum on the site.

☎ (0434) 632349
Open: all year, Apr-Sep, daily 10-6; Oct-
Mar, Tue-Sun 10-4. (Closed 24-26 Dec &
1 Jan).
Admission: £1.80 (ch 90p, pen, students &
UB40 £1.40).
🅿 ♿ ⛶
(EH)

GILSLAND   Birdoswald Roman Fort

This unique section of Hadrian's Wall enjoys a most
picturesque setting overlooking the Irthing Gorge. There
is no other point along the Wall where all the components
of the Roman frontier system can be found together. But
Birdoswald isn't just about the Romans, it's also about
border raids in the Middle Ages, about the Victorians, and
about recent archaeological discoveries. A new Visitor
Centre brings its fascinating history to life.

(.25m S in Cumbria)
☎ (06977) 47602
Open: Apr-1 Nov, daily 10-5.30. Winter
opening by prior arrangement only.
Admission: £1.50 (ch 75p, concessions £1).
🅿 ♿ toilets for disabled shop

HADRIAN'S WALL   see Bardon Mill, Carrawbrough, Corbridge, Gilsland,
   Housesteads & Walwick.

HOUSESTEADS   Roman Wall (Housesteads Fort & Museum)

Housesteads was the Roman fort of *Vercovicium* It has a spectacular site on Hadrian's Wall, and is also one of the best preserved Roman forts. It covers five acres, including the only known Roman hospital in Britain, and a 24-seater latrine with a flushing tank. There is also a museum.

Nr Bardon Mills
☎ **Bardon Mill (0434) 344363**

Open: all year, Good Fri-Sep, daily 10-6; Oct-Maundy Thu, daily 10-4. (Closed 24-26 Dec & 1 Jan).
Admission: ✳ £1.60 (ch 16 80p, students, pen & UB40s £1.20). Party reductions in winter.
shop ⊮
(EH & NT)

ROTHBURY   Cragside House, County Park & Garden

This splendid Victorian masterpiece was built for Sir William (later the first Lord) Armstrong in stages, between 1864 and 1895. It was designed for him by the architect Richard Norman Shaw and the interior of the house reflects the taste and style of both its architect and its owner. The drawing room is huge, with a curved glass roof and 10-ton marble-lined inglenook designed to soak up the heat of the peat fires. This was the first house in the world to be lit by electricity generated by water-power. The grounds, now 900 acres of country park, were transformed by Lord Armstrong. He planted seven million trees, diverted streams and created lakes, a waterfall, terraces, winding paths, gardens and orchards. Open in 1992: formal garden including greenhouses, Italian terraces and rose loggia.

(Entrance for cars 2m N on B6341)
☎ **(0669) 20333**

Open: all year, Country Park & garden: daily, 10.30-7; Nov & Dec, Tue & wknds 10.30-4. House: Apr-Oct, daily (ex Mon, Open BH Mon's) 1-5.30. Last admission 5pm. Armstrong Energy Centre open Apr-Oct daily, 10.30-5.30; Nov & Dec, Tues & wknds, 10.30-4;
Admission: House, Country Park, Garden & Energy Centre £5.20. Country Park, Garden & Energy Centre only £3.20. Party.
🅿 ☞ ✗ licensed ⅋ toilets for disabled shop ⊮
(NT)

WALWICK   Chesters Roman Fort & Museum

One of the Roman forts on Hadrian's Wall is now in the park of Chesters, an 18th-century mansion. The fort named *Cilurnum* housed 500 soldiers and covered nearly 6 acres. The excavations were started in the 19th century by the owner of Chesters, and have revealed a great deal about life in a Roman fort.

A large wall and six gatehouses were built to defend the fort, but evidence revealed that it was destroyed and rebuilt three times. The standard of living appears to have been high: water was brought in by aqueduct, the commandant had underfloor heating in his house, and the soldiers' bath house had hot, cold, dry or steam baths, and latrines. The remains of the bath house are very substantial. There is a museum exhibiting artefacts from the site.

(.5m E)
☎ **Humshaugh (0434) 681379**

Open: all year, Apr-Sep, daily 10-6; Oct-Mar, daily 10-4. (Closed 24-26 Dec & 1 Jan).
Admission: £1.80 (ch 90p, pen, students & UB40 £1.40).
🅿 ⅋ shop ⊮
(EH)

SYMBOLS

☎ Telephone number	✳ Indicates 1991 price	☞ Refreshments ⊮ No Dogs
⅋ Suitable for visitors in wheelchairs	🅿 Parking at Establishment	✗ Restaurant ⛟ No coaches

NOTTINGHAMSHIRE

FARNSFIELD   White Post Modern Farm Centre

This working farm gives an introduction to a variety of modern farming methods. It explains how farms work, with exhibits such as llamas, deer, pigs, cows, snails, quails, snakes and fish, through to 20 arable crop plots. A kennel is provided for dogs. There is also lots to see indoors including the owl houses, incubator room, mousetown and a reptile house. Barn dances and wildlife and craft weekends will take place during the year (tel. for details).

(1m W)
☎ Mansfield (0623) 882977 & 882026
Open: all year, Mon-Fri 10-5. Wknds & BH's 10-6.
Admission: £1.95 (ch 4-16 £1.20, under 4 free, pen & people with special needs £1.50). Party 10 + .
P ♥ & toilets for disabled shop ⅓ (kennels available)

NOTTINGHAM   Brewhouse Yard Museum

Housed in 17th-century buildings on a two acre site with unusual local plants, the museum depicts everyday life in Nottingham in post-medieval times. Rock-cut cellars show their past uses and there are thematic displays. Many items may be operated by the public, and temporary exhibitions are changed regularly.

Castle Boulevard
☎ (0602) 483504 ext 3602 or 3600
Open: all year 10-5. Last admission 4.45pm. (Closed Xmas).
& toilets for disabled ⅓
Details not confirmed for 1992

NOTTINGHAM   Canal Museum

The history of the River Trent from the Ice Age to the present day is told in the ground and first floors and wharf of this 19th-century warehouse. Life size dioramas, models and an audio-visual presentation add impact to the displays which include local canal and river navigation, boats, bridges and archaeology.

Canal St
☎ (0602) 598835
Open: all year, Apr-Sep, Wed-Sat 10-12 & 1-5.45, Sun 1-5.45; Oct-Mar, Wed, Thu & Sat 10-12 & 1-5, Sun 1-5.
Admission: Free.
& (wheelchairs available) toilets for disabled shop ⅓

NOTTINGHAM   Nottingham Industrial Museum

Housed in the 18th-century stable block, displays illustrate Nottingham's industrial history, in particular those of lace and hosiery. Exhibits on the pharmaceutical industry, engineering, printing and the tobacco industry are also here. A beam (pumping) engine and heavy agricultural machinery are housed in a new extension. Victorian street furniture is displayed in a yard outside, along with a horse gin from a local coalmine.

Courtyard Buildings, Wollaton Park
(3m W off A609 Ilkeston Rd)
☎ (0602) 284602
Open: all year, Apr-Sep, Mon-Sat 10-6, Sun 2-6; Oct-Mar, Thu & Sat 10-4.30, Sun 1.30-4.30. 19th-century beam pump engine in steam last Sun in each month & BH.
Admission: ✳ Free, Mon-Sat 50p (ch 20p) Sun & BH. Ticket includes Natural History Museum Wollaton Hall.
P & (hand & powered wheelchairs available) toilets for disabled shop ⅓

NOTTINGHAM   The Tales of Robin Hood

A marvel of special effects transporting the visitor to medieval Nottingham and the magical glades of the greenwood in search of Robin Hood. Travelling in the unique adventure cars the experience happens below, around and above you as the commentary is piped into each car by portable compact disc players.

Maid Marian Way
☎ (0602) 483284
Open: all year, daily 10-5.
Admission: £3.95 (ch £2.50). Family ticket £9.95.
☻ & (chairlift) toilets for disabled shop ✗

RAMPTON   Sundown Kiddies Adventureland

Created specially with young children in mind, the attractions include animated nursery rhymes. Noah's Ark play area, Westown Street with 'Crazy Critters' Show. Large forts with climbing frames etc., Smugglers' Cove, a Fantasy Castle guarded by a watchful dragon, a Tudor Street with secret passages and a miniature farm with live animals are just some of the goodies to delight youngsters, including the recently opened indoor play jungle.

(Sundown Pets Garden), Treswell Rd
(3m off A57 at Dunham crossroads)
☎ (077784) 274 due to change to 8274
Open: all year, daily 10-6, earlier in winter. (Closed 25-26 Dec).
Admission: £2.75 (ch under 2 free).
🅿 ☻ & toilets for disabled shop ✗

SUTTON-CUM-LOUND   Wetlands Waterfowl Reserve & Exotic Bird Park

The collection of waterfowl includes ducks, geese, swans, and flamingos on two lagoons covering some 32 acres, and many wild birds live here. There are also parrots, a variety of trees and plants, and a children's farm.

Off Loundlow Rd
☎ Retford (0777) 818099
Open: all year, daily 10-6 (or dusk whichever is earlier). (Closed 25 Dec). Guided tours available on weekdays, bookings only.
🅿 ☻ & (wheelchair available) shop ✗
Details not confirmed for 1992

OXFORDSHIRE

Burford   Cotswold Wildlife Park

The 180-acre landscaped zoological park, surrounding a Gothic-style manor house, has a varied collection of animals from all over the world, with tropical birds, a large reptile collection, aquarium and insect house. Other attractions include an adventure playground, animal brass-rubbing centre in the manor house and train rides during the summer months. Also during the summer there are Snake Days, car rallies, Morris dancers and falconry displays – dates on application.

(2m S off A40 & A361)
☎ (0993) 823006
Open: all year, daily (ex Xmas Day) 10-6 or dusk if earlier.
Admission: £3.80 (ch 4 & pen £2.20). Party 20+
🅿 ☻ ✗ licensed & toilets for disabled shop

ABBREVIATIONS					
AM	Ancient Monument	BH	Bank Holidays	ch 15 20p	Children under 15 20p
AM(CadW)	Ancient Monument	PH	Public Holidays	Pen	Senior Citizens
	(Wales)	Etr	Easter	Party	Special or reduced rates for
EH	English Heritage	ex	except		parties booked in advance
NT	National Trust	Free	Admission free	Party 30+	Special or reduced rates for
NTS	National Trust for	10p	Admission 10p		parties of 30 or more booked
	Scotland	ch 20p	Children 20p		in advance

The main attraction of Oxford is undoubtedly its colleges, and it is pleasure enough just to wander around the streets and alleyways, soaking up the atmosphere of those ancient walls. The heart of the university can be found between Broad Street and The High in a series of buildings which include the domed Radcliffe Camera and the beautiful Sheldonian Theatre, designed by Sir Christopher Wren in the 1660s. A cobbled lane behind The High leads to Merton College, the oldest of all, which dates from the late 13th century, and the imposing Christ Church College (its medieval chapel is also Oxford's cathedral). At the end of The High is Magdalen (pronounced 'mordlin'), said by some to be the most beautiful of all, where, at 6am on May Day the college choir sings from the top of the tower. Colleges are normally open from 2-5pm, but visitors are asked to respect the privacy and peace of those who live and work there. Guided walks start at regular intervals from the Tourist Information Office and there are open-topped bus tours. Boating on the river is also a popular pastime.

Oxford is not just the university – it is a thriving commercial and industrial city with an excellent shopping centre and lots of events and entertainments.

Tourist information: St Aldates Telephone: (0865) 726871

☆ STAR ATTRACTIONS

Ashmolean Museum of Art & Archaeology _____
First opened in 1683 and the oldest museum in the country, the Ashmolean Museum was re-housed in C R Cockerell's building of 1845. Archaeological exhibits from Britain, Europe, the Mediterranean, Egypt and the Near East are on show and the Herbeden Coin Room contains coins and medals from all countries and periods. Italian, Dutch, Flemish, French and English oil paintings adorn the walls along with Old Masters and modern drawings, water-colours, prints and miniatures. Chinese and Japanese porcelain, paintings and laquer-work are gathered here as well as European ceramics, Tibetan art, Indian sculpture and paintings, metalwork, and pottery from Islam and Chinese bronzes. Temporary exhibitions are held throughout the year, including The Art of Laughter (Feb-May), the Maxwell Webb Collection (May-Aug), and Indian Paintings from the Howard Hodgkin Collection (Oct-Dec).

Beaumont St
☎ (0865) 278000

Open: all year, Tue-Sat 10-4, Sun 2-4. (Closed Etr & during St.Giles Fair in early Sep, Xmas & 1 Jan).
Admission: ✳ Free. Guided tours by arrangement.
&. shop ✺

The Oxford Story _____
The 800-year history of Oxford University is brought to life at this innovative exhibition. Sights, sounds . . . and smells from the past are described by Sir Alec Guinness or Timmy Mallett as visitors take a seat and ride through the exhibition. Foreign language commentaries are available.

6 Broad St
☎ (0865) 728822

Open: all year, Apr-Jun & Sep-Oct daily 9.30-5, Jul-Aug 9.30-7 & Nov-Mar daily 10-4. (Closed 25 Dec)
Admission: £3.75 (ch under 16 £2.50, pen & students £3.25). Family ticket £11
&. toilets for disabled shop ✺

University of Oxford Botanic Garden _____
Founded in 1621, these gardens are the oldest in the country and are of great botanical interest. There is a collection of over 8000 species of plants from all over the world.

High St (by Magdalen Bridge)
☎ (0865) 276920

Open: all year, daily 9-5 (9-4.30 Oct-Mar), Greenhouses, daily 2-4. (Closed Good Fri & 25 Dec).
Admission: Jul-Aug £1, otherwise free
&. Entry at wknds using Radar key. ✺

DIDCOT   Didcot Railway Centre

The biggest collection anywhere of Great Western Railway stock is housed in the GWR engine shed, including 20 steam locomotives, a diesel railcar, and a large amount of passenger and freight rolling stock. A typical GWR station has been re-created and original track has been relaid. Events for 1992 include 'steamings' Spring Holidays (23-25 May) and Christmas (29 Nov-20 Dec), Steamdays for Midsummer (20 Jun), and for the disabled (5 Jul), a Teddy Bears' Picnic (12 Jul), an Autumn Gala (26-7 Sep), and a Photographers' Evening (31 Oct).

(on A4130 at Didcot Parkway Station)
☎ **(0235) 817200**
Open: all year, 4 Apr-27 Sep, daily 11-5 dusk in winter. Steam days first & last Sun of each month from Mar, BH's, all Sun's Jun-Aug & Wed in Aug.
Admission: £2.70-£4.50 depending on event (ch £1.90-£4.50, over 60's £2.20-£3.60)
☎ & (advance notice recommended) toilets for disabled shop

IPSDEN   Wellplace Bird Farm

Tropical birds, lambs, goats, monkeys, donkeys, otters, ponies and llamas are just some of the hundred varieties of animals and birds who make their homes at Wellplace Bird Farm; a delightful place for adults and children.

☎ **Checkendon (0491) 680473**
Open: all year, Apr-Sep, daily 10-5, Sun 10-6; Oct-Apr, wknds weather permitting.
Admission: ✳ £2 (ch 50p)
P ☎ & toilets for disabled shop garden centre ⍥

LONG WITTENHAM   Pendon Museum of Miniature Landscape & Transport

This charming exhibition shows a highly detailed model railway and miniature village scenes transporting the visitor back into a 1930s country landscape. Skilled modellers can often be seen at work on the exhibits.

☎ **Clifton Hampden (086730) 7365**
Open: Sat & Sun 2-5, each day of summer BH wknds 11-5 (Closed 14 Dec-9 Jan).
Admission: £1.50 (ch 16 & pen £1, ch under 6 free).
P ☎ shop ⍥

WITNEY   Cogges Farm Museum

Farmhouse kitchens, a dairy, walled gardens and local breeds of animals form the central features of this Edwardian Oxfordshire farm. There is an historic trail, and daily agricultural and craft demonstrations.

Church Ln, Cogges (0.5m SE off A4022)
Open: Apr-Nov, Tue-Fri & BH Mon 10.30-5.30. Sat & Sun noon-5.30. Mon, booked parties only.
Admission: ✳ under review
P ☎ & toilets for disabled shop

WOODSTOCK   Blenheim Palace

Once a Royal Manor, Woodstock was given to the Duke of Marlborough by Queen Anne as a reward for his brilliant military achievements in defeating the French. The Palace, begun in 1705, was designed by Sir John Vanbrugh. It was built on a very grand scale, covering three acres of ground, and was completed in 1722. The Palace has splendid State

☎ **(0993) 811325**
Open: Palace & Gardens mid Mar-Oct, daily 10.30-5.30 (last admission 4.45pm). Park all year 9-5.

Rooms, a Long Library, magnificent tapestries and paintings as well as period furniture. Of particular interest are the door frames carved by Grinling Gibbons and the Hall ceiling painted to depict the Battle of Blenheim by Sir James Thornhill.

The Palace is set in a 2000-acre park landscaped by Capability Brown who created a lake spanned by a 390-ft bridge. There are also formal Italian gardens and terraced water gardens. Sir Winston Churchill was born in the Palace in 1874 and he is buried nearby, at Bladon.

There is a garden centre, an adventure playground and nature trail through the parkland. Other attractions include a Motor launch, train and Butterfly House. Various events are held in the park throughout the year.

Admission: £6 (ch 5-15 £3, ch under 5 free, pen £4.50)
P ☕ ✖ licensed ♿ toilets for disabled shop garden centre ✻ (ex in park)

SHROPSHIRE

ACTON SCOTT   Acton Scott Historic Working Farm

Expertly laid out in an old estate farm, the working museum gives a vivid introduction to traditional rural life. The animals are rare breeds, and the crops are types grown around 1900. They are cultivated on the old crop rotation system, and all the work is done by hand or horse power, or with old machines such as steam-threshers. Butter-making takes place throughout the season, with daily craft demonstrations, and old machinery and equipment are displayed. Visitors may take part in some of the work, by becoming resident volunteers. Purpose-built toilets and picnic bench for wheelchair users; three wheelchairs for use on site; guide books in braille. Throughout the season there will be a variety of craft displays, weekend demonstrations of spinning, pottery and more, and seasonal festivals.

Wenlock Lodge (off A49)
☎ Marshbook (06946) 306 & 307

Open: Apr-Nov, Tues-Sat 10-5; Sun & BH Mon 10-6.
Admission: £2.50 (ch & pen £1)
P ☕ ♿ (Braille guide) toilets for disabled shop ✻

BRIDGNORTH   Midland Motor Museum

A notable collection of over 100 well-restored sports and sports racing cars, and racing motor cycles dating from 1920 to 1980 (also a steam traction engine and a collection of toy model cars) are housed in the converted stables of Stanmore Hall and surrounded by beautiful grounds with a nature trail and camping park. There are gatherings of various motor clubs at weekends from April to September.

Stanmore Hall, Stourbridge Rd (2m on A458 Stourbridge Rd)
☎ (0746) 761761

Open: all year, daily 10-5. (Closed 25 Dec). Evenings by appointment.
Admission: £3.50 (ch £1.75, pen £2.80). Family ticket £9.95.
P ☕ ♿ toilets for disabled shop ✻

BRIDGNORTH   Severn Valley Railway

The leading standard gauge steam railway, with one of the largest collections of locomotives and rolling stock in the country. Services operate from Kidderminster and Bewdley to Bridgnorth through 16 miles of picturesque

☎ Bewdley (0299) 403816 & (0746) 764361

Open: wknds early Mar-Oct & daily mid May-early Oct. Also 21-28 Oct. Santa Steam

scenery along the River Severn. Special steam Galas take place in Apr, Jun and Sep and there is a Vintage Vehicle Weekend on 11 Oct. Saturday evening 'Wine and Dine' and 'Sunday Luncheon' trains are a speciality. Steam, diesel and vehicle galas are arranged for 1992

& Mince Pie Specials wknds, end Nov-22 Dec, daily 16-20 Dec & 23-24 Dec. *Admission:* ✳ fee payable. Refundable in full if train tickets subsequently purchased. 🅿 🍴 ✗ licensed ♿ toilets for disabled shop

COSFORD   Aerospace Museum

This is one of the largest aviation collections in the UK. Exhibits include the Victor and Vulcan bombers, the Hastings, York and British Airways airliners, the Belfast freighter and the last airworthy Britannia. The research and development collection include the notable TSR2, Fairey Delta 2, Bristol 188 and many more important aircraft. There is a British Airways exhibition hall, and a comprehensive missile display. 21 June is Royal Air Force Cosford open day.

(off A41)
☎ **Albrighton (0902) 374872 & 374112**

Open: all year daily, 10-4 (last admission). (Closed 24-26 Dec & 1 Jan).
Admission: £3.50 (ch, & pen £1.75). Family ticket £9. Party 20+.
🅿 🍴 ♿ toilets for disabled shop ✟

IRONBRIDGE   Ironbridge Gorge Museum

Ironbridge became famous when the world's first iron bridge was cast and built here in 1779, to span a narrow gorge over the River Severn. Now it is the site of a remarkable series of museums covering some six square miles. Perhaps the most appealing is the Blists Hill Open Air Museum. Set in 42 acres of woodland, the recreated Victorian town offers the visitor a chance to step into the past and see how people lived and worked in the 1890s. The Coalbrookdale Furnace Site uses a light and sound display to show the technique of smelting iron ore, perfected here by Abraham Darby. Associated with the furnace is the Museum of Iron. Another of the museums is housed in the original buildings of the Coalport China Company, based in the area until the mid-1920s. It features workshop and social history displays. There is also the Jackfield Tile Museum. An introduction to the Ironbridge Gorge is given at the visitor centre in the Museum of the River, brought to life by a sound and light display.

☎ **(0952) 433522 & 432751 (wknds)**

Open: all year, Jun-Aug 10-6, Sep-May 10-5.
Admission: ✳ £7.10 (ch £4.60, pen £6.10, family £20.50). Passport to all sites. A passport will admit visitors to all sites, in any order until all have been visited. It is therefore possible to return to Ironbridge on different days to ensure the whole atmosphere of this unique museum may be captured.
🅿 🍴 ✗ licensed ♿ toilets for disabled shop ✟ (ex at Blists Hill)

SOMERSET

CHEDDAR   Cheddar Showcaves

Britain's two most beautiful caves, Gough's Cave with its cathedral-like caverns and Cox's Cave with its delicate stalagmites and stalactites, are beneath the limestone cliffs of Cheddar Gorge. Climb Jacob's Ladder for spectacular views of this conservation area. There is an exhibition of 'Cheddar Man' Britain's oldest complete skelton, and his world 9,000 years ago. 'The Crystal Quest' is new. It is a fantasy adventure underground, while for the more daring, there is an exciting Adventure Caving Expedition (minimum age 12).

Cheddar Gorge
☎ **(0934) 742343**

Open: all year, Etr-Sep 10-5.30; rest of year 10.30-4.30. (Closed 24 & 25 Dec).
Admission: Combined ticket for all attractions £4.50 (ch 5-15 & pen £2.80, ch under 5 free). Adventure Caving Expeditions (min 12yrs) £5.50. Inclusive ticket incl all attractions plus Adventure Caving & Orienteering £9 (ch 12-15 £7). Reductions for disabled on application.
🅿 🍴 ✗ licensed ♿ toilets for disabled shop

CRANMORE   East Somerset Railway

Nine steam locomotives and rolling stock can be seen at Cranmore station, which has an engine shed and workshops. The new art gallery displays David Shepherd's work. Steam train services (see timetable for Steam Days) include Santa Specials in December, and also here are a museum, wildlife information centre and play area.

Cranmore Railway Station (on A361)
☎ (074988) 417

Open: daily May-Aug, 10-5.30. Apr, Sep & Oct 10-4. (wknds Nov, Dec & Mar 10-4). (Closed 2 Jan-Feb).
Admission: £3.30 (ch 4-16 & pen £1.70). Non-steam days £1.30 (ch 70p).
🅿 ✕ ♿ toilets for disabled shop

CRICKET ST THOMAS   Wild Life Park

The old and beautiful park of Cricket House has become a home for a wide variety of animals and birds, including elephants, camels, llamas, parrots and other exotic creatures. The wildlife enclosures have been designed to blend in with the surroundings as far as possible, and there have been successes with breeding, most notably of black swans. Shire horses can be seen at the National Heavy Horse Centre, and there is a woodland railway. The house became well known as 'Grantleigh Manor' in the BBC television series *To The Manor Born*. To celebrate 25 years of being open to the public, 25 charitable events are to be held in 1992, in addition to various other events such as the Wessex Custom and American Car Show on 10 May.

(on A30)
☎ Winsham (0460) 30755

Open: all year Apr-Oct, daily 10-6; Nov-Mar 10-5 or dusk (whichever is earlier).
Admission: £5.50 (ch 3-14 £3 & pen £4.50). Wheelchair users free. Party 20+.
🅿 ☕ ✕ licensed ♿ toilets for disabled shop garden centre

EAST HUNTSPILL   New Road Farm

One of the oldest farms in the area, this family run farm demonstrates both modern and traditional methods of farming. There are over 60 different breeds of animals and visitors are free to explore and make contact with the animals – or even try hand milking the cows. Somerset County Council's Levels Visitor Centre is also here, offering unusual audio-visual effects and 'hands-on' experiences for all ages. There is an 'I Spy' farm trail, an observation badger sett and a barn owl release scheme. Special events for 1992 include, amongst others, a sheepshearing demonstration at Whitsun, and a demonstration of bee keeping, horse shoeing and craft spinning in August.

New Rd (signposted from A38)
☎ Burnham-on-Sea (0278) 783250

Open: Feb-Etr, wknds 10-5. Etr-Oct daily 10-6.
Admission: £3 (ch £2, pen £2.50). Party.
🅿 ☕ ✕ ♿ toilets for disabled shop garden centre

MONKSILVER   Combe Sydenham Country Park

The 16th-century house was the home of Sir Francis Drake's second wife, Elizabeth, and is currently being restored. The Elizabethan-style garden has woodland walks, a corn mill and a children's play area. There is also fly fishing for the beginner, plus day tickets for the more experienced fisherman, and a trout farm for the unsuccessful.

☎ Stogumber (0984) 56284

Open: 9 Apr-2 Nov. Country Park: Sun-Fri. Court Room & Gardens: Mon-Fri. 10-5 (Last admission to Court Room & Garden 4pm).
🅿 ✕ shop garden centre 🐾 (ex in park)
Details not confirmed for 1992

RODE   Tropical Bird Gardens

The Tropical Bird Gardens consist of 17 acres of grounds, planted with trees and shrubs, in a pretty and little-visited village. An ornamental lake and a number of ponds surround the aviaries, where more than 200 species are kept.

There is also a Pets Corner, a children's play area and an information centre. Plants are for sale; children must be accompanied by an adult. A Woodland steam railway operates daily (Etr-mid Sep), weather permitting. Events for 1992 include a Parrot Weekend (30-31 May), and a Clematis Weekend (11-12 Jul).

☎ Frome (0373) 830326
Open: all year daily (ex 25 Dec); Summer 10-6.30pm (last admission 5.30pm); Winter 10-dusk (last admission 1hr before closing time).
Admission: £3.50 (ch 15 £1.75, pen £3).
🅿 ☕ ♿ toilets for disabled shop ✸

WASHFORD   Tropiquaria

Housed in a 1930s BBC transmitting station, the main hall has been converted into an indoor jungle with a 15-foot waterfall, tropical plants and free-flying birds. (Snakes, lizards, iguanas, spiders, toads and terrapins are caged!) Downstairs is the submarine crypt with local and tropical marine life. Other features include landscaped gardens, outdoor aviaries, a children's playground and the Shadowstring Puppet Theatre.

(on A39)
☎ (0984) 40688
Open: all year, Mar-Oct daily 10-6; Nov, Jan-Feb wknds & school hols 10-4; 27-31 Dec, 10-4. Closed 1-26 Dec.
Admission: £2.90 (ch £1.50, student & pen £2.40).
🅿 ☕ ♿ shop ✸

WOOKEY HOLE   Wookey Hole Caves & Papermill

The Caves are the main feature of Wookey Hole. Visitors enjoy a half mile tour through the Chambers, accompanied by a knowledgeable guide who points out the amazing stalagmites and stalactites, including the famous Witch of Wookey. The guides use remote controlled lighting to highlight geological features and illustrate the history and myths associated with the caves.

Visitors also take in the Traditional Papermill, at one time amongst the largest handmade paper mills in Europe, which sold exquisite paper all over the world. Also in the Mill are the Fairground Memories, historically important late 19th century and early 20th century fairground rides. The latest attraction is the Magical Mirror Maze, an enclosed passage of multiple image mirrors creating an illusion of endless reflections. After the fun of the maze, visitors move on to a typical Old Penny Arcade where they can purchase old pennies to operate the original machines.

☎ Wells (0749) 672243
Open: all year, Mar-Oct 9.30-5.30; Nov-Feb 10.30-4.30. (Closed 17-25 Dec).
Admission: ✤ £4.60 (ch £3, pen £4). Party 10 +. Disabled £3 (ch in wheelchairs & helpers free).
🅿 ✕ licensed ♿ (ex Papermill) toilets for disabled shop ✸ (ex in grounds)

YEOVILTON   Fleet Air Arm Museum

Based at the Royal Naval Air Station, the museum portrays the history and achievements of the Royal Naval Air Service, with examples from the early days of kites and airships to the present day. A collection of more than 50 historical aircraft, plus ship and aircraft models, paintings and photographs tell the story of aviation at sea from 1908. There are many special exhibitions including World War's

Royal Naval Air Station (on B3151)
☎ Ilchester (0935) 840565
Open: all year, daily (ex 24-26 Dec) 10-5.30 (4.30pm Nov-Feb).

I and II the Falklands War, the Wrens, War in the Pacific and the Swordfish story. Most recent exhibitions include The Harrier Jump-Jet Story and the Underwater Experience. Of particular interest is the prototype of Concorde 002 and the exhibition of the development of supersonic flight. There are airfield viewing galleries where the aircraft from the Naval base may be observed, a flight simulator and a children's adventure playground.

Admission: £4.50 (ch, students & UB40's £2.50, pen £3.50). Disabled £2. Family ticket £12.50.
🅿 ☕ ✕ licensed ♿ toilets for disabled shop 🐾

SOUTH YORKSHIRE

CUSWORTH   Cusworth Hall Museum

The 18th-century house is the home of this museum of South Yorkshire life. There are sections of special interest to children, and the extensive grounds have fishing (in ponds), cricket and football pitches. A children's study base and research facilities are provided and a programme of special exhibitions and events is planned for 1992.

☎ Doncaster (0302) 782342

Open: all year, Mon-Fri 10-5, Sat 11-5 & Sun 1-5. (4pm Dec & Jan) (Closed Good Fri, Xmas & 1 Jan).
Admission: Free.
🅿 ♿ (wheelchair available) shop 🐾 (ex park)

SHEFFIELD   Abbeydale Industrial Hamlet

One of the first places to be preserved, and made accessible to the public, as an example of industrial archaeology, built around a late 18th-century and early 19th-century water-powered scythe and steelworks. The works, with their machinery, show production from raw material stage to the finished product. Some of the worker's houses and the manager's house have been restored and furnished in period style. There are special Abbeydale Working Days, when visitors can see craftsmen at their forges.

Abbeydale Rd South (4m SW of Sheffield off A621)
☎ (0742) 367731

Open: all year, Wed-Sat 10-5 & Sun 11-5. Also open BH Mon. (Closed Xmas & New Year).
Admission: £1.80 (ch & pen 90p). Family ticket £3.60. On working days £2.10 (ch & pen £1.05). Family ticket £4.20.
🅿 ☕ ♿ shop 🐾

STAFFORDSHIRE

ALTON   Alton Towers

This is the most famous and longest-established of Britain's theme parks, voted 'Britain's most outstanding tourist attraction' by the British Tourist Authority.

There are more than 125 attractions, grouped into five theme areas, centred on the ruined mansion which was formerly the home of the Earl of Shrewsbury. For those who don't enjoy the prospect of the rides, the lovely and extensive terraced gardens are a delight. For most people, however, Alton Towers means white-knuckle and white-water rides. Most famous of all is the Corkscrew Roller-coaster, but rivalling it for sheer terror is the Black Hole, introduced for the Alton Towers 1988 Silver Jubilee Year. White-water rides include the Grand Canyon Rapids and Log Flume, and on both of these you are liable to get quite

☎ Oakamoor (0538) 702200

Open: mid Mar-early Nov 9am until 1 hr after attractions close. Attractions 10-5, 6 or 7 as shown daily at main entrance gate. Grounds & gardens daily mid Nov-mid Mar at reduced rates.
🅿 ☕ ✕ licensed ♿ toilets for disabled shop Details not confirmed for 1992

wet – something to remember if the weather is cold. There are lots of gentler amusements too – from the Swanboat to the Scenic Skyride that takes you all around the park. For those who only want the illusion of adventure, there is a fantastic 3-D cinema with an enormous screen, and Kiddies Kingdom provides for the younger visitor.

DRAYTON MANOR PARK & ZOO

A family leisure park with 160 acres of parkland, lakes, open-plan zoo and amusements. There are over 40 rides, including the Pirate Adventure, the looping roller coaster, log flume, Paratower, cable cars, Dinosaurland, Jungle Cruise, Flying Dutchman, Jungle Palladium Theatre, and the Pirate Ship. Wristbands for unlimited rides are available or discount tickets for multiple or single rides.

(on A4091)
☎ Tamworth (0827) 287979

Open: Park & Zoo open Etr-Sep, daily 10.30-6 (Also Oct wknds & school holiday). Park (rides) 10.30-5, 6 or 7 (depending on season).
Admission: Free.
P (charged) ☕ ✕ licensed ♿ toilets for disabled shop garden centre 🚫🐕 (ex in park)

HIMLEY Himley Hall

The extensive parkland offers a range of attractions, from a model village to a nine-hole golf course and coarse fishing. The hall is *not* open to the public.

Himley Rd (off A449)
☎ Dudley (0384) 456000 ext 5514

Open: all year, daily 8-8pm or half hour before dusk.
P (charged) ☕ ♿
Details not confirmed for 1992

SHUGBOROUGH Shugborough Hall & Staffordshire County Museum

Shugborough Hall is the stately home of the Earls of Lichfield. It was begun in 1693 but was enlarged in the 18th and 19th centuries, largely by the architect Samuel Wyatt. There are magnificent state rooms with notable plasterwork, elegant Louis XV and XVI furniture, fine 18th- and 19th-century silver and glassware and a collection of paintings. Among the offices, the kitchens, butler's pantry, laundry and brewhouse have been restored as museums but are fully operational.

The landscaped grounds are unusual in that they have seven large monuments scattered through them. These include a Chinese House, probably influenced by Admiral Anson's stay in China in the early 1700s, and also four monuments designed by James 'Athenian' Stuart in the Greek Revival style. There is also a working rare breeds farm, an agricultural museum and a restored corn mill in the park. Many special events, exhibitions and concerts take place throughout the year, including a classic car show (3-4 May), a goose fair (19 Jul), and The Great Bread Race (20 Sep).

(6m E of Stafford off A513)
☎ Little Haywood (0889) 881388

Open: 28 Mar-Oct, daily 11-5. Site open all year to pre-booked parties from 10.30am on weekdays.
Admission: ✻ Entry to Estate £1 per car. Mansion £3 (ch, pen & UB40's £2); Museum £3 (ch, pen & UB40's £2); Farm £3 (ch, pen & UB40's £2). Combined ticket £7.50 (ch, pen & UB40's £5). Family ticket £15.
P (charged) ☕ ✕ ♿ (wheelchairs provided) toilets for disabled shop garden centre 🚫🐕 (ex in parkland)
(NT)

SYMBOLS

☎ Telephone number	✻ Indicates 1991 price	☕ Refreshments	🚫🐕 No Dogs
♿ Suitable for visitors in wheelchairs	P Parking at Establishment	✕ Restaurant	🚫🚌 No coaches

STOKE-ON-TRENT   Chatterley Whitfield Mining Museum

Chatterley Whitfield opened in 1979 as Britain's first underground mining museum on the site of the former million ton per annum Whitfield Colliery Complex. Established to preserve and present the story of coal mining in North Staffordshire, Chatterley Whitfield's purpose has broadened during the site's 11-year history as a working museum of the mining industry. With British Coal's decision in 1989 to relocate their national collection of mining artefacts to Whitfield, the museum is now emerging as a major national archive for students of mining history.

The museum can offer visitors tours led by retired miner guides which include pit cage and manrider locomotive rides, together with retired pit ponies in their underground stalls. On the surface visitors can enjoy the sight of restored winding and compressor engines or marvel at the Museum's working steam railway. Visiting school and leisure groups can participate in Whitfield's Sandford award-winning Heritage Education Services. All visitors can take refreshments in the site's 1930s pit canteen. Events for 1992 include a rock and mineral fair on 2 May, and a bus rally on 7 June.

Chatterley Whitfield Colliery, Tunstall (on A527)
☎ (0782) 813337

Open: all year, daily 10-5, last tour 4pm (Closed 25-26 Dec).
Admission: ✳ £3.95 (ch 5-16 £2.95, pen, students & UB40 £2.95). Family ticket £11.95. Party.
🅿 ☕ & (surface only) toilets for disabled shop

TAMWORTH   Tamworth Castle

The castle is a mixture of Norman Gothic, Tudor, Jacobean and early 19th- century architecture, showing the tastes of its inhabitants over 700 years. It started as a Norman motte-and-bailey castle, with the walls of its keep 10ft thick at the base, and outer walls and a gatehouse were added in the 13th- century. The Tudor period brought additions of a more domestic sort, with a splendid, timber-roofed great hall and a warden's lodge.

The Jacobean state apartments have fine woodwork, furniture and heraldic friezes, including 55 oak panels painted with the arms of the lords of the castle up to 1787. There is a Norman exhibition with 'speaking' knight, a haunted bedroom, The Chapel, Annie Cook's bedroom and a Victorian nursery.

Outside are floral terraces and pleasure grounds with swimming pool and adventure playground.

The Holloway
☎ (0827) 63563

Open: all year, Mon-Sat 10-5.30; Sun 2-5.30. Last admission 4.30pm. (Closed 25 Dec).
& shop ✹
Details not confirmed for 1992

WESTON PARK

Built in 1671, this fine mansion stands in elegant gardens and a vast park designed by 'Capability' Brown. Three lakes, a miniature railway, and a woodland adventure playground are to be found in the grounds, and in the house itself there is a notable collection of pictures, furniture and tapestries. Additional attractions are special events, including point-to-points, festivals of transport, craft fairs, dog shows, and others.

(7m W of junc 12 of M6; 3m N of junc 3 on M54)
☎ Weston-under-Lizard (095276) 207

Open: 17 Apr-21 Apr; 25 Apr-14 Jun wknds & BH (ex 4 May & Spring BH wk); 15 Jun-Jul daily (ex Mon & Fri); Aug daily; 1-20 Sep wknds only. Park 11-7 (last admission 5pm); House 1pm (last admission 5pm).
Admission: Park £3 (ch & pen £2). House £1 (ch & pen 75p).
🅿 ☕ & (disabled route) toilets for disabled shop

SUFFOLK

BUNGAY The Otter Trail

Otters are a rare sight in the wild nowadays, but at the Otter Trust it is possible to see these beautiful creatures at close quarters. While they are entertaining to watch, one of the Trust's main aims is to breed this endangered species in captivity in sufficient numbers so that it can re-introduce young otters into the wild every year wherever suitable habitat remains to reinforce the vanishing wild population. This re-introduction programme has been running very successfully since 1983 and is carried out in conjunction with English Nature. The Trust has now introduced captive-bred otters into the wild in Norfolk, Suffolk, Dorset, Hampshire and Hertfordshire and subsequent scientific monitoring has shown that nearly all these animals are breeding successfully. This has resulted in the wild otter population of Norfolk increasing to almost what it was twenty years ago. The Otter Trust covers 23 acres on the banks of the river Waveney. As well as the otter pens there are three lakes with a large collection of European waterfowl, lovely riverside walks and picnic areas.

Earsham (off A143)
☎ (0986) 893470

Open: Apr (or Good Fri if earlier)-Oct, daily 10.30-6.
Admission: ✻ £3 (ch £1.50, pen £2.50). Disabled person & pusher free.
🅿 ☕ ♿ toilets for disabled shop 🚫

EASTON Easton Farm Park

Visitors can watch cows being milked at a modern dairy operation, alongside a Victorian dairy established by the Duke of Hamilton in 1870. Victorian dairy equipment is also on display, and the farm park has a collection of farming implements and vehicles. There is also a new exhibition on food and farming: Foodchains. There are Suffolk Punch horses and rare breeds of farm animals and other attractions include a picnic area, and adventure playground. There are also nature trails to follow through damp woodland and pasture alongside the River Deben. Interesting woodland and wetland plants and animals may be seen. There will be a country fair on 21 June.

☎ Wickham Market (0728) 746475

Open: 22 Mar-27 Sep, daily 10.30-6. Last admission 4.30pm.
Admission: £3.50 (ch3-16 £2, pen £2.75). Party 20+.
🅿 ☕ ♿ toilets for disabled shop

HORRINGER Ickworth

Ickworth was designed to show off works of art: it is a 100ft-high oval rotunda with two curved corridors, which were meant to be painting and sculpture galleries. The building was commissioned in 1796 by Frederick Hervey (pronounced Harvey), who collected many items for Ickworth, most of which were confiscated by Napoleon. The house is filled with treasures amassed by the family, however. It has fine furniture and porcelain, one of England's most splendid silver collections, sculptures, and paintings by Velasquez, Lawrence, Kauffmann, Gainsborough and others. The formal gardens are noted for fine trees and there are extensive park walks, a deer enclosure and a children's play area.

(2.5m S of Bury St Edmunds)
☎ (028488) 270

Open: House & Garden 28 Mar, Apr & Oct wknds only; Mar-Sep Tue, Wed, Fri, Sat, Sun & BH Mons 1.30-5.30. Park open daily 7-7pm.
Admission: House, Garden & Park £4.10 (ch £2); Garden & park £1.50. Party 15+
🅿 🍴 licensed ♿ toilets for disabled shop 🚫
(NT)

LONG MELFORD   Kentwell Hall

The major appeal of this Tudor manor house is its lived-in feeling: it is indeed a much-loved family home and great efforts have been made to retain its unique atmosphere. The mellow, red-brick, E-shaped building is surrounded by a broad moat and externally little has been altered. Appropriately enough, the house displays an exhibition of Tudor style costume, while outside a brick-pave mosaic maze and rare breeds of farm animals are the chief attractions.

(off A134)
☎ Sudbury (0787) 310207
Open: House, Moat House, Gardens & Farm; 2-5 Apr, 28 May-2 Jun, 17 Jul-29 Sep, daily 12-5. Also 7 Apr-19 May, 9-16 Jun & 6-27 Oct, Sun only 12-5.
P ■ & shop ✘
Details not confirmed for 1992

LOWESTOFT   East Anglia Transport Museum

A particular attraction of this museum is the reconstructed 1930s street scene which is used as a setting for working vehicles: visitors can ride by tram, trolley-bus and narrow gauge railway. Other motor, steam and electrical vehicles are exhibited on the three-acre woodland site. On 4-5 July the London Event will be staged to commemorate the last day of tram operation in London in 1952. There will be London Transport vehicles to see, model displays and sales stands.

Chapel Rd, Carlton Colville (3m SW, on B1384)
☎ (0502) 518459
Open: Etr Sun & Mon then all BH's & Sun's from May-Sep from 11; Jun-Sep Sat; weekends during last week in Jul-Aug, from 2pm
Admission: £2.50 (ch & pen £1.20). Party
P ■ & shop

LOWESTOFT   Pleasurewood Hills American Theme Park

After the initial admission fee there is nothing more to pay at this exciting theme park. Apart from the breathtaking rides like the Waveswinger, Star Ride Enterprise and the Tempest visitors can slow down the pace at the Land that Time Forgot of Woody's Fairytale Fantasy. Other attractions include the Sealion and Parrot shows, a Fun Factory and Cine 180. Train rides and chairlift make it easier to get around the park.

Corton Rd (on A12)
☎ (0502) 513626
Open: 29 Mar-7 Apr, 4 May-22 Sep & 21-27 Oct, daily. 13-14, 20-21, 27-28 Apr & 28-29 Sep, wknds. 6, 13 & 20 Oct, Sun. 10-6 (4 or 5 according to season).
P ■ & toilets for disabled shop ✘
Details not confirmed for 1992

SAXMUNDHAM   Bruisyard Winery, Vineyard & Herb Centre

This picturesque, 10-acre winery produces the award-winning Bruisyard St Peter English wine. There is also a herb garden, water gardens, a wooded picnic area, and a children's play area. English wine, herbs, crafts and souvenirs are for sale.

Church Rd, Bruisyard (between Framlingham & Peasenhall)
☎ Badingham (072875) 281
Open: Etr-Nov, daily 10.30-5.
Admission: ✳ £2.90 (ch £1.50 pen £2.65)
P ✗ licensed & shop garden centre ✘ (ex in vineyard)

STOWMARKET   Museum of East Anglian Life

The extensive, 70-acre, all-weather museum is set in an attractive river-valley site. There are reconstructed buildings, including a water mill, a smithy and also a wind pump, and the Boby Building houses craft workshops, with a resident wood turner. There are videos of a cooper and basket maker at work, as well as a historic film show in a

☎ (0449) 612229
Open: 22 Mar-1 Nov, daily 10-5.
Admission: £3.25 (ch 3-16 £1.60, students & pen £2). Party.
P ■ & (wheelchairs available, special parking facilities) toilets for disabled shop

Bioscope cinema. Also here are displays on Victorian domestic life, gypsies, farming and industry. These include working steam traction engines, the only surviving pair of Burrell ploughing engines of 1879, and a working Suffolk Punch horse.

SUFFOLK WILDLIFE & RARE BREEDS PARK

Set in an area of outstanding natural beauty this wildlife park has a wide selection of animals and birds, some of which are very rare. There are plenty of good sites for picnics, a children's play area, and also a 'Meet the Animals' show daily.

Kessingland (on A12)
☎ **Lowestoft (0502) 740291**

Open: Etr-Oct, daily 10-6 (5pm Sep-Oct).
Admission: ✽ £3.50 (ch £2)
🅿 ☂ ⅋ toilets for disabled shop ⅍

WEST STOW   West Stow Anglo-Saxon Village

The village is a reconstruction of a pagan Anglo-Saxon settlement dated 420-650 AD. Six buildings have been reconstructed on the site of the excavated settlement, using the same techniques, tools and building materials as were used in the original farming village (free audio guides available).

The village is situated in the 125-acre West Stow Country Park. There is a special Open Day each year and a new Visitors' Centre and children's play area. Facilities for the disabled include purpose-built toilets for wheelchair users and a braille guide to the park.

West Stow Country Park (on A1101)
☎ **Culford (0284) 728718**

Open: all year, daily 10-5.
Admission: £2 (ch, pen & students £1.20).
🅿 ⅋ toilets for disabled shop ⅍

SURREY

CHARLWOOD   Gatwick Zoo & Aviaries

The zoo covers almost 10 acres and has hundreds of birds and mammals. The monkey island has spider and squirrel monkeys, and other animals and birds can be seen in large, naturalised settings. Nearly all species breed each year. A play area for children up to 12 years old has been added.

Russ Hill
☎ **Crawley (0293) 862312**

Open: all year, Mar-Oct, daily 10.30-6 (earlier by appointment for schools). Nov-Mar, wknds & school hols 10.30-4 or dusk if earlier. (Closed 25-26 Dec). No butterflies during winter.
Admission: £3.50 (ch 3-14 £2.50, pen £3 ex Sun & BH). Admission price includes Butterfly House.
🅿 ☂ ⅋ toilets for disabled shop ⅍

ABBREVIATIONS					
AM	Ancient Monument	BH	Bank Holidays	ch 15 20p	Children under 15 20p
AM(CadW)	Ancient Monument	PH	Public Holidays	Pen	Senior Citizens
	(Wales)	Etr	Easter	Party	Special or reduced rates for
EH	English Heritage	ex	except		parties booked in advance
NT	National Trust	Free	Admission free	Party 30 +	Special or reduced rates for
NTS	National Trust for	10p	Admission 10p		parties of 30 or more booked
	Scotland	ch 20p	Children 20p		in advance

CHERTSEY   Thorpe Park

The park offers 500 acres of family fun; over 70 attractions are included in the admission price. The attractions include Loggers Leap, the highest log theme ride in the UK, Thunder River, Tea Cup ride, Thorpe Farm, Canada Creek Railway, Carousel Kingdom, Magic Mills, lots of shows, and much more. There is free transport round the park by land train or water bus. The park is located one and three-quarter miles north of Chertsey on the A320.

Staines Rd (on A320, off junc 11 or 13 of M25)
☎ **(0932) 562633 & 569393**

Open: 23 Mar-27 Oct, daily 10-6 (5 early & late season).
🅿 ☕ ✘ ♿ toilets for disabled shop 🐾
Details not confirmed for 1992

FARNHAM   Birdworld & Underwaterworld

Eighteen acres of garden and parkland are home to a wide variety of birds, from the tiny tanager to the great ostrich and many rare and unusual species. There are waterfowl as well as land birds; a Sea Shore Walk and Tropical Walk; and an aquarium with tropical, freshwater and marine fish. The Owls Nest bookshop sells books on wildlife. Plant lovers will enjoy the extensive gardens. There are purpose-built toilets for wheelchair users, wheelchairs are available on loan and there are good, solid paths around the grounds. Special events for 1992 will include: 14 Jun, Garden Day; 19 Jul, Teddy Bears Picnic, and at the end of August a Mad Hatter's party.

Holt Pound (5m S on A325)
☎ **Bentley (0420) 22140**

Open: all year, daily from 9.30. (Closed 25 Dec).
Admission: Birdworld £3.40 (ch £1.80, pen £2.60); Underwater World 95p (ch 50p).
🅿 ☕ ♿ (wheelchairs available) toilets for disabled shop 🐾

GUILDFORD   Loseley House

Familiar to many from ice cream and yoghurt pots, the Elizabethan house has notable panelling, decorated ceilings, a carved chalk chimney piece and tapestries. It is also home of the Loseley dairy products, and there are farm tours.

(2.5m SW)
☎ **(0483) 304440**

Open: House: 29 May-28 Sep, Wed-Sat 2-5. Also BH Mon (27 May & 26 Aug). Farm Tours: also May-Oct, Mon-Sat.
🅿 ✘ licensed ♿ (wheelchair available, parking outside house) toilets for disabled shop 🐾
Details not confirmed for 1992

HASCOMBE   Winkworth Arboretum

This lovely woodland covers a hillside of nearly 100 acres, with fine views over the North Downs. The best times to visit are May, for the azaleas, bluebells and other flowers, and October for the autumn colours.

(1m NW on B2130)
☎ **(048632) 477**

Open: all year, daily during daylight hours.
Admission: ✳ £2.
🅿 ☕ shop (Apr-15 Nov, Tue-Sun 2-6) (NT)

ABBREVIATIONS

AM	Ancient Monument	BH	Bank Holidays	ch 15 20p	Children under 15 20p
AM(CadW)	Ancient Monument (Wales)	PH	Public Holidays	Pen	Senior Citizens
		Etr	Easter	Party	Special or reduced rates for parties booked in advance
EH	English Heritage	ex	except		
NT	National Trust	Free	Admission free	Party 30 +	Special or reduced rates for parties of 30 or more booked in advance
NTS	National Trust for Scotland	10p	Admission 10p		
		ch 20p	Children 20p		

TYNE & WEAR

NEWCASTLE UPON TYNE Museum of Science & Engineering

This museum houses a wealth of artefacts and images from the industrial heritage of the North East. Beautiful ship models, powerful steam turbines, guns, engines and even the humble light bulb are displayed to tell the fascinating story on one of Britain's greatest industrial centres. Visitors can also discover that science is fun in the popular Science Factory Interactive Science Centre – the only one in the North East. In spring there will be the North East Craft Roadshow and in summer 1992, the Time Tunnel display will open.

Blandford House, Blandford Sq (off A6115/A6125)
☎ 091-232 6789

Open: all year, Tue-Fri 10-5.30, Sat 10-4.30, BH Mons 10-5.30. (Closed 25-26 Dec & 1 Jan).
Admission: Free.
P ☕ ♿ toilets for disabled shop 🐕

WASHINGTON The Wildfowl & Wetlands Trust

Set in a busy industrial area, this Wildfowl Trust park is a welcome refuge on the north bank of the River Wear. The 100-acre park has over 100 species of wildfowl, which form one of the largest collections in the world. The attractive landscaped park includes 70 acres for wild birds, which can be viewed from several public hides. The Visitor Centre, housed in an attractive log cabin, also has a viewing gallery and large picture windows giving excellent views over the main collection area. The centre provides information on the birds, talks and guided walks as well as a souvenir shop and bookshop.

☎ 091-416 5454

Open: all year, daily 9.30-5 or dusk if earlier. (Closed 24-25 Dec).
P ☕ ♿ toilets for disabled shop 🐕
Details not confirmed for 1992

WARWICKSHIRE

ALCESTER Ragley Hall

Ragley Hall is set in four hundred acres of parkland and gardens. The Great Hall contains some of England's finest Baroque plasterwork designed by James Gibbs. Graham Rust's mural *The Temptation* can be seen on the south staircase. Ample picnic areas beside the lake, as well as an Adventure Playground, maze and woodland walks. Events planned for 1992 include horse trials in May and a craft fair in June.

(1.5m SW, on A435)
☎ (0789) 762090

Open: Etr-Sep, Tue-Thu, Sat, Sun & BH Mon; Jul-Aug park & garden open everyday. House 12-5, park & gardens 10-6.
Admission: Garden & Park £3.50 (ch & pen £2.50). House (including garden & park) £4.50 (ch & pen £3.50).
P ☕ ♿ toilets for disabled shop 🐕 (ex in park & gardens)

MIDDLETON Ash End House Farm

Ash End House is a children's farm, specifically set up with children in mind. They love to learn and experience new things, and what better way than when having fun. Children's guided tours give them a unique opportunity to get close to friendly farm animals. A host of animals from

Middleton Ln, Middleton (signposted from A4091)
☎ 021-329 3240

Open: daily 10-6 or dusk in winter. (Closed 25 & 26 Dec).

the gigantic shire horse, through to hatching tiny chicks and fluffy ducklings can be seen daily. There are also rare breeds such as Bagot goats, Saddleback pigs and Soay sheep. To celebrate the farm's 10th anniversary, from spring 1992, there will be a display of British wild animals in a natural scene in the old stables. Birthday party bookings are accepted and tours can also be arranged for Beavers, Brownies, Cubs etc.

Admission: ✽ £1.10(ch £2.20 includes animal feed, badge, pony ride & fresh egg when available).
P ☛ ⅙ (shop not accessible) toilets for disabled shop ✖

SHOTTERY   Anne Hathaway's Cottage

Before her marriage to William Shakespeare, Anne Hathaway lived in this substantial 12-roomed thatched Tudor farmhouse with her prosperous yeoman family. The house now shows many aspects of domestic life in 16th-century England, and has a lovely garden and Shakespeare tree garden.

☎ Stratford-upon-Avon (0789) 292100
Open: all year, Mar-Oct Mon-Sat 9-5.30, Sun 10-5.30; Nov-Feb Mon-Sat 9.30-4, Sun 10.30-4. (Closed Good Fri am, 24-26 Dec & 1 Jan am).
Admission: ✽ £2 (ch 90p). Inclusive ticket to all 5 Shakespearian properties £6 (ch £3). School and student party rates for groups visiting all five properties.
P (charged) ☛ shop ✖

STRATFORD-UPON-AVON   The National Teddy Bear Museum

Ten settings are devoted to bears of all shapes and sizes. Many of the old bears are displayed and there are also mechanical and musical bears. Some of the bears belonged to famous people or are famous in their own right, such as 'Aloysius' from the television adaptation of *Brideshead Revisited*. This bear is actually named 'Delicatessen' and belonged to the actor Peter Bull. A bear festival will be held in the Civic Hall on 1 Feb.

19 Greenhill St
☎ (0789) 293160
Open: all year, daily 9.30-6
Admission: ✽ £1.90 (ch 95p) Party 20 +
shop ✖

STRATFORD-UPON-AVON   Royal Shakespeare Company Collection

The permanent exhibition in the RSC Collection, Stages and Staging, contains over 1,000 items including costumes, props, pictures, photographs and sound recordings. They are used to illustrate the changes in staging from medieval times to the present use of a thrust stage in the Swan Theatre, and comparisons of past RSC productions with the current season's plays. Temporary exhibitions include the work of the current artist(s) in residence.

Royal Shakespeare Theatre, Waterside
☎ (0789) 296655
Open: all year, Mon-Sat 9.15-8, Sun 12-5 (Nov-Mar Sun 11-4).(Closed 25 Dec).
Admission: Exhibition £1.50 (ch, pen & students £1). Theatre Tours £3.50 (ch, pen & students £2.50).
P (charged) ☛ ✗ licensed ⅙ toilets for disabled shop ✖

ABBREVIATIONS					
AM	Ancient Monument	BH	Bank Holidays	ch 15 20p	Children under 15 20p
AM(CadW)	Ancient Monument	PH	Public Holidays	Pen	Senior Citizens
	(Wales)	Etr	Easter	Party	Special or reduced rates for
EH	English Heritage	ex	except		parties booked in advance
NT	National Trust	Free	Admission free	Party 30 +	Special or reduced rates for
NTS	National Trust for	10p	Admission 10p		parties of 30 or more booked
	Scotland	ch 20p	Children 20p		in advance

STRATFORD-UPON-AVON   Shakespeare's Birthplace

Shakespeare was born in the timber-framed house in 1564. It contains numerous exhibits of the Elizabethan period and Shakespeare memorabilia, and a BBC Television Costume Exhibition is included in the admission price.

Henley St
☎ (0789) 204016

Open: all year, Mar-Oct Mon-Sat 9-5.30, Sun 10-5.30; Nov-Feb Mon-Sat 9.30-4, Sun 10.30-4. (Closed Good Fri am, 24-26 Dec & 1 Jan am).
Admission: £2.40 (ch £1). Town Heritage Walking Tour (inc 3 town properties) £4.50 (ch £2). Inclusive tickets to all 5 Shakespearian properties £6.50 (ch £3). School & student party rates for groups visiting all 5 properties.
& toilets for disabled shop ✹

STRATFORD-UPON-AVON   World of Shakespeare

The atmosphere of Elizabethan England is recreated here with 25 life-size tableaux. Each one is brought to life by a combination of dramatic lighting, sound techniques, original music and an audio-visual presentation.

13 Waterside
☎ (0789) 269190

Open: all year, daily 9.05-5.30. Shows every hour & half hour. (Closed 25 Dec).
Admission: £3 (ch, students & pen £2). Family ticket £7. Party 10 + .Children under 5 free.
& toilets for disabled shop ✹

WARWICK   Warwick Castle

The first fortifications at Warwick were built by Ethelfleda, daughter of Alfred the Great, but the great castle that now stands over the River Avon was not begun until the end of the 11th century by William the Conqueror. The land was given then to Henry de Burgh, later the 1st Earl of Warwick; in the 16th century the castle was given to the Dudley family. None of the present buildings date from before the 13th century, when extensive work began on the castle. The outstanding buildings are Caesar's Tower, built in 1356 (128ft high), and Guy's Tower (1394), which are on either side of the Gatehouse, or Clock Tower. The south range, overlooking the River Avon, houses the State Rooms, Private Apartments and Great Hall. In the Private Apartments there is an award-winning display by Madame Tussaud's entitled 'A Royal Weekend Party – 1898'.

There are also dungeons with a torture display and an armoury display. There is a rampart walk from Guy's Tower, and outside are magnificent grounds laid out by Capability Brown in the 18th century. The gardens are noted for their peacocks. Medieval banquets are held every Friday and Saturday night in the 14th-century Undercroft. Special events are planned for the summer – telephone for details.

Off Castle Hill
☎ (0926) 495421

Open: daily 10-5.30 (4.30 Nov-Feb). (Closed 25 Dec).
Admission: ✳ £5.75 (ch 4-16 £3.50 & pen £4). Family ticket £16-£18. Party 20 +
🅿 ♨ ✗ licensed & toilets for disabled shop ✹

SYMBOLS

☎ Telephone number	✳ Indicates 1991 price	♨ Refreshments	✹ No Dogs
& Suitable for visitors in wheelchairs	🅿 Parking at Establishment	✗ Restaurant	🚌 No coaches

WEST MIDLANDS

BIRMINGHAM   Birmingham Botanical Gardens & Glasshouses

The gardens are a 15-acre 'oasis of delight' just 2 miles from the centre of Birmingham. Originally opened in 1832 they continue to be run by an independent educational charity. The Tropical House has a 24ft-wide lily pool and its lush tropical vegetation includes bromeliads, bananas, cocoa and other economic plants. Palm trees, ferns, orchids and insectiverous plants are displayed in the Palm House. The Orangery features a wide variety of citrus fruits and the Cactus House gives a desert scene with its giant agaves and opuntias. Outside there is colourful bedding on the Terrace and a tour of the gardens includes rhododendrons and azalea borders, Rose Garden, Rock Garden and a collection of over 200 trees. There are Domestic Theme Gardens, Herb and Cottage Gardens, a Children's Adventure Playground and Aviaries. Plant centre, gift shop, gallery and refreshment pavilion. Bands play every Sunday afternoon throughout the summer.

Westbourne Rd, Edgbaston
☎ 021-454 1860

Open: all year, wkdays 9-8 or dusk, Sun 10-8 or dusk whichever is earlier. (Closed 25 Dec).
Admission: £2.70 (£3 summer Sun, concessions £1.40). Party.
🅿 ☛ ✗ licensed & (3 wheelchairs available free) toilets for disabled shop garden centre ✻

BIRMINGHAM   Birmingham Nature Centre

Animals of the British Isles and Europe can be seen in indoor and outdoor enclosures which are designed to resemble natural habitats. The grounds also have various ponds and a stream, to attract wild birds, butterflies and other creatures.

Pershore Rd, Edgbaston (off A441, in Cannon Hill Pk)
☎ 021-472 7775

Open: 23 Mar-3 Nov, daily 10-5. (Winter Sat & Sun 10-dusk).
🅿 ☛ & toilets for disabled shop ✻
Details not confirmed for 1992

BIRMINGHAM   Birmingham Railway Museum

This is a working railway museum with a fully equipped workshop. There are 12 steam locomotives and 36 historic carriages, wagons and other vehicles. Steam-hauled train rides can be taken.

670 Warwick Rd, Tyseley
☎ 021-707 4696

Open: daily 10-5. (Closed 25 & 26 Dec & 1 Jan). Steam Days every Sun & BH Etr-Oct & Dec.
🅿 ☛ ✗ & shop
Details not confirmed for 1992

BIRMINGHAM   Museum of Science & Industry

The displays range from the Industrial Revolution to the present day, with an emphasis on Birmingham's contribution to science and engineering. The Engineering Hall is a former Victorian plating works, and contains machine tools, electrical equipment, and working steam, gas and hot air engines. The Locomotive Hall was built to house the Stanier Pacific loco 'City of Birmingham; and the

Newhall St (close to Post Office Tower)
☎ 021-236 1022

Open: all year, Mon-Sat 9.30-5, Sun 2-5 (Closed Xmas & 1 Jan).
& toilets for disabled shop ✻
Details not confirmed for 1992

aircraft section has a World War II Spitfire and a Hurricane, as well as aircraft engines. The James Watt building houses the earliest still-functioning steam engine in the world, dated 1799. Other sections cover science, transport and arms. There are steam weekends in March and October, and an engine rally in May. Engines are steamed on the first and third Wednesday of each month.

BIRMINGHAM   The Patrick Collection

Three halls are devoted to motoring from the beginning of the century to the present day, with cars ranging from a 1904 Wolseley to a 1991 Alfa Romeo SZ. There are also terraced gardens, a children's play area, children's electric go-karts and a new jetty for feeding the lakeside wildlife and fish. In spring 1992 a nature trail (accessible to disabled visitors) will be opening. The Engine House, newly refurbished, will be exhibiting cut away engines and gear boxes from Jaguar, Scania, Rover etc.

180 Lifford Ln, Kings Norton
☎ 021-459 9111
Open: 17 Apr-Oct, Wed, Sat & Sun 10.30-5.30. Also school holidays & BH's; Nov-Etr, Sun 10.30-5.30.
Admission: £3.50 (ch 14 £2.10, under 5 free, pen students & disabled £2.50). Family ticket £9. Party 10+.
P ⛟ ✗ licensed & (lift) toilets for disabled shop ⅙

BOURNVILLE   Cadbury World

Not just a chocolate factory tour by any means. Visitors to Cadbury World are first of all transported to a tropical rainforest to see the Aztecs of the 16th century growing and trading cocoa beans, and may even sample Emperor Montezuma's favourite drink – a mixture of cocoa, honey and chilli peppers! The introduction of chocolate to Europe follows, with a reconstruction of a cobbled square in Georgian England complete with the notorious White's Chocolate House. Here the story of the Cadbury family and their chocolate enterprise, including the creation of the Bournville factory and village, is related. There are further displays on packaging and marketing, early machinery, health and safety etc. Although there are no tours of the modern factory, the hand-processing unit shows all stages in the production of hand-made chocolates.

Linden Rd
☎ 021-433 4334
Open: all year, Mon-Sat 10-5.30, Sun 12-6 (Closed 25 Dec).
Admission: £4 (ch 5-15 £3, pen £3.60). Family ticket £12.85.
P ⛟ ✗ licensed & (ex packaging plant) toilets for disabled shop ⅙

COVENTRY   Coventry Cathedral & Visitor Centre

Coventry's old cathedral was bombed during an air raid of November 1940 which devastated the city. The remains have been carefully preserved. The new cathedral was designed by Sir Basil Spence and consecrated in May 1962. It contains outstanding modern works of art, including a huge tapestry designed by Graham Sutherland, the west screen (a wall of glass engraved by John Hutton with saints and angels), bronzes by Epstein, and windows by John Piper and others. There is also an opportunity to enjoy the art of modern technology in the visitors' centre.

7 Priory Row
☎ (0203) 227597
Open: all year, daily, Etr-Sep 9.30-7; Oct-Etr 9.30-5.30.
Admission: ✳ Visitor centre £1.25 (ch under 6 free, ch 6-16, students & pen 75p). Party 10+. Cathedral £2 donation. Camera charge £1.
✗ licensed & (lift) toilets for disabled shop ⅙

COVENTRY   Coventry Toy Museum

A collection of toys dating from 1740 to 1980, including trains, dolls, dolls' houses and games, housed in a 14th-century monastery gatehouse.

Much Park St
☎ (0203) 227560
Open: all year, daily 2-6.
Admission: ✱ £1 (ch & pen 50p).
shop ✖

COVENTRY   Museum of British Road Transport

The museum illustrates the role of Coventry and the West Midlands in the development of transport throughout the world. There are over 400 exhibits, in displays of motor cars, commercial vehicles, motor cycles and associated items. New for 1992 – a display of die-cast models.

St Agnes Ln, Hales St
☎ (0203) 832425
Open: all year, daily 10-5.
Admission: £2.50 (ch & pen £1.50). Family ticket £6.50.
& toilets for disabled shop ✖

DUDLEY   Black Country Museum

The museum is really a reconstruction of a Victorian Black Country village, complete with cottages, a chapel, chemist, baker and a pub serving real ale. One of the buildings is a chainmaker's house with a brewhouse, and demonstrations of chainmaking and glass cutting are given in traditional workshops. There is also a canal boat dock with a range of narrowboats, and boats set off daily for canal trips into the Dudley Tunnel, an eerie underground ride. Transport around the village is provided by an electric tramway. You can go underground in an 1850s mine, and see a replica of the world's first steam engine venture into a pit-pulled cottage (affected by subsidence due to mining). There will be a Working Boat gathering 26-27 Sep.

Tipton Rd (opposite Dudley Guest Hospital)
☎ 021-557 9643 & 021-520 8054
Open: all year, Mar-Oct daily 10-5; Nov-Feb, Wed-Sun 10-4. (Closed 25 Dec).
Admission: £4.75 (ch under 5 free, ch 18 £3.25, pen £4.25). Party 20+
🅿 ☕ & toilets for disabled shop ✖

DUDLEY   Dudley Zoo & Castle

The wooded grounds of Dudley Castle make a wonderful setting for the long-established, traditional zoo, which has animals from every continent. The castle ruins are impressive, and a chairlift and land train take you to the top of Castle Hill. An audio visual show of the castle's history is shown free of charge.

2 The Broadway
☎(0384) 252401
Open: all year, Etr-mid Sep, daily 10-4.30; mid Sep-Etr, daily 10-3.30. (Closed 25 Dec).
Admission: ✱ £4 (ch & pen £2). Family ticket £11.50. Party 15+.
🅿 (charged) ☕ ✗ licensed & (land train from gates to castle) toilets for disabled shop ✖

WEST SUSSEX

AMBERLEY   Amberley Chalk Pits Museum

A former chalk quarry and limeworks is the setting for this eye-opening display of industries in south-east England. A working blacksmith, potter and printer are based here, and there is a cobbler's shop. Narrow-gauge railway; various events all year.

Houghton Bridge (off B2139)
☎ Bury (0798) 831370
Open: 20 Mar-27 Oct, Wed-Sun & BH Mon 10-6. Also Mon & Tue in school summer holidays. Last admission 5pm.
🅿 ☛ ♿ toilets for disabled shop
Details not confirmed for 1992

ANSTY   Legh Manor

Three rooms and the hall can be visited in the interesting old house, and there is a garden laid out by Gertrude Jekyll.

☎ Haywards Heath (0444) 413428
Open: May-Sep, 2nd and 3rd Wed and 2nd Sat in each month 2.30-5.30.
🅿 ⚠
Details not confirmed for 1992

ARDINGLY   Wakehurst Place Garden

Woodland and lakes linked by a pretty watercourse make this large garden a beautiful place to walk, and it also has an amazing variety of interesting trees and shrubs. It is administered and maintained by the Royal Botanic Gardens at Kew.

(1.5m NW, on B2028)
☎ (0444) 892701
Open: all year, Nov-Jan 10-4; Feb & Oct 10-5; Mar 10-6; Apr-Sep 10-7. (Closed 25 Dec & 1 Jan). Last admission 30 mins before closing.
Admission: ✱ £3
🅿 ☛ ♿ toilets for disabled shop ⚠
(NT)

ARUNDEL   Arundel Castle

This great Castle, home of the Dukes of Norfolk, dates from the Norman Conquest. Containing a very fine collection of furniture and paintings, it is still a family home reflecting the changes of nearly a thousand years.

☎ (0903) 883136
Open: Apr-last Fri in Oct, Sun-Fri 12-5. Last admission 4pm (Closed Sat).
Admission: £3.60 (ch 5-15 £2.60, pen £3.10). Party 20+
🅿 (charged) ☛ ✗ licensed shop ⚠

ARUNDEL   Arundel Toy & Military Museum

A Georgian cottage in the heart of town displays a vast private collection of interesting old toys, games, dolls, teddy bears and toy soldiers. There are also royal commemoratives, boats, 'Goss' models, puppets, pocillovy (egg-cups), small militaria and curiosities collected from all over the world. During the Arundel festival in August, the museum will hold a 'Design a Garden' competition – details on application.

23 High St
☎ (0903) 883101 & 882908
Open: every weekend 12-5, school & BH; Jun-Aug daily 10.30-5. Most days in Spring & Sep-Oct.
Admission: £1.25 (ch 15, students & pen £1). Party.
♿ shop

ARUNDEL   Wildfowl & Wetlands Trust

More than a thousand ducks, geese and swans from all over the world live here in 55 acres of well-landscaped pens, lakes and paddocks, and the site is also a sanctuary for many wild birds. Wild diving duck are attracted by the clear, spring-fed pools, while waders come to feed in the damp meadows and 'wader scrape'. Rarities include the shy water rail, which makes its nest among the reed beds. Its grunting, squealing call may be heard. There are hides overlooking the different habitats, and the site also has a large viewing gallery and education complex. Facilities for the disabled include purpose-built toilet for wheelchair users, free wheelchair loan, access throughout the centre (including hides), and waitress service at the restaurant.

Mill Rd
☎ (0903) 883355
Open: all year, daily. Summer 9.30-6.30; Winter 9.30-5.30. Last admission Summer 5.30; Winter 4pm. (Closed 25 Dec).
🅿 ✕ licensed ♿ toilets for disabled shop 🐾
Details not confirmed for 1992

CHICHESTER   Mechanical Music & Doll Collection

Here is a unique opportunity to see and hear barrel, fair and Dutch street organs, musical boxes, polyphons etc – all fully restored and playing for your pleasure. The Doll Collection contains over one hundred fine examples of French and German bisque-headed dolls. Also phonographs, stereoscopic viewers, veteran cycles and natural history exhibits.

Church Rd, Portfield (1m E off A27)
☎ (0243) 785421
Open: all year, Etr-Sep, daily 10-5; Oct-Etr wknds only 10-5; Evening bookings by arrangement.
Admission: fee payable.
🅿 ♿ shop 🐾

FISHBOURNE   Roman Palace

This is the largest known Roman residence in Britain, but the reason for building such a magnificent house here is not known. It was occupied from the 1st to the 3rd centuries AD, when its hundred or so rooms must have been a wonderful sight with their mosaic floors and painted walls; 25 of these mosaic floors can still be seen in varying states of completeness, including others rescued from elsewhere in the area. The museum gives an account of the history of the palace, and there is also an audio-visual theatre. There is a full-size reconstruction of a Roman dining room. The garden has been re-planted to its original first-century plan. There is a new mosaic making area for children.

Salthill Rd
☎ Chichester (0243) 785859
Open: all year, daily, Mar-Apr & Oct 10-5; May-Sep 10-6; Nov 10-4; Dec-Feb, Sun only 10-4.
Admission: £3 (ch £1.20, pen & students £2.30). Family ticket £7.50.
🅿 ☕ ♿ (self guiding tapes & tactile objects for the blind) toilets for disabled shop 🐾

HENFIELD   Woods Mill Countryside Centre

The centre consists of a wildlife and countryside exhibition in an 18th- century watermill, and a trail through varied habitats. Nets are provided for a pond where children can identify specimens. Special events are held throughout the season, including Focus on Bats (16-17 May), and Victorian Haymaking Day (19 Jul).

Shoreham Rd (1.5m S Henfield on A2037)
☎ (0273) 492630
Open: 17 Apr-27 Sep, Tue, Wed, Thu & Sat 2-6; Sun & BH's 11-6.
Admission: £1.80 (ch 90p, pen £1.40). Family £5.
🅿 ☕ ♿ shop 🐾

PETWORTH   Petworth House

A 13-mile wall surrounds Petworth's acres. Rebuilt by the Duke of Somerset in the 17th century, all that remains of the 13th-century building is the chapel. The imposing 320ft west front faces the lake and great park, and was redesigned by Anthony Salvin between 1869 and 1872. The state rooms and galleries contain one of the finest art collections in England, including works by Gainsborough, Rembrandt and Van Dyck. Turner was a frequent visitor to Petworth, and a notable collection of his works is kept here. The carved room is said to be the most impressive in the house, with its lovely decoration by Grinling Gibbons. On 26-27 July open air concerts will be held, (telephone 0798 43748 for information).

☎ (0798) 42207

Open: Apr-Oct, daily (ex Mon & Fri; Open Good Fri & BH Mons, closed Tue following) 1-5.30. Gardens daily. Park 8-sunset.
Admission: ✳ £3.80.
🅿 ☛ 占 toilets for disabled shop ⚑ (ex in park)
(NT)

PULBOROUGH   Parham House & Gardens

Surrounded by a deer park, fine gardens and pleasure grounds in a beautiful downland setting, this Elizabethan family home contains a good collection of paintings, furniture, carpets and rare needlework. A brick and turf maze has been created in the grounds – designed with children in mind, it is called 'Veronica's Maze'. The garden at Parham has won the prestigious Christie's 1990 Garden of the Year Award. Plans for the garden in 1992 include a vegetable garden, with vegetable sales from the new garden shop. There is also a rose garden. Special events in the park include a steam rally in June, the Sussex Down RAFA Fete and a craft show. Details available from the Estate Office, 0903 742866.

Parham Park (3m SE off A283)
☎ **Storrington (0903) 742021**

Open: Etr Sun-1st Sun in Oct, Wed, Thu, Sun & BH. Gardens 1-6; House 2-6 (last entry 5.30pm). Guided tours on Wed & Thu mornings by special arrangement.
Admission: ✳ House & Gardens £3.20 (ch 5-15 £1.50 & pen £2.50). Gardens £1.60 (ch 75p). Party 20+.
🅿 ☛ 占 (by arrangement) shop garden centre ⚑ (ex in grounds)

SINGLETON   Weald & Downland Open Air Museum

Situated in a beautiful Downland setting, this museum is of rescued historic buildings from south-east England. The buildings, ranging from early medieval houses to a 19th-century schoolhouse, have been re-erected to form a village and outlying farms and agricultural buildings. Among the exhibits there is a medieval farmstead working watermill, where corn is ground and flour is sold, a Tudor market hall, a blacksmith's forge, tollhouse and timber-framed building. There are displays of rural industries, including a charcoal burner's camp, and traditional crafts. Special events for 1992 include: 25 May, Sheep Dog Trials; 7 Jun, Heavy Horses; 26 July, Show for Rare and Traditional Breeds; 24-25 Oct, Steam Threshing and Ploughing.

(6m N of Chichester on A286)
☎ **(024363) 348**

Open: all year, Mar-Oct, daily 11-6; Nov-Feb, Wed & Sun 11-5. Also open BH's. Last admission 1hr before closing.
Admission: ✳ £3.50 (ch £1.75, pen £2.75). Family ticket £8.50. Party.
🅿 ☛ 占 toilets for disabled shop

SYMBOLS			
☎ Telephone number	✳ Indicates 1991 price	☛ Refreshments	⚑ No Dogs
占 Suitable for visitors in wheelchairs	🅿 Parking at Establishment	✗ Restaurant	No coaches

WEST YORKSHIRE

BRADFORD   Industrial Museum

The museum illustrates the growth of the woollen and worsted textile industry, and is housed in a former spinning mill. Motive power and transport are covered as well. The mill owner's house is also open and gives an idea of domestic life around 1900. The Victorian street is complete with a tramway and back-to-back workers' cottages, and there are also working Victorian stables with three Shire horses. Visitors can ride on a horse-drawn tram, and there are also waggon rides. Temporary exhibitions are held monthly at weekends.

Moorside Rd, Eccleshill
☎ (0274) 631756
Open: all year, Tue-Sun & BH Mon 10-5. (Closed Mon ex BH)
Admission: free. Charges made for rides.
🅿 ☕ ♿ (induction loop in lecture theatre) toilets for disabled shop ✗

BRADFORD   National Museum of Photography, Film & Television

The National Museum of Photography, Film and Television portrays the past, present and future of the media using interactive displays and dramatic reconstructions – ride on a magic carpet, become a newsreader for the day or try your hand at vision mixing. Action Replay, the Museum's own theatre company, regularly performs highlights from the galleries. At the heart of the Museum is IMAX, UK's largest cinema screen, which is over five storeys high. Vast brilliant images sweep you into another world, exploring the realms of space to the depths of the ocean or indeed any subject big enough to be turned into this extraordinary experience. Special event for 1992 is the opening of the new cinema development in April.

Prince's View
☎ (0274) 727488
Open: all year, Tue-Sun & BH's 11-6. (Closed Mon).
Admission: ✱ Museum free, IMAX Cinema £3.30 (ch 16 £1.75, concessions £2.25).
☕ ♿ toilets for disabled shop ✗

HAREWOOD   Harewood House & Bird Garden

The 18th-century home of the Earl and Countess of Harewood contains fine furniture, porcelain and paintings, and its Capability Brown grounds offer lakeside and woodland walks. The Bird Garden has aviaries for over 150 species, and a tropical house. Adventure playground. Special events take place throughout the year.

(junc A61/A659 Leeds/Harrogate Rd)
☎ (0532) 886225
Open: Etr-Oct, daily Bird Garden from 10am, House from 11am.
🅿 ☕ ✗ licensed ♿ toilets for disabled shop garden centre ✗ (in House or bird garden)
Details not confirmed for 1992

HAWORTH   Keighley & Worth Valley Railway & Museum

The line was built mainly to serve the valley's mills, and goes through the heart of Brontë country. It begins at Keighley (also a BR station), and then climbs up to Haworth, the railway headquarters. The terminus is at Oxenhope, which has a museum and restoration building. There are 36 steam engines and eight diesels. Special events are planned throughout 1992.

Keighley, Haworth, Oxenhope & Ingrow West
☎ Keighley (0535) 645214
Open: all year wknd service, but daily all BH wks & Jul-1st wk Sep.
✱ Full line ticket £3.50 reduced fares for ch & pen. Family ticket £9. Other fares on request.
🅿 (charged) ☕ ♿ (wheelchairs can be accommodated in brake car). toilets for disabled shop

KEIGHLEY   Cliffe Castle Museum & Gallery

French furniture from the Victoria and Albert Museum is displayed, together with collections of local and natural history, ceramics, dolls, geological items and minerals. The grounds of this 19th-century mansion contain a play area and an aviary.

Spring Gardens Ln (NW of town on A629)
☎ **Bradford (0274) 758230**

Open: all year, Apr-Sep Tue-Sun 10-6; Oct-Mar Tue-Sun 10-5. Also open BH Mon. (Closed Good Fri, 25 & 26 Dec).
🅿 ♥ ⅊ toilets for disabled shop ⚔
Details not confirmed for 1992

LEEDS   Armley Mills Museum

Once the world's largest woollen mill, when the shuttles fly and the bobbins spin Armley Mills evokes memories of the 18th-century woollen industry showing the progress of wool from the sheep to knitted clothing. The museum also illustrates the history of cinema projection, including the first moving pictures taken in Leeds, as well as 1920s silent movies. There are demonstrations of static engines and steam locomotives, and a unique exhibition of underground haulage.

Canal Rd, Armley (2m W of city centre)
☎ **(0532) 637861**

Open: all year, summer – Tue-Sat 10-6, Sun 2-6; winter – Tue-Sat 10-5, Sun 2-5. Last entry 1 hr before closing. (Closed Mon, 25-26 Dec & 1 Jan)
Admission: ✱ £1 (concessions 45p)
🅿 ⅊ toilets for disabled shop ⚔

LEEDS   Middleton Colliery Railway

This was the first railway authorised by an Act of Parliament (in 1758) and the first to succeed with steam locomotives (in 1812). Steam trains run each weekend in season from Tunstall Road roundabout to Middleton Park. Facilities include a picnic area, nature trail, playgrounds and fishing. Extensive programme of special events.

Moor Rd, Hunslet
☎ **(0532) 710320 (ansaphone)**

Open: 6 Apr-29 Sep, Sat 1.30-4.30 & Sun 1-4.30 & Wed (Aug only), 1.30-4.30. Train trips every 45 minutes Sat & Wed (diesel-hauled), 30 minutes Sun. BH wknds from 11am.
🅿 ⅊ shop
Details not confirmed for 1992

LEEDS   Temple Newsam House & Park

This Tudor and Jacobean mansion boasts extensive collections of decorative arts in their original room settings, including the incomparable Chippendale collection. An extensive programme of renovation is restoring each room to its former glory, using original wall coverings and furniture.

Set in 1,200 acres of parkland (landscaped by Capability Brown), the Rare Breed Centre in the Home Farm delights visitors. The gardens have a magnificent display of rhododendrons, whilst a riot of roses bloom amid vibrant borders in the old walled garden. Events for 1992 include a steam spectacular (23- 25 May), and Threshing Day (13 Sep). A programme of chamber music is planned for the 2nd Tuesday every month from Sep to May. Telephone for details.

(off A63)
☎ **(0532) 647321 (House)**
& 645535 (Park)

Open: all year – House, daily 10.30-6.15 or dusk, Wed, May-Sep until 8.30. (Closed Mon ex BH Mons). Home Farm – summer Tue-Sun 10-5, winter Tue-Sun 10-4, last entry 30 mins before closing. Estate – daily dawn-dusk.
Admission: ✱ £1 (ch if accompanied & pen 45p). Estate & Home Farm, free.
🅿 ♥ ⅊ toilets for disabled shop ⚔

MIDDLESTOWN   The Yorkshire Mining Museum

A unique opportunity to go 450ft underground down one of Britain's oldest working mine shafts, where models and machinery depict methods and conditions of mining from the early 1800s to the present day. Visitors are strongly advised to wear sensible footwear and warm clothing. Surface displays (both indoor and outdoor), pit ponies, 'paddy' train rides, steam winder, nature trail and adventure playground. Many events are planned for 1992 including a Yorkshire Day on 1 August.

Caphouse Colliery, New Rd (on A642 between Wakefield & Huddersfield)
☎ Wakefield (0924) 848806
Open: all year, daily 10-5. (Closed 25-26 Dec & 1 Jan).
Admission: ✳ £4.45 (ch £3.65, concessions £3.80). Party.
🅿 ☕ ♿ (induction loop, arrange in advance for underground tour) toilets for disabled shop

OAKWELL HALL

A moated Elizabethan manor house, furnished as it might have looked in the 1690s. Extensive Country Park with countryside centre. There are period gardens, an equestrian arena and an adventure playground. A full events programme is planned for 1992 including historical re-enactments, a country fair, craft days and summer holiday events.

Nutter Ln, Birstall, Batley (6m SE of Bradford)
☎ Batley (0924) 474926
Open: all year, daily, telephone for opening times. (Closed Xmas).
Admission: ✳ fee payable Mar-Oct. Otherwise Free ex major event days.
🅿 ☕ ♿ (herb garden for the blind) toilets for disabled shop (ex in gardens)

SHIPLEY   Sooty's World

Sooty's World is now Sooty's official home, and fans can follow his rise to super-stardom through the sets, props, scripts, photos and films which chart the puppet's 40 year history. This permanent exhibition displays the many tiny special effects which have been used in Sooty shows over the years, including a miniature saxophone which cost more than a full-size instrument. Special events for 1992: for Sooty's 40th anniversary on television in 1992, many special events will be organised. Ring Bradford (0274) 531122 for details.

Windhill Manor, Leeds Rd
☎ (0274) 531122
Open: all year, Sat & Sun 10-5, Mon-Thu 10.30-4.30, Fri (school hols) 10.30-4.30. (Closed 25-26 Dec & 1 Jan).
Admission: ✳ £1.75 (ch, pen & disabled £1.25)
☕ ♿ shop ✗

ISLE OF WIGHT

ARRETON   Haseley Manor

This is the oldest and largest manor open to the public on the island. Parts of the south wing have some of the original building, c1350, but the rest of the house is a mixture of styles including Georgian and Victorian. The manor fell into disuse and was derelict by the 1970s but has since been carefully restored and now 20 rooms can be viewed, furnished in period style. Tableaux of figures in costume appear in many of the rooms.

☎ Isle of Wight (0983) 865420
Open: daily 10-5.30 Etr-Oct; Mon-Fri 10-5.30 Nov-Etr.
Admission: ✳ £3 (ch £2.50, pen £2.60). Party.
🅿 ☕ ✗ ♿ toilets for disabled shop

Outside, there is a re-constructed 18th-century farm complete with animals, and a well-stocked herb garden. There is also a children's play area with a tree house, a small lake with an island castle and a floating Noah's Ark. Visitors can also see pottery and sweet-making demonstrations.

ARRETON   Robin Hill Adventure Park

The 88 acres of magnificent downs and woodland incorporate a fascinating range of wildlife and activities. There is an exhilarating toboggan ride, a giant hillbilly slide, a Commando assault course, a maze, a boating lake, archery, BMX bikes, in fact everything for the adventurous! A 10-acre walk-through enclosure is home to fallow deer, sheep, llamas, wallabies, peacocks, geese, and ducks; snake handling demonstrations are held in a large tropical jungle house; there's a parrot playschool, and a nature trail through woodland. Events for 1992 include various 'fun days', a steam traction rally (3 May), and a clown convention (11 Jul).

Robin Hill
☎ Isle of Wight (0983) 527352 & 528029

Open: Mar-Oct, daily from 10am.
Admission: £3.90 (ch 4-14 & pen £2.90).
Party 15 +
🅿 ☕ ᕫ toilets for disabled shop

BEMBRIDGE   Bembridge Windmill

The only windmill on the island to survive, Bembridge mill was built about 1700 and was in use until 1913. The stone-built tower with its wooden cap and machinery have been restored since it was given to the National Trust in 1961.

(off B3395)
☎ Isle of Wight (0983) 873945

Open: Apr-Oct, daily (ex Sat) & Etr Sat & Jul-Aug, daily 10-5. Last admission 4.45pm.
Admission: £1 (ch 50p)
🅿 shop 🎯
(NT)

BEMBRIDGE   Isle of Wight Shipwreck Centre & Maritime Museum

Situated at the centre of Bembridge village, this fine museum brings alive the maritime history of the Isle of Wight. There are six galleries displaying a unique collection of salvage and shipwreck items, early diving equipment, ship models, HMS *Swordfish*, and a model of the harbour.

Providence House, Sherborne St
☎ Isle of Wight (0983) 872223 & 873125

Open: Mar-Oct, daily 10-5. (Other times by appointment)
Admission: £1.85 (ch £1 & pen £1.40).
🅿 ☕ ✘ licensed ᕫ shop 🎯

BLACKGANG   Blackgang Chine Fantasy Park

Opened as scenic gardens in 1843 covering some 30 acres, the park is now divided into different theme areas. Set on the steep wooded slopes of the chine are Jungleland, Smugglerland (complete with pirate ship), Nurseryland, Dinosaurland and Frontierland. There is also Fantasy Land, Water Gardens and a maze. And the park incorporates two heritage exhibitions – Timberworld and St Catherine's Quay – set in the 1890s. Winner of the Isle of Wight Best Attraction Award.

(on A3055)
☎ Isle of Wight (0983) 730330

Open: 6 Apr-Oct daily, 10-5, late May-late Sep, daily 10-10 (floodlit).
Admission: Combined ticket to chine, sawmill & quay £3.99 (ch 3-13 £2.99).
🅿 (charged) ☕ ✘ licensed ᕫ toilets for disabled shop 🎯

BRADING   Isle of Wight Wax Museum

Full of mystery and intrigue, this world-famous wax museum is set in the Ancient Rectory Mansion, part-dating from 1066. See the Chamber of Horrors in the Castle Dungeons. The picturesque courtyards are floodlit at night.

High St (on A3055)
☎ Isle of Wight (0983) 407286

Open: all year, May-Sep 10-10pm; Oct-Apr 10-5.
Admission: ✳ £3.30 (ch 14 £2.35, under 3 free). Party 20 + . Combined ticket with Animal World of Natural History available £3.70 (ch £2.65)
🅿 ᕫ

CARISBROOKE   Carisbrooke Castle

A Norman castle adapted from a Saxon fort, Carisbrooke is the only medieval castle on the island. It is set on a hill 150ft high, and the 12th-century keep is built on an artificial mound of about 60ft. The keep overlooks the later Elizabethan and Jacobean additions and the strong castle walls.

There are two medieval wells in the castle. The keep has a 160ft-deep well, reached by climbing 71 steps, and the other is housed in a 16th-century wellhouse in the courtyard. The winding gear was traditionally driven by a donkey, and a team of donkeys now gives displays of the machinery working. Charles I was a prisoner in the castle from 1647-48, and the castle was the home of the Governor of the island. His lodge is now the Isle of Wight Museum.

(on B3401)
☎ (0983) 522107
Open: all year, Apr-Sep, daily 10-6; Oct-Mar, daily 10-4. (Closed 24-26 Dec & 1 Jan).
Admission: £3 (ch £1.50, pen, students & UB40 £2.30).
🅿 ♥ ᕕ
(EH)

HAVENSTREET   Isle of Wight Steam Railway

When the Newport to Ryde railway was closed, Haven Street Station was taken over by a private company, the Isle of Wight Steam Railway. A number of volunteers restored the station, locomotives and rolling stock, and steam trains now run the five miles from Wootton, via Haven Street to Smallbrook Junction where there is a direct interchange with the BR Ryde-Shanklin line. Locomotives in operation include former LSWR tank engine *Calbourne*, built in 1891, and LSBCR/Freshwater, Yarmouth & Newport Railway locomotive *Freshwater,* built in 1875. The rolling stock includes 60 70-year-old LBSCR/ SECR carriages, plus vintage goods wagons. At Haven Street, the old gas works houses a display of Island railway memorabilia.

The Railway Station
☎ Isle of Wight (0983) 882204
Open: 26 Mar-30 Apr, Thu, Sun & BH's; also 21 & 22 Apr; May, Wed, Thu & Sun also BH Mon & Tue, 5 & 26 May; 2 Jun-16 Jul, Tue-Thu & Sun; 19 Jul-4 Sep, daily (ex Sat); 6-30 Sep, Wed, Thu & Sun; Oct, Thu & Sun.
Return Fares £4 (ch 5-15 £3). Family ticket £14. Unlimited travel on day of issue.
🅿 ♥ ᕕ (with assistance) toilets for disabled shop

OSBORNE HOUSE

Designed by Prince Albert and Thomas Cubitt and built between 1845 and 1848, Osborne was the Royal Family's private residence and Queen Victoria's favourite home. She lived at Osborne most of the time and died there in 1901. The house was designed to resemble an Italian villa, with terraced gardens overlooking Osborne Bay. The state and private apartments, which have been largely untouched since Victoria's death, are open to the public. The private apartments upstairs are cosy and comfortable and filled with all the paraphernalia of daily life. The large grounds are filled with every kind of English tree, a miniature fort and a Swiss cottage, where the Royal children learnt cooking and gardening. A horse-drawn carriage takes visitors to the Swiss cottage gardens and museum.

(1m SE of E Cowes)
☎ Isle of Wight (0983) 200022
Open: Apr-Sep, daily 10-5 (last admission 4.30pm), Grounds 10-6; Oct, House & Grounds daily 10-5 (last admission 4pm).
Admission: £5 (ch £2.50, students, pen & UB40 £3.80).
🅿 ♥ ᕕ shop ✗
(EH)

ST LAWRENCE   Tropical Bird Park

A bird park situated in the heart of the almost sub-tropical undercliff, in the grounds of Old Park. Enclosed by high stone walls are over 400 birds such as toucans, macaws and cockatoos. Woodland Trail is the home of eagles, storks, vultures and owls. On an ornamental lake are spoonbills, flamingoes and ducks. An extra attraction is a showroom where Isle of Wight glass is blown and displayed.

Old Park
☎ **Isle of Wight (0983) 852583 & 853752**
Open: Etr-Oct, 10-5; Oct-Etr, 10-4. (Closed 25 Dec).
Admission: ✻ £2.20 (ch 7-15 £1.50, pen £1.75).
🅿 (charged) ☕ ♿ shop ✘

SHORWELL   Yafford Water Mill Farm Park

The mill is situated in attractive surroundings with a large mill pond. The great overshot wheel still turns and all the milling machinery is in working order. An unusual attraction is the millpond, which is home to a pair of seals and their pup. The millstream has pools and falls with flowers and trees along its banks. There is a nature trail along the stream and among the pools – home to ducks, coots and moorhen. Old farm wagons and machinery are displayed and there are some rare breeds of sheep and cattle and a trout farm. Across the lane there is a picnic area and an adventure playground.

☎ **Isle of Wight (0983) 62117**
Open: Etr-Oct, daily 10-6. (Last admission 5pm).
Admission: £1.85 (ch & pen £1.25). Party 12 +.
🅿 ☕ ♿ shop ✘

YARMOUTH   Fort Victoria Country Park

Based around the remains of a fort built in 1852-3 to protect the western approach to Portsmouth, the wide grassy areas, coastal slopes, beach and sea wall have been made into a country park. Affording superb views of the Solent, there are picnic and barbeque facilities, also guided walks, exhibitions and a Marine Aquarium.

Sconce Point (1m W, off A3054)
☎ **Isle of Wight (0983) 760860**
Open: Park daily. Aquarium open end Mar-Nov 10-6.
Admission: ✻ Park free. Aquarium £1.10 (ch 60p, pen 60p). Museum 80p (ch 40p, pen 50p).
🅿 ☕ ♿ toilets for disabled shop

WILTSHIRE

AVEBURY   Avebury Manor

Avebury Manor has a monastic origin, and has been much altered since then. The present buildings date from the early 16th century, with notable Queen Anne alterations and Edwardian renovation. The flower gardens contain medieval walls, and there are examples of topiary.

☎ **(06723) 388**
Open: Garden – Apr-1 Nov, Tue-Wed & Fri-Sun 11-5.30 (last admission 5pm). House – due to restoration work, telephone for opening details.
Admission: House & garden £3 (ch £2.30); garden only £2 (ch £1.30).

(NT)

AVEBURY   Avebury Museum

This is one of the most important prehistoric sites in Europe, and was built before Stonehenge. In the midst of it is the pretty village of Avebury, which is surrounded by circles of massive sarsen stones and an impressive circular embankment and ditch. An avenue of great stones leads to the site, which must have been a place of great religious significance. The small museum has recently been refurbished and contains many new exhibits. It is named after Alexander Keiller, the first archaeologist to analyse the site in a modern way. It shows finds from Avebury and from Windmill Hill, a Neolithic causewayed enclosure about 1.5 miles away, which is also part of the National Trust property. Educational facilities are provided.

(Alexander Keiller Museum)
☎ (06723) 250
Open: all year, Apr-Sep, daily 10-6; Oct-Mar, daily 10-4. (Closed 24-26 Dec & 1 Jan).
Admission: £1.20 (ch 60p, students, pen & UB40 90p).
🅿 🚻 ⅋
(EH & NT)

AVEBURY   Great Barn Museum of Wiltshire Life

Close to the prehistoric stones, the museum is housed in a fine 17th-century thatched barn with a splendid roof structure. There are displays on cheesemaking, thatching, saddlery, sheep and shepherds, and the work of black-smiths, wheelwrights and other rural craftsmen. Regular craft sessions take place on Sundays between April and September, and there is a rare breeds weekend on the early May Bank Holiday, followed by a craft fair at the end of the month. The Wiltshire Country Food Fair takes place on August Bank Holiday.

☎ (06723) 555
Open: all year, mid Mar-Oct, daily 10-6. Nov-mid Mar, Sat 11-5, Sun 11-5.
Admission: 95p (ch & pen 50p). Family ticket £2.30.
✗ licensed 🚻 shop

BEDWYN, GREAT   Crofton Beam Engines

The oldest working steam engine in the world, the Boulton and Watt 1812, is to be found in this rural spot. Its companion is a Harvey's of Hayle of 1845. Both are coal-fired, and pump water into the Kennet and Avon Canal with a lift of 40ft. During steam weekends telephone Marlborough (0672) 870300 for information. The surroundings are pleasant, and walks can be taken on the canal towpath nearby. Trips can also be taken on the boat *Jubilee*: telephone 081-290 0031 to book places.

(6m SE of Marlborough, signposted from A338)
☎ Devizes (0380) 721279
Open: 17-20 Apr; 23-25 May; 25-28 Jun; 29-31 Aug; 25-27 Sep; 24-25 Oct.
Admission: ✶ £2.50 (ch £1, pen £1.50). Family ticket £5.
🅿 🛒 🚻 shop ⅋ (ex in grounds)

BROKERSWOOD   Woodland Heritage Museum & Woodland Park

Woodland Heritage Museum and Woodland Park nature walks lead through 80 acres of woodlands, with a lake and wildfowl. Facilities include a woodland visitor centre (covering wildlife and forestry), a children's adventure playground and guided walks and the Smokey Oak railway, over a third of a mile long. (Special catering facilities for parties of 10 or more). Barbeque sites and fishing permits available.

☎ Westbury (0373) 822238 & 823880
Open: all year; Park open daily 10-sunset. Museum open Mon-Fri 9-4; Sat 2-6, Sun 10-6 (summer); Sun 2-4.30 (winter).
Admission: £2 (unaccompanied ch £1.25, accompanied ch free, pen £1.75).
🅿 🛒 🚻 shop

CALNE   Bowood House & Gardens

Originally built in 1624, the house was unfinished when it was bought by the first Earl of Shelburne in 1754. He employed celebrated architects, notably Robert Adam, to complete the work, and what the visitor sees now is a handsome Georgian house. Adam's library is particularly admired, and also in the house is the laboratory where Dr Joseph Priestley discovered oxygen in 1774. There are fine paintings, sculpture, costume and other displays. The chief glory of Bowood, however, is its 2,000-acre expanse, 100 acres of which are pleasure gardens. They were laid out by Capability Brown in the 1760s and are carpeted with daffodils, narcissi and bluebells in spring. The centrepiece is a lake, while terraces, roses, clipped yews and sculpture are a perfect complement to the house. There is also a hermit's cave, a temple and cascade; and for children there is a huge adventure playground.

(off A4 in Derry Hill village)
☎ (0249) 812102

Open: Apr-Nov, daily 11-6, including BH. Rhododendron Gardens (separate entrance off A342) open 6 weeks during May & Jun 11-6.
Admission: ✳ House & Grounds £4 (ch £1.90 pen £3.30). Party.
🅿 ☕ ✗ licensed ☔ (parking by arrangement) toilets for disabled shop garden centre ⅋

LACOCK   Lackham Gardens, Museum & Woodland

Various visitor attractions are situated within the 210-hectare estate of the Lackham College of Agriculture. Thatched and refurbished farm buildings accommodate the farm museum and the grounds feature a walled garden, glasshouses, rhododendron glades, riverside and woodland walks, a children's adventure playground and two hectares of grassland devoted to rare breeds. There is a major collection of historical roses in the Italian Garden. Also grown in this garden was the largest citron (large lemon) which earned a place in the Guinness Book of Records. The gardens are open in aid of the National Gardens Scheme on 3 May, 12 July and 4 October and on 17 May there is an open day with displays, tractor rides and more.

(3m S of Chippenham on A350)
☎ Chippenham (0249) 443111

Open: 21 Mar-1 Nov, 11-5 (last admission 4pm).
Admission: £3 (ch £1, concessions £2). Family ticket £8.
🅿 ☕ ✗ ☔ (wheelchair available) toilets for disabled shop garden centre ⅋

LONGLEAT HOUSE

The present Marquess of Bath was the first peer to open his house to the public on a regular basis, a trend which many would follow. The Longleat estate has now grown to offer the visitor a safari park (home to hundreds of wild animals, including Britain's only white tiger); an exciting Adventure Castle; a maze; pleasure boat; narrow-gauge railway and a multitude of exhibitions and other attractions. The centrepiece of all this tourist activity is the majestic Elizabethan house, built by Sir John Thynne in 1580 and decorated in the Italian Renaissance style in the late-19th century. It contains a mixture of furnishings and artefacts reflecting the tastes and interests of the Thynne family through the centuries, and the fully restored Victorian kitchens offer an interesting glimpse of life 'below stairs'. The magnificent grounds, laid out by Capability Brown, offer many lovely walks. Heaven's Gate is particularly spectacular when the rhododendrons are flowering. Rallies and other special events are planned throughout 1992 include the Radio Society of Great Britain Amateur Radio Rally on 28 June.

(Entrance on Warminster-Frome Rd A362)
☎ Warminster (0985) 844551

Open: all year. House daily Etr-Oct 10-6, Nov-Etr 10-4. Safari park, mid Mar- end Oct 10-6, last car admitted 5.30 or sunset if earlier. All other attractions Etr-Oct 11-6 (some close or accept last visitor at 5.30pm).
Admission: House: £3.50 (ch £1.50, pen £3). Safari Park: £5 (ch £3.50, pen £4). Discount tickets for all attractions: £10 (ch & pen £8). All attractions can be paid for separately.
🅿 ☕ ✗ licensed ☔ toilets for disabled shop

LYDIARD PARK   Lydiard House & Park

Set in beautiful country park land, this fine Georgian house belonged to the St John family for 500 years up until 1943 when the house and parkland were purchased by the Swindon Corporation. Since then the sadly delapidated house has been gradually restored and refurbished with period furniture (in many cases original to the house) and a large St John family portrait collection (also original to the house). Exceptional plasterwork, early wallpaper and rare painted glass windows can also be seen. Adjacent, the church of St Marys has many fine and unusual memorials to the St John family. The Park, now operating as a Country Park, offers a variety of pleasant woodland walks, spacious lawns, lakes and children's adventure playground.

Lydiard Tregoze
☎ **Swindon (0793) 770401**
Open: all year, Mon-Sat 10-1 & 2-5.30, Sun 2-5.30. (Closed Good Fri & Xmas). Winter closing 4pm.
Admission: Free.
🅿 ☂ ♿ shop ✻

TEFFONT MAGNA   Farmer Giles Farmstead

Working dairy farm with 20,000sq ft under cover without steps. The 150 cows are milked from 2.30 to 5pm, and there are calves, highland cattle, shire horses, donkeys, Shetland ponies, pigs, sheep, goats, rabbits and poultry in the paddocks. Children may bottle feed the lambs. Features include 'Dairying Through the Ages', exhibitions and displays in the undercover area, and an adventure playground with tractor and beech belt nature walk. Special events including craft displays and a steam rally are held throughout the year.

☎ **(0722) 716338**
Open: 28 Mar-2 Nov, daily 10.30-6, wknds until Xmas. Party bookings all year.
Admission: £2.50 (ch £1.50, pen £2)
🅿 ✗ ♿ toilets for disabled shop

WILTON (near Salisbury)   Wilton House

Built on the site of an abbey founded by King Alfred, the present Wilton House is the home of the Earl of Pembroke. The Pembroke family have lived at Wilton since the mid 1500s, when the abbey grounds were given to the 1st Earl by Henry VIII. The original house was probably designed by Hans Holbein, but a fire in 1647 destroyed most of it and little remains apart from a porch. After the fire, the house was redesigned by Inigo Jones and John Webb. Their contribution still remains in the seven state rooms, of which the unusual double and single cube rooms are the most magnificent. The single cube is exactly 30ft in height, length and width.

In 1800 James Wyatt made further extensive improvements, particularly to the north and west fronts. Inside the house there is a world-famous collection of paintings by Rubens, Van Dyck and Tinteretto among others, and some fine furniture and sculptures. There is also a display of 7,000 model soldiers and a dolls' palace.

The grounds are laid mainly to lawn, with superb old cedar trees and a Palladian bridge over the river as dramatic features. Documentary drama film presentations are planned for 1992.

(2.5m W of Salisbury, on A30)
☎ **Salisbury (0722) 743115**
Open: 7 Apr-18 Oct, Mon-Sat 11-6, Sun 12-6. Last admission 4.30pm.
Admission: ✽ £4.50 (ch 5-16 £3.20, under 5 free, students & pen £4.20).
🅿 ✗ licensed ♿ toilets for disabled shop garden centre ✻

CHANNEL ISLANDS Guernsey

CÂTEL (CASTEL) Le Friquet Butterfly Centre

European and tropical butterfies fly freely in the lush setting of the Butterfly Farm greenhouse, and may be seen hatching from their chrysalids. Other attractions include putting and croquet.

☎ Guernsey (0481) 54378

Open: Etr-Oct, daily 10-5.
Admission: £1.75 (ch & pen £1.25).
P ☕ ✕ licensed ♿ shop

ST MARTIN Sausmarez Manor

The Manor has been owned by the same family for many centuries, a family which has included artists, generals, admirals, privateers, judges, sportsmen, inventors, cartographers, explorers, adventurers and politicians – most of whom have left some mark on the house or its contents. Each room is a happy contrast in style to its neighbour, with collections of Oriental, French and English furniture and an eclectic variety of paintings. The Formal Garden has herbaceous borders in the style of Gertrude Jekyll, while the Woodland Garden, set around two small lakes and a stream, is inter-planted with colourful shrubs, bulbs and wild flowers, many designed to encourage butterflies, birds and other animal life. In a section of the wood, a 7.25 gauge ride-on railway runs for over a quarter of a mile over embankments and through cuttings, while in the 16th-century Tudor Barn there is a 310sq ft model railway layout, with up to eight trains running continuously through meticulously scaled countryside, towns and villages. Another special layout of the Robus Playmobile Train Set is available for visitors to operate. New for 1992 is the Old Guernsey Working Museum with daily live demonstrations of a variety of old Guernsey crafts and activities, plus, in the Little Barn, a collection of dolls' houses dating from 1820 to the present day. There are a number of special events planned for 1992 ranging from fashion to bonsai to craft.

Sausmarez Rd
☎ Guernsey (0481) 35571

Open: last BH in May-last Thu in Sep, Tue-Thu & BH Mons.
Admission: ❄ House £2 (ch 70p). Old Guernsey Museum £1.50. Dolls House £1. Railways £1.
P ☕ ✕ ♿ shop

CHANNEL ISLANDS Jersey

ST OUEN Jersey Shire Horse Centre

There are Shire horses and their foals to meet, and carriage rides can be taken along country lanes. There are also displays of harness, farming implements and a museum.

Champ Donne, Rue de Trodez
☎ Jersey (0534) 82372

Open: Mar-Oct, daily (ex Sat) 10-5.30. Also all BH's.
Admission: £2.50 (ch £1.50, ch under 3 free, pen £2). Wheelchair users and the blind free.
P ☕ shop 🐕

ST OUEN   Kempt Tower Interpretation Centre

The centre has displays on the past, and the wildlife, of St Ouen's Bay, including Les Mielles, which is Jersey's miniature national park. Nature walks are held every Thursday (May to September), with bird walks most Sunday afternoons. Check local press for details.

Five Mile Rd
☎ Jersey (0534) 483651
Open: 2 Apr & 27 Sep-29 Oct, Thu & Sun only 2-5; May-27 Sep, daily (ex Mon) 2-5.
Admission: Free.
🅿 shop ⚑

TRINITY   Jersey Zoological Park

Les Augres Manor is the home of Gerald Durrell, and the Jersey Wildlife Preservation Trust, which has established here a unique sanctuary and breeding centre for endangered animals. Among the many exciting and attractive exhibits are Jambo, the world-famous Lowland gorilla and his large family, the Spectacled bears and their cubs, Snow leopards, marmosets and tamarins. The most important and prestigious new building is The Princess Royal Pavilion, where the fascinating story of the work of the Trust is unfolded in a superb audio-visual presentation.

Les Augres Manor
☎ Jersey (0534) 64666 **due to change to 864666**
Open: all year, daily 10-6 (dusk in winter). (Closed 25 Dec).
Admission: ✳ £4 (ch & pen £2).
🅿 ☛ ♿ (trail for the blind, auditory loop in pavilion) toilets for disabled shop ⚑

ISLE OF MAN

BALLAUGH   Curaghs Wild Life Park

Developed adjacent to the reserve area of the Ballaugh Curraghs is the wildlife park, which exhibits a variety of animals and birds in natural settings.

☎ Sulby (062489) 7323
Open: Etr-Sep, daily 10-6. Last admission 5.15pm.
Admission: £2 (ch £1). Party 25+.
🅿 ☛ ♿ toilets for disabled shop ⚑

CREGNEISH   Cregneash Village Folk Museum

A group of traditional Manx cottages with their gardens and walled enclosures. Inside the cottages furniture and the everyday equipment used by typical Manx crofting communities are displayed. A crofter-fisherman's home, a farmstead, a turner's shed, smithy and a weaver's shed are all represented in realistic settings. Spinning demonstrations are given on certain days and sometimes a blacksmith can be seen at work. In the field adjoining the turner's shed, Manx Loghtan sheep can often be viewed; this ancient breed survives in very small numbers. The rams have a tendency to produce four, or even six, horns.

(2m from Port Erin/Port St Mary)
☎ Douglas (0624) 675522
Open: Etr-Sep, daily 10-5.
✳ £1.50 (ch & pen 75p).
🅿 ☛ ✗ ♿ shop ⚑ (ex in grounds)

LAXEY   Laxey Wheel

Constructed to keep the lead mines free from water, this big wheel, known as the 'Lady Isabella', is an impressive sight at 72.5ft in diameter. It is the largest working wheel in the world.

☎ Douglas (0624) 675522
Open: Etr-Sep, daily 10-5.
Admission: ✳ £1.50 (ch & pen 75p).
🅿 ♿ shop ⚑

SCOTLAND

BORDERS

DUNS Manderston

This grandest of grand houses gives a fascinating picture of Edwardian life both above and below stairs. It was built for the millionaire racehorse owner Sir James Miller. The architect was told to spare no expense, and so the house boasts features such as the world's only silver staircase, a ballroom painted in Sir James's racing colours, and painted ceilings. The state rooms are magnificent, and the domestic quarters are also quite lavish. Outside buildings include the handsome stable block and marble dairy, and there are fine formal gardens, with a woodland garden and lakeside walks.

(1.25m E off A6105)
☎ (0361) 83450

Open: 9 May-29 Sep, Thu & Sun 2-5.30 (also May & Aug BH Mon).
Admission: ✻ House & grounds £3.75. Grounds only £2.
🅿 ☕ ♿ shop

JEDBURGH Castle Jail & Museum

The social history of 19th-century Jedburgh, a town with a colourful past, is revealed in a museum at the Castle Jail. The jail itself is interesting as possibly the last surviving example of its kind. Built in the 1820s on the site of a medieval castle, it served as a county prison, and the three blocks were used to incarcerate different types of offenders.

Castlegate
☎ (0835) 63254

Open: Etr-Sep, Mon-Sat 10-5, Sun 1-5.
Admission: 70p (ch, pen, students & UB40's 35p). Party 20+.
♿ 🚫🐕

JEDBURGH Jedburgh Abbey

Standing as the most entire of the Border monasteries, although it has been sacked and rebuilt many times, Jedburgh Abbey has been described as 'the most perfect and beautiful example of the Saxon and early Gothic in Scotland'. It was founded as a priory in the 12th century by David I and remains of some of the domestic buildings have been uncovered during excavations.

4-5 Abbey Bridgend
☎ 031-244 3101

Open: all year, Apr-Sep, weekdays 9.30-6, Sun 2-6; Oct-Mar, weekdays 9.30-4, Sun 2-4. (Closed 25-26 Dec & 1-2 Jan).
Admission: £1.70 (concessions 90p). Family ticket £4.50.
🅿 ♿ (limited access) toilets for disabled shop 🚫🐕
(AM)

JEDBURGH Mary Queen of Scots House

Mary Queen of Scots visited Jedburgh in 1566, and had to prolong her stay because of ill-health. Her home here is now a museum devoted to her memory and tragic history. An unusual feature of this 16th-century fortified dwelling ('bastle house') is the left-handed spiral staircase: the owners of the house, the Ker clan, were left-handed and

Queen St
☎ (0835) 63331

Open: Etr-mid Nov, daily 10-5.
Admission: £1.10 (ch, pen, students & UB40's 55p). Party 20+.
♿ shop 🚫🐕

the special staircase allowed the men to use their sword hands. The museum presents a thought-provoking interpretation of her tragic life, and as 1992 is the 450th anniversary of the birth of Mary Queen of Scots, special events will be held, including medieval fayres, music and dancing in the house and grounds, and children's competitions.

KELSO   Floors Castle

Sir Walter Scott described this fairy-tale castle as 'altogether a kingdom for Oberon and Titania to dwell in'. Today it is the home of the 10th Duke of Roxburghe and its lived-in atmosphere enhances the superb collection of tapestries and paintings contained inside. The house was designed by William Adam in 1721 and extended by W H Playfair over a century later; it boasts a window for each day of the year and looks out over the graceful River Tweed. A holly tree in the grounds is said to mark the spot where James II was killed; and a magnificent walled garden, garden centre and play area are among the attractions outside. Pipe bands play on 3 and 24 May, 7 Jun, 12 Jul, and 30 Aug.

☎ (0573) 23333

Open: Etr & Apr-Jun & Sep (Sun-Thu), Jul-Aug (daily) 10.30-5.30; Oct, Sun & Wed, 10.30-4. Walled Garden & Garden Centre open daily.
Admission: £3 (ch £1.50, pen £2.40). Family ticket £8. Party.
🅿 ☕ ✗ licensed ও (lift) toilets for disabled shop garden centre ✗ (ex in grounds)

LAUDER   Thirlestane Castle

This fairy-tale castle has been the home of the Maitland family, the Earls of Lauderdale, since the 12th century, and part of the family still live in one of the wings. Some of the most splendid plasterwork ceilings in Britain may be seen in the 17th-century state rooms. The former family nurseries now house a sizeable collection of antique toys and dolls, while in the basement there are several interesting displays illustrating Border country life. The informal grounds, with their riverside setting and views of nearby grouse moors, include a woodland walk.

(off A68)
☎ (05782) 430

Open: 17-20 Apr, May-Jun & Sep, Wed-Thu & Sun; Jul-Aug, daily (ex Sat) 2-5 (last admission 4.30pm). Grounds open on dates listed above noon-6.
Admission: £3. Family ticket £8. Grounds only £1. Party.
🅿 ☕ ও toilets for disabled shop ✗ (ex in grounds)

MELROSE   Melrose Abbey & Abbey Museum

The ruin of this Cistercian abbey is probably one of Scotland's finest, and has been given added glamour by its connection with Sir Walter Scott. The abbey was repeatedly wrecked during the Scottish wars of independence, but parts of the nave and choir survive from the 14th century, and include some of the best and most elaborate traceried stonework in Scotland. Most of the ruins belong to a 15th-century reconstruction. The abbey has many interesting features: the heart of Robert the Bruce is buried somewhere within the church; note too the figure of a pig playing the bagpipes, set on the roof. The museum, sited at the entrance to the ruins and housed in the 16th-century Commendator's House, is an interesting addition to this historic ruin.

☎ 031-244 3101

Open: all year, Apr-Sep weekdays 9.30-6, Sun 2-6; Oct-Mar, weekdays 9.30-4, Sun 2-4.
Admission: £1.70 (concessions 90p). Family ticket £4.50.
🅿 ও shop ✗
(AM)

MELROSE Melrose Motor Museum

A short walk from the abbey ruins, this is a fascinating collection of cars, cycles, motorcycles and accessories.

Annay Rd
☎ St Boswells (089682) 2624

Open: Etr-Whitsun, please telephone for opening times. Whitsun-Oct, daily 10-5.30. Last admission 4.45pm.
Admission: £1.80 (ch 50p, pen £1.30). Party 10+ by arrangement.
P ♿ shop 🐕̸

SELKIRK Bowhill House & Country Park

An outstanding collection of pictures, including works by Van Dyck, Canaletto, Reynolds, Gainsborough and Claude Lorraine, are displayed in this, the Border home of the Duke of Buccleuch and Queensberry KT. In addition to these there is an equally stunning collection of porcelain and furniture, much of it made in the Paris workshop of André Boulle. Memorabilia and relics of people such as Queen Victoria and Sir Walter Scott, and a restored Victorian kitchen add further interest inside the house. Outside, the wooded grounds are perfect for walking, cycling and riding (there is bicycle hire and a riding centre). Children will enjoy the adventure playground and, no doubt, the gift shop. There is also a theatre and an audio-visual display. Art courses are held here.

(3m W of Selkirk off A708)
☎ (0750) 20732

Open: Grounds: May-Aug 12-5 (ex Fri), Riding centre all year. House & grounds: Jul, daily 1-4.30.
Admission: House & grounds £3 (ch under 5 free, pen £2). Grounds only £1. Party 20+.
P ☕ ✕ licensed ♿ (guided tours for the blind) toilets for disabled shop (Jul) 🐕̸ (ex in grounds)

TRAQUAIR Traquair House

This is said to be Scotland's oldest inhabited, and most romantic, house. It dates back to the 10th century and 27 English and Scottish kings have stayed here. William the Lion Heart held court at Traquair, and the house has rich associations with Mary Queen of Scots and the Jacobite risings. The large Bear Gates were closed in 1745, not to be reopened until the Stuarts should once again ascend the throne.

The house contains a fine collection of historical treasures and a unique 18th-century brewhouse which is licensed to make and sell its own beer. Outside there is a maze, croquet, and the opportunity for woodland walks by the River Tweed. There are also craft workshops and an art gallery. Events for 1992 include Traquair Fair (1-2 Aug) and a sheep and wool day (26 Jul).

(1m S of Innerleithen on B709)
☎ Innerleithen (0896) 830323 & 830785

Open: Etr wk & 18-26 Apr, Sun & Mons in May, then daily from 30 May-Sep, 1.30-5.30 (ex Jul & Aug 10.30-5.30). Last admission 5pm. Grounds open Apr-Sep, 10.30-5.30.
Admission: £3 (ch £1.50). Party.
P ☕ ✕ licensed ♿ shop

ABBREVIATIONS

AM	Ancient Monument	BH	Bank Holidays	ch 15 20p	Children under 15 20p
AM(CadW)	Ancient Monument (Wales)	PH	Public Holidays	Pen	Senior Citizens
EH	English Heritage	Etr	Easter	Party	Special or reduced rates for parties booked in advance
NT	National Trust	ex	except	Party 30+	Special or reduced rates for parties of 30 or more booked in advance
NTS	National Trust for Scotland	Free	Admission free		
		10p	Admission 10p		
		ch 20p	Children 20p		

CENTRAL

BIRKHILL   The Birkhill Clay Mine

No simulations here, this is a real clay mine deep in the steep wooded Avon Gorge. Experience life underground, and visit the original mill, clay handling buildings and haulage gear. Work is in progress on a car park, picnic area, underground walks and a nature trail.

☎ Bo'ness (0506) 825855
Open: Etr-Sep, Sat & Sun 12-4; daily, mid Jul-Aug 12-4.
🅿 shop
Details not confirmed for 1992

BLAIR DRUMMOND   Blair Drummond Safari & Leisure Park

Wild animals can be seen roaming in natural surroundings. There is a lion and a tiger reserve with an aerial walkway above the lions. Other attractions include a pets' farm, boat safari around Chimp Island, sealion shows, Splash Cats and pedal boats, Astra Glide, and flying fox cable slide across the lake. Amusement area and Adventure Playground.

(Exit 10 off M9, A84 between Doune/Stirling)
☎ Doune (0786) 841456
Open: late Apr-5 Oct, daily 10-5.30. Last admission 4.30pm.
Admission: £5 (ch 3-14 & pen £3).
🅿 🍴 ♿ toilets for disabled shop ✗

BO'NESS   Bo'ness & Kinneill Railway

The Scottish Railway Preservation Society has reclaimed land on the foreshore at Bo'ness and used it to re-create the days of steam, with many relocated historic railway buildings and Scotland's largest collection of locomotives and rolling stock. There is a seven-mile round trip by steam train through woodland and countryside for a visit underground to Birkhill Fireclay Mine. Work is in progress to extend the line to Manuel Junction (5.5 miles). Santa Specials are held at weekends in December, and other special events take place throughout the year, including a Victorian Day (24 May), a vintage vehicle rally (21 Jun), and a diesel enthusiasts' weekend.

Bo'ness Station, Union St
☎ (0506) 822298
Open: wknds 11 Apr-18 Oct; Mon 20 Apr, 4 & 25 May; daily 18 Jul-Aug; School weeks Mon-Fri 25-29 May & 1-5 Jun.
Return fare £3 (ch 5-15 £1.50, pen £2). Family ticket £7.50. Event days £4 (ch 3-15 & pen £2). Family ticket £10.
🅿 🍴 ♿ shop

STIRLING   Smith Art Gallery & Museum

This lively, award-winning museum and gallery presents a variety of exhibitions drawing on its own rich collections and works from elsewhere. A range of programmes and events offers the opportunity to see, find out about and join in art, history, craft and design. There is a small shop.

Dumbarton Rd
☎ (0786) 71917
Open: all year, Apr-Oct, Tue-Sat 10.30-5, Sun 2-5; Nov-Mar Tue-Fri 12-5, Sat 10.30-5 & Sun 2-5.
🍴 ♿ (wheelchair lift) toilets for disabled shop ✗
Details not confirmed for 1992

STIRLING   Stirling Castle

Sitting on top of a 250ft rock, Stirling Castle has a strategic position on the Firth of Forth. As a result it has been the scene of many events in Scotland's history. Much of the castle that remains today is from the 15th and 16th

Upper Castle Hill
☎ 031-244 3101
Open: all year, Oct-Dec & 4 Jan-Mar, Mon-Sat 9.30-4.20 (last ticket sold), Sun

centuries, when it became a favourite royal residence. James II was born at the castle in 1430. Mary Queen of Scots spent some years there, and it was James IV's childhood home. The old towers were built by James IV, as was the fine great hall. Among its finest features are the splendid Renaissance palace built by James V, and the Chapel Royal, rebuilt by James VI.

12.30-3.35 (last ticket sold). Apr-Sep, Mon-Sat 9.30-5.15, (last ticket sold). Sun 10.30-4.45 (last ticket sold). (Closed 24-26 Dec & 31 Dec-3 Jan).
Admission: £2.30 (concessions £1.20). Family ticket £6.
P ♥ shop ✗
(AM)

STIRLING   Stirling Castle Visitor Centre

The centre has an exhibition with an audio-visual display on the history of Stirling Castle. It is situated in a restored old building overlooking the River Forth. There is also a shop.

Upper Castle Hill, Castle Esplanade
☎ (0786) 62517

Open: Visitor Centre all year (ex Jan); Oct-Mar, Mon-Sat 9.30-5.05, Sun 12.30-4.20; Apr-Sep, Mon-Sat 9.30-6 & Sun 10.30-5.30. (Last entry 45 minutes before closing).
Admission: Charge for audio visual, 60p (ch & pen 30p).
P ♥ & (Induction loop for the hard of hearing) shop ✗
(NTS)

DUMFRIES & GALLOWAY

CAERLAVEROCK   Wildfowl & Wetlands Trust

This is an exciting wildlife refuge of over 100 acres on the north Solway shore. There are outstanding hide facilities, observation towers and an observatory giving impressive views of the huge numbers of wildfowl that spend most of the winter here. The barnacle geese are the most impressive sight. Thousands of them fly in from their Spitsbergen breeding grounds to rest and feed in the waters and marshes. Pink-footed and greylag geese can also be seen, as can waders, whooper swans and ducks such as pintails and wigeons. These in turn may attract interesting predators such as peregrines and merlins. The 'merse', or salt marsh, is also a home of the rare natterjack toad.

Eastpark Farm
☎ Glencaple (038777) 200

Open: mid Sep-Apr, 9.30-5 (Closed 24-25 Dec).
P & ✗
Details not confirmed for 1992

KIRKBEAN   Arbigland Gardens

Extensive woodland, formal and water gardens are set around a delightful sandy bay which is ideal for children. John Paul Jones, the US Admiral, worked in the gardens as a young boy (his father was the gardener here in the 1740s). His birthplace can be seen nearby; it will be opened officially as a museum mid-July.

(1m SE, adjacent to Paul Jones cottage)
☎ (038788) 283

Open: Gardens May-Sep, Wed-Sun 2-6. House 21-31 May. Also open BH Mon.
Admission: £2 (ch 50p).
P ♥ & toilets for disabled shop

THORNHILL Drumlanrig Castle

This unusual, pink sandstone castle was built in the late 17th century in Renaissance style. Ringed by rugged hills, the castle was erected on the site of earlier Douglas strongholds. It contains a celebrated collection of paintings by Rembrandt, Da Vinci, Holbein, Murillo and many others. There is also French furniture, mainly Louis XIV, as well as silver and relics of Bonnie Prince Charlie. The old stable block has a craft centre with resident craft workers, a gift shop, tearoom and a visitor's centre. The grounds offer an extensive garden, and adventure woodland play area and woodland walks.

(4m NW off A76 on west bank of River Nith)
☎ (0848) 31682 & 30248

Open: Castle May-Aug, wkdays 11-5, Sun 1-5 (Closed Sat). Last admission 4pm. Grounds May-Sep, daily.
Admission: ✻ House & Grounds £3 (ch 5-16 £1, pen & student £2). Grounds only £1. Party.
P ☕ ♿ (lift) toilets for disabled shop 🚫🐕 (ex in park)

WANLOCKHEAD Museum of Lead Mining

The museum conserves, displays and interprets the physical and written evidence of lead mining in Scotland. There is also an interesting collection of local gold, silver and other minerals on display. A one-and-a-half-mile walkway takes the visitor to an 18th-century lead mine, smelt mill and miners' cottages furnished in the styles of 1740 and 1890. An unusual feature is a Miners' Reading Society library, which was founded in 1756. In 1992 the museum will display a new collection of rare minerals, all found locally. There will also be a new exhibition on gold to celebrate Wanlockhead's hosting of the 1992 world gold panning championships.

(on B797 at N end of Mennock Pass)
☎ Leadhills (0659) 74387

Open: 17 Apr-mid Oct, daily 11-4.30 (last mine tour 4pm).
Admission: £2.50 (ch 5-16 £1, concessions £1.80).
P ♿ toilets for disabled shop

WHITHORN Whithorn Dig

Archaeologists are carefully uncovering 1,500 years of history of Scotland's first-recorded Christian settlement. There are site tours and viewing platforms. Admission also includes the new visitor centre, picture show, exhibitions, Whithorn Priory (see below), museum and crypts, herb garden, gift shop, craft demonstrations and children's play area.

45-47 George St
☎ (09885) 508

Open: Etr-Oct.
Admission: ✻ £2.50 (ch, pen & UB40's £1.25). Family ticket £7. Season ticket. Party.
♿ toilets for disabled shop

WHITHORN Whithorn Priory

The first Christian church in Scotland was founded here by St Ninian in 397, but the present ruins date from the 12th century. The ruins are scanty but there is a notable Norman door, the Latinus stone of the 5th century and other early Christian monuments.

☎ 031-244 3101

Open: all year, Apr-Sep weekdays 9.30-6, Sun 2-6; Oct-Mar, wkdys 9.30-4, Sun 2-4. (Closed Mon-Fri in winter, 25-26 Dec & 1-2 Jan).
Admission: £1 (concessions 50p).
♿ 🚫🐕 (AM)

SYMBOLS

☎ Telephone number
♿ Suitable for visitors in wheelchairs
✻ Indicates 1991 price
P Parking at Establishment
☕ Refreshments
✕ Restaurant
🚫🐕 No Dogs
🚫🚌 No coaches

FIFE

BURNTISLAND Burntisland Edwardian Fair Museum

All the fun of the fair at this Scottish Museum of the Year award winner. Burntisland Museum has recreated a walk through the sights and sounds of the town's fair in 1910, based on a painting of the scene by local artist Andrew Young. See rides, stalls and side shows of the time and view the local history gallery.

102 High St
☎ Kirkcaldy (0592) 260732

Open: all year, Mon-Sat 10-1 & 2-5. (Closed Sun & BH Mon's).
Admission: Free.
P 🐕

CUPAR Hill of Tarvit Mansion House & Garden

Sir Robert Lorimer virtually rebuilt this Edwardian house. It has a notable collection of furniture, tapestries and paintings, regular exhibitions of local artists' work, a walled garden, nursery, video and adventure playground.

(2.5m S off A916)
☎ (0334) 53127

Open: 4-30 Apr, Sat & Sun; 17-20 Apr & May-Oct, daily 2-6. (Last admission 5.30pm). Garden & grounds all year, daily 10-sunset.
Admission: ❄ House & Garden £2.80 (ch & pen £1.40). Garden only £1 (ch 50p). Party.
P ☕ ♿ shop 🐕
(NTS)

CUPAR The Scottish Deer Centre

Guided tours take about 30 minutes and allow visitors to meet and stroke deer. Children can help with bottle-feeding young fawns, and facilities include farm, nature and heritage trails. A film presentation and exhibition are provided. Aerial walkways and observation platforms are a special feature, allowing better views of several species of deer and the landscape. There is a large Adventureland and indoor playroom for children.

Bow-of-Fife (3m W on A91)
☎ Letham (033781) 391

Open: daily, Apr-Oct 10-5 (summer 6pm). Nov-Dec & Mar Sat-Sun only 10-5 (or dusk). (Closed Jan-Feb).
Admission: ❄ £3.05 (ch £1.95, concessions £2.50). Family ticket £8.25. Party 10+.
P ✕ licensed ♿ (special parking bay, loan of wheelchairs) toilets for disabled shop 🐕

LEUCHARS Earlshall Castle

Built with 5ft-thick walls, battlements and gun loops, Earlshall Castle is a fine example of a 16th-century Scottish stronghold. A renowned feature of its interior is the painted ceiling in the Long Gallery depicting mythological beasts and the arms of the principal families of Scotland. There is also a wealth of old timber panelling, Jacobite relics, arms and armour, antique furniture, porcelain and paintings exhibited throughout the castle. The gardens contain a notable feature too, in the form of topiary yew chessmen, and the wooded parkland has a nature trail and picnic facilities. There is a Craft Festival 13 Jul-3 August.

☎ (0334) 839205

Open: Etr Fri-Mon, Sun in Apr then daily May-Sep, 2-6. (Last admission 5.15pm).
Admission: £2.80 (ch £1, pen £2.20). Party.
P ☕ shop 🐕

GRAMPIAN

ABERDEEN   Satrosphere ('Hands-On' Science & Technology Centre)

Satrosphere, the Discovery Place, is different from many museums or exhibition centres. It is a Science and Technology Exhibition Centre where everything is 'hands-on'. Displays aren't locked in glass cases and there are certainly no *Do Not Touch* signs. The emphasis is on doing and finding out, not just looking and standing back. There is a shop with exciting and unusual presents. Special events include visits by 'Starlab' (an inflatable planetarium), Captain Cook, Sir Isaac Newton and many others. Theme events run for approximately one month and include such topics as Colour, Communication (Jan), Electricity (Feb), Festival of Toys, Health (Mar), and The Ground Beneath Your Feet (Apr).

19 Justice Mill Ln
☎ (0224) 213232
Open: all year, Mon-Sat 10-4, Sun 1.30-5. (Closed Tue, 25-26 & 31 Dec & 1 Jan). *Admission:* ✱ £2.75 (ch £1.25, concessions £1.25). Family ticket £4.25-£7.50. **P** (charged) ☕ ᴕ toilets for disabled shop ✻

ALFORD   Alford Valley Railway

Narrow-gauge passenger railway in two sections: Alford Haughton Park and Haughton Park-Murray Park approx one mile each. Steam on peak weekends. Diesel traction. Exhibitions.

☎ (09755) 62326
Open: Apr, May & Sep wknds from 1-5, Jun-Aug daily from 11 (30 min service). Party bookings also available at other times. *Admission:* £1.30 (ch 70p) return fare. **P** ᴕ shop

BALMORAL   Balmoral Castle Grounds & Exhibition

Balmoral is the focal point of what is now known as Royal Deeside, a landscape of woodlands and plantations sweeping up to grouse moors and distant mountains. Queen Victoria and Prince Albert first rented Balmoral Castle in 1848, and Prince Albert bought the property four years later. He commissioned William Smith to build a new castle, which was completed by 1855 and is still the Royal Family's Highland residence. The wooded grounds and gardens can be visited from May to July when the Royal Family is not in residence. Country walks and pony trekking can be enjoyed, and an exhibition of paintings and other works of art can be seen in the castle ballroom.

(on A93)
☎ Crathie (03397) 42334 & 42335
Open: May-Jul, Mon-Sat 10-5. *Admission:* £1.75 (ch free, pen £1.25). ☕ ᴕ (wheelchairs available) toilets for disabled shop ✻ (ex in grounds)

BRODIE CASTLE

The Brodie family were granted land in this area in 1160, and lived in the castle for hundreds of years. It was passed to the National Trust for Scotland by the 25th Chief of the family in 1980. It is a handsome, gabled Scottish castle, and contains numerous treasures acquired over the centuries: fine furniture, porcelain, and an impressive collection of paintings including 17th-century Dutch works, 19th-

(4.5m W of Forres, off A96)
☎ Brodie (03094) 371
Open: Apr-27 Sep, Mon-Sat 11-6, Sun 2-6; 3-18 Oct, Sat 11-6, Sun 2-6 (last admission 5.15pm). Other times by prior appointment. Grounds open all year, 9.30-sunset.

century English watercolours and French Impressionists. The extensive grounds have woodland walks, daffodils and a wildlife hide. There is also an adventure playground. Facilities for the disabled include wheelchair loan, purpose-built toilets for wheelchair users, audio tape and information in braille.

Admission: £3 (ch & pen £1.50). Party.
🅿 ☕ ♿ (audio tape & information sheet in Braille) 🐾
(NTS)

CRATHES   Crathes Castle & Garden

This impressive 16th-century castle with magnificent interiors and painted ceilings has royal associations dating from 1323. There is a walled garden of over 3 acres and a notable collection of unusual plants. Yew hedges date from 1702, and seasonal herbaceous borders are a special feature. Wild gardens, extensive grounds and five nature trails, including one for the disabled, are among the attractions, plus a wayfaring course and children's adventure playground. There is entertainment within the grounds on most Sundays.

(3m E of Banchory on A93)
☎ **(033044) 525**

Open: Castle & Visitor Centre 17 Apr-Oct, daily 11-6. (Last admission 5.15pm). Other times by appointment only. Garden & grounds open all year, daily 9.30-sunset.
Admission: Castle, Garden & Grounds £3.50 (ch & pen £1.80). Grounds £1.30 (ch & pen 70p). Party.
🅿 ✗ licensed ♿ toilets for disabled shop 🐾 (ex in grounds)
(NTS)

KILDRUMMY   Kildrummy Castle

An important part of Scottish history, at least until it was dismantled in 1717, this fortress was the seat of the Earls of Mar. Now it is a ruined, but splendid example of a 13th-century castle, with four round towers, hall and chapel all discernible. Some parts of the building, including the Great Gatehouse, are from the 15th and 16th centuries.

(10m W of Alford)
☎ **031-244 3101**

Open: all year, Apr-Sep, weekdays 9.30-6, Sun 2-6; Oct-Mar, Sat 9.30-4, Sun 2-4. (Closed 25-26 Dec & 1-2 Jan).
Admission: £1 (ch & pen 50p).
🅿 ♿ toilets for disabled shop 🐾
(AM)

KILDRUMMY   Kildrummy Castle Garden Trust

With the picturesque ruin as a backdrop, these gardens are not only beautiful but also noted for their botanic interest. An alpine garden in an ancient quarry and a water garden are just two of its features, while the surrounding woods give interesting short walks. There is also a small museum, a video room showing a 15-minute film of the changes in the garden through the seasons, a children's play area and a sales area selling unusual plants.

(on A97)
☎ **(09755) 71264 & 71277**

Open: Apr-Oct, daily 10-5.
Admission: £1.50 (ch 3-9 20p, 10-16 50p).
🅿 ♿ toilets for disabled shop

MARYCULTER   Storybook Glen

This is a children's fantasy land, where favourite nursery rhyme and fairytale characters are brought to life. Grown-ups can enjoy the nostalgia and also the 20 acres of Deeside country, full of flowers, plants, trees and waterfalls.

(5m W of Aberdeen on B9077)
☎ **Aberdeen (0224) 732941**

Open: Mar-Oct, daily 10-6; Nov-Feb, Sat & Sun only 11-4.
Admission: £2.10 (ch £1.05).
🅿 ☕ ✗ licensed ♿ toilets for disabled shop 🐾

METHLICK Haddo House

Haddo House is renowned for its Choral Society and is the venue for international concerts which attract top performers from around the world. It is a splendid Palladian-style mansion built in the 1730s to designs by William Adam. Home to the Earls of Aberdeen, the house was refurbished in the 1880s in the 'Adam Revival' style and still retains much of its original flavour. The adjoining country park, run by Grampian Regional Council, offers a network of enchanting woodland paths and attracts all kinds of wildlife. Hundreds of birds can be seen roosting on the loch and there is an observation hide for visitors. James Giles exhibition.

(4m N of Pitmedden off B999)
☎ Tarves (06515) 440

Open: House 17 Apr-May & Sep, daily 2-6; Jun-Aug, daily 11-6; Oct, Sat-Sun 2-5 (last admission 30 mins before closing). Garden & country park open all year, daily 9.30-sunset.
Admission: £3 (ch & pen £1.50). Garden by donation. Party.
🅿 ☕ ✕ ♿ (lift & wheelchair) toilets for disabled shop 🐕 (ex in grounds)
(NTS)

MINTLAW Aden Country Park

The grounds of a former estate provide over 200 acres of beautiful woodland and open farmland for the visitor to explore. A network of footpaths winds through a specially developed nature trail, and gives a chance of seeing many varieties of plants and animals. A countryside ranger service is available by appointment. New wildlife centre is open weekends only.

(1m W Mintlaw off A950)
☎ (0771) 22857

Open: all year. Farm Heritage centre May-Sep, daily 11-5; Apr & Oct wknds only 12-5. Last admission 30 mins before closing.
Admission: ✻ Park free. Admsiion charge to Farm Heritage Centre.
🅿 ☕ ♿ (access via Radar key. Garden for blind) toilets for disabled shop 🐕 (ex in park)

MINTLAW NE Scotland Agricultural Heritage Centre

The award-winning heritage centre is housed in 19th-century farm buildings, once part of the estate which now makes up the Aden Country Park (above). Two centuries of farming history and innovation are illustrated in an exciting exhibition, a pleasant way to take a break from enjoying the surrounding countryside. The story of the Aden estate is also interestingly illustrated. The newly reconstructed farm of Hareshowe shows how a family in the north-east might have farmed during the 1950s – access by guided tour only.

Aden Country Park (1m W on A950)
☎ (0771) 22857 & Banff (0261) 812521

Open: May-Sep, daily 11-5; Apr & Oct, wknds only noon-5. Park open all year. Last admission 30 mins before closing.
Admission: ✻ £1 (ch 16 free).
🅿 ☕ ♿ (garden for blind) toilets for disabled shop 🐕

HIGHLAND

ALNESS Dalmore Farm Centre

An old-fashioned Highland welcome awaits visitors to this family-run working farm. Attractions include a restaurant serving home cooking and baking, a farm shop, garden centre, farm museum, children's play area and pets' corner. Visitors will see the animals in their natural surroundings and are welcome to watch farm activities, such as sheep clipping and sheep dipping.

☎ (0349) 883978

Open: all year, Mon-Sat 10-5, Sun 1-5. Farm open Etr-Oct.
Admission: Free.
🅿 ☕ ✕ ♿ toilets for disabled shop garden centre

AVIEMORE   Strathspey Steam Railway

This steam railway covers the five miles from Boat of Garten to Aviemore, where trains can also be boarded. The journey takes about 20 minutes, but allow around an hour for the round trip. Timetables are available from the station and the tourist information centre. Special events for 1992 include a Boat of Garten beer festival, a crafts fair and a Thomas the Tank Engine weekend – please telephone for details.

Aviemore Speyside Station, Dalfaber Rd
☎ (0479) 810725

Open: 23 May-4 Sep daily; 28 Mar-28 Oct selected days. Also 19-20, 26-27 & 31 Dec. *Admission:* £3.60 Basic return; £9 Family return.
🅿 ☕ ✗ ᵹ shop

CARRBRIDGE   Landmark Visitor Centre

The innovative centre has an exhibition on the history of the Highlands and a multi-screen, sound-and-vision presentation, 'The Highlander', which tells of the break-up of Europe's last tribal society. The Forestry Heritage Park has a 65ft forest viewing tower, a working steam-powered sawmill and various exhibitions and buildings. Attractions include trails, a maze, an adventure play area, a craft and book shop, restaurant, and snack bar with picnic area.

(off A9)
☎ (047984) 614

Open: all year, daily, Apr-Jun & Sep-Oct 9.30-6; Jul-Aug 9.30-8 & Nov-Mar 9.30-5. *Admission:* Apr-Jun £3.85 (ch £2.40); Jul-Sep £3.95 (£2.60).
🅿 ✗ licensed ᵹ toilets for disabled shop

CAWDOR   Cawdor Castle

Home of the Thanes of Cawdor since the 14th century, the castle has a drawbridge, an ancient tower built round a tree, and a freshwater well inside the house. There are nature trails, pitch-and-putt and a putting green.

(on B9090 off A96)
☎ (06677) 615

Open: May-4 Oct, daily 10-5.30. (Last admission 5pm). *Admission:* £3.50 (ch 5-15 £1.90, pen £2.80). Family ticket £10. Party 20+. Gardens, grounds & nature trails only £1.80.
🅿 ☕ ᵹ toilets for disabled shop 🐾

DRUMNADROCHIT   Official Loch Ness Monster Exhibition

A fascinating computer-controlled, multi-media presentation lasting 40 minutes. Ten themed areas cover the story from the pre-history of Scotland, through the cultural roots of the legend of the monster in Highland folklore, and into the fifty year controversy which surrounds it. The exhibition was totally renewed in July 1989 and the centre encompasses the Nessie Giftshop, Iceberg Glassblowers and a kilt-maker.

Loch Ness Centre
☎ (04562) 573 & 218

Open: all year, peak season 9am-9.30pm, otherwise times on application. *Admission:* ✳ £3.50 (ch reduced rate, students £2.50).
🅿 ☕ ✗ licensed ᵹ toilets for disabled shop 🐾 (ex in grounds)

KINCRAIG   Highland Wildlife Park

In a magnificent natural setting, native animals from Scotland's past and present can be viewed: wolves, bears, reindeer, wildcats and European bison are some of the many animals who have their home and breed here. Eagles and capercaillie are kept in the aviaries. For children, a pets' corner provides amusement, and grown-ups will find the 'Man and Fauna' exhibition fascinating.

(on B9152)
☎ (05404) 270 due to change to (0540) 651270

Open: Apr-Oct, daily 10-6. *Admission:* ✳ £8 per car.
🅿 ☕ ᵹ toilets for disabled shop 🐾

KINGUSSIE   Highland Folk Museum

The Highland way of life is illustrated with an interesting display of crafts and furnishings, a farming museum, a reconstructed Hebridean mill and a primitive 'black house'. Demonstrations of crafts are held every day throughout Jul and Aug, including weaving, spinning and baking.

Duke St
☎ (0540) 661307

Open: all year, Apr-Oct, Mon-Sat 10-6, Sun 2-6; Nov-Mar, Mon-Fri 10-3. (Closed Xmas-New Year).
Admission: £1.70 (ch & pen 85p). Subject to review.
🅿 ᒼ toilets for disabled shop

LOTHIAN

DALKEITH   Dalkeith Park

The extensive grounds of Dalkeith House offer pleasant woodland and riverside walks, and nature trails. A beautiful Adam bridge and an orangery can be seen, and there is a fine woodland adventure playground and a farm park. Ranger-led walks are available, as are hay rides.

Buccleuch Estate
☎ 031-663 5684 & 031-665 3277

Open: end Mar-Oct, daily 10-6.
Admission: £1.50. Family ticket £4. Party 20+.
🅿 ᒼ toilets for disabled

DALKEITH   Edinburgh Butterfly & Insect World

Richly coloured butterflies from all over the world can be seen flying among exotic plants, trees and flowers. The tropical pools are filled with giant waterlilies and colourful fish, and surrounded by lush vegetation. Also displayed are scorpions, tarantulas and other dangerous creatures, and there is a unique honeybee display.

(At Dobbie's Melville Gdn World 1m N on A7)
☎ 031-663 4932

Open: 12 Mar-Oct, daily 10-5.30.
Admission: £2.85 (ch under 5 free, ch £1.60, pen & students £2.20). Family ticket £8.20. Party 10+.
🅿 ᒼ ᒼ toilets for disabled shop garden centre ✗

EDINBURGH   see page 166

NEWTONGRANGE   Scottish Mining Museum

Newtongrange is the largest surviving coal company village in Scotland, and after a working life of almost 90 years, Lady Victoria Colliery is being restored and developed as a museum. An exhibition of talking tableaux in the visitor centre portrays characters involved in the creation of the mine and its day-to-day organisation. The steam winding machine and pit-head can also be visited. Guided tours by a former miner are available.

Lady Victoria Colliery (on A7)
☎ 031-663 7519

Open: Apr-Sep, daily 11-4. Last tour 3pm.
Admission: £1.95 (ch & pen £1).
🅿 ᒼ ᒼ toilets for disabled shop ✗

PRESTONPANS   Scottish Mining Museum

The oldest documented coal mining site in Britain with 800 years of history, this museum shows a Cornish Beam Engine and on-site evidence of associated industries such as brickmaking and pottery, plus a 16th-century customs port. The 'Cutting the Coal' exhibition, in the David Spence Gallery, has an underground gallery, a coalface, a reconstruction of a colliery workshop and a wonderful collection of coal-cutting machines and equipment. There is a guided tour of the site by a former miner. Special events for 1992 include: Apr-Sept, Steam Sundays on the first Sunday of each month.

Prestongrange (on B1348)
☎ 031-663 7519

Open: Apr-Sep, daily 11-4. Last tour 3pm.
Admission: £1 (ch & concessions 50p).
🅿 ☕ & toilets for disabled shop 🐾

SOUTH QUEENSFERRY   Dalmeny House

This is the home of the Earl and the Countess of Rosebery, whose family have lived here for over 300 years. The house, however, only dates from 1815 when it was built in Tudor Gothic style. There are vaulted corridors and a splendid Gothic hammerbeamed hall, but the main rooms are in classical style. Dalmeny House has a magnificent situation on the Firth of Forth and there are delightful walks in the wooded grounds and along the shore. Inside, it has fine French furniture, tapestries and porcelain from the Rothschild Mentmore collection. Early Scottish furniture is also shown, with 18th-century portraits, Rosebery racing momentoes and a display of pictures and items associated with Napoleon.

☎ 031-331 1888

Open: May-Sep, Sun-Thu 2-5.
Admission: ✴ £3 (ch £1.50, students £2.50). Party 20+.
🅿 ☕ & toilets for disabled 🐾 (ex in grounds)

SOUTH QUEENSFERRY   Hopetoun House

Scotland's greatest Adam mansion is the home of the 4th Marquess of Linlithgow. It was built in 1699 to a design by William Bruce, but between 1721 and 1754 it was enlarged by William and Robert Adam. The magnificent reception rooms have notable paintings by artists such as Canaletto, Gainsborough and Raeburn, and there are also fine examples of furniture and a collection of china. A museum in the stables features an exhibition entitled 'Horse and Man' in Lowland Scotland.

The grounds are extensive, and include deer parks with red and fallow deer, and a herd of the rare St Kilda sheep. There are formal gardens as well, and it is possible to play croquet or petanque for a fee. Walks along the coast give views of the Forth bridges, which can also be seen from a special viewing platform. Facilities include a garden centre, a nature trail and a free Ranger Service. If prior notice is given special arrangements can be made for blind and disabled visitors.

(2m W on unclass road)
☎ 031-331 2451

Open: 17 Apr-4 Oct, daily 10-5.30 (last admission 4.45pm).
Admission: £3.30 (ch £1.60). Grounds £1.70 (ch 50p).
🅿 ☕ & toilets for disabled shop garden centre

SYMBOLS

☎ Telephone number	✴ Indicates 1991 price	☕ Refreshments 🐾 No Dogs
& Suitable for visitors in wheelchairs	🅿 Parking at Establishment	✗ Restaurant 🚫 No coaches

Scotland's ancient capital is a splendid city with an enormous amount to see and do – historic buildings, great national museums and art collections, culture and folklore – and one festival after another throughout the year.

The city is dominated by Edinburgh Castle, perched high up on Castle Rock. Away from it stretches the Royal Mile, the spine of the Old Town, at the far end of which is the Palace of Holyroodhouse, once the home of Mary, Queen of Scots and still a Royal residence. Allow time to walk down the Royal Mile if you can, exploring the little courts and alleys on the way; numerous plaques tell about past events and residents. The New Town is an elegant Georgian townscape and one house, on Charlotte Square has been restored and is open to the public.

Edinburgh has begun to market itself as a 'child friendly city'. Among the huge number of museums, large and small, are some designed specifically for younger visitors, such as the Museum of Childhood, and Edinburgh even has an International Children's Festival.

A variety of guided tours – some with guides in traditional Scottish dress – are available and there are open-top bus tours and boat trips on the Firth of Forth. The *Maid of the Forth* will take you to Inchcolm Island to see the Abbey and colony of seals. Twenty-minute helicopter tours are also available – for a price!

Tourist information: Waverley Shopping Centre, 3 Princes Street Telephone: 031-557 1700

☆ *STAR ATTRACTIONS*

Edinburgh Castle

This historic stronghold stands on the precipitous crag of Castle Rock. One of the oldest parts is the 11th-century chapel of the saintly Queen Margaret, but most of the present castle evolved later, during its stormy history of sieges and wars, and was altered again in Victorian times. The apartments of Mary Queen of Scots can be seen, including the bedroom where James I of England and VI of Scotland was born. Also on the rock is James IV's 16th-century great hall. The vaults underneath have graffiti by 19th-century French prisoners of war. The Scottish crown and other royal regalia are displayed in the Crown Room, and the spectacular Military Tattoo is held on the Esplanade, built in 1753 – shortly after the castle's last siege in 1745. Also notable is the Scottish National War Memorial, opened in 1927 on the site of the castle's church. There is still a military presence in the castle, and some areas cannot be visited.

☎ 031-244 3101

Open: all year, 4 Jan-Mar & Oct-Dec, Mon-Sat 9.30-4.20 (last ticket sold), Sun 12.30-3.35 (last ticket sold). Apr-Sep, Mon-Sat 9.30-5.05 (last ticket sold), Sun 10.30-4.45 (last ticket sold). Castle closes 45 mins after above times.
Admission: £3.40 (ch & pen £1.70). Family ticket £5.50. War Memorial Free.
🅿 (charged) ♿ (with limitations) toilets for disabled shop ✗
(AM)

Royal Botanic Garden

The gardens offer 70 acres of peace and greenery close to the city centre. They were founded as a physick garden in 1670 at Holyrood, and came to Inverleith in 1823. The largest rhododendron collection in Britain can be seen here, and the different areas include an arboretum, a peat garden, a woodland garden, and rock and heath gardens. There is a splendid herbaceous border, and the plant houses have orchids, cacti and other specialities from a variety of climates. The gardens have colour all year round, even in winter when the plants with coloured bark come into their own. The exhibition hall has informative displays, and Inverleith House Gallery has art exhibitions. All major routes and areas of interest are accessible to wheelchairs, and there are purpose-built toilets for wheelchair users. Wheelchairs are available at the entrance.

Inverleith Row
☎ 031-552 7171

Open: all year Garden. (Closed 25 Dec & 1 Jan).
Admission: Free. Donations.
✗ licensed ♿ (wheelchairs available at east/west gates) toilets for disabled shop ✗

Edinburgh Zoo

The zoo is set in 80 acres of grounds, and is notable for its colony of penguins, which perform the Penguin Parade daily at 2.30pm in summer. A visitor centre explains the role of zoos in conservation, research and education, and there are panoramic views of Edinburgh and the countryside.

The Scottish National Zoological Park, Corstorphine Rd (2m W on A8)
☎ 031-334 9171

Open: all year, Mon-Sat 9-6, Sun 9.30-6 in summer, but closes 5pm or dusk in winter.
Admission: ✻ £3.85 (ch, pen & UB40's £2). Party 10+.
🅿 (charged) ☛ ✗ licensed ⬥ toilets for disabled shop garden centre 🦮

Museum of Childhood

One of the first museums of its kind, it was reopened in 1986 after major expansion and reorganisation. It has a wonderful collection of toys, games and other belongings of children through the ages, to delight visitors both old and young.

42 High St (Royal Mile)
☎ 031-225 2424 ext 6645

Open: all year, Mon-Sat, Jun-Sep 10-6; Oct-May 10-5. (During Festival period only Sun 2-5. (Closed Xmas).
Admission: Free.
⬥ (3 floors only) toilets for disabled shop 🦮

Palace of Holyroodhouse

The palace grew from the guesthouse of the Abbey of Holyrood, said to have been founded by David I after a miraculous apparition. Mary, Queen of Scots, had her court here from 1561 to 1567, and Bonnie Prince Charlie held levees at the palace during his occupation of Edinburgh. The castle is still used by the royal family, but can be visited when they are not in residence. Little remains of the original abbey except the ruined 13th-century nave of the church. The oldest part of the palace proper is James V's tower, with Mary's rooms on the second floor. A plaque marks the spot where Rizzio was murdered. The audience chamber where she debated with John Knox can also be seen. There are fine 17th-century state rooms, and the picture gallery is notable for its series of Scottish monarchs, starting in 330 BC with Fergus I. The work was done by Jacob de Wet in 1684-5, so many of the likenesses are based on imagination. The grounds are used for royal garden parties in summer. Special events for 1992.

(at east end of Canongate)
☎ 031-556 7371 & 031-556 1096 (info)

Open: Winter, 6 Jan-28 Mar 9.30-3.45. (Closed Sun). Summer 29 Mar-Oct, wkdays 9.30-5.15, Sun 10.30-4.30. (Closed 11-26 May & 9 Jun-28 Jul). Subject to closure at short notice at other times telephone 031-556 1096.
Admission: £2.50 (ch £1.30, pen £2). Family ticket £6.50.
⬥ shop 🦮

The People's Story

The museum, housed in the 16th-century tolbooth, tells the story of the ordinary people of Edinburgh from the late 18th century to the present day. Reconstructions include a prison cell, 1930s pub and 1940s kitchen supported by photographs, displays, sounds, smells and a video.

Canongate Tolbooth, 163 Canongate
☎ 031-225 2424 ext 6638/6687
031-225 1131 after 5 pm & wknds

Open: Jun-Sep, Mon-Sat 10-6; Oct & May, Mon-Sat 10-5. Also, open Sun during Edinburgh Festival 2-5.
Admission: Free.
⬥ (first floor accessible by lift) toilets for disabled shop 🦮

Royal Observatory Visitor Centre

The visitor centre explains the work of Scotland's national observatory both at home and overseas. There are displays on the latest discoveries about the universe, and a wide range of exhibits including two large telescopes and many antique examples. The Visitor Centre rooftop gives panoramic views over the city and the Braid Hills. A permanent exhibition includes the latest NASA photography, and there are also videos and computer games. Evening observing and winter breaks from October to March. Special events for 1992.

Blackford Hill
☎ 031-668 8405

Open: all year, Apr-Sep, Mon-Fri 10-4, wknds & PHs noon-5; Oct-Mar, daily 1-5.
Admission: £1.50 (ch 75p). Season ticket £5. Family season ticket £10.
🅿 ⬥ (lift) toilets for disabled shop

STRATHCLYDE

AUCHINDRAIN Old West Highland Township

Auchindrain is an original West Highland township, or village of great antiquity, and the only communal tenancy township to have survived on its centuries-old site. The township buildings, which have been restored and preserved, are furnished and equipped in the style of various periods to give the visitor a taste of what life was really like for the Highlander in past ages.

(5.5m SW of Inverary)
☎ Furnace (04995) 235

Open: Apr-May & Sep, Sun-Fri 10-5; Jun-Aug, daily 10-5.
Admission: £2.20 (ch £1.40, pen £1.70). Family ticket £6.80.
P ☕ shop

BALLOCH Balloch Castle Country Park

Set beside Loch Lomond, the country park spreads over a hillside with woodland trails, a walled garden, and lawns for picnics giving wonderful views. Overlooking the lawns is Balloch Castle, built in 1808. Its visitor centre gives an introduction to local history and wildlife.

☎ Alexandria (0389) 58216

Open: Visitor Centre, Apr-Sep daily 10-6. Country Park 8-dusk. Garden 10-6 (4.30 winter).
Admission: Free.
P ♿ toilets for disabled shop

BARCALDINE Sea Life Centre

This ultra-modern centre has Britain's largest collection of native marine life. The unique layout is designed for greater understanding, and includes a tidepool touch tank and intertidal dump tank. Seals can be seen underwater, with a twice-daily talk and feeding time. During the summer young seals can be viewed prior to their release back into the wild. A full talks programme is available throughout the day during the peak season.

Loch Creran (10m N of Oban on A828)
☎ Ledaig (0631) 72386

Open: mid Feb-late Nov, daily 9-6. (Jul-Aug 7pm).
Admission: fee payable.
P ✕ licensed ♿ toilets for disabled shop 🐕

CULZEAN CASTLE

This great 18th-century castle stands on a clifftop site in spacious grounds (see below) and was designed by Robert Adam for David, 10th Earl of Cassillis. It is noted for its oval staircase, circular drawing room and plasterwork. The Eisenhower Room explores the general's links with Culzean. There are numerous events taking place here throughout the year.

(4m W of Maybole, off A77)
☎ Kirkosald (06556) 274

Open: Castle, Visitor Centre, restaurant & shops Apr-25 Oct, daily 10.30-5.30 (last admission 5pm). Other times by appointment.
Admission: £3 (ch & pen £1.50). Party.
P (charged) ☕ ✕ licensed ♿ (lift) toilets for disabled shop 🐕 (NTS)

CULZEAN CASTLE Culzean Country Park

The country park and castle together make one of the most popular days out in Scotland. Culzean was Scotland's first country park, and covers 563 acres with a wide range of attractions – shoreline, woodland walks, parkland, an

(4m W of Maybole, off A77)
☎ Kirkoswald (06556) 269

Open: all year.

adventure playground, and gardens, including a walled garden of 1783. The visitor centre has various facilities and information, and is also the base of the ranger naturalists who provide guided walks and other services. Various events are held each year.

Admission: Country Park £4.50 per car, £7 minibus/caravan, £1.10 motor cycles, free to members & pedestrians. Party.
P (charged) **♥ ✗** licensed **♿** (wheelchairs available) toilets for disabled shop garden centre **✻** (NTS)

GLASGOW   see page 170

INVERARY   Inverary Castle

The third Duke of Argyll (the chief of Clan Campbell) engaged Roger Morris to build the present castle in 1743; in the process the old Burgh of Inverary was demolished and a new town built nearby. The beautiful interior decoration was commissioned by the 5th Duke from Robert Mylne; the great armoury hall and staterooms are of particular note but the furniture, tapestries and paintings throughout are well worth viewing. The gardens are open by appointment.

☎ (0499) 2203

Open: Apr-Jun & Sep-Oct, Sat-Thu, 10-1 & 2-6, Sun 1-6; Jul-Aug, Mon-Sat 10-6, Sun 1-6. Last admissions 30 mins before closing. *Admission:* £3 (ch 16 £1.50, pen £2). Family ticket £7.50.
P ♥ ♿ shop **✻**

INVERARY   Inverary Jail

Enter Inveraray Jail and step back in time. See furnished cells and experience prison sounds and smells. Ask the 'prisoner' how to pick oakum, or help him make herring nets. Turn the heavy handle of an original crank machine, take 40 winks in a hammock or listen to Matron's tales of day-to-day prison life as she keeps one eye on the nursing mother, barefoot thieves and the lunatic in her care. Visit the magnificent 1820 courtroom, see trials in progress and imaginative exhibitions including 'Torture, Death and Damnation'.

Church Sq
☎ (0499) 2381

Open: all year, Nov-Mar, daily 10-5 (last admisssion 4); Apr-Oct, daily 9.30-6 (last admission 5pm). (Closed 25-26 Dec & 1 Jan). Extended hours in summer. *Admission:* £3.25 (ch £1.60, pen £1.75). Family ticket £8.90. Party.
P ♿ toilets for disabled shop

KILMARNOCK   Dean Castle

This fine castle has a 14th-century fortified keep and 15th-century palace, and is the ancestral home of the Boyd family. The restoration work which has taken place shows the building in almost its original splendour, and inside there is an outstanding collection of medieval arms and armour, musical instruments, tapestries and a display of Burns' manuscripts. The castle is set in a beautiful wooded country park with rivers, gardens, woodlands, adventure playground, children's corner and avaries. A jazz festival will be held on 1st and 2nd August.

Dean Rd
☎ (0563) 26401 ext 136 & 22702

Open: all year, daily noon-5. (Closed 25-26 Dec & 1-2 Jan).
Admission: ✢ £1 (ch free).
P ♥ ♿ (special disabled garden) toilets for disabled shop **✻** (ex in grounds)

KILMUN   Arborteum & Forest Walks

The Argyll Forest Park extends over a large area of hill ground and forest, noted for its rugged beauty. Numerous forest walks and picnic sites allow the forest to be explored in detail. The Arboretum walks and the route from the Younger Botanic Gardens to Packs Glen are of special scenic quality.

(on A880 1m from junc with A815)
☎ (036984) 666

Open: all year.
Admission: Free.
P ▭

Glasgow is a city which has undergone a major transformation in recent years – in image as well as in reality. It is now an exciting place with plenty to see and do – no less than 35 museums and galleries as well as a fine 12th-century cathedral, historic houses to visit, parks and gardens, ad a lively cultural programme of events and entertainments all year round. The city's theatres, halls and streets really come alive during the annual Mayfest, Streetbiz and International Jazz Festival.

Predominantly Victorian, the best area to see Glasgow's architecture in its full grandeur is the Merchant City. George Square, with its splendid City Chambers along one side, is one of the city's showpieces and the unique Art Nouveau buildings of Charles Rennis Mackintosh include the Glasgow School of Art in Renfrew Street and the Willow Tearooms in Sauchiehall Street.

Glasgow has over 70 parks and gardens, including Kelvingrove Park near Sauchiehall Street, superbly set in the Kelvin valley and home of Glasgow Art Gallery and Museum, and Pollok Country Park, 360 acres around Pollok House and the setting for the famous Burrell Collection. The Botanic Gardens are splendid and a fun place to take children is Lamont City Farm in Erskine.

There is a range of sightseeing tours available including guided walks, coach tours of the city, helicopter trips and boat trips along the Clyde. The historic paddle steamer, PS *Waverley*, is a popular option.

Tourist information: 35 St Vincent Place Telephone: 041-204 4400

☆ *STAR ATTRACTIONS*

Botanic Gardens

Queen Margaret Dr, off Great Western Rd
☎ 041-334 2422

The gardens were established in 1817 from an older university physick garden, and moved to this site in 1842. There is an outstanding plant collection, but the most remarkable feature is the 23,000 sq ft Kibble Palace, a spectacular glasshouse with soaring tree ferns inside, set off by a number of Victorian sculptures. There are more conventional glasshouses too, showing orchids and other exotica. The grounds are laid out with lawns and beds, including a chronological border and a herb garden. At the northern edge the ground slopes down to the River Kibble, which is crossed by footbridges.

Open: The Kibble Palace 10-4.45 (4.15 in winter).The main glasshouse open Mon-Sat 1-4.45 (4.15 in winter), Sun 12-4.45 (4.15 in winter). Gardens open daily 7-dusk.
&. toilets for disabled ✗ (ex in grounds)
Details not confirmed for 1992

Haggs Castle

100 St Andrews Dr
☎ 041-427 2725

Adults are welcome, but the museum is really meant for children. The house was built in the 1580s, taken over by the Army in World War II, converted into flats and finally transformed into a museum in the 1970s. Children are encouraged to find out its history through worksheets and quizzes, and can explore the house, from the old-style kitchen up to the 17th-century bedroom and Victorian nursery. The hands-on approach to education extends to weekend and holiday activities, including learning traditional crafts. Regular temporary exhibitions are held.

Open: all year, Mon-Sat 10-5, Sun noon-6. (Closed 25 Dec & 1 Jan).
Admission: Free.
&. shop ✗

HMS Plymouth

Here is a chance to see Scotland's own Falklands frigate, bombed and battered but home safely.

Plantation Quay, Govan Rd
☎ 041-427 1407

Open: all year, daily 10-dusk.
Admission: ✻ £2 (ch & pen £1).
🅿 ☕ ✕ shop 🐕

Linn Park

The park covers 200 acres of hillside by White Cart Water, with riverside and woodland walks, a nature trail, a children's zoo and a collection of British ponies and Highland cattle. The 18-hole golf course is another attraction, and also in the park is a ruined 14th-century castle. Countryside ranger service; various events. Adventure playground for the disabled adjacent to park (Netherlee Road).

Cathcart (southern outskirts of Glasgow)
☎ 041-637 1147

Open: all year, daily 7am-dusk.
🅿 ♿ (some parts of river walkway unsuitable)
Details not confirmed for 1992

Museum of Transport

The first Museum of Transport was an old tram depot, but in 1988 the collections were handsomely rehoused in Kelvin Hall. The new museum is a feast of nostalgia for older Glaswegians and a fascinating look at the past for younger visitors, with Glasgow buses, a reconstruction of a Glasgow side street in the year 1938, and Glasgow trams (last used in 1962, when they made their way around the city in a grand, final procession). There are Scottish-made cars, fire engines, horse-drawn vehicles, cycles and motorcycles, and a walk-in car showroom with vehicles from the 1930s to the present day. Railways are represented by steam locomotives and a Glasgow subway station; and the already notable collection of ship models has been expanded.

Kelvin Hall, 1 Bunhouse Rd
☎ 041-357 3929

Open: all year, Mon-Sat 10-5, Sun noon-6. (Closed 25 Dec & 1 Jan).
Admission: Free.
🅿 ☕ ♿ (wheelchair available) toilets for disabled shop 🐕

Pollok Country Park

The leafy 361-acre park was presented to the city in 1966 by Mrs Anne Maxwell Macdonald, whose family owned the Pollok estates for nearly 700 years. It is home to two major museums, the Burrell Collection and Pollok House, and its many outdoor attractions range from a jogging track to a display rose garden and a demonstration garden. Amateurs are given advice here on a wide range of gardening matters. There are waterside and woodland trails to follow. The Countryside Rangers' Centre gives information on these and on the park's history and wildlife (ranger service available). The park is also home to a championship herd of Highland cattle, which represents the City of Glasgow at agricultural shows around the country.

2060 Pollokshaws Rd
☎ 041-632 9299 & 041-649 0331

Open: Park always. Demonstrations & display garden open Mon-Thu 8-4, Fri 8-3, wknds 8-6.30 (winter wknds 8-4pm).
🅿 ✕ ♿ toilets for disabled shop (at Ranger Centre)
Details not confirmed for 1992

Rouken Glen Park

Fine walks can be taken along riverside pathways through the deep, wooded glen, and the waterfall at the head of the glen is a noted beauty spot. The park also offers the pleasures of a large walled garden and spreading lawns, a picturesque loch for boating, a large enclosed children's play area (dog free) and an 18-hole pitch and putt course.

Giffnock
☎ 041-638 1101

Open: all year, daily, dawn-dusk.
Admission: Free.
☕ ✕ licensed ♿ shop garden centre

KILSYTH   Colzium House & Estate

The old castle was associated with Montrose's victory over the Covenanters in 1645; the museum, courtyard, ice-house and walled garden make interesting viewing and the grounds include a children's zoo and forest walks.

Colzium-Lennox Estate (on A803)
☎ (0236) 823281

Open: House Etr wknd-Sep wknd, Mon-Fri, 9-5 & Sun, 10-6. (Closed when booked for private functions). Grounds open at all times. Museum open Wed 2-8.
Admission: Free.
🅿 ☕ &

LANGBANK   Finlaystone Country Estate

A charming exhibition of Victorian flower books and an international collection of dolls, are displayed in a homely family house with historical connections to John Knox and Robert Burns. The house, though, is only a foil to the considerable natural beauty; most visitors to Finlaystone are drawn by the formal gardens, walled gardens, woodland walks and adventure playgrounds. Disabled visitors will enjoy the small scented garden, and there is a purpose-built toilet for wheelchair users in the visitor centre; lift to second floor in the Mansion House.

(1m W on A8)
☎ (047554) 285 & 505

Open: all year. Woodland & Gardens daily. House with doll collections Apr-Aug, Suns only 2.30-4.30 or by appointment.
Admission: ✷ Garden & Woods £1.20 (ch & pen 80p); House £1.20 (ch & pen 80p).
🅿 ☕ & (lift to second floor) toilets for disabled

LARGS   Kelburn Country Centre

Eighteenth-century farm buildings have been neatly converted here to resemble a village square, with craft shops, workshops, display rooms, special exhibitions and a café. The setting is the historic estate of the Earls of Glasgow, which also provides the visitor with beautiful gardens and magnificent scenery. The most famous part of the estate is Kelburn Glen, areas of which are still in a wild state, with waterfalls and pools. There are also rare trees, nature trails, a pets' corner, pony-trekking centre and adventure playgrounds. For those looking for some real action, there is a Marine Commando assault course and various special events during the year, including a Scottish teddy bears' picnic (May 10), and a Viking day (Aug 30).

(2m S off A78)
☎ Fairlie (0475) 568685

Open: all year, Etr-mid Oct, daily 10-6; Grounds only mid Oct-Etr, daily 11-5. Kelburn Castle 20 Apr-27 May.
Admission: £3 (ch & pen £1.50). Low season £1.50 (ch & pen £1).
🅿 ☕ ✗ licensed & shop

LOCHAWE   Cruachan Power Station

A vast cavern inside Ben Cruachan contains a 400,000 kilowatt hydro-electric power station which is driven by water drawn from a high-level reservoir up the mountain. A guided minibus tour starts from the visitor centre which also provides fascinating displays on the site. The picnic area gives spectacular views.

(3m W off A85, near Pass of Brander)
☎ Taynuilt (08662) 673

Open: late Mar-late Oct, daily 9-4.30.
Admission: ✷ £1.50 (ch 8-16 50p).
🅿 ☕ & toilets for disabled shop ⚡

	SYMBOLS		
☎ Telephone number	✷ Indicates 1991 price	☕ Refreshments	⚡ No Dogs
& Suitable for visitors in wheelchairs	🅿 Parking at Establishment	✗ Restaurant	No coaches

LOCHWINNOCH   Lochwinnoch Community Museum

Local agriculture, industry and village life are reflected in the series of changing exhibitions displayed in this enterprising museum.

Main St
☎ (0505) 842615

Open: all year, Mon, Wed & Fri 10-1, 2-5 & 6-8; Tue & Sat 10-1 & 2-5.
Admission: Free.
🅿 ᕑ ⚙

LOCHWINNOCH   RSPB Nature Centre

An attractive Norwegian timber building in the Lochwinnoch Nature Reserve, incorporating an observation tower offering fine views of the reserve and the surrounding countryside, an RSPB shop, and an exhibition and lecture room with a video system and displays. A nature trail leads from the centre, through deciduous woodland to two observation hides. An attractive second trail, featuring a boardwalk across the marsh, leads from the centre to a third birdwatching hide; this one has been designed specifically for the convenience of disabled visitors.

Largs Rd (on A760)
☎ (0505) 842663

Open: all year, Sun-Wed & Fri-Sat 10-5. (Closed Thu & Xmas-New Year).
Admission: £1 (ch 50p).
🅿 ᕑ (wheelchairs available) toilets for disabled shop ⚙

UDDINGSTON   Glasgow Zoo

The developing, open-plan zoo has birds, mammals and reptiles housed in spacious new enclosures and buildings. There are many rare animals and the zoo's specialities are cats and reptiles. Other attractions include ample picnic sites, children's shows and free guided tours.

Calderpark
☎ 041-771 1185

Open: all year, daily 10-5 (or 6pm depending on season).
🅿 ✕ ᕑ shop ⚙
Details not confirmed for 1992

TAYSIDE

BLAIR ATHOLL   Atholl Country Collection

Artefacts and photographs illustrate local life and trades from 1850 onwards. Displays include a crofter's kitchen, a 'smiddy' (smithy), dress, communications, a byre (with stuffed Highland cow) and a gamekeeper's corner. There is a Kiddies' Kist, where everything can be lifted up and examined.

The Old School
☎ (079681) 232

Open: end May-mid Oct 1.30-5.30 also from 9.30am Jul-Aug & Sep weekdays.
Admission: £1 (ch 50p).
🅿 ᕑ toilets for disabled shop

BLAIR ATHOLL   Blair Castle

Home of the Duke of Atholl, chief of the Murrays, and his unique private army, the Atholl Highlanders. The castle dates back to the 13th century but was altered in the 18th century and later given a castellated exterior. The oldest part is Cumming's Tower, built in about 1270. There are

(7m NW of Pitlochry, off A9)
☎ (079681) 207 **due to change to**
(0796) 481207

Open: 28 Mar-25 Oct, daily 10-6 (Sun in Apr, May & Oct 2-6). Last admission 5pm.

32 rooms open to the public, with paintings, Jacobite relics, lace, tapestries, china, arms and armour, and Masonic regalia to be seen. The extensive grounds include a deer park, and visitors may follow nature trails or go pony trekking. Numerous events are held throughout the year, including Highland games (May 24), a charity day (Jul 2), and the Glenfiddich Fiddle Championships (Nov 1).

Admission: ✳ £4 (ch & pen £2.50). Family ticket £11.50. Party.
P ⬤ ✗ licensed ♿ (restaurant accessible to disabled) toilets for disabled shop ✖ (ex in grounds)

DUNDEE   Camperdown Country Park

The 19th-century mansion of Camperdown House was built for the son of Admiral Lord Duncan, who defeated the Dutch at the Battle of Camperdown in 1797. The house is set in nearly 400 acres of fine parkland with a wide variety of trees, some of them rare. Most notable is the Camperdown elm, a weeping form of wych-elm. The park also offers attractions such as a golf course, a wildlife centre with a big collection of native and domestic animals, and an award-winning adventure play area with the Battle of Camperdown as its theme. There is an extensive network of footpaths and forest trails to follow, and the house itself has a restaurant and function area. The Templeton Ranger Centre has interpretive displays and offers guided walks.

(off A923)
☎ **(0382) 621993 & 23141 ext 4296**

Open: all year – park. Wildlife Centre – daily 10-4.
Admission: ✳ Park free. Wildlife Centre £1 (ch 20p). Party 12 + .
P ⬤ ✗ ♿ toilets for disabled shop

DUNDEE   HM Frigate Unicorn

The *Unicorn* is the oldest British warship still afloat, and is Scotland's only example of a wooden warship. Today she makes an apt setting for a fascinating museum of life in the Royal Navy during the days of sail, with guns, models and displays.

Victoria Dock
☎ **(0382) 200900**

Open: all year, daily 10-5.
Admission: ✳ £1.50 (concessions £1).
P ♿ shop ✖

DUNDEE   Royal Research Ship Discovery

Built by the Dundee Shipbuilding Company, the *Discovery* was the first purpose-built research vessel to be constructed in Britain. She was commissioned for Captain Scott's 1901-4 Antarctic expedition, and came to be seen as a symbol of shipbuilding quality and of human endurance. The *Discovery* is undergoing a five-year restoration, but can be visited and is already a focal point of the docks.

Victoria Dock
☎ **(0382) 201175**

Open: 27 Mar-3 May & 2 Sep-13 Oct, wkdays 1-5, wknds & PHs 11-5; Jun-1 Sep, daily 10-5.
Admission: £2.20 (concessions £1.70).
P ♿ (induction loop, radio hearing link with guides) toilets for disabled shop ✖

GLENGOULANDIE DEER PARK

Various native birds and animals are kept in surroundings as similar to their natural environment as possible, and there are herds of red deer and Highland cattle. Pets must not be allowed out of cars.

(8m NW of Aberfeldy on B846)
☎ **Kenmore (08873) 509 & 261**

Open: Apr-Oct, 9am-1hr before sunset.
Admission: ✳ 75p. Cars £3.
P shop ✖

KILLIECRANKIE   Killiecrankie Visitor Centre

The visitors' centre at this historic spot features an exhibition illustrating the battle that took place near here in 1689; there are also displays on the natural history of the area and ranger services. The battle site was where the Jacobite army, led by 'Bonnie Dundee' (who was mortally wounded in the attack) routed King William's troops. The wooded gorge is a notable beauty spot admired by Queen Victoria, and there are some splendid walks.

(3m N of Pitlochry on A9)
☎ **Pitlochry (0796) 3233**
Open: Visitor Centre, Exhibition, shop & snack bar Apr-May & Sep-Oct, daily 10-5; (Jun-Aug, daily 9.30-6).
Admission: 30p (ch free)
🅿 (charged) ☕ shop
(NTS)

PITLOCHRY   Faskally

On the shores of man-made Loch Faskally, the woodland incorporates forest walks, a nature trail and picnic facilities.

Forestry Commission (1m N on the B8019)
☎ **Dunkeld (03502) 284**
Open: Apr-Oct, dawn to dusk.
Admission: Free.
🅿 ♿ toilets for disabled 🚮

PITLOCHRY   Power Station, Dam & Fish Pass

The hydro-electric visitor centre consists of a souvenir shop; an exhibition showing how electricity is brought from the power station to the customer; access to the turbine viewing gallery and video shows. The salmon ladder viewing chamber allows visitors to see the fish as they travel upstream to their spawning ground. There is also a walkway across the top of the dam.

☎ **(0796) 3152**
Open: Apr-25 Oct, daily 9.40-5.30.
Admission: £1.50 (ch 60p, student £1).
Family ticket £2.50.
🅿 ♿ toilets for disabled shop 🐕

QUEEN'S VIEW   Queen's View Visitor Centre

Queen Victoria admired the view on a visit here in 1866, and there is a splendid viewpoint which also has access for the disabled. Forest walks take the visitor to viewpoints, an excavated ring fort and a reconstructed 18th- century farm village. The Visitor Centre has an exhibition describing the history of the area and places to visit.

(7m W of Pitlochry on B8019)
☎ **Dunkeld (03502) 284**
Open: 25 Mar-26 Oct, daily 10-5.30.
Free.
🅿 (charged) ☕ ♿ toilets for disabled shop

SCONE   Scone Palace

Scottish kings were crowned at Scone until 1651; it was the seat of government in Pictish times; and it was the site of the famous coronation Stone of Destiny, brought there in the 9th century until it was seized by the English in 1296. The castellated edifice of the present palace dates from 1803 but incorporates the 16th-century and earlier buildings. The displays inside include a magnificent collection of porcelain, furniture, ivories, clocks and 16th-century needlework; one of the bed hangings was worked by Mary Queen of Scots. The grounds include an outstanding Pinetum, woodland garden and brilliant displays of rhododendrons and azaleas (at the right time of the year). Although one of the most historical houses in Scotland, its chief attraction lies in its much-loved and 'lived-in' atmosphere – it still remains a family home. Events for 1992 include horse trials (May 2-3), a Coronation pageant (Jun 28), and a Scottish game fair (Jul 4-5).

☎ **(0738) 52300**
Open: 17 Apr-12 Oct, Mon-Sat 9.30-5, Sun 1.30-5 (Jul-Aug 10-5). Special parties outside normal opening hours & during winter by arrangement.
Admission: Palace & Grounds £3.70 (ch £2). Grounds only £1.85 (ch £1). Family £11. Party 20+.
🅿 ☕ ✕ licensed ♿ toilets for disabled shop 🐕 (ex in grounds)

SCOTTISH ISLANDS Arran

BRODICK   Brodick Castle, Garden & Country Park

The site of Brodick Castle has been fortified since Viking times, but the present castle dates from the 13th century, with extensions added in 1652 and 1844. It was a stronghold of the Dukes of Hamilton and more recently became the home of the late Duchess of Montrose. Splendid silver, fine porcelain and paintings acquired by generations of owners can be seen, including many sporting pictures and trophies.

There is a formal garden, dating from the 18th century and restored in Victorian style, but the most impressive part of the grounds is the woodland garden. It was started by the Duchess in 1923, and is world-famous for its rhododendrons and azaleas. A self-guided walk leads to its heart, and there are weekly guided walks in summer. The grounds also have an ice house and an adventure playground, ranger service and display centre.

☎ (0770) 2202
Open: all year, Country Park & Goatfell, daily 9.30-sunset. Castle open 1-17 Apr & 3-24 Oct, Mon, Wed, Sat 1-5; 18 Apr-Sep, daily 1-5. (Last admission 4.30).
Admission: House & Gardens £3 (ch & pen £1.50). Garden only £2 (ch & pen 90p).
P ☛ (Braille sheets & wheelchairs available) shop ✗ (ex in park)
(NTS)

BRODICK   Isle of Arran Heritage Museum

The setting is an 18th-century croft farm, including a cottage restored to its pre-1920 state and a 'smiddy' where a blacksmith worked until the late 1960s. There are farming and shipping displays, as well as a heritage project carried out in conjunction with a local high school. There are also occasional demonstrations of horseshoeing, sheepshearing and of the horse mill working.

Rosaburn
☎ (0770) 2636
Open: Apr-Oct, Mon-Sat 10-5.
Admission: ✻ £1 (ch 50p, pen 75p).
P ☛ & shop

SCOTTISH ISLANDS Mull

CRAIGNURE   Mull & West Highland Narrow Gauge Railway

The first passenger railway on a Scottish island opened in 1983. Both steam and diesel trains operate on the ten-and-a-quarter inch gauge line, which runs from Craignure to Torosay Castle. The line is 1.25 miles long, and there are extensive and dramatic woodland and mountain views.

Craignure (old Pier) Station
☎ (06802) 494 (in season) or Aros (0680) 300389
Open: Etr-mid Oct.
Return £1.75 (ch £1.20); Single £1.20 (ch 90p). Family ticket return £4.70, single £3.30.
P & (provision to carry person seated in wheelchair on trains) shop

---

SYMBOLS

☎ Telephone number	✻ Indicates 1991 price	☛ Refreshments	✗ No Dogs
& Suitable for visitors in wheelchairs	P Parking at Establishment	✗ Restaurant	No coaches

CRAIGNURE   Torosay Castle & Gardens

Much of this Victorian castle is open to the public together with its delightful Italian terraced gardens, designed by Lorimer. The Scottish baronial architecture is complemented by the magnificent setting and inside the house there are displays of portraits and wildlife pictures, family scrapbooks and a study of the Antarctic. The Edwardian library and archive rooms particularly capture the flavour of their era. Allures of the garden include a statue walk and water garden, an avenue of Australian gum trees, a Japanese garden and many rare shrubs.

(1m S of Ferry Terminal at Craignure)
☎ (06802) 421
Open: May-Oct, daily 10.30-5.30. Gardens all year.
Admission: ✳ Castle & garden £3.50. Garden only £1.50 (Reductions for ch, pen, students & groups).
🅿 ☕ ♿ toilets for disabled shop 🐕 (ex in gardens)

SCOTTISH ISLANDS Skye

ARMADALE   Clan Donald Centre

Skye's award-winning Visitor Centre is situated at the south end of the island. Armadale Castle and Gardens were built in 1815 as the home of Lord Macdonald. The sculptured ruins of the castle now house the Museum of the Isles, with an exhibition and slide-show. A library and study centre offer genealogical research and access to historical records. Surrounding the castle are 40 acres of beautiful woodland gardens and nature trails. The Countryside Ranger Service provides a full summer programme of walks, talks and children's afternoons. The stables serve as a gift shop and licensed restaurant during the day, and in the evenings as a theatre for plays and music. Events for 1992 include classical pipes and harp competitions, and sheep dog trials. Telephone for details.

(0.5m from Armadale Pier A851)
☎ Ardvasar (04714) 305 & 227
Open: Mar-Oct, daily 9.30-5.30. Limited winter opening.
Admission: £2 (concessions £2). Family ticket £8. Party.
🅿 ☕ ✗ licensed ♿ (wheelchairs available) toilets for disabled shop

DUNVEGAN   Dunvegan Castle

This fortress stronghold set on the sea loch of Dunvegan has been the home of the Chief of Macleod for 790 years. On view are books, pictures, arms and treasured relics of the clan. There is a display that traces the history of the family and the clan from their days as Norsemen until the present day. There are boat trips from the jetty to a nearby seal colony, and musical events in July and August. There are also shops and a restaurant.

☎ (047022) 206
Open: 23 Mar-Oct, Mon-Sat 10-5.30, Sun, castle 1-5.30, gardens 10-5.30. Last admission 5pm. Nov-Mar by appointment only.
Admission: ✳ £3.30 (ch £1.70, pen £2.80). Gardens £1.70 (ch 90p). Seal boats £2.80 (ch £1.70)
🅿 ☕ ✗ licensed shop 🐕 (ex in grounds)

ABBREVIATIONS					
AM	Ancient Monument	BH	Bank Holidays	ch 15 20p	Children under 15 20p
AM(CadW)	Ancient Monument	PH	Public Holidays	Pen	Senior Citizens
	(Wales)	Etr	Easter	Party	Special or reduced rates for
EH	English Heritage	ex	except		parties booked in advance
NT	National Trust	Free	Admission free	Party 30+	Special or reduced rates for
NTS	National Trust for	10p	Admission 10p		parties of 30 or more booked
	Scotland	ch 20p	Children 20p		in advance

WALES

CLWYD

BODELWYDDAN Bodelwyddan Castle

The castle has been authentically restored as a Victorian mansion and it houses a major collection of 19th-century portraits and photography from the National Portrait Gallery. These are complemented with a remarkable collection of furniture from the Victoria and Albert Museum and the Royal Academy of Arts. The extensive walled gardens have been restored to their former glory and provide a magnificent display of flowering plants, water features, aviary and woodland walks. For children, there is an adventure woodland and play areas. Temporary exhibitions and events throughout the year.

Special events for 1992 include: 11 Apr-1 Sep, Discovery Dome, hands on science exhibition; 30-31 May, North Wales Antiques Fair; 24-25 October, Conservation and Countryside Fair.

(adjacent to A55)
☎ St Asaph (0745) 584060)

Open: all year, Etr-Jun & Sep-1 Nov, daily (ex Fri) Jul-Aug daily 10-5. Last admission one hour before closing. Please phone for details of winter opening.
Admission: £3.50 (ch 4-16, pen, student & UB40 £2). Family ticket £9. Grounds only £2 (ch 4-16, pen, student & UB40 £1). Family ticket £5. Party.
P ☕ ✕ licensed ♿ (lift to first floor) toilets for disabled shop garden centre 🐕

CERRIGYDRUDION Llyn Brenig Information Centre

The 1,800-acre estate has a unique archaeological trail and round-the-lake walks of 10 miles (completion certificate available). There is also a nature trail and a nature reserve with a number of rare plants and birds. A hide is available: best viewing is November to March. Disabled anglers are catered for with a specially adapted boat and an annual open day. The centre has a bi-lingual exhibition on geology, archaeology, history and natural history.

(on B4051)
☎ (049082) 463

Open: all year, mid Mar-3 Oct daily 8-6; 1 Nov-mid Mar, Mon-Fri 8-4. (Access in winter may be limited by snow; cross-country skiing is then available).
Admission: ✻ Free. (ex water sports & fishing).
P (charged) ☕ ♿ (boats for disabled & fishing open days) toilets for disabled shop 🐕

COLWYN BAY Welsh Mountain Zoo & Flagstaff Gardens

The zoo and gardens are set in a 37-acre estate overlooking Colwyn Bay, with magnificent panoramic views. The animals are housed in natural settings, interspersed with gardens and woodland. The traditional range of zoo animals can be seen, from lions and elephants to penguins and parrots, and the zoo also attracts a variety of local wildlife. There are falconry displays during the summer months, and Californian sealions can be seen performing tricks at feeding time. A new attraction is the Chimpanzee World complex, featuring the unique Chimp Encounter. There is also a Jungle Adventureland and Tarzan Trail activity area, and a Children's Farm. Special events for 1992 include: 10 Oct, Cub Scouts' Fun Day.

Old Highway (off bypass, A55)
☎ (0492) 532938

Open: all year, 9.30-last admission 5pm. (4pm Nov-Feb).
Admission: ✻ £4 (pen & ch £2). Party
P ☕ ✕ licensed ♿ (free admission for the blind & wheelchair visitors) toilets for disabled shop 🐕

GLYN CEIRIOG Chwarel Wynne Mine & Museum

This is a mine, museum and education centre, where visitors can watch a video on the history of the slate industry, and take a half-hour conducted tour of the underground workings. The mine has a beautiful setting in a 12-acre site, and there is a nature trail.

Wynne Quarry (on B4500)
☎ (069172) 343

Open: Etr-Oct, daily 10-5. Parties welcome at other times by prior appointment.
Admission: ❄ £2 (ch & students £1, pen £1.50) Party & family tickets available.
P ☕ ♿ shop garden centre

LLANGOLLEN Horse Drawn Boats and Canal Exhibition Centre

Visitors can enjoy horsedrawn boat trips along the beautiful Vale of Llangollen, as well as a fascinating museum illustrating the heyday of canals in Britain. The imaginative displays include working and static models, photographs, murals and slides.

The Wharf, Wharf Hill
☎ (0978) 860702 & 823548 (eve)

Open: wknd afternoons Apr-Oct (pm daily Jul-Aug). Trips also run during May, Jun & Sep at various times, phone for details
Admission: ❄ Museum 70p (ch 45p).
☕ ♿ shop

LLANGOLLEN Llangollen Station

The restored Great Western Railway Station is situated in the town centre and beside the River Dee. Locomotives and rolling stock are displayed, and passenger trains run on a seven-mile round trip between Llangollen and Deeside Halt. A special coach for the disabled is sometimes available. Events for 1992 will include Thomas the Tank Engine weekends, Santa Specials, and special 'Wine and Dine' trains on Saturday evenings (summer only) and Sunday lunchtimes.

☎ (0978) 860951 & 860979

Open: Station wkds, Steam hauled trains Mar-Oct Sun & daily in Jul & Aug, diesel trains May-Oct Sat, daily during Jun. Santa specials during Dec.
Admission: ❄ Station Free; Return Fares 1st class £3.70 (ch £1.85) 2nd class £3.20 (ch £1.60). Single Fare 1st class £2.50 (ch £1.40) 2nd class £2.20 (ch £1.20)
☕ ♿ (special coach for disabled parties) toilets for disabled shop (at stations)

WREXHAM Erddig

Owned by the National Trust, Erddig is a treasure house of furnishings, utensils and tools of a country house since the 1700s. Built in 1680, the house was enlarged and improved during the next half century by a wealthy London lawyer with a passion for gilt and silver furniture. The house still has its original furnishings including a magnificent state bed in Chinese silk.

The house is especially notable for the view it gives of both 'upstairs' and 'downstairs' life. There is a range of restored outbuildings which show the workings of the laundry, the bakehouse – where bread is still baked – and the estate smithy and sawmill.

The gardens are unusual in that they have been very little changed since the 18th century.

(off the A525, 2m S of Wrexham)
☎ (0978) 355314

Open: Apr-Sep, daily (ex Thu & Fri, open Good Fri); 11-6 (house 12-5); last entry 4pm. Family rooms close in Oct, 3 Oct-1 Nov belowstairs servants quarters only.
Admission: Family rooms (inc below stairs, outbuildings & gardens) £4.50 (ch £2.25). Below stairs (inc gardens & outbuildings) £2.80 (ch £1.40). Party.
P ✕ licensed ♿ toilets for disabled shop (no dogs)
(NT)

DYFED

CAPEL BANGOR   Rheidol Power Station & Information Centre

A guided tour of the power station can be taken. It lies in a secluded valley, and other facilities include a fish farm, forest walks and a lakeside picnic area. There is an information centre.

Cwm Rheidol (off A44 at Capel Bangor)
☎ (097084) 667

Open: Etr-Sep, daily 11-4.30 & Oct noon-4pm for tours of the Power Station & information centre.
Admission: £1.50 (ch 16 50p, pen & students £1). Family ticket £3.50.
🅿 ᕦ shop

CARDIGAN   Cardigan Wildlife Park

This is an unusual park and sanctuary, with a wide range of animals, birds and plants. It also has nature walks and fishing on the River Teifi. The ancient art of coracle fishing is demonstrated regularly during the season, and various events are held through the year.

Cilgerran (entrance near village off A478)
☎ (0239) 614449

Open: from Etr, daily 10-sunset (last admission 5.30pm).
🅿 ☞ ᕦ shop ✗
Details not confirmed for 1992

CAREW   Carew Castle & Tidal Mill

This magnificent Norman castle – later an Elizabethan residence – has royal links with Henry Tudor and was the setting for the Great Tournament of 1507. Special events for the year include theatre interpretation, a schools programme, holiday activities and concerts – details available spring 1992.

Nearby is the Carew Cross (Cadw), an impressive 13ft Celtic cross dating from the 11th century. Carew Mill is one of only three restored tidal mills in Britain, with records dating back to 1558. The fine four-storey building houses a theatre showing an introductory film, and there are talking points explaining the milling process.

(on A4075, 5m E of Pembroke)
☎ (0646) 651657 & 651782

Open: Etr-Oct, daily 10-5.
Admission: ✳ £1.75 (ch & pen 90p). Single ticket (castle or mill) £1.15 (ch 60p).
🅿 ᕦ shop

CARREG CENNEN CASTLE

A steep path leads up to the castle, which is spectacularly sited on a limestone crag. It was first built as a stronghold of the native Welsh and then rebuilt in the late 13th century. Most remarkable among the impressive remains is a mysterious passage, cut into the side of the cliff and lit by loopholes. The farm at the site operates a rare breeds centre and a tea room.

☎ Llandeilo (0558) 822291

Open: all year, 27 Oct-24 Mar wkdays 9.30-4, Sun 2-4; 25 Mar-26 Oct daily 9.30-6.30. (Closed 24-26 Dec & 1 Jan).
🅿 ☞ shop ✗
(AM Cadw)
Details not confirmed for 1992

CRYMYCH Castell Henllys Fort

This Iron Age hill fort is set in the beautiful Pembrokeshire Coast National Park. Excavations began in 1981 and three roundhouses have been reconstructed. A forge, smithy, and primitive looms can be seen, with other attractions such as adventure trails and a herb garden.

Pant-Glas, Meline (off A487)
☎ Crosswell (023979) 319

Open: Etr-Oct, daily 10-6 (closes 5pm from mid-Sep).
Admission: ✻ £2 (ch & pen £1).
P shop

KIDWELLY Kidwelly Industrial Museum

Two of the great industries of Wales are represented in this museum: tinplate and coal mining. The original buildings and machinery of the Kidwelly tinplate works, where tinplate was hand made, are now on display to the public. There is also an exhibition of coal mining with pit-head gear and a winding engine, while the more general history of the area is shown in a separate exhibition.

☎ (0554) 891078

Open: Etr-Sep, Mon-Fri 10-5 (6pm Jul-Aug), Sat-Sun 2-5 (6pm Jul-Aug). Last admission 4pm (5pm Jul-Aug). Other times by arrangement for parties only.
Admission: ✻ £1 (ch, pen, students & UB40s 50p). Family ticket £2.50. Party.
P ♿ toilets for disabled shop 🐕̸ (ex in grounds)

NARBERTH Oakwood Adventure & Leisure Park

The activities offered here are numerous and include rollercoaster, waterfall and bobsleigh rides, miniature trains, go-karts and assault courses. There is a huge undercover playland as well as an outdoor children's play area. A 400- seat theatre has recently opened.

Canaston Bridge (signposted off the A40)
☎ Martletwy (0834) 891376

Open: 11 Apr-Sep, daily from 10am. Restricted in Oct.
Admission: fee payable.
P ✕ licensed ♿ toilets for disabled shop 🐕̸

NEWCASTLE EMLYN Felin Geri Mill

Felin Geri Mill is one of the last watermills in the UK to use the original methods of production to grind corn on a regular, commercial basis. Visitors are shown all the stages of production of stoneground wholemeal flour. There is also a water-powered sawmill and a mill museum. Children can have fun in the large adventure playground and there are walks to enjoy. With trout ponds, a woodland interpretation centre and craft workshops there is plenty to see and do.

Cwmcou (2m N on unclass rd off B4333 at Cwmcou)
☎ (0239) 710810

Open: Etr-Oct, daily 10-6.
P ✕ licensed ♿ shop
Details not confirmed for 1992

PONTERWYD Bwlch Nant-Yr-Arian Forest Visitor Centre

Operated by the Forestry Commission, the centre interprets all the aspects of the forest. There are forest walks in the vicinity.

(3m W)
☎ Crossword (09743) 404

Open: Etr-Sep, daily 10-5 (6pm in Jul-Aug).
Admission: Free.
P ♿ toilets for disabled shop 🐕̸ (ex in grounds)

PONTERWYD   Llywernog Silver-Lead Mine

The Llywernog Silver-Lead Mine is an internationally known mining heritage centre. The mountains of Mid Wales form a backdrop to the museum displays, Miner's Trail, underground tunnel, working water-wheels, tea rooms and picnic site. Displays and demonstrations of silver panning take place regularly in season. A special event for 1992 is Miners' Gala Day on 4 July.

(11m E of Aberystwyth on A44)
☎ (097085) 620

Open: Etr-Oct, daily 10-6 (Oct 5pm). Last admission 1 hour before closing time. Winter by appointment.
Admission: £2.75 (ch 5-15 £1.50, students & pen £2.25). Family ticket £7.50.
🅿 ☕ ᶑ shop

PUMSAINT   Dolaucothi Gold Mines

Here is an opportunity to spend a day exploring the gold mines and to wear a miner's helmet and lamp while touring the underground workings. The information centre and a walk along the Miners' Way disclose the secrets of 2,000 years of gold mining. A unique blend of history and beauty, this is the only place in Britain where the Romans mined gold.

☎ (05585) 359

Open: 30 Mar-Oct, daily (incl BH's) 10-6. Underground tours May-Sep, daily every half hour. (Last admission 5pm).
Admission: ✻ £2-£4 (ch £1.20-£2).
🅿 ☕ shop 🐾
(NT)

ST FLORENCE   Manor House Wildlife & Leisure Park

The park is set in 12 acres of delightful wooded grounds and award-winning gardens. The wildlife includes exotic birds, reptiles and fish. Also here are a pets' corner, a children's playground, amusements and radio-controlled models. Other attractions include a giant astraglide slide, a go-kart track and model railway exhibition. There are falconry displays twice a day (except Sat).

Ivy Tower (on B4318)
☎ Carew (0646) 651201

Open: Etr-Sep, daily 10-6.
Admission: £2 (ch & pen £1). Party 20+.
🅿 ☕ ᶑ toilets for disabled shop garden centre 🐾

SCOLTON   Scolton Manor Museum & Country Park

The early Victorian mansion, stables and a large exhibition hall are given over to illustrating the history and natural history of Pembrokeshire. The 60 acres of grounds are rich in fine trees and ornamental shrubs while a 'tree and nature trail' provide interesting diversions.

(5m N of Haverfordwest, on B4329)
☎ Clarbeston (0437) 731328 (Mus) & 731457 (Park)

Open: all year, Country Park. Museum: May-Sep, Tue-Sun & BH's 10-4.30.
Admission: ✻ 50p (ch free, pen & UB40 25p). Party 10+.
🅿 ☕ ᶑ shop 🐾 (ex in grounds)

SOLVA   Solva Nectarium

At the Nectarium, live butterflies from all around the world can be seen at close quarters. There are specimens from places as far apart as the rain forests of India, Malaysia and the Amazon, as well as many from more temperate climates. In an insect gallery, butterflies can be seen emerging from their pupae. There are several shops in the complex selling perfumery, designer clothing and furnishings for the home.

☎ St Davids (0437) 721323

Open: Etr-Sep, Mon-Sat 10-6, Sun 2-6. (Last admission 5pm).
Admission: ✻ £2 (ch 5-14 £1, under 5 free, pen £1.50).
☕ shop

GWENT

BLAENAVON Big Pit Mining Museum

The 'Big Pit' closed as a working mine in 1980, but today visitors can don safety helmets and cap lamps, and descend the 300ft shaft to find out what life was like for generations of miners in South Wales. There is an exhibition in the old pithead baths and changing rooms, and a reconstructed miner's cottage can also be seen. Stout shoes and warm clothes are recommended for tours of the mine.

☎ (0495) 790311

Open: Mar-Oct, daily 9.30-5. (Last tour 3.30). Nov-Feb telephone for opening details.
Admission: Underground & surface £4.50 (ch £3.25 & pen & students £4.25) surface only £1.50 (ch 75p, pen & students £1.25). Family ticket £14.
P ☕ ♿ (underground tours by prior arrangement) toilets for disabled shop

CALDICOT Caldicot Castle, Museum & Countryside Park

The restored Norman border castle has a sandstone keep which was probably built by Humphrey de Bohun in the 13th century. It houses a museum and exhibitions, and overlooks a country park where herons and other water-loving birds may be seen. There is also an adventure playground. Around the castle are tranquil gardens, the scene of fashionable parties in the 19th century.

(on B4245)
☎ (0291) 420241

Open: Mar-Oct, Mon-Fri 11-12.30 & 1.30-5, Sat & BH 10-1 & 1.30-5, Sun 1.30-5.
P ♿ toilets for disabled shop
Details not confirmed for 1992

CWMCARN Cwmcarn Forest Drive

A seven-mile scenic drive with spectacular views over the Bristol Channel and surrounding countryside. Facilities include barbecues, picnic and play areas, and forest and mountain walks. The area is run by the Forestry Commission.

(9m N of Newport on A467)
☎ Newport (0633) 400205

Open: Etr-Oct, daily 11-7pm.
Admission: ✻ Cars & Motorcycles £2, Minibus fr £6, Coaches £20.
P ♿ shop

NEWPORT Tredegar House & Park

Tredegar was home to one of the greatest of Welsh families, the Morgans, later Lords Tredegar, for over five centuries, but for years their house has remained relatively unknown. Today it stands out as one of the most magnificent 17th-century houses in Britain. A tour of the interior vividly illustrates what life was like for the Morgans and their servants, giving visitors a fascinating insight into life 'above' and 'below' stairs.

The gardens are currently being restored but their past history – and that of the Orangery and Stables – and of the famous Cefn Mill Mabli shovelboard, is magically brought to life. The house and gardens are set within a 90-acre landscape park. Carriage rides, self-guided trails, craft workshops, boating, and an exciting adventure playfarm provide a wide variety of things to do and see. Special events for 1992 include: 15-17 May, Folk Festival; 20-21 Jun, Antiques Fayre; 28-30 Aug, Newport Show.

Coedkernew
☎ (0633) 815880

Open: Good Fri-end Sep, Wed-Sun & BHs 11.30-4.(Tue during school holidays. Wknds only in Oct. Special Xmas opening).
Admission: ✻ House £3.20 (ch & pen £2.20) Family ticket £8. Garden only £1.
P (charged) ☕ ✕ licensed ♿ (wheelchairs for loan) toilets for disabled shop

TINTERN Tintern Abbey

Standing serenely beside the banks of the River Wye, the ruins of the Cistercian monastery church are still surprisingly intact. The monastery was established in 1131 and it continued to thrive and become increasingly wealthy well into the 15th century. During the Dissolution, the monastery was closed and most of the buildings, other than the church, were completely destroyed. During the 18th century the ruins of Tintern were considered to be one of the essential sites to visit. Many poets and artists came to see the majestic arches, fine doorways and elegant windows, and recorded their experiences in poetry and paintings. An exhibition, situated near the new shop, illustrates the lifestyles of the monks.

(via A466)
☎ (0291) 689251

Open: all year, 27 Oct-24 Mar wkdays 9.30-4, Sun 2-4; 25 Mar-26 Oct, daily 9.30-6.30. (Closed 24-26 Dec & 1 Jan).
🅿 ♿ toilets for disabled shop 🚫
(AM Cadw)
Details not confirmed for 1992

GWYNEDD

BANGOR Penrhyn Castle

The splendid castle with its towers and battlements was commissioned in 1827 as a sumptuous family home. The architect was Thomas Hopper, who was also responsible for the panelling, plasterwork and furniture, still mostly in the 'Norman' style of the mid-19th century. Notable rooms include the great hall, heated by the Roman method of hot air under the floor, the library with its heavily decorated ceiling and great arches, and the dining room, which is covered with neo-Norman decoration. Among the furniture is a slate bed weighing over a ton, and a decorated brass bed made specially for Edward VII at the then huge cost of £600.

A natural history collection in the house shows species native to Snowdonia and there are two museums. Lady Penrhyn's bedroom suite is a doll museum and has dolls from all parts of the world, with an annexe showing Victorian nursery toys. The Penrhyn Castle Industrial Railway Museum occupies the stableyard.

The 40-acre grounds include a walled garden, wild garden and attractive woodland. There are wonderful views over Anglesey, Puffin Island, the North Wales coast and Snowdonia.

(3m E at Landegai on A5122)
☎ (0248) 353084

Open: Apr-1 Nov, daily (ex Tue) 12-5 (Jul-Aug 11-5). Last admission 4.30pm. Last audio tour 4pm. Grounds open 11-6.
Admission: £3.80 (ch £1.90). Family ticket £9.50. Party. Garden only £2 (ch £1).
🅿 ☕ ♿ toilets for disabled shop 🚫
(NT)

BEAUMARIS Beaumaris Castle

Beaumaris was the last of the great castles built by Edward I around the coast of North Wales, and there is an exhibition on his castles in the Chapel Tower. The building took from 1295 to 1312 to complete and involved a huge workforce: a record for 1296 mentions 400 masons and 2,000 labourers, besides 100 carts and wagons and 30 boats carrying stone and seacoal. In the early 1400s it was captured by Owain Glyndwr and then retaken, and in later

☎ (0248) 810361

Open: all year, 27 Oct-24 Mar wkdays 9.30-4, Sun 2-4; 25 Mar-26 Oct daily 9.30-6.30. (Closed 24-26 Dec & 1 Jan).
🅿 ♿ 🚫
(AM Cadw)
Details not confirmed for 1992

centuries it was plundered for its lead, timber and stone. Despite this it remains one of the most impressive and complete castles built by Edward I. It has a perfectly symmetrical, concentric plan, with a square inner bailey and curtain walls, round corner towers and D-shaped towers in between. There are also two great gatehouses, but these were never finished. Around it is an outer curtain wall with small towers, and a moat which has been restored. The original defended dock for shipping has also survived.

BEAUMARIS   Beaumaris Gaol & Courthouse

With its treadmill and grim cells, the gaol is a vivid reminder of the tough penalties exacted by 19th-century law. One particularly gruesome feature is the route that condemned prisoners took to the scaffold. Also here is the George Scott exhibition of police memorabilia. The courthouse, built in 1614 and renovated early in the 19th-century, is a unique survival of a Victorian court room.

☎ (0248) 750262 ext 269

Open: Etr, end May-Sep, daily 11-6. Court 11.30-5.30 (ex when in session). Other times by arrangement only.
Admission: Gaol £2.20 (ch & pen £1.50). Courthouse £1.30 (ch & pen £1). Combined ticket £2.70 (ch & pen £2). Family ticket £6.50.
& (audio tape tour available) shop ✖

BEAUMARIS   Museum of Childhood

Many rare and valuable exhibits are shown in the nine rooms of the museum, which illustrates the life and interests of children and families over 150 years. They include money boxes, dolls, educational toys and games, early clockwork trains, cars and aeroplanes, push toys and cycles. Also shown are things that were used rather than played with by children, such as pottery and glassware, and pieces of furniture. A gallery shows paintings and prints of children, with early samplers and needlework pictures worked by children. Winner of the BTA and National Heritage Museum of the Year Awards. In 1990, the museum was voted 'Star Choice' out of 35 top museums by the Sunday Express Magazine travel writers.

1 Castle St (on B4375)
☎ Bangor (0248) 7123498

Open: daily 10-6, Sun 12-5. (Closed 25 Dec & 2nd wk Jan-2nd wk Mar).
Admission: ✳ £2.50 (ch £1.25, pen £1.50). Family ticket £6. Free entry for wheelchairs.
🅿 & shop ✖

BEDDGELERT   Sygun Copper Mine

With the help of an expert guide, visitors can explore the workings of this 19th-century copper mine set deep within the Gwynant Valley. The less energetic can enjoy a continuous audio-visual presentation and a display of artefacts found during excavations.

☎ (076686) 595

Open: all year, daily 10-6. (Last tour 5.15pm).
Admission: ✳ £3.60 (ch £2.25, pen £3).
🅿 & toilets for disabled shop ✖

BETWS-Y-COED   Conwy Valley Railway Museum

The two large museum buildings have displays on both the narrow- and standard-gauge railways of North Wales, including railway stock and other memorabilia. There are working model railway layouts and a steam-hauled miniature railway in the grounds, which cover over four acres. The latest addition is a 15in gauge tramway to the woods.

Old Goods Yard
☎ (0690) 710568

Open: Etr-Oct, daily 10-5.30.
Admission: £1 (ch & pen 50p). Family ticket £2.50. Steam train/Tram ride 75p.
🅿 ☕ & toilets for disabled shop

BLAENAU FFESTINIOG   Ffestiniog Pumped Storage Power Station

The scheme was the first hydro-electric pumped storage scheme, and was opened by Her Majesty the Queen in 1963. Water is released from an upper dam, through turbines, to generate electricity when needed, and then pumped back up when demand is low. Guided tours are available, and the information centre includes a souvenir shop and café.

Ffestiniog Information Centre, Tan-Y-Grisiau (off A496)
☎ (0766) 830310

Open: Etr-Oct 10-4.30. Other times by prior arrangement.
🄿 ☕ shop 🐾 (ex in grounds)
Details not confirmed for 1992

BLAENAU FFESTINIOG   Gloddfa Ganol Slate Mine

Visitors can put on safety helmets and go into the extensive underground workings of this slate mine, which is the world's largest. There are special conducted tours by Land Rover for the more adventurous, which explore some of the miles of chambers and tunnels hundreds of feet up in the mountain. The massive machinery used in slate mining is displayed in the mill, and the art of slate splitting is demonstrated. Gloddfa Ganol is an active mine. Today's open cast blasting operations can be seen from the safety of the Mining Museum, and with the help of video films, exhibitions and demonstrations visitors achieve a valuable insight into the complex nature of the slate industry.

(1m N on A470)
☎ (0766) 830664

Open: Etr-Oct, Mon-Fri, also Sun 19 Jul-1 Sep 10-5.30.
Admission: £3 (ch £1.75).
🄿 ☕ ✗ licensed ⅙ shop

BLAENAU FFESTINIOG   Llechwedd Slate Caverns

The miners' underground tramway carries visitors into areas where early conditions have been recreated, while the Deep Mine is reached by an incline railway and has an unusual audio-visual presentation. Free surface attractions include several exhibitions and museums, slate mill and the Victorian village which has Victorian shops, money-house, Miners Arms pub, lock-up and working smithy.

☎ (0766) 830306

Open: all year, daily from 10am. Last tour 5.15 (Oct-Feb 4.15). (Closed 25-26 Dec & 1 Jan).
Admission: Single Tour £4.25 (ch £3, pen £3.75). Combined Tour £6.50 (ch £4.50, pen £5.25).
🄿 ☕ ✗ licensed ⅙ toilets for disabled shop
🐾 (ex on surface)

BODORGAN   Hen Blas Country Park

The focal point is the manor house, which dates back to the 15th century, and is one of Anglesey's oldest properties. There are 230 acres of parkland, with an 18th-century barn, shire horses, and a nature reserve and trail. There is also a large undercover play area.

☎ (0407) 840152

Open: all year, daily 10-5.30. (Restricted facilities at other times).
🄿 ☕ ✗ ⅙ shop
Details not confirmed for 1992

BRYNSIENCYN   Anglesey Sea Zoo

The sea zoo is a unique collection of marine life found around Anglesey and the North Wales coast. The sea creatures are housed in glass-sided and open-topped tanks of all shapes and sizes, which are intended to provide as natural and unrestricted an environment as possible. Another important consideration has been providing cover for visitors. There are also shoaling tanks, a wave tank,

The Oyster Hatchery
☎ (0248) 430411

Open: 7 Jan-Dec, from 10am. Last admission 5pm (Nov-Feb 3pm).
Admission: £3.80 (ch £2.60, pen £3.30). Family ticket £10.50. Party 12 + .

tide tank, wreck room and touch pools. A new attraction is an exhibit called 'The Big Fish Forest'. This is a huge kelp forest enclosed by the largest unsupported acrylic panel in Britain.

🅿 ✖ licensed ♿ (wheelchair available) toilets for disabled shop

CAERNARFON   Caernarfon Castle

Edward I began building the castle and extensive town walls in 1283 after defeating Llywelyn the Last (last of the native Welsh princes). Completed in 1328, it has unusual polygonal towers, notably the 10-sided Eagle Tower, and the walls have bands of colour. There is a theory that these features were copied from the walls of Constantinople, to reflect a tradition that Constantine the Great was born nearby, at the Roman fort of Segontium. Caernarfon was the largest of Edward I's castles in Wales, and the Chamberlain Tower has an exhibition on the castles of Edward I. His son and heir was born and presented to the Welsh people here, setting a precedent that was followed in 1969, when Prince Charles was invested as Prince of Wales – there is a 'Prince of Wales' exhibition in the North-East Tower and a display of investiture robes. A wall walkway links the Eagle Tower to the Queen's Tower, which houses the museum of the Royal Welsh Fusiliers. The regiment dates back to 1689 and eight Victoria Crosses are on display. There is also a 'Prospect of Caernarfon' exhibition on the ground floor of the Eagle Tower.

☎ (0286) 77617

Open: all year, 27 Oct-24 Mar wkdays 9.30-4, Sun 2-4; 25 Mar-26 Oct daily 9.30-6.30. (Closed 24-26 Dec & 1 Jan)
🅿 shop 🐾
(AM Cadw)
Details not confirmed for 1992

COED-Y-BRENIN   Coed-y-Brenin Forest Park & Visitor Centre

Located in the heart of Coed-y-Brenin the visitor centre provides an excellent introduction to the area with its range of displays and audio-visual programmes. Coed-y-Brenin means King's Forest, and it was named to commemorate the Silver Jubilee of King George V in 1935. There are over 50 miles of waymarked walks, delightful picnic spots and a wildlife conservation hide. Guide leaflets in the surrounding trails are provided by the centre, where visitors can also see a fascinating display on the gold mines which were once worked in this area.

☎ Dolgellau (0341) 422289

Open: Etr-Oct 10-5. Other dates by prior bookings.
🅿 (charged) ☕ ♿ toilets for disabled shop
Details not confirmed for 1992

CONWY   Conwy Castle

The castle is a magnificent fortress, built from 1283-9 by Edward I. There is an exhibition on Edward I and his castles in Wales within the shop area. The castle forms part of the same defensive system as the extensive town walls, 1,400yds long and some 30ft high, which are among the most complete in Europe. They have 21 (originally 22) towers, and sweep up and down hills as they encircle the town. The best view of the castle and walls is from the other side of the river, which is spanned by three bridges designed to complement the scene. The graceful suspension bridge was built by Telford in 1826, the tubular bridge by Stephenson in 1848, and the road bridge was completed in 1958.

(by A55 or B5106)
☎ (0492) 592358

Open: all year, 27 Oct-24 Mar, wkdays 9.30-4, Sun 2-4; 25 Mar-26 Oct daily 9.30-6.30. (Closed 24-26 Dec & 1 Jan)
🅿 shop 🐾
(AM Cadw)
Details not confirmed for 1992

DINAS MAWDDWY   Meirion Mill

This working woollen mill stands in the grounds of the old Mawddwy railway station in a pretty village at the southern end of Snowdonia National Park. Facilities include a visitor centre, shop, children's adventure playground, and dog exercise area. There is a packhorse bridge which is an ancient monument.

☎ (06504) 311

Open: Etr-Oct, daily incl BH. Limited during winter.
Admission: Free.
🅿 ♥ ✕ licensed & shop

FAIRBOURNE   Fairbourne Railway

One of the most unusual of Wales's 'little trains' – it was built in 1890 as a horse-drawn railway to carry building materials for the seaside resort of Fairbourne. It was later converted to steam, and now runs one-and-a-half miles from Fairbourne to the end of the peninsula and the ferry for Barmouth. Its route passes one of the loveliest beaches in Wales, with views of the beautiful Mawddach Estuary. An enjoyable round trip can be made from Barmouth in summer, crossing the Mawddach by ferry, catching the miniature train to Fairbourne and then taking the British Rail train – or walking – across the Mawddach Viaduct. At Gorsaf Newydd terminus visitors can see locomotive sheds and engineering works.

Beach Rd
☎ (0341) 250362

Open: Etr-Sep, times vary according to season and events.
🅿 ✕ licensed & shop
Details not confirmed for 1992

GLAN CONWY   Felin Isaf Watermill

This award-winning 17th-century mill has recently been restored, and stands in its own secluded gardens. There is a mini golf course, fishing and craft shops. A working water wheel will be ready for 1992. School groups are a speciality. Children can take part in a Discovery Project.

(on A470, 1m S from junc A55 & A470)
☎ Aberconwy (0492) 580646

Open: Etr-Nov, daily 10-dusk.
Admission: £1.50 (ch & disabled £1).
🅿 & shop 🐾

LLANBEDR   Maes Artro Village

An old wartime RAF camp has been imaginatively converted to display a varied range of exhibitions and activities. An original air raid shelter has been restored with light and sound effects; the history of RAF Llanbedr is illustrated; and a Spitfire, used in the TV series *A Piece of Cake*, is on show. Old farm implements, a 'Village of Yesteryear', a log fort playground and nature trails are all set among the lovely wooded grounds. Most recent attraction is the Marine Life Aquarium. Musicians play live in the village most days.

☎ (034123) 467

Open: Etr-Sep, daily 10-5.30
Admission: ✳ £2.30 (ch & pen £1.70).
🅿 ♥ ✕ licensed & toilets for disabled shop garden centre

LLANBERIS   Dolbadarn Castle

Built by Llywelyn the Great in the early 13th century, this Welsh castle overlooks Llyn Padarn in the Llanberis pass.

Open: all year, 27 Oct-24 Mar, wkdays 9.30-4, Sun 2-4; 25 Mar-26 Oct, daily 9.30-6.30. (Closed 24-26 Dec & 1 Jan).
🅿 🐾
(AM Cadw)
Details not confirmed for 1992

LLANBERIS   Llanberis Lake Railway

Steam locomotives dating from 1889 to 1948 carry passengers on a four-mile return journey to Gilfach Ddu, adjacent to the Welsh Slate Museum and the centre of the Padarn Country Park. The railway was formerly used to carry slate.

Padarn Country Park (off A4086)
☎ (0286) 870549

Open: Etr-late Oct. Trains run frequently every day (ex Sat), 11-4.30 in peak season. *Admission:* £3.40 (ch £2). Family ticket. 🅿 ♨ ✦ toilets for disabled shop ♴ (train & shop)

LLANBERIS   Snowdon Mountain Railway

On the route of an old pony track, Britain's only rack-and-pinion railway is operated by 7 vintage steam and 3 modern diesel locomotives. The journey of just over four-and-a-half miles takes passengers more than 3000ft up to the summit of Snowdon; breathtaking views include, on a clear day, the Isle of Man and the Wicklow Mountains in Ireland. The railway was opened in 1896.

(on A4086)
☎ (0286) 870223

Open: 15 Mar-1 Nov, daily from 9am (weather permitting). *Admission:* ✱ Return £12 (ch £8.50). Single (Llanberis-summit) £8.50 (ch £6). Party 15+ by prior arrangement (out of season only). 🅿 (charged) ♨ ✦ (2 carriages suitable for disabled) toilets for disabled shop ♴

LLANBERIS   Welsh Slate Museum

Until its closure in 1969 the Dinorwic Quarry was one of the largest in Britain, employing over three thousand men in its heyday. The workshops, most of the machinery and plant have been preserved, including the foundry and the Dinorwic water wheel. The museum which was subsequently founded on the site includes displays and audio-visual presentations depicting the life here, and much of the original atmosphere still prevails. Nearby is a group of craft workshops and a woodcraft centre where visitors can watch craftsmen at work.

Gilfach Ddu (.25m off A4086)
☎ (0286) 870630

Open: daily, Etr Sat-Apr 9.30-5.30; May-Sep 9.30-6.30. (Closed May Day). *Admission:* ✱ £1 (ch 50p, pen 75p). 🅿 ✦ shop (AM Cadw)

LLANDUDNO   Childhood Revisited

The Llandudno Doll Museum and the Llandudno Motorcycle Museum form part of this 'collection of collections'. Exhibits range from 16th-century dolls and those made from wood, wax, china, bisque and terracotta to present day dolls, and there are various playthings and accessories of childhood. The centrepiece of the display is a model working railway, combined with hundreds of old toys, models, games and books.

5 Bodhyfryd Rd
☎ (0492) 870424

Open: Mar-1 Nov, daily 10-6 (last admission 5pm). *Admission:* £2.50 (ch 3-15 £1.50 & pen £2) ♨ ✦ shop

LLANUWCHLLYN   Bala Lake Railway

Steam locomotives which once worked in the slate quarries of North Wales now haul passenger coaches for four-and-a-half miles from Llanwchllyn Station along the lake to Bala. The railway has one of the four remaining GWR signal boxes, installed in 1896. Some of the coaches are open and

The Station (off A494)
☎ (06784) 666

Open: 23 Mar-7 Apr, 25 May-2 Jun & 29 Jul-8 Sep,daily; 9 Apr-23 May, 4-27 Jun & 18-29 Sep, daily (ex Mon & Fri).

some closed, so passengers can enjoy the beautiful views of the lake and mountains in all weathers; the latest corridor coach has facilities for the disabled. Special events for 1992 include: 20-21 Jun, Grand Summer Gala; 5-6 Sep, Model Engineers' Weekend.

Admission: £4 return (ch £2). Family ticket £9.10. (single fares also available).
P ☛ &. shop

PORTHMADOG   Ffestiniog Railway

Opened in 1836 to serve the slate mines at Blaenau Ffestiniog, the line carried slate to the sea at Porthmadog on trucks which ran from the production point by gravity. The railway carried its first passengers on steam trains in 1865 and was closed in 1946. The narrow-gauge railway was re-opened by enthusiasts and operates steam locomotives including a unique Fairlie-type articulated locomotive. Most trains carry licensed buffet cars.

Harbour Station
☎ **(0766) 512340 & 831654**

Open: late Mar-early Nov, daily service and also 26 Dec-1 Jan & wnds Mar. Also limited service on certain days in Nov & Feb.
Admission: ✳ Charges vary according to distance travelled. First & third class available.
P ☛ &. shop

PORTHMADOG   Ffestiniog Railway Museum

The harbour station is home to exhibits including an old four-wheeled hearse converted from a quarryman's coach, one of the original steam locos from 1863, a slate wagon and model steam engine. Maps and diagrams illustrate the history of the famous narrow-gauge railway.

Harbour Station
☎ **(0766) 512340**

Open: Mar-Nov when train services operating (see Ffestiniog Railway).
Admission: Donations.
P ☛ &. shop

PORTMEIRION

Welsh architect Sir Clough Williams Ellis built his fairy-tale, Italianate village on a rocky, tree-clad peninsula on the shores of Cardigan Bay. The nucleus of the estate is a sumptuous waterfront hotel, rebuilt from the original house and containing a fine 18th-century fireplace and a library moved here from the Great Exhibition of 1851. A bell-tower, castle and lighthouse mingle with a watch-tower, grottoes and cobbled squares among pastel-shaded picturesque cottages let as holiday accommodation. A number of shops sell a variety of goods and the whole village is set in 175 acres of sub-tropical coastal cliff and wooded gardens.

One of the finest wild gardens in Wales is here – the 60-acre Gwyllt Gardens. They include miles of dense woodland paths and are famous for their fine displays of rhododendrons, azaleas, hydrangeas and sub-tropical flora. There is a mile of sandy beach and a playground for children. Toll-paying visitors can see the place where Noel Coward wrote 'Blithe Spirit', and the location for the cult TV series 'The Prisoner'.

☎ **Porthmadog (0766) 770457**

Open: all year, daily 9.30-5.30.
Admission: £2.70 (ch £1.20, pen £2.20).
Party 20 + .
P ☛ ✗ licensed &. toilets for disabled shop
🐾

SYMBOLS			
☎ Telephone number	✳ Indicates 1991 price	☛ Refreshments	🐾 No Dogs
&. Suitable for visitors in wheelchairs	P Parking at Establishment	✗ Restaurant	🚌 No coaches

TAL-Y-CAFN   Bodnant Garden

Situated above the River Conwy with beautiful views over Snowdonia, these gardens are a delight. They were first laid out in 1875 but in 1900 the 2nd Lord Aberconway started to improve them dramatically. Five terraces in the Italian style were constructed below the house, and between two large, existing cedars he placed a lily pool. On the lowest terrace is a canal pool with an open-air stage at one end and a reconstructed Pin Mill at the other. Part of the grounds have been made into a beautiful woodland garden in a sheltered valley. This is notable for its rhododendrons and other delicate shrubs. There are also many azaleas, a rock garden, and a laburnum walk.

(8m S of Llandudno & Colwyn Bay on A470)
☎ Tyngros (0492) 650460
Open: 14 Mar-Oct, daily 10-5 (last admission 4.30pm).
Admission: £3 (ch £1.50). Party 20+.
🅿 ☕ ✕ ⅋ shop garden centre 🐕
(NT)

TYWYN   Talyllyn Railway

This is the oldest 27in gauge railway in the world. It was built in 1865 to run from Tywyn on Cardigan Bay to Abergynolwyn slate mine some seven miles inland. The railway was also the first to be saved by a voluntary preservation society, after the slate quarry closed in 1947. The railway climbs the steep sides of the Fathew valley and on the way there are stops to admire the Dolgoch falls or to allow passengers to visit the Nant Gwernol forest. The train takes 2 hours and 30 minutes to cover the round trip. Each year in August there is a 'Race the Train' charity competition. This will be held on 15 August in 1992. Nearly 1,000 runners follow the track and usually as many as 100 will beat the train.

Wharf Station
☎ (0654) 710472
Open: 6 Apr-Oct, daily. Santa special 19 Dec, Xmas holiday serice 26 Dec-3 Jan. Timetable available.
Admission: ✳ £5.50 return ticket. Family ticket £12.50-£14.50.
🅿 (charged) ☕ ⅋ (by prior arrangement on trains) toilets for disabled shop

MID GLAMORGAN

MERTHYR TYDFIL   Brecon Mountain Railway

After eight years of planning and construction, this narrow-gauge railway was opened in 1980. It follows part of an old British Rail route which was closed in 1964 when the iron industry in South Wales fell into decline. The present route starts at Pant Station, three miles north of Merthyr Tydfil, and continues through the beautiful scenery of the Brecon Beacons National Park, as far as the two-and-a-half-mile long Taf Fechan reservoir. The train is pulled by a vintage steam locomotive, a delight in itself, and for lovers of vintage locomotives the workshops at Pant Station are well worth a visit. The display includes engines built in Germany and the USA as well as Great Britain, and some have spent their days on railways in far-flung corners of the earth.

Pant Station Dowlais (2.5m NE to the N of A465)
☎ (0685) 4854 due to change to 384854
Open: times on application to The Brecon Mountain Railway, Pant Station, Merthyr Tydfil, Mid Glamorgan.
Admission: Return fares £3.60 (ch 16 £1.80, free when travelling with adult paying full return fare). Party.
🅿 ☕ ✕ licensed ⅋ toilets for disabled shop

MERTHYR TYDFIL   Garwnant Forest Centre

Old farm buildings on the southern edge of the Brecon Beacons National Park have been converted into this visitor centre for the surrounding forest area. It offers a wealth of information about the facilities and forest trails,

Cwm Taf (5m N, off A470)
☎ (0685) 723060

and has displays of models and photographs to illustrate the main features of the area: farming, forestry and water. The verandah looks out over the Llwyn-On reservoir, and the character of the old buildings has been carefully preserved. It is a pleasant spot to start a walk in the surrounding forest, the Coed Taf Fawr. There is also a children's adventure play area.

Open: Etr-Sep wkdys 10.30-4.45. Apr, May & Sep, wknds 2-5 (inc BH). Jun-Aug, wknds 2-6 (inc BH).
🅿 ▼ ❤ shop
Details not confirmed for 1992

POWYS

ABERCRAF   Dan-Yr-Ogof Showcaves

Winner of eleven major tourism awards, Dan-Yr-Ogof Showcave is the longest in Britain. Cathedral Showcave is the largest single chamber in any British showcave and Bone Cave was home to man 3,000 years ago. There is also a Dinosaur Park, a museum and audio-visual theatre, and a craft shop with information centre. Instruction is also given on the artificial ski slope (opening times on request). Special event for 1992 is 'Music in the Mountains' on 30-31 August.

(3m N on A4067)
☎ **(0639) 720284**
Open: Apr-Oct, daily from 10am.
Admission: £4.50 (ch £3).
🅿 ▼ ❤ toilets for disabled shop

LLANFAIR CAEREINION   Welshpool & Llanfair Light (Steam) Railway

Austrian and Colonial locomotives are among those operated on the eight miles of track between Welshpool and Llanfair Caereinion.

(on A458)
☎ **(0938) 810441**
Open: Etr-4 Oct, wknds; Etr, May Day BH, Spring BH wk; 16 Jun-16 Jul, Tue-Thu; 18 Jul-6 Sep, daily. 8-17 Sep, Tue-Thu. Trains from Llanfair at 10.45, 1.30 & 4.15pm; from Welshpool 12, 2.45 & 5.15. Extra trains at BHs.
£5.80 return (ch 5-15 £2.90). Family ticket £14.
🅿 ▼ ❤ (one coach adapted for wheelchairs) toilets for disabled shop (at Llanfair station)

WELSHPOOL   Powis Castle

This medieval castle was built in about 1200 for a Welsh prince and has been continuously inhabited ever since. Later improvements to the castle have added 16th-century plasterwork and panelling and a fine 17th-century staircase. There are also murals by Lanscroon. Over the centuries many articles and treasures have been collected by both the Herbert family and the Clive family, who lived here and formed one of the finest country-house collections in Wales, including paintings, tapestries and early Georgian furniture. The most celebrated of the Clive family was Clive of India, and there are relics of his life and career in the house. The gardens at Powis, with their magnificent early 18th-century terraces, are of great horticultural and historical importance.

☎ **(0938) 554336**
Open: Apr-Jun & Sep-1 Nov, Wed-Sun; Jul-Aug, Tue-Sun & BH Mon. Castle: noon-5; Museum & garden: 11-6. Last admission 30 mins prior to closing. Gardens & Museum Sun 2-4 in winter.
Admission: Castle, Museum & Gardens £5.40 (ch 2.70). Museum & Gardens only £3.20 (ch £1.60) Family ticket £8. Party.
🅿 ▼ ❤ toilets for disabled shop ✗ (NT)

SOUTH GLAMORGAN

BARRY   Welsh Hawking Centre

There are over 200 birds of prey here, including eagles, owls and buzzards as well as hawks and falcons. They can be seen and photographed in the mews and some of the breeding aviaries, and there are flying demonstrations at regular intervals during the day. A variety of tame, friendly animals, such as donkeys, goats, pigs, lambs, cows and rabbits will delight younger visitors.

Weycock Rd (on A4226)
☎ **(0446) 734687**
Open: all year, daily 10.30-5, 1hr before dusk in winter. (Closed 25 Dec).
Admission: £2.75 (ch & pen £1.75).
🅿 ☕ ♿ shop

CARDIFF   see page 194

PENARTH   Cosmeston Medieval Village

Deserted during the plagues and famines of the 14th century, the original village was rediscovered through archaeological excavations. Now the buildings have been faithfully reconstructed on the excavated remains, within the Cosmeston Lakes Country Park, creating a living museum of medieval village life. Special events throughout the year.

Cosmeston Lakes Country Park, Lavernock Rd
☎ **Cardiff (0222) 708686**
Open: all year, Mon-Fri 8.30-4.30 & Sat-Sun 9-5. (Closed Sat, Nov-Mar, 24-26 Dec, 31 Dec & 1 Jan).
☕ ♿ toilets for disabled shop
Details not confirmed for 1992

ST FAGANS   Welsh Folk Museum

Once the home of the Earls of Plymouth, St Fagans is a 16th-century house built within the curtain walls of the original 13th-century castle. Donated to the National Museum in 1947, it is now the home of the extensive Welsh Folk Museum.

The museum is designed to represent the life and culture of Wales, and there is a huge amount to see. Old farmhouses, cottages, a tannery, a school and a chapel have been reconstructed, and are just a part of the range of the building styles and living conditions to be seen. Numerous skills are also demonstated throughout the year, and traditional Welsh cooking is part of the facilities. Events for 1992 include the Old May Day Fair (1-4 May), a Midsummer Folk Festival (20 Jun), and a Harvest Festival (26-27 Sep).

(junc 33 of M4)
☎ **Cardiff (0222) 569441**
Open: all year, Apr-Oct, daily 10-5; Nov-Mar, Mon-Sat 10-5. (Closed Good Fri, 24-26 Dec & 1 Jan).
Admission: £3.50 (ch £1.75, pen £2.60).
🅿 ☕ ✕ licensed ♿ (wheelchairs available) toilets for disabled shop 🐕 (ex in grounds)

ABBREVIATIONS					
AM	Ancient Monument	BH	Bank Holidays	ch 15 20p	Children under 15 20p
AM(CadW)	Ancient Monument	PH	Public Holidays	Pen	Senior Citizens
	(Wales)	Etr	Easter	Party	Special or reduced rates for
EH	English Heritage	ex	except		parties booked in advance
NT	National Trust	Free	Admission free	Party 30 +	Special or reduced rates for
NTS	National Trust for	10p	Admission 10p		parties of 30 or more booked
	Scotland	ch 20p	Children 20p		in advance

Cardiff is Europe's youngest capital city – it achieved the status in the 1950s. It prospered during the Industrial Revolution, when its docks were in great demand for the transportation of Welsh coal and iron ore. The docks declined, but are now being revitalised to become a huge complex of houses, offices, shops, restaurants, entertainment venues and activity centres and are already attracting large numbers of visitors to the Welsh Industrial and Maritime Museum and Techniquest, a fascinating 'hands-on' science centre.

Cathays Park is the home of the National Museum of Wales, full of treasures, and Llandaff Cathedral, on the outskirts of the city, is well worth a visit. Open-top bus tours and guided walks are available.

Cardiff has a rich cultural life and there is a lively programme of events throughout the year, including the Summer Festival, Lord Mayor's Parade and the Butetown Carnival, all in August, and the Cardiff Festival in September and October.

Tourist information: Bridge Street Telephone: (0222) 227281

☆ STAR ATTRACTIONS

Cardiff Castle
The Norman castle was built on the site of a Roman fort, and Roman walls some 10ft thick can still be seen. There is also a Norman keep and a 13th-century tower. Apartments were started in the 15th century, but the present-day character of the castle comes from its transformation in the 19th century, when the immensely rich 3rd Marquess of Bute employed William Burges to restore and rebuild it. Together they created a romantic fantasy of a medieval castle. Special events for 1992 include: 27 Jun, Beating Retreat Ceremony; 17-19 Jul, Hot Air Balloon Festival; 30-31 Jul, Marching Massed Bands Display.

Castle St
☎ (0222) 822083

Open: all year, daily (ex Xmas & New Year BH's). Conducted tours Mar, Apr & Oct, daily 10-12.30 & 2-4 (Castle closes 5). May-Sep, daily 10-12.40 & 2-5 (Castle closes 6); Nov-Feb daily 10.30-3.15 (Castle closes 4.30).
Admission: Conducted tour, military museums, green, Roman Wall & Norman Keep £3 (ch & pen £1.50). £2 (ch & pen £1) without conducted tour.
🍷 ⛏ shop ⚔ (ex in grounds)

Techniquest
Science and technology made accessible – and fun – at Britain's largest hands-on science centre, where visitors of all ages can participate in the activities and experiment with the exhibits. See yourself as others see you, instead of the mirror-image you are used to. Understand how aircraft fly . . . Techniquest makes it easy. Special events take place throughout the year.

72 Bute St, Pier Head
☎ (0222) 460211

Open: all year, Tue-Fri 9.30-4.30; Sat-Sun & BH's 10.30-5. Also Mon during school hols.
🅿 🍷 ⛏ toilets for disabled shop ⚔
Details not confirmed for 1992

Welsh Industrial & Maritime Museum
The museum tells the story of industrial and maritime Wales. Within a Hall of Power, working exhibits show the evolution of methods of driving machinery. A transport gallery includes a replica of Trevithick's Locomotive and the Railway and Shipping galleries complete the picture. Newly opened is '126 Bute Street – Coal out of Cardiff' which tells the tale of Cardiff's growth from small town quay to coal port, with photographic displays, a mock street scene and the replica wheelhouse of a typical Cardiff tramp steamer where a West Walian sea captain regales visitors with stories of his voyages.
'Q Shed' was once the warehouse and booking office for the much-loved P and A Campbell pleasure steamers. Today a wide range of frequently changing, exciting and dynamic events are held here.

Bute St
☎ (0222) 481919

Open: all year, Tue-Fri 10-5, Sun 2.30-5. (Closed Mon (ex BHs), 24-26 Dec, 1 Jan, Good Fri).
Admission: £1 (ch 50p, pen 75p).
⛏ (wheelchair available) toilets for disabled shop ⚔

WEST GLAMORGAN

ABERDULAIS   Aberdulais Falls

A short walk through the wooded gorge reveals one of the most famous waterfalls in the Vale of Neath, whose waters have been harnessed since the 16th century for a range of industries, from copper-smelting to tinplate. A unique hydro-electric scheme is currently underway.

☎ Neath (0639) 636674

Open: Apr-Oct, Mon-Fri 10-5, Sat-Sun & PH 11-6; Nov-24 Dec, daily 11-4. Due to development work, site may have to close. Telephone for details.
Admission: ✿ £2 (ch 70p).
& shop. (NT)

CILFREW   Penscynor Wildlife Park

Tropical birds, penguins, sea lions and parrots are seen here in an attractive setting among trees, streams and ponds, where visitors can also feed rainbow trout or see their tropical relatives. A chair lift goes to the cliff top for bobsleigh rides, and there is a children's playground.

☎ Neath (0639) 642189

Open: all year, daily 10-6, dusk in winter. (Closed 25 Dec).
Admission: ✿ £3 (ch under 3 free, ch & pen £2). Party 20+.
🅿 (charged) ☕ & toilets for disabled shop 🐾

CYNONVILLE   Welsh Miners Museum & Afan Argoed Country Park

The picturesquely placed museum gives a vivid picture of mining life, with coal faces, pit gear and miners' equipment. The country park has forest walks and picnic areas, and a visitor centre.

(on A4107)
☎ Cymmer (0639) 850564 & 850875

Open: Mar-Oct 10.30-6; Nov-Feb Sat & Sun only 10.30-5 (Bookings accepted in winter by arrangement).
🅿 ☕ ✗ & toilets for disabled shop 🐾
Details not confirmed for 1992

MARGAM   Margam Park

Margam Park's 850 acres of open parkland and forest are full of natural and historic treasures. The castle and abbey ruins, the waymarked walks, gardens and adventure playground, all go toward a memorable day out for the visitor. Fairytale Land, Nursery Rhyme Village, a large hedge maze and the Margam Orangery, the largest of its kind in Britain, add to the appeal of this notable beauty spot. There is entertainment for children daily during school summer holidays, and other events take place throughout the year, including a kite festival (13-14 Jun), and the Margam country fair (31 Aug).

(E off junc 38 M4)
☎ Port Talbot (0639) 881635

Open: all year, Apr-Sep daily 10-6 (last admission 5pm). Oct-Mar, Wed-Sun 10-5 (last admission 3pm).
Admission: Jan-Mar £1.20 (ch 3-16 & pen 60p); Apr-Sep £2.50 (ch under 3 free). Family ticket £8. Walker £1.25 (ch under 3 free). Family walker ticket £4; Oct-Dec £1 (ch 3-16 & pen 50p). Season ticket.
🅿 ✗ licensed & (free wheelchair loan) toilets for disabled shop

SWANSEA   Swansea Maritime & Industrial Museum Service

This museum complex in the Swansea docks contains a complete, working woollen mill as well as a selection of floating boats to explore from April to October. These include a trawler, a tug and a lifeboat. There are displays relating to the Port of Swansea, its industries and its environment, transport exhibits, and maritime and agricultural sections.

Museum Square, Maritime Quarter
☎ (0792) 650351

Open: all year, daily 10.30-5.30 (Closed 25, 26 Dec & 1 Jan).
& shop 🐾
Details not confirmed for 1992

INDEX

D

E

F

G

H

N

T

courants et prenez le temps d'apprendre comment agir selon les circonstances pour augmenter les chances qu'on découvre votre valeur.

Passer à l'action

Quand vous prévoyez rencontrer une personne qui pourrait être intéressante, préparez-vous. Accordez-vous une période de repos avant la rencontre et efforcez-vous de paraître à votre meilleur, même physiquement. Le premier contact qui s'établit entre deux personnes est d'abord visuel. Il ne s'agit pas d'afficher du tape-à-l'œil mais de refléter l'image de la personne intéressante que vous êtes.

Comment se mettre en mouvement vers l'autre, toucher son cœur et son esprit? Il n'y a pas qu'un chemin qui mène à l'autre. Heureusement, vous avez toujours ce petit explorateur en vous. Laissez sa curiosité vous guider.

Mentionnons d'abord ces signaux anodins qui ne visent qu'à attirer l'attention et à annoncer notre disponibilité. Tous les moyens sont bons. Tous les endroits peuvent être propices aux rencontres. Il n'y a que votre imagination qui vous limite. Mentionnons quelques exemples (Fortin, 1993).

— Arts ou artisanats (cours de théâtre, musées, concerts);
— clubs sportifs (conditionnement physique, gymnases, yoga, judo, karaté);

— conférences, colloques et activités professionnelles (formations, dîners, groupes d'intérêts);
— conférences et cours aux adultes (relations humaines, relaxation, dessin, décoration, poterie, cuisine, langues, yoga);
— cours et soirées de danse;
— encans, marchés aux puces, centres commerciaux;
— groupes de discussion (arts, lettres, défense des droits des animaux, écologie, spiritualité, etc.);
— groupes sociaux ou communautaires mixtes (parents monoparentaux, bénévolat, organismes de charité, mouvements religieux);
— jeux de société (échecs, dames, etc.);
— observation, admiration, contemplation (animaux, zoo, oiseaux, coucher de soleil, étoiles);
— organismes spécialisés (agences de rencontre, petites annonces, lettres, etc.);
— rencontre des amis des amis, en agrandissant progressivement notre territoire. Annonce informant les gens de notre intérêt à rencontrer des personnes intéressantes;
— voyages et déplacements, visite de certains endroits (tourisme, campagne, plage, pêche, parcs).

Souriez et présentez-vous à votre meilleur. Abordez la personne en lui demandant si elle connaît un bon restaurant aux alentours, si elle vous prendrait en photo, mettez votre chien ou votre enfant sur son chemin, parlez de la pluie et du beau temps, peu importe. Il s'agit d'augmenter vos chances d'ouvrir une porte vers quelqu'un qui semble intéressant. Reconnaissez sa réponse comme un commentaire sur sa disponibilité, son intérêt et ses goûts, et non comme une évaluation de votre valeur personnelle.

Pour faciliter la prise de contact, posez des questions ouvertes auxquelles la personne ne pourra pas répondre par oui ou par non (Boisvert et Beaudry, 1979). Pensez par exemple aux questions qui commencent par «comment» ou par «qu'est-ce qui» ou «qu'est-ce que». Voyons quelques exemples:

— Comment trouvez-vous la musique (l'ambiance, la nourriture, la conférence) ce soir?
— Comment avez-vous entendu parler de cette activité?
— Comment en êtes-vous venu à vous intéresser à la fine cuisine (ou au judo, à l'observation des étoiles ou au tarot)?
— Qu'est-ce qui vous a amené à choisir cette discothèque (ce repas, cette conférence, cette agence de rencontre)?

Ce genre de questions amène la personne à vous parler plus longuement et à vous fournir de l'information sur elle-même. Soyez attentifs. Cela ne vous sert à rien de poser une multitude de questions si vous n'écoutez pas les réponses. Votre but n'est pas d'éloigner l'autre en lui faisant subir un interrogatoire en règle. Vous souhaitez au contraire que ces questions créent des liens.

Donnez de l'information sur vous. Répondez à vos propres questions. Prenez soin de ne pas effrayer l'autre en abordant trop rapidement des questions personnelles. Il est préférable de se dévoiler lentement, au même rythme que votre interlocuteur le fera.

Aucune stratégie ne vous enlèvera la responsabilité de prendre le temps de bien connaître la personne avant de la laisser entrer davantage dans votre vie. Rappelons que ce ne sont pas nécessairement les personnes les plus flamboyantes ou les plus rapides à établir un contact qui correspondront à vos besoins.

Le meilleur conseil que nous puissions vous donner pour approfondir vos relations se résume probablement à la formule: parler de soi et parler de souhaits. Parler de soi, c'est accepter de vous dévoiler progressivement. À celui qui le mérite, faites le cadeau de vous laisser connaître peu à peu. Vous aurez ainsi plus de chance de toucher son cœur et son esprit. Ce n'est qu'en vous laissant vibrer que vous pourrez susciter une réaction semblable chez l'autre.

Le partage des souhaits plutôt que des insatisfactions et des inquiétudes suscite l'espoir et évite les propos blessants. Cela crée un projet commun autour duquel vous pouvez vous réunir. Cela indique clairement les comportements souhaités plutôt que de ne dire que ce que l'autre ne doit pas faire, et de lui laisser deviner ce qu'il faut faire. Les gens que vous croisez ne se comporteront pas toujours selon vos souhaits. Il y a toutefois plus de chances que les personnes de bonne volonté fassent des efforts pour vous plaire si vous leur donnez la bonne information sur ce qui vous plaît, sur vos valeurs ainsi que sur vos souhaits.

Vous doutez de votre capacité de toucher le cœur et l'esprit de l'autre? C'est sans doute que vous oubliez tout ce que vous pouvez faire. Laissez-nous vous rappeler quelques-uns des pouvoirs que vous avez en vous. Cette liste s'inspire des principes émis par Virginia Satir (1971, 1988).

Vous pouvez communiquer. Vous pouvez demander ce dont vous avez besoin et choisir de répondre aux besoins des autres. Vous pouvez donner de l'information. Vous pouvez parler, bouger, être expressif. Vous pouvez recevoir des informations. Vous pouvez voir, goûter, sentir, toucher et écouter. Vous pouvez donner un message clair. Vous n'êtes pas obligés d'enrober ce que vous avez à dire de tellement de détours que l'autre ne peut vous comprendre. Vous pouvez écouter, et surtout écouter sans interrompre. Vous pouvez garder un contact des yeux avec la personne avec qui vous communiquez. Vous pouvez parler en votre propre nom. Vous n'êtes pas obligés de ramasser des alliés (nous, on, les gens, etc.). Vous pouvez assumer la responsabilité de vos idées et de votre vécu. L'autre parlera pour lui-même.

Vous pouvez métacommuniquer, c'est-à-dire communiquer sur la communication en cours. Ce deuxième niveau vous permet de vous situer et de communiquer avec l'autre sur votre relation. Il s'agit de faire un pas de côté et de se dire ce qui se passe entre vous. C'est souvent un moment important lorsque l'on peut dire: «Je me sens bien avec toi» ou «Je me sens mal à l'aise lorsque tu agis ainsi». Sa réaction vous donnera de l'information sur la possibilité de développer une relation solide avec cette personne.

Soyez à l'écoute de la personne que vous fréquentez. Apprenez quelque chose sur elle à chacune de vos rencontres. Demandez-vous: «Est-ce que cette personne est capable d'identifier et de partager ses sentiments? Est-elle intéressée à développer ses capacités? Est-elle honnête et digne de confiance? Est-elle autonome? A-t-elle une attitude positive envers la vie? Partage-t-elle mes valeurs? Est-elle disponible et prête à s'engager?»

Comme nous l'avons déjà souligné, il ne s'agit pas de courir après un rêve ou de se faire une liste rigide de critères prédéterminés. Il s'agit plutôt de se méfier de nos points aveugles et de se donner l'occasion de bien percevoir la réalité de la personne dont nous souhaitons toucher le cœur et l'esprit.

Lucien

Lorraine n'était pas intéressée par Lucien, un employé du même centre d'accueil. Elle le trouvait trop sérieux, et d'apparence quelconque. Il était toutefois présent autour d'elle d'une façon persistante et il demeurait près d'elle malgré les aventures qui amenaient Lorraine à partager la vie d'autres personnes.

La persistance de l'attention de Lucien finit par attirer celle de Lorraine qui dîna avec lui à quelques reprises. Elle découvrit chez lui un humour qu'elle ne soupçonnait pas. La nature de leur relation changea suite à un événement banal. Lucien changea ses lunettes pour des verres de contact et modifia sa coiffure. Il devint subitement plus attirant pour Lorraine.

Lucien a réussi à toucher le cœur et l'esprit de Lorraine d'abord par son engagement et sa persistance polie et amicale. Une fois qu'il fut assez près d'elle pour être informé de ses goûts, il put en tenir compte et modifier son apparence. Ce n'est que par la suite que leur relation devint plus intime.

11

En guise de conclusion

Nous vous avons encouragés dans ce livre à prendre le temps de vous informer et de réfléchir. Nous vous avons invités à vous épanouir, parfois à persévérer dans vos choix et parfois à les modifier. Nous vous avons suggéré de vous relier aux autres, de remettre en question les pensées nuisibles et de mettre de côté certains de vos rêves irréalistes pour mieux faire face à la vie. Nous vous avons également incités à regarder vers l'avenir, à tenir compte de vos émotions et à vivre vos deuils, pour finalement vous préparer à toucher le cœur et l'esprit d'autrui.

Est-ce suffisant pour ne plus jamais être seul? Nous visons surtout à vous aider à ne plus sombrer dans la détresse à l'idée d'être seul, et à envisager la solitude différemment. Nous souhaitons principalement que vous ne vous sentiez plus jamais seul et sans ressources.

Il n'y a pas de recette magique, de solution instantanée qui permettraient à tous de vivre sans douleur, sans effort et d'oublier rapidement les départs que nous subirons tout au long de notre vie. Savoir créer des liens sans s'accrocher et apprendre à laisser aller sans s'effondrer, voilà les défis que nous affrontons quotidiennement.

L'histoire de nos deuils, c'est l'histoire de nos attachements et du dénouement de ces précieux liens qui nous rattachent les uns aux autres ainsi qu'à la vie. C'est l'histoire de notre vie.

Nous remplissons tous différents rôles dans notre vie: père ou mère, citoyen, étudiant, travailleur, auditeur ou téléspectateur, lecteur, consommateur, etc. Chacun de ces rôles nous relie les uns aux autres. Ils nous permettent, à travers des modèles associés à notre culture, d'échanger à l'intérieur d'un groupe social. Notre culture utilise ces moyens pour nous relier les uns aux autres. C'est ainsi que nous nous attendons à ce que le vendeur au dépanneur du coin nous rende certains services spécifiques, et que nous adoptons face à lui une certaine conduite précise.

Chaque fois que nous jouons un de nos rôles sociaux, nous reconnaissons la présence d'un être humain, notre appartenance à une culture commune et la possibilité d'échanger. Ces échanges sont toutefois restreints.

Chaque fois que l'un d'entre nous va au-delà de ces rôles en reconnaissant la présence d'un individu unique, particulier, nous nous relions à l'autre. Un seul lien suffit pour nous sortir tous deux de la solitude. À chaque lien que vous créez, vous augmentez la qualité du réseau social qui vous entoure, et tous en profitent.

Chaque fois que l'un d'entre nous témoigne de sa détermination à profiter de la vie et de la présence des autres, malgré les départs, les abandons et les trahisons, en utilisant pleinement ses ressources et celles de son entourage, il éveille autour de lui le goût irrépressible de faire de même, de vivre à plein. Chacun de nous peut ainsi contribuer à transformer le monde en un lieu où il fait bon vivre. C'est ce que nous vous invitons à faire, et nous vous en remercions à l'avance.

Bibliographie

BANDLER, R. (1985), *Using Your Brain — For a Change*, Moab, Utah, Real People Press.

BANDURA, A. (1990), «Conclusion», *in* R.J. STERNBERG et J. KOLLIGAN, *Competence Considered* (p. 315-362), New Haven, Yale University Press.

BOISVERT, J.-M. et M. BEAUDRY (1979), *S'affirmer et communiquer*, Montréal, les Éditions de l'Homme.

BOWLBY, J. (1984), *La perte. Tristesse et dépression* (Attachement et perte, Tome III), Paris, PUF.

BUGEN, L.A. (1977), «Human Grief: A Model for Prediction and Intervention», *American Journal of Orthopsychiatry*, 47, 196-206.

DE ANGELIS, B. (1993), *Making Love Work*, Baltimore, Inphomation, inc.

DÉSORMEAU, L. et B. FORTIN (1993), *Vivre à plein malgré ses limites*, Montréal, Éditions Fides.

EDINBERG, M. (1985), *Mental Health Practice with the Elderly*, Englewood Cliffs, NJ, Prentice-Hall.

FORTIN, B. (1993), *Prendre soin de sa santé mentale*, Laval, Éditions du Méridien.

FORTIN, B. et L. DÉSORMEAU (1994), *Vivre et grandir avec son enfant*, Montréal, Éditions Fides.

FORTIN, B. et S. NÉRON (1990), *Vivre avec la cancer*, Laval, Éditions du Méridien.

—— (1991), *Vivre avec un malade... sans le devenir!*, Laval, Éditions du Méridien.

GARNEAU, J. et M. LARIVEY (1979), *L'auto-développement. Psychothérapie de la vie quotidienne*, Montréal, Ressources en Développement.

GRAY, J. (1993), *Men, Women and Relationships*, Hillsboro, Oregon, Beyond Words Publishing.

HOAGLAND, A.C. (1983), «Bereavement and Personal Constructs: Old Theories and New Concepts», *Death Education*, 7(2-3), 175-193.

Joie de Vivre Canada (1994), *Guide des animateurs et animatrices*, Ottawa, Joie de Vivre Canada Inc.

KÜBLER-ROSS, E. (1973), *On Death and Dying*, New York, Tavistock Publications.

—— (1975), *Death: The Final State of Growth*, New Jersey, Prentice Hall.

LAZARUS, R.S. et B.N. LAZARUS (1994), *Passion & Reason*, New York, Oxford University Press.

LAZARUS, R.S. et S. FOLKMAN (1984), *Stress, Appraisal and Coping*, New York, Springer Publishing Company.

LEHMAN, D.R., C.B. WORTMAN et A.F. WILLIAMS (1987), «Long-Term Effects of Losing a Spouse or Child in a Motor Vehicle Crash», *Journal of Personality and Social Psychology*, 52, 218-231.

LEHRER, P.M. et R.L. WOOLFOLK (1993), *Principles and Practice of Stress Management*, New York, The Guilford Press.

McCARTHY, J. B. (1980), *Death Anxiety, the Loss of the Self*, New York, Gardner Press.

MENDELSON, M. (1974), *Psychoanalytic Concepts of Depression* (2ᵉ éd.), New York, Halsted Press.

MONBOURQUETTE, J. (1992), *Comment pardonner?* Montréal, Novalis.

MOUNT, E. (1983), «Individualism and our Fears of Death», *Death Education*, 7, 25-31.

NEALE, R.E. (1973), *The Art of Dying*, New York, Harper & Row.

NÉRON, S. et B. FORTIN (1993), «Vivre avec le cancer: stratégies d'adaptation pour le malade et pour les aidants naturels», *Perspectives psychiatriques*, 39 (4), 242-251.

PARKES, C.M. (1969), «Separation Anxiety: An Aspect of the Search for a Lost Object», *in* M.H.J. LADER (dir.), *Studies of Anxiety* (p. 87-92), Londres, Meadley.

PARKES, C.M. (1970), «"Seeking" and "Finding" a Lost

Object: Evidence from Recent Studies of the Reaction to Bereavement», *Social Science and Medicine*, 4, 287-301.

PRÉVOST, Jean-Pierre (1994), *Dire ou maudire sa souffrance?*, Montréal, Éditions Paulines.

ROSKIES, E. (1987), *Stress Management for the Healthy Type A.*, New York, The Guilford Press.

ROWE, D. (1983), «Constructing Life and Death», *Death Education*, 7(2-3), 97-113.

SATIR, V. (1971), *Thérapie du couple et de la famille*, Paris, Épi.

—— (1988), *The New Peoplemaking*, Montain View, Californie, Science and Behavior Books.

SCHMALE, A.H. (1980), «The Dying Patients», *Advances in Psychosomatic Medicine*, 10, 99-110.

SCHULZ, C.M. (1978), «Death Anxiety and the Structuring of a Death Concerns Cognitive Domain», *Essence*, 1(3), 171-188.

SEVERINO, S.K., R. FRIEDMAN et P. MOORE (1986). «The dying patient: Physician's suffering». *Loss, Grief and Care*, 1(1-2), 25-29.

WINNICOTT, D.W. (1969), *De la pédiatrie à la psychanalyse*, Paris, Payot.

WOODFIELD, R.L. et L.L.VINEY (1984), «A Personal Construct Approach to the conjugally bereaved woman», *Omega*, 15 (1), 1-13.

WORDEN, J.W. (1982), *Grief Counseling and Grief Therapy: A Handbook for the Mental Health Practitioner*, New York, Springer Publishing Company.

WORTMAN, C.B. et R.C. SILVER (1989), «The Myths of Coping with Loss», *Journal of Consulting and Clinical Psychology*, 57(3), 349-357.

YALOM, I.D. (1980), *Existential Psychotherapy*, New York, Basic.

Table des matières

ACHEVÉ D'IMPRIMER
CHEZ
MARC VEILLEUX,
IMPRIMEUR À BOUCHERVILLE,
EN AVRIL MIL NEUF CENT QUATRE-VINGT-QUINZE